Educational Governance in China

Ming Yang · Hao Ni

Educational Governance in China

Ming Yang
College of Education
Zhejiang University
Hangzhou, Zhejiang, China

Hao Ni
China Academy of West Region
  Development
Zhejiang University
Hangzhou, Zhejiang, China

ISBN 978-981-13-0841-3   ISBN 978-981-13-0842-0   (eBook)
https://doi.org/10.1007/978-981-13-0842-0

Jointly published with Higher Education Press, Beijing, China

The print edition is not for sale in China Mainland. Customers from China Mainland please order the print book from: Higher Education Press Limited Company.

Library of Congress Control Number: 2018950218

This Springer imprint is published by the registered company Springer Nature Singapore Pte Ltd.
The registered company address is: 152 Beach Road, #21-01/04 Gateway East, Singapore 189721, Singapore

Foreword

Of all human activities, Education is among the highest and noblest. As a social factor, it has been seen as "an engine of social development," "a purifier of human harmony," and "an expression of culture." Without education, the prospects for humanity would be bleak and world prosperity might be a mere dream. Civilization, social development, and personal advancement are continuous with education: they precede and follow it. Nations, families, and individuals stake their hopes on education. Because of its special role at all levels of human progress, education has been given priority in all ages in countries the world over.

As a result, humanity has accumulated a wealth of positive experience and, in the world's long history, many intractable problems have been solved, setbacks have been tackled, and challenges have been turned into opportunities. But we cannot rest on our laurels or stop addressing the present and the future. New challenges and problems have come as a consequence of the faster pace of change and expansion, which characterizes the new century. To promote steady and sustainable development and foster understanding among peoples in this increasingly global world of ours, we should never give up exploring new avenues and finding new opportunities. Education, as history shows, is perhaps the single best approach we can rely on to achieve our goals. With this background, mutual exchange and cooperation become all the more important.

China's rise in the recent past has benefited from educational development spanning a period of nearly 70 years, beginning with the birth of the People's Republic of China. China has made considerable strides and achieved enviable goals in the field of education during often very difficult times. Now, with the largest education system in the world, China is well on track in successfully achieving the "popularization of compulsory education" and the "massification of higher education." Some of China's achievements may surprise us: a modern education system is basically in place; vocational and technical education policy tries to meet the demands of social and economic development; the internationalization of education has set out along a broad avenue; educational policies and legislation are being regularly improved, etc. At the same time, however, China is still facing many hurdles and challenges in her task of further developing the education system. Education is part of China's overall development, and as such it requires her own efforts, wisdom, and innovation in order to set up and manage a modern education system able to respond to the unique challenges she faces. To sustain development, China needs to learn from the experiences, the achievements, the researches, and experimentation of other countries, without underestimating, in the process, her own achievements and characteristics. With significant Chinese characteristics, Chinese educational development will also play an important role in the global educational system.

This year marks the 40th anniversary of The Reform and Opening Up and the 5th anniversary of the Belt and Road Initiative. Along with the fast social and economic development in the past years, Chinese education has witnessed tremendous achievements due to the increasing public financial support, changing attitude toward education, and the progress of information technology. Mutual understanding is the precondition for international exchange and cooperation. However, up to now, foreigners have encountered many hurdles in trying to improve their knowledge of Chinese education. On the one hand, not many of them manage to achieve a working knowledge of the Chinese language and, on the other hand, there is an undeniable shortage of English literature on Chinese Education.

In order to help foreign friends and scholars know more about today's Chinese education, *Chinese Education Series* comes into being. These series include four volumes, namely, **Educational Policies and Legislation in China**, **Educational Governance in China**, **Higher Education in China**, and **Technical and Vocational Education in China.** The various volumes endeavor to explain the context of Chinese education, to introduce educational development in the present situation, to analyze the problems as they develop, and to look forward to the future of Chinese education in different areas, with each author offering his or her own original perspective. We hope that the series have to some extent help global society to better know the outline and features of modern Chinese education, which it has aroused interest in it, and has encouraged readers to explore the legislation governing its development.

Many thanks are due to Higher Education Press and Springer, for undertaking the publication of the *Chinese Education Series*. I would also like to express my sincere appreciation to the authors who carefully revise the volumes with true professionalism and selflessness, while handling busy schedules, and to all the friends and colleagues who have offered invaluable criticism, advice, and encouragement.

Hangzhou, China   Xiaozhou Xu

Professor Xiaozhou Xu is an outstanding scholar in the field of comparative education and entrepreneurship education. He is Dean of the Academy of Humanities and Social Sciences at Zhejiang University, and Yangtze River Scholar Chair Professor of Ministry of Education of China. He is currently the holder of UNESCO Chair in Entrepreneurship Education and President of UNESCO Entrepreneurship Education Network National Chapter of China. He undertook international and national research projects from UNESCO, the World Bank, and the National Social Science Fund of China. He edited a range of influential series which cover Entrepreneurship Education Research, Changes in Higher Education Policy, 60 Years of Education in China and Research on Strategy and Decision of Education Development. He has published over a hundred essays in academic journals, and over ten monographs including *Building the Entrepreneurship Education System in University*, *Strategies of College Students' Entrepreneurial Skill Development*, etc. Over ten research outcomes were rewarded by Ministry of Education of China and Zhejiang Province Government.

Preface

In the past 68 years, the educational system in China has undergone profound transformation of institutions. In the period of 1949–1956, China emphasized the restructuring of its economy and education. The founding of the People's Republic of China was an epoch-making historical affair. During the celebrating ceremony of the establishment of the new China, Mao Zedong said that the Chinese People had finally stood up in the world. The Chinese government pursued the movement of learning from the Soviet Union with all the enthusiasm although China had once been characterized as imitation of the Western world in earlier decades. In a very short period of time, the Chinese government reinstituted regular order in schools and rapidly facilitated educational expansion at all levels.

The period of 1957–1965 is marked by the complete construction of a socialist country. During the Great Leap Forward in 1958, the educational reform was regarded as part of a comprehensive new strategy of mass mobilization for economic development. On September 19, 1958, the Ministry of Education issued *Directive on Educational Undertakings* and launched the educational reform. During this period, the Chinese Communist Party's leadership on education was strengthened. Productive labor became part of the curriculum in every school at all levels. More specifically, a number of half-work and half-study schools were founded for the masses. Educational scale underwent great expansion.

The decade between 1966 and 1976 was perceived as a period when educational expansion slowed down. The enrollment of higher education institutions decreased. The number of vocational secondary schools also lessened.

From 1977 to 1991, China implemented the new policy of reform and opening up to the outside world. Educational reconstruction was an urgent priority. In the later 1970s, under the leadership of Deng Xiaoping, universalization of primary education was conducted in China, and during this period China learned from the West, in search for a scientific and technical development model. In 1985, the Central Committee of the Chinese Communist Party adopted the document *Decision on Educational Reform,* aimed at providing the mix of skills for a rapidly changing society; improving efficiency, quality, and equity; and releasing resources required to develop and enhance education at all levels.

Since 1992, China has made great efforts to construct a socialist market economy. In February 1993, the Central Committee of the Chinese Communist Party and the State Council issued *Program for China's Educational Reform and Development*. The document set up goals of educational development such as popularizing 9-year compulsory education, increasing the enrollment of students in vocational schools, and building 100 key universities and key courses of studies. In order to fulfill these goals, reforms were initiated in the system of running of schools, the system of management, the system of higher education, the system of students' enrollment and graduation, and the system of financing of education. Moreover, teachers' professional development and increase in educational input was emphasized. In the later 1990s, examination-oriented education brought much more pressures on schools, teachers, and students. In May 1999, the Central Committee of the Chinese Communist Party and the State Council issued *Decision on Deepening Educational Reform and Implementing Competency Education*. Competency education in schools at all levels was pursued with all efforts. Since 2001, the Ministry of Education has put forward to a new program on curriculum reform in primary schools and high schools. However, up till now China has clearly encountered some problems and challenges in the building new institutions required for education expansion and reform.

In order to understand educational reform and development in China more clearly, it is necessary to know how educational activities are conducted under institutional constraints. Institutional analysis is a very useful disciplinary approach in understanding educational systems. Institutions are human relationships that structure opportunity via constraints and enablement. A constraint on one person is an opportunity for another. Institutions enable individuals to do what they cannot do alone. They structure incentives and affect personal beliefs and preferences. Analysts are called upon to determine what kinds of institutions are to be established and contribute to the current educational performance, and to suggest institutional changes to educational policy-makers and citizens that can help achieve a particular educational performance.

The purpose of this book is to provide a better understanding of China's contemporary educational system in the last 68 years. Except for the introduction, this book covers nine concrete educational systems.

In each chapter, five sections are included.

In the first section, the concept, kinds, and functions of different systems are defined.

In the second section, the historical development of each concrete educational system is explored. The historical development of the educational system is classified into five stages. On June 27, 1981, at the 3rd Plenary Session of the 11th Congress of the Central Committee of the Chinese Communist Party issued a very important document named the *Resolutions on Some Historical Problems Facing the Central Committee of the Chinese Communist Party since the Founding of the People's Republic of China* (Editorial Board of China's Education Yearbook, 1982). The document made a very authoritative classification of the stages of development in China. The period of 1949–1976 could be divided into three stages, namely, the stage of completing socialist restructuring (1949–1956), the stage of building a socialist country (1957–1966), and the stage of the *Cultural Revolution* (1966–1976). The period of 1976–1977 was a short transitional period. The past system and policies were under critical scrutiny in this period. China has been implementing the policy of reform and opening up to the outside world effectively since 1978. The period of 1978–2016 may be divided into two stages, one is the stage of building socialist commodity markets (1977–1991) and the other is the stage of building a socialist market economy (1992–2016). The division criterion was based on the fact that in 1992 the 14th Congress of the Central Committee of the Chinese Communist Party declared that China should establish a socialist market economy hereafter. In each stage, the basic context, process, main activities, and progress of each educational system is reviewed in detail.

In the third section, the current situations of each educational system are described so as to give complete information on what is going on in respective educational systems.

In the fourth section, the problems facing China in each educational system are discussed.

In the fifth section, the relevant strategies and measures for resolution of these problems are put forward.

This book consists of 10 chapters. Chapter 1 is an introduction to the educational system. Chapters 2 and 3 review the external governance structure and internal governance structure in terms of macro-management of the educational system and micro-management of schools at various levels. Chapter 4 examines the system of educational provision. Running of schools is the most important part in the operation of an educational system. Chapters 5 and 6 demonstrate the enrollment of students and graduation of students. Chapter 7 explores the system of financing education. Funds are the first and continuous driving force in educational expansion. Chapter 8 demonstrates the system of examination. The establishment of the system of examination aims at making sure whether schools and students have achieved definite goals set by the society at large. Chapters 9 and 10 examine the quality assurance process in primary schools, secondary schools as well as higher education institutions.

Many, many thanks to Prof. Xu Xiaozhou, Dean of Academy of Humanities and Social Sciences, Zhejiang University for his creative idea and effective guidance on this program. Thanks to Prof. Tian Zhengping and Prof. Zhou Guping, two former deans of the College of Education, for giving good advice on research on the history of educational development in China. Thanks to my colleagues Prof. Gu Jianmin and Prof. Wu Xueping for suggestions on writing. Thanks to Zhou Qiong who gave me critical review on the manuscript. Thanks to Prof. Wu Hua's novel ideas on private educational development.

Hangzhou, China   Ming Yang

Contents

1   Defining Educational System   1
  1.1   The Origins of Research on Educational System   1
  1.2   Significance of the Reform of Educational System   1
  1.3   The Concept of Educational System   3
  1.4   Elements of Educational System   5
  1.5   Relationship Between Educational System and
         Economic System   6
  1.6   Classification of Educational System   7
  1.7   Various Educational Systems   9
  1.8   Policy Perspective on Educational System   10
  1.9   Institutional Perspective on Educational System   11
  1.10 Characteristics of the Educational System in China
         Before the Reform and Opening up to the Outside World   11
  1.11 The Beginning of the Educational Reform Since 1978
         in China   12
  1.12 Direction of the Reform of the Educational System
         After the Initiation of Economic Reform   12
  1.13 Goals, Tasks and Measures for the Reform of Educational
         System in 1985   13
  1.14 Deepening the Reform of Educational System in 1990s   14
  1.15 "National Guidelines" Enforcement and Local Educational
         Reform Initiation   15
  1.16 The Outline of This Book   15
  References   16

**2   Pursuing Good Governance: Educational Administration
System in China**   17
  2.1   Introduction to the System of Educational Administration   17
        2.1.1   The Concept of the System of Educational
              Administration   17

2.1.2   Classification of the System of Educational
Administration 18
2.1.3   The Functions of the System of Educational
Administration 20
2.2   The System of Educational Administration at the Stage of
Completing Socialist Restructuring (1949–1956). 20
2.2.1   The Context, Tasks, Guideline and Achievements in
Educational Reform and Development in
This Period 21
2.2.2   Establishment of Educational Administrative
Institutions at Various Levels 23
2.2.3   Measures Taken by the New Educational
Administrative Departments to Reform Public and
Private Education 29
2.3   Educational Administration at the Stage of the Socialist
Construction (1957–1965) 29
2.3.1   The Organization and Policy Changes in
This Period 30
2.3.2   The Administrative System of Education in Primary
and Secondary Education (1957–1965) 31
2.3.3   Educational Administration in Higher Education
Institutions (1957–1965) 33
2.4   Educational Administration During the "Cultural Revolution"
(1966–1976). 34
2.4.1   Organization and Policy Changes in Educational
Administration (1966–1976) 34
2.4.2   Administration of Primary Education and Secondary
Education (1966–1976). 35
2.4.3   Educational Administration in Higher Education
Institutions (1966–1976) 36
2.5   Educational Administration at the Stage of Building the
Socialist Commodity Markets (1977–1991) 37
2.5.1   Organization and Policy Changes in Terms of
Educational Administration (1977–1991) 37
2.5.2   Reform of the System of Administration of Primary
and Secondary Education (1977–1997) 40
2.5.3   Reform of Educational Administration in Higher
Education Institutions (1977–1991) 41
2.6   The System of Educational Administration at the Stage of
Building Socialist Market Economy (1992–2016) 43
2.6.1   Organizational and Policy Changes in Terms of
Educational Administration (1992–2016) 44
2.6.2   Reform of Educational Administration in Primary
Schools and Secondary Schools (1992–2016). 45

        2.6.3   Reform of Administration in Higher Education
                Institutions (1992–2016)   47
        2.6.4   The Historical Experiences of Reform of the System
                of Educational Administration   50
    2.7 Current Situation of Reform of the System of
         Educational Administration   50
        2.7.1   Current Situation of the System of Educational
                Leadership and Administration   50
        2.7.2   Current Situation of Educational Administration in
                Primary Schools and Secondary Schools   52
        2.7.3   Current Situation of Educational Administration in
                Higher Education Institutions   52
    2.8 Problems Facing China in the Reform of Educational
         Administration   53
        2.8.1   Problems Facing China Due to Governments'
                Position in Educational Development.   53
        2.8.2   Problems Facing China Due to Governments'
                Macro-management of Education   53
        2.8.3   Problems in the System of Educational
                Administration in Primary and Secondary Schools
                in China   55
        2.8.4   Problems in the System of Educational
                Administration in Higher Education Institutions
                in China   55
    2.9 Strategies and Measures for Further Reforms of the System of
         Educational Administration   56
        2.9.1   Addressing Problems of Governmental Functions
                in Educational Administration   56
        2.9.2   Strengthening Governments' Macro-management   57
        2.9.3   Strategies and Measures for Reform of the System
                of Educational Administ-Ration in Primary Schools
                and Secondary Schools   58
        2.9.4   Strategies and Measures for the Reform of the
                System of Educational Administration in Higher
                Education Institutions   59
    References   60
3   Increasing Education Vigor: Internal Management
    System in Schools in China   61
    3.1 Introduction to the System of Internal Management   61
        3.1.1   The Concept of the System of Internal Management . . .   61
        3.1.2   Classification of the System of Internal Management . . .   63
        3.1.3   Functions of the System of Internal Management   64

3.2   The System of Internal Management in Primary and Secondary
       Schools at the Stage of Completing Socialist Restructuring
       (1949–1956)..   65
       3.2.1   The System of Internal Management in Primary
               Schools and Secondary Schools (1949–1956)........   65
       3.2.2   The System of Internal Management in Higher
               Education Institutions (1949–1956)   68
3.3   The System of Internal Management in Primary Schools and
       Secondary Schools at the Stage of Completing the Socialist
       Construction (1957–1965)   69
       3.3.1   The System of Internal Management in Primary
               Schools and Secondary Schools (1957–1965)........   69
       3.3.2   The System of Internal Management in Higher
               Education Institutions (1957–1965)   71
3.4   The System of Internal Management in Schools at
       Various Levels at the Stage of the "Cultural Revolution"
       (1966–1976)..   72
       3.4.1   The System of Internal Management in Primary
               Schools and Secondary Schools (1966–1976)........   72
       3.4.2   The System of Internal Management in HEIs
               (1966–1976)   72
3.5   The System of Internal Management in Schools at Various
       Levels at the Stage of Building Socialist Commodity
       Markets (1977–1991)   72
       3.5.1   The System of Internal Management in Primary
               Schools and Secondary Schools (1977–1991)........   73
       3.5.2   The System of Internal Management in Higher
               Education Institutions (1977–1991)   75
3.6   The System of Internal Management at Various Levels at the
       Stage of Building Socialist Market Economy (1992–2016)   77
       3.6.1   The System of Internal Management in Primary
               Schools and Secondary Schools (1992–2016)........   77
       3.6.2   The System of Internal Management in HEIs
               (1992–2016)   79
       3.6.3   Historical Experiences in the Reform and
               Development of the System of Internal
               Management in China........................   81
3.7   Current Situation of the System of Internal Management
       in China...   81
       3.7.1   Current Situation of the System of Internal
               Management in Primary and Secondary Schools   82
       3.7.2   Current Situation of the System of Internal
               Management in Higher Education Institutions   84

3.8   The Problems Facing China in the System of Internal
Management   85
     3.8.1   The Problems Facing China in the System of Internal
             Management in Primary and Secondary Schools   85
     3.8.2   The Problems Facing China in the System of Internal
             Management in Higher Education Institutions   87
3.9   The Strategies and Measures for Reform of System of Internal
Management in China   89
     3.9.1   The Strategies and Measures for the Reform of the
             System of Internal Management in Primary and
             Secondary Schools in China   89
     3.9.2   The Strategies and Measures for Reform of System of
             Internal Management Reform in HEIs in China   91
References   94

4   Engaging Social Actors: Educational Provision System in China . . .   **95**
4.1   Introduction to the System of Educational Provision   95
     4.1.1   The Concept of the System of Educational Provision . . .   95
     4.1.2   Classification of the System of Educational Provision . . .   97
     4.1.3   The Factors Affecting the System of Educational
             Provision   97
4.2   The System of Educational Provision at the Stage of
Completing Socialist Restructuring (1949–1956).   98
     4.2.1   The Reform of the System of Provision of Public
             Education and Private Education in Primary and
             Secondary Schools (1949–1956)   98
     4.2.2   The Reform of the System of Provision of Education
             in Pubic and Private Universities and Colleges
             (1949–1956)   104
4.3   The System of Educational Provision at the Stage of Building
Socialist Country with All Efforts (1957–1965)   106
     4.3.1   The Organization and Policy Changes (1957–1965) . . .   106
     4.3.2   The Reform of the System of Provision of Public
             Education and Private Education in Primary and
             Secondary Schools from 1957 to 1965   107
     4.3.3   The Reform of the System of Provision of Public
             Education and Private Education in HEIs
             (1957–1965)   111
4.4   The System of Educational Provision at the Stage of the
"Cultural Revolution" (1966–1976)   114
     4.4.1   Reform of the System of Provision of Public and
             Private Education in Primary and Secondary Schools . . .   114
     4.4.2   The Reform of the System of Provision of Higher
             Education   115

4.5   The System of Educational Provision at the Stage of Building
       Socialist Commodity Markets (1977–1991) 115
       4.5.1   Formulation of Policies on Mutual Sponsoring and
                Running of Schools by Both State
                and Private Agents 116
       4.5.2   Reform of the System of Educational Provision in
                Primary and Secondary Schools (1977–1991) 116
       4.5.3   Reform of the System of Educational Provision in
                HEIs (1977–1991) 119
4.6   The System of Educational Provision at the Stage of Building
       Socialist Market Economy (1992–2016)................. 122
       4.6.1   Formulation of Policies for Running of Schools
                Mutually by the State and Private Agents
                (1992–2016) 122
       4.6.2   Reform of the System of Provision of Public and
                Private Education in Primary Schools and Secondary
                Schools (1992–2016) 124
       4.6.3   Reform of System of Provision of Higher Education
                (1992–2016) 126
       4.6.4   Historical Experiences of the System of
                Educational Provision 128
4.7   Current Situation of the System of Provision of Education 128
       4.7.1   Current Situation of the System of Educational
                Provision in Primary and Secondary Schools 128
4.8   Problems Facing China in the System of Educational
       Provision 131
       4.8.1   Problems Facing China in the System of Educational
                Provision in Primary and Secondary Schools 131
       4.8.2   Problems Facing China in the System of Educational
                Provision in Public and Private Higher Education
                Institutions 134
4.9   Strategies and Measures for Reform of the System of
       Educational Provision 136
       4.9.1   Strategies and Measures for Reform of the
                System of Educational Provision in Primary
                and Secondary Schools 136
       4.9.2   Strategies and Measures for Reform in the System of
                Educational Provision in Higher Education 138
References 140

5 Strengthening Educational Autonomy: Educational Enrollment System in China 141

5.1 Introduction to the System of Enrollment 141

    5.1.1 The Concept of the System of Enrollment 141

    5.1.2 Classification of the System of Enrollment. 141

    5.1.3 Functions of the System of Enrollment 142

5.2 System of Enrollment at the Stage of Completing Socialist Restructuring (1949–1956) 142

    5.2.1 The System of Enrollment of Students in Primary and Secondary Schools (1949–1956) 142

    5.2.2 The System of Enrollment in HEIs (1949–1956) 144

5.3 The System of Enrollment at the Stage of Completion of Building Socialism (1957–1965) 148

    5.3.1 The System of Enrollment of Students in Primary and Secondary Schools (1957–1965) 148

    5.3.2 The System of Enrollment of Students in Higher Education Institutions (1957–1965) 148

5.4 The System of Enrollment at the Stage of the "Cultural Revolution" (1966–1976) 150

    5.4.1 The System of Enrollment of Students in Primary and Secondary Schools (1966–1976) 150

    5.4.2 The System of Enrollment of Students in HEIs (1966–1976) 150

5.5 The System of Enrollment at the Stage of Building Socialist Commodity Economy (1977–1991) 151

    5.5.1 The System of Enrollment of Students in Primary and Secondary Schools (1977–1991) 151

    5.5.2 The System of Enrollment of Students in Higher Education Institutions (1977–1991) 152

5.6 The System of Enrollment at the Stage of Building Socialist Market Economy (1992–2016) 157

    5.6.1 The System of Enrollment of Students in Primary and Secondary Schools (1992–2016) 157

    5.6.2 The System of Enrollment of Students in HEIs (1992–2016) 159

    5.6.3 Historical Experiences of Reform of the System of Enrollment 160

5.7 Current Situation of the System of Enrollment 161

    5.7.1 Current Situation of the System of Enrollment in Primary and Secondary Schools 162

    5.7.2 Current Situation of the System of Enrollment for Students in HEIs 163

5.8   Problems Facing China in the System of Enrollment.   164
      5.8.1   Problems Facing China in the System of Enrollment
              in Primary and Secondary Schools   164
      5.8.2   Problems Facing China in the System of Enrollment
              in Higher Education Institutions   166
5.9   Strategies and Measures for Further Reform of the
      System of Enrollment   167
      5.9.1   Strategies and Measures for Further Reform of the
              System of Enrollment in Primary and
              Secondary Education   167
      5.9.2   Strategies and Measures for Further Reforms of the
              System of Enrollment in Higher Education   168
Reference   169

6   **Moving Towards Market Orientation: The System of
    Employment in China**   171
    6.1   Introduction to the System of Employment.   171
          6.1.1   The Concept of the System of Employment   171
          6.1.2   Classification of the System of Employment   171
          6.1.3   Functions of the System of Employment   172
    6.2   The System of Employment During the Completion of
          Socialist Restructuring (1949–1956)   172
          6.2.1   The System of Employment for Students in Primary
                  and Secondary Schools (1949–1956)   172
          6.2.2   The System of Employment for Students in HEIs
                  (1949–1956)   174
    6.3   The System of Employment at the Stage of Completion of
          Building Socialism (1957–1965)   176
          6.3.1   The System of Employment of Students in Primary
                  and Secondary Schools   176
          6.3.2   The System of Employment of Students in HEIs
                  (1949–1965)   176
    6.4   The System of Employment at the Stage of the "Cultural
          Revolution" (1966–1976)   179
          6.4.1   The System of Employment for Students in Primary
                  and Secondary Schools (1966–1976)   179
          6.4.2   The System of Employment for Students in HEIs
                  (1966–1976)   180
    6.5   The System of Employment at the Stage of Building Socialist
          Commodity Economy (1977–1991)   180
          6.5.1   The System of Employment for Students in Primary
                  and Secondary Schools (1977–1991)   180
          6.5.2   The System of Employment for Students in HEIs
                  (1977–1991)   181

6.6   The System of Employment at the Stage of Building Socialist
Market Economy (1992–2016) 182
    6.6.1   The System of Employment for Students in Primary
and Secondary Schools (1992–2016) 182
    6.6.2   The System of Employment of Students in HEIs
(1992–2016) 183
6.7   Current Situation of the System of Employment 184
    6.7.1   Current Situation of the System of Employment for
Graduates in Primary and Secondary Schools........ 184
    6.7.2   Current Situation of the System of Employment for
Graduates in HEIs 185
6.8   Problems Facing China in the System of Employment 187
    6.8.1   Problems Facing China in the System of Employment
in HEIs 187
    6.8.2   Lack of Strong Guidance by Governments.......... 187
6.9   Strategies and Measures for Further Reforms of the System of
Employment..................................... 189
    6.9.1   Strategies and Measures for Further Reforms of the
System of Employment For Graduates in Higher
Education Institutions 189
Reference... 191

7   **Expanding the Channels: Education Financing System
in China** 193
7.1   Introduction to the System of Financing of Education 193
    7.1.1   The Concept of the System of Financing
of Education 193
    7.1.2   Classification of the System of Financing
of Education 194
    7.1.3   Functions of the System of Financing of Education ... 195
    7.1.4   Factors Influencing the System of Financing
of Education 195
7.2   The System of Financing of Education at the Completion of
Socialist Restructuring (1949–1956)..................... 195
    7.2.1   The Reform of the System of Financing of Education
(1949–1956) 195
    7.2.2   Financing of Primary Education and Secondary
Education (1949–1956)........................ 201
    7.2.3   Financing of Higher Education in This Period 203
7.3   The System of Financing of Education at the Stage of
Completion of Socialist Restructuring (1957–1965).......... 203
    7.3.1   Reform of the System of Financing of Education
(1957–1965) 203

7.3.2   Financing of Primary Education and Secondary
        Education (1957–1965).   205
7.3.3   Financing of Higher Education (1957–1965)   206
7.4   The System of Financing of Education at the Stage of the
      "Cultural Revolution" (1966–1976)   206
      7.4.1   Reform of the System of Financing of Education
              (1966–1976)   206
      7.4.2   Financing of Primary Education and Secondary
              Education (1966–1976).   207
      7.4.3   Financing of Higher Education (1966–1976)   207
7.5   The System of Financing Education at the Stage of Building
      Socialist Commodity Markets (1977–1991)   207
      7.5.1   Reform of the System of Financing of Education
              (1977–1991)   208
      7.5.2   Financing of Primary Education and Secondary
              Education (1977–1991).   211
      7.5.3   Financing of Higher Education (1977–1991)   212
7.6   The System of Financing of Education at the Stage of Building
      Socialist Market Economy (1992–2016).   214
      7.6.1   Reform of the System of Financing of Education
              (1992–2016)   214
      7.6.2   Financing of Primary Education and Secondary
              Education (1992–2016).   219
      7.6.3   Financing of Higher Education (1992–2016)   221
7.7   Current Situation of the System of Financing of Education   223
      7.7.1   Law and Policies for the System of Financing of
              Education and Basic Sources of Revenues   223
      7.7.2   Financing of Primary Education and Secondary
              Education   225
      7.7.3   Financing of Higher Education   226
7.8   Some Problems Facing China in the System of Financing
      of Education.   227
      7.8.1   Problems Facing China in the Macro-management
              in Financing of Education.   227
      7.8.2   Problems Facing China in Financing Primary
              Education and Secondary Education   229
      7.8.3   Problems Facing China in Financing Higher
              Education   230
7.9   Strategies and Measures for Reform of the System of
      Financing of Education   231
      7.9.1   Strategies and Measures for Reform of Macro-
              management of Financing of Education   231
      7.9.2   Strategies and Measures for Reform of the System of
              Financing Primary and Secondary Education   232

7.9.3   Strategies and Measures for Reform of the System of
        Financing of Higher Education in China   233
References   234

8 **Balancing Between Social Equality and Meritocracy:
   The System of Examination in China**   235
   8.1   Introduction to the System of Examination   235
         8.1.1   The Concept of the System of Examination   235
         8.1.2   Classification of the System of Examinations   235
         8.1.3   Functions of the System of Examinations   236
   8.2   The System of Examination at the Stage of Completing
         Socialist Restructuring (1949–1956)   236
         8.2.1   The System of Examination in Primary and
                 Secondary Schools from 1949 to 1956   236
         8.2.2   The System of Examination in HEIs (1949–1956)   238
   8.3   The System of Exanimation at the Completion of Building
         Socialism (1957–1965)   241
         8.3.1   The System of Examination in Primary Schools and
                 Secondary Schools (1957–1965)   241
         8.3.2   The System of Examination in HEIs (1957–1965)   242
   8.4   The System of Examination at the Time of the Great Cultural
         Revolution (1966–1976)   243
         8.4.1   The System of Examination in Primary and
                 Secondary Schools (1966–1976)   243
         8.4.2   The System of Examination in HEIs (1966–1976)   243
   8.5   The System of Examination at the Stage of Building Socialist
         Commodity Markets (1977–1991)   244
         8.5.1   The System of Examination in Primary Schools and
                 Secondary Schools (1977–1991)   244
         8.5.2   The System of Examination in Higher Education
                 (1977–1991)   246
   8.6   The System of Examination at the Stage of Building Socialist
         Market Economy (1992–2016)   248
         8.6.1   Reform of the System of Examination in Primary
                 Schools and Secondary Schools (1992–2016)   248
         8.6.2   Reform of the System of Examination in HEIs
                 (1992–2016)   249
   8.7   Current Situation in the System of Examination   250
         8.7.1   Current Situation in System of Examination in
                 Primary Education and Secondary Education   250
         8.7.2   Current Situation in the System of Examination in
                 Higher Education Institutions   252

8.8   Problems Facing China in the System of Examination   254
       8.8.1   Problem Facing China in the System of Examination
                of Primary and Secondary Schools   254
       8.8.2   Problems Facing China in the System of Examination
                in Higher Education   256
8.9   Strategies and Measures for Reform of the System of
       Examination   256
       8.9.1   Strategies and Measures for Reform of the System of
                Examination in Primary and Secondary Education   256
       8.9.2   Strategies and Measures for Reform of the System of
                Examination in Higher Education   259
References   261

9   **Aiming at School Improvement: Educational Evaluation System
     in Primary and Secondary Schools**   263
     9.1   Introduction to the System of Educational Evaluation   263
            9.1.1   The Concept of the System of Educational
                     Evaluation   263
            9.1.2   Classification of the System of Educational
                     Evaluation   263
            9.1.3   Functions of the System of Educational Evaluation . . .   264
     9.2   The System of Educational Evaluation in Primary Schools and
            Secondary Schools (1949–1956)   264
            9.2.1   The System of Evaluation of Primary Schools and
                     Secondary Schools (1949–1956)   264
            9.2.2   The System of Evaluation of Teachers (1949–1956) . . .   265
            9.2.3   The System of Evaluation of Students (1949–1956) . . .   265
     9.3   The System of Educational Evaluation in Primary and
            Secondary Schools (1957–1965)   266
            9.3.1   The System of Educational Evaluation in Schools
                     (1957–1965)   266
            9.3.2   The System of Evaluation of Teachers (1957–1965) . . .   266
            9.3.3   The System of Evaluation of Students (1957–1965) . . .   267
     9.4   The System of Educational Evaluation in Primary Secondary
            Schools (1966–1976)   267
     9.5   The System Educational of Evaluation in Primary and
            Secondary Schools (1977–1991)   267
            9.5.1   The System of Evaluation of Primary and Secondary
                     Schools (1977–1991)   267
            9.5.2   The System of Evaluation of Teachers (1977–1991) . . .   267
            9.5.3   The System of Evaluation of Students (1977–1991) . . .   269

9.6   The System of Educational Evaluation in Primary and
        Secondary Schools (1992–2016) 269
        9.6.1   The System of Evaluation of Primary and Secondary
                Schools (1992–2016) 269
        9.6.2   The System of Evaluation of Teachers (1992–2016)... 270
        9.6.3   The System of Evaluation of Students (1992–2016) ... 271
9.7   Current Situations of the System of Evaluation............. 271
        9.7.1   Current Situation of the System of Evaluation in
                Primary Schools and Secondary Schools 271
        9.7.2   Current Situation of the System of Evaluation of
                Teachers 272
        9.7.3   Current Situation of the System of Evaluation of
                Students................................. 274
9.8   Problems Facing China in the System of Evaluation in Primary
        and Secondary Schools 276
        9.8.1   Problems Facing China in the Evaluation of Schools... 276
        9.8.2   Problems Facing China in Evaluation of Teachers 277
        9.8.3   Problems Facing China in the System of Evaluation of
                Students................................. 279
9.9   Strategies and Measures for Reform of the System of
        Educational Evaluation 280
        9.9.1   Strategies and Measures for Reform of the System of
                Educational Evaluation in Schools................ 280
        9.9.2   Strategies and Measures for Reform of the System of
                Evaluation of Teachers 281
        9.9.3   Strategies and Measures for Reform of the System of
                Evaluation of Students 283
References 283

10   Ensuring Higher Education Performance: Quality Assurance
     System of Higher Education in China...................... 285
     10.1   Introduction to the System of Quality Assurance of
             Higher Education 285
             10.1.1   The Concept of System of Quality Assurance of
                      Higher Education 285
             10.1.2   Classification of the System of Quality Assurance of
                      Higher Education 285
             10.1.3   Functions of the System of Quality of Assurance of
                      Higher Education 286
     10.2   The System of Assurance of Higher Education (1949–1956) ... 287
     10.3   The System of Assurance of Higher Education (1957–1965) ... 287
     10.4   The System of Assurance of Higher Education (1966–1976) ... 288
     10.5   The System of Assurance of Higher Education from
             1977 to 1991 288

          10.5.1   Preparatory Stage (1977–1984)   288
          10.5.2   All-Round Development Stage (1985–1991)   289
   10.6   The System of Assurance of Higher Education (1992–2016) . . .   290
   10.7   Current Situations of the System of Quality Assurance of
          Higher Education   293
          10.7.1   Accreditation of Higher Education Institutions
                   in China   293
          10.7.2   Accreditation and Evaluation of Graduate Education . . .   295
          10.7.3   The Evaluation of Instruction at Various Levels   297
          10.7.4   University Rankings   301
          10.7.5   The Assessment of Key Construction Projects   303
   10.8   Some Problems Facing China in the System of Quality
          Assurance of Higher Education   303
   10.9   Strategies and Measures for Improving Quality of
          Higher Education   306
   References   307

References   309

Index   315

About the Authors

Dr. Ming Yang is a Professor at the College of Education of Zhejiang University, China. In 1998 and 2005, he worked as a Visiting Scholar at Kiel University, Germany. His main focus is on theories of education and educational systems. He is the author of the works *Educational System in China* published in 2009 (in English), and in 2012 (in Italian). Further works include *Government and Market: Research on Financial Policy of Higher Education* (2007), *Exam-Oriented and Quality-Oriented: Secondary Education in China over the Past 60 Years* (2009), and *Analysis of Educational Development Theory and Implementation Strategy* (2010).

Dr. Hao Ni is Assistant Professor at China Academy of West Region Development, Zhejiang University. He got his doctoral degree in international and comparative education from College of Education, Zhejiang University. He has served as an Intern in UNESCO Asia and Pacific Regional Bureau for Education in Bangkok, Thailand and spend 1 year in University of Wisconsin-Madison as a Visiting Scholar. His work has been published in journals such as The Asia Pacific Education Researcher, Higher Education, Asia Pacific Education Review, International Entrepreneurship and Management Journal, International and Comparative Education (Chinese), and China Higher Education Research (Chinese). His main research interests cover entrepreneurship in universities and comparative higher education.

Chapter 1
Defining Educational System

1.1 The Origins of Research on Educational System

Systematic research on educational system is of relatively recent origin. In the initial stage of educational system analysis, people borrowed the relevant research methodology and techniques from other social sciences such as economics and sociology.

Since the early 1980s, when the market-oriented reform of educational system was introduced in the United States, the United Kingdom and other countries, the reform of educational system became a hotly debated issue across the world.

Although comparative research on capitalism and socialism began in the 1920s, and in 1938 Locke and Hought published an important book named Comparative Research on Economy, systematic research on economic systems was a new research area mainly established in the 1960s and the 1970s (Gregory and Stuart 1980). Comparative research on economic systems aims at finding out how different economic systems have affected economic development in different countries. Research on economic systems focuses on the structures and functions of the economy. Borrowing the principles and methods of research on economic and social systems, some educational researchers have been doing research on education systems since the late 1960s. As the great transformation from planning economy to market economy was taking place in many countries, reform of educational systems had become a special research field in educational sciences in China since the late 1970s.

1.2 Significance of the Reform of Educational System

Educational system is the basic educational organization form in a country. Any social system has three dimensions, namely, material technological dimension, system dimension and concept dimension.

© Springer Nature Singapore Pte Ltd. and Higher Education Press 2018
M. Yang and H. Ni, *Educational Governance in China*,
https://doi.org/10.1007/978-981-13-0842-0_1

1

Educational system reflects the basic relations in educational operation mechanism. Educational system determines the basic operational order of education in a country.

Reform of educational system is the institutional guarantee of educational development. Educational system may have great influences on educational outcomes.

The historical development of education in China has shown that scientific management of education is of great importance to the holistic development of education. A minor mistake in the macro-management of education may cause harm to educational undertaking. Educational development has both macro-aspects and micro-aspects. In China, there are some problems with the micro-aspects of educational development; but the main problems exist in the macro-aspects of educational development. If problems in the macro-aspects of educational development are not solved, the healthy reform and development of education cannot be guaranteed.

From 1985 on, it was decided that the educational system should be systematically reformed so as to establish a modern educational system. After two decades of exploration and practice, the reform has produced great achievements.

A comparative research on the educational system will be helpful in understanding how other countries formulate educational policies and guidelines and implement them and how educational development goals have been put forward and achieved. Reform on educational system reflects the different ways of solving educational problems. Educational system is an important variable for educational development. To find out how this kind of variable affects educational outcome is a difficult, yet challenging, task for educational researchers. The choice of educational systems and educational development strategies are factors affecting both educational input and educational output. Educational system may affect the coordination of education and economy as well as the fulfillment of social and economic functions of education.

The reform of educational system is the key element in educational reform. Educational development must be adapting to the economic, political and cultural development in a specific society. This adaptation process has two aspects. On the one hand, as a subsystem of the social system, educational system is restricted by economic, political and cultural development. Education is based on economic development. On the other hand, education must serve economic, political and cultural development. The reform of educational system aims at creating the necessary conditions for the reform of other educational elements, such as the reform of educational contents, educational methods and educational structures. Educational system should eventually bring about good and rapid social and economic development.

The reform of the total educational system is systematic engineering. The piece by piece reform has only a limited role in establishing a new system adapted to social and economic development (Wan 1992).

The reform of educational system is the key factor for educational reform. Reform of educational system can create the necessary conditions for other educational reforms. A good educational system is characterized by three features. A good educational system should adapt to the needs of political system, economic system, scientific system and cultural system. A good educational system should be an equitable system. A good educational system should bring about high efficiency and effectiveness for educational development.

1.3 The Concept of Educational System

What does a system mean? *Longman Dictionary of Contemporary English* gives five meanings to the concept of "system": (1) a group of related parts working together; (2) an ordered set of ideas, methods, or ways of working; (3) a plan; (4) the body with its usual ways of working; (5) orderly methods (Procter 1978, P. 567). Educational system is a social system. It has both positive connotations and normative connotations. As far as social phenomenon is concerned, social system is made of a group of parts working together in society and is an orderly set of ways of working. So two important parts are included in a social system, one part is the organizational factors; the other part is institutional factors.

In *Great Chinese Dictionary*, a system is defined as the total elements concerning the related parts, institutions and methods that pertain to the structural establishment, leaderships of different institutions, power and responsibilities in State institutions, enterprises and other public institutions. (Editorial Board of Great Chinese Dictionary 1991).

Pan Maoyuan points out that a system consists of various institutions; among these institutions, administrative institutions are regarded as core institutions (Pan 1995). Generally speaking, a system denotes the management power and task of concerned departments so that these departments can achieve great effectiveness.

Wang Jisheng thinks that a system is a very broad concept. It denotes the institutions whereby rules, positions, functions, rights, obligations within an entity are specified (Wang 2002).

Liu Haibo maintains that a system is the total institution in terms of organizational elements and their relations (Liu 1999). Here institution means rules.

The *Great Educational Dictionary* points out that various educational systems are the various institutions that pertain to the structural establishment and division of management power (Gu 1992). It concerns with educational leadership, organizational structures and division of responsibilities among the social actors.

An educational system is the combination of educational institutions and educational rules. Educational institutions include both educational institutions that conduct educational activities and management institutions that conduct management activities. Educational rules stipulate educational institutions' powers and the responsibilities of personnel within these institutions. The combination of educational institutions and rules may construct a system of schooling; the combination of management institutions and rules may construct a system of education management. The system of educational management consists of a system of education administration and a system of internal management. As far as the educational system is concerned, educational institutions are the carriers of educational systems, and rules are at the core of the educational system. Without educational institutions, educational system would lack organization basis; without educational rules, educational institutions cannot be established smoothly.

Higher education is a part of the educational system in the country. Some researchers give definitions on system of higher education system. According to Pan Maoyuan, higher education system is the relatively stable structural models of higher education; it is formulated by the State power institutions and leadership structure; it defines the power of higher education management, regulates higher education activities and facilitates higher education development (Pan 1995).

Tian Jianguo points out that higher education system consists of the total of all the parts of higher education (Tian 1990). It includes the educational organizations and institutions in terms of higher education. Higher education organization refers to the various parts of higher education and their positions and relations. Higher education institutions refer to the laws and regulations concerning management of higher education. These laws and regulations pertain to the running of schools, regulations of investment, regulations of managements, regulations of development plans.

Wang Yapu maintains that higher education system is the total structural relations of higher education, and its main part consists of educational organizations and ways of management (Wang 2002).

As reform of economic system is deepening and the concomitant reform of educational system is carried out, the concepts and related issues about resource allocation, operation mechanism and transformation of system have become hotly debated issues. Up to now these concepts have not been defined scientifically; many persons still have different opinions about these concepts. So it is urgent to give accurate definitions of these basic concepts.

Economic system consists of the ways, methods and institutions of state's organizing and managing economy.

Educational undertakings are human activities with specific purposes. Educational activities aims at making younger generation integrate into the community or the society. Educational system is a way of organizing human activities. So educational system can be defined as the ways, methods and institutions by which people are organizing and managing education.

In order to bring about an accurate definition of educational system, we must distinguish between educational system, educational structure, and educational policy. Educational system is different from educational structure. An educational system refers to the ways, methods and institutions through which education is organized and managed. Educational system is affected mainly by the political system and economic system in a State while educational structure is affected mainly by the levels of economic and social development in a state in a definite period.

Educational system is different from educational goal. Educational goal refers to the ends that need to be achieved. Educational system is related to the realization of educational goal, but it is not the educational goal itself.

1.4 Elements of Educational System

Educational system consists of the following four factors. The first factor is the educational decision-making system. It is the most important part in the process of reforming the educational system. The decision-making process is a process of making arrangements for educational action schemes. Educational action schemes can be classified as educational research schemes and educational practice schemes. The purpose of educational research is to obtain theoretical knowledge about education. The purpose of educational practice is to obtain knowledge about basic facts of education and bring about changes of education.

The decision making system deals with the distribution of educational decision making power. It aims to answer questions regarding who has the power of decision-making and how the decisions are made. The decision-makers in educational system include the government administrators, school managers and educators. Educational decision-making system includes educational decision-making structures, educational decision-making mechanisms, educational decision-making functions. The structures pertain to the distribution of power; the mechanisms pertain to the use of educational decisions and the functions pertain to the actions.

The second factor is information and feedback in decision making and implementation of decisions. The information in an educational system is the basis for making educational decisions. Educational information system aims to answer questions about how to obtain information and where to obtain information. According to the information transmission process, the system of information can be classified as system of horizontal information and system of vertical information. The system of horizontal information is a system whereby the information is transmitted among schools of the same level. The system of vertical information is a system whereby the information is transmitted between upper levels and lower levels. No matter what kind of information system exists, the accurate and rapid transmission of information is necessary.

The third factor is the regulation system. The regulation system concerns how to execute policies after the relevant decisions have been formed. In the process of implementation of policies it is necessary for decision-makers to set up different regulation systems. There are three kinds of regulation systems. The first regulation system is planning regulation system; it is directive-based regulation system. The second regulation system is market-oriented regulation system; it is the system regulated by market mechanism. The third regulation system is the mixture of planning regulation system with market-oriented regulation system.

The fourth factor is the organization system. It is organization that makes implementation of education policies. Organization system includes the educational institutions and their relationship.

1.5 Relationship Between Educational System and Economic System

The relationship between educational development and economic development is a basic relationship between education and the society at large.

Every country has its own systems of management of economy and education. But as the social systems differ from country to country, the level of social development and economic development also differ; the contents, methods, goals and means of managing economy and education also differ in society.

Economic system is a major factor affecting educational system. Although political system and science-technology system affect educational system, it is the economic system that determines the nature and basic features of educational system. When the economic system in a country changes, the educational system will also change eventually.

Presently, the main problem facing China is how to reform its educational system so as to adapt it to the economic system and help to facilitate the reform of economic system.

The relationship between economic system and educational system is an important aspect of the relationship between economy and education. This relationship can be defined as a two-sided relationship. On the one hand, economic system determines educational system; educational system adapts to the economic system. On the other hand, educational system is different from economic system, and it has its own independent characteristics. The reform of educational system can be beneficial to the reform of economic system (Wan 1989).

The basic function of education is to provide skilled manpower and high level professionals for economic development. Education is a basic means of social reproduction of labor force. Educational process is also a process of input, production and output similar to the process of material production. Educational input is a part of social and economic resource. Educational production is the use of input so as to bring about products and services. Educational output is an important part of economic input which is called human resource. So the basic model and framework of educational system is determined by economic system.

In a broad sense, economic system determines educational system. As economic system changes, the education system too will experience changes, sooner or later.

Educational activities have their own characteristics. Although there are input and output in the process of education, education is not a process for providing material products; it is not a kind of pure economic activity. Education is also an activity with cultural connotations. The subjects of educational activities are educators, the objects of educational activities are the students, and both are persons.

The teaching and learning materials are used by both educators and the students. The goal of education is to cultivate and provide manpower and professionals.

The educational system is an important condition for economic system. As far as educational system is concerned, it pertains to the training of skilled labor force and professionals. The quantity, quality and structure of skilled labor force and professionals determine economic development to a certain extent. A rational and effective educational system can be beneficial to the rapid economic development. Otherwise it may hinder economic development.

As for the relation between reform of economic system and reform of educational system, there are both a complementary relationship and a competitive relationship. The reform of economic system can be beneficial to the reform of educational system for it provides the necessary economic environment and economic conditions. The reform of educational system can also be beneficial to the reform of economic system.

In the case of China, Brown pointed out that tying education to the demands of economic modernization has proved to be a double-edged sword. On the one hand, it has led to the welcome restoration of policies of reform on curriculum and administration in line with the economic reform they are intended to support. On the other hand, the application of the principles of economic reform to education has been used to justify the withholding of adequate government's funding from non-elite educational institutions, and to withdraw or reduce student support service.

At present China has been making great efforts to establish a socialist market economic system. Educational system must be adapting to this new type of economic system. So the reform of educational resource allocation mechanism is the core of the reform of educational system. From macro-management perspective, the system of establishment and management of schools at various levels should be perfected. The system of financing of education should be reformed. From the micro-management perspective, the system of personnel management and system of teachers' salaries should be reformed.

The relationship between educational system and political system is also important. Within a social system, political system is of foremost importance. Political system is the basic social system that affects many social activities in a society; it is also the basic factor that affects the educational system. The political system affects educational aims, constrains the educational contents and forms, and affects students' political and ideological consciousness.

1.6   Classification of Educational System

There are different ways of classifying educational systems. According to the levels of regular schools, educational system can be divided into preschool education system, primary education system, secondary education system and higher education system.

Educational system can also be classified as compulsory educational system and non-compulsory. Compulsory education is a kind of public goods. In view of public goods, governments provide compulsory education to citizens at a certain age. Non-compulsory education is not considered complete public goods; both governments and individuals can provide this kind of goods.

According to the ways of examination and approval of educational standards and outcome, educational systems can be classified as system of educational supervision in primary schools and secondary schools and system of educational evaluation in higher education institutions. At present, in China, there is an independent system of supervision which monitors primary education and secondary education. Local governments especially the governments of counties take the main responsibility in monitoring basic education reform and development. The responsibility of monitoring higher education is not taken by governments of counties but by the central government and provincial governments as well as some governments of municipalities. Viewed from the perspective of government administration, the system of evaluation of higher education is different from system of supervision of basic education.

According to the criteria of evaluation of teachers and students, educational system can be classified as the system of certification and system of academic degrees. Only after one meets the need of basic qualification of teachers can he or she become teachers after necessary selection procedures.

Educational system can be classified as external or internal educational system. External educational system is affected greatly by economic system and political system. Internal educational system is related to the management of schools.

According to the role of governments and the role of markets in educational development, educational system can be classified as government-oriented or market-oriented educational system. If governments dominate educational operations, this educational system can be called a government-oriented system. If markets dominate educational operations, the system can be called market-oriented educational system.

Government-oriented educational system has the following features. Firstly, decisions about what kind of education should be provided, how schools should be run, what is the purpose in running of schools, are determined by governments. Secondly, governments have a definite production function for educational development. Thirdly, the information for operation of education is transmitted from upper-level governments to lower-level governments. Fourthly, the transmission of information is based on the relation between various levels of governments. Fifthly, the incentives for teachers and students are instituted within the administrative framework and institutions. Sixthly, the criterion of reward depends on to what extent educational development plans have been fulfilled (Zhao 2003).

The government-oriented educational system has the following strengths. It is useful for mobilizing resources for fulfilling the educational development goals. The educational structure can be adjusted to the needs of governments and society at large. The externalities can be internalized by restructuring of schools at various levels. The educational resources can be used in key fields to enhance educational quality in a short time.

The government-oriented educational system has some shortcomings. It tends to be too rigid and the frequent interventions by governments leads to low efficiency in educational operation and will finally hinder educational development.

The market-dominated educational system has some features. Firstly, the power of decision making is dispersed among government, social groups, enterprises, families, individuals. Secondly, educational development is based on wide educational development goals and functions. Thirdly, the transmission of information in the process of educational development across the same level of stakeholders influences decision-making. Fourthly, educational actors can obtain sufficient information about choice of actions. Fifthly, the reward of educational activities is based on the various means of encouragement. Sixthly, the reward is connected with the evaluation results in market operation.

The market-dominated educational system has the following strengths. It is beneficial to guaranteeing consumer's freedom of choice. It is flexible in adapting to the requirement for manpower. It is beneficial to avoiding great mistakes. It is beneficial to educational innovation. It is beneficial to enhancement of efficiency of education.

There are some shortcomings with the market-oriented educational system. Under complete market competition, there will be serious problems with regard to equality of educational opportunities (Xiao 2004).

1.7 Various Educational Systems

Educational system in a State includes some concrete systems. The first kind of concrete educational system is the system of educational administration. According to theories of public goods, compulsory education is public goods, senior regular secondary education is semi-public goods, and regular higher education is quasi-public goods. Vocational and technical education is mainly private goods.

In nearly every country, public schools are the main part of schools especially in terms of primary schools and junior secondary schools. Central government and local governments should provide the funds for these schools. Governments also have administrative functions in social and economic management.

The school is a kind of social organization. Schools are educational institutions that use scarce resources such as teachers, staffs, students as well as materials and funds to make rational choice for provision of educational service so as to meet the needs of individuals and society at large. The educational institutions are using the form of bureaucratic management. Internal management is vital for the control and coordination of educational institutions.

The system of educational administration and system of internal management is connected to each other intimately. Usually the system of educational administration determines internal management system. The system of internal management aims at fulfilling the goals determined by governments in many cases.

In the process of running of schools, the enrollment of students is the prerequisite for operation of schools. Education is a kind of social service. The consumers of educational service are chiefly the students. Without students' participation schools cannot function properly. The system of enrollment tackles the questions of what kind of students are qualified to be enrolled in an educational institution, how to recruit these students, how to screen the candidates.

Students are destined to graduate from schools within a specific period of schooling. After finishing the summative education students will find jobs outside of schools. So the system of employment is a natural part of the operation of schools and society at large.

In order to run schools, funds are a necessary input. In a narrow sense, funds are the first and continuous driving force of educational development. How to raise funds and how to use these funds become main issues in the system of financing of education.

The aim of examination is for teachers to find out whether students are achieving the prescribed standards of learning. The system of examination is an important part of operation of schools.

The system of supervision is a monitoring system and feedback mechanism. The system of evaluation at school level is an important part of management. The evaluation includes evaluation of schools, teachers and students.

1.8 Policy Perspective on Educational System

The term 'policy' is an elusive one and demands some clarification. Even a brief investigation will reveal that the word 'policy' is used in many ways. This is the case both in everyday language and in scholars' writing. The word 'policy' is sometime used in a narrow sense to refer to formal statements of action to be followed, while other persons use the word as a synonym for words such as plan or program. Here the term policy is used to refer to the implicit or explicit specification of courses of purposive action being followed and directed towards the accomplishment of some intended or desired set of goals. Policy could be thought of as a position or stance developed in response to a problem or issue of conflict, and directed towards a particular objective (Hough 1984).

For policy system, there are some related concepts. Laws or regulations refer to the formal or legal expressions providing authorization to policies. Decisions refer to specific actions taken to set goals, develop plans, implement and evaluate programs. Programs refer to authorized means, strategies and details of procedure for achieving goals. Plans or proposals refer to specified means for achieving goals. The circular issued by educational administrative department do not have the force of law, they have a persuasive effect on subordinate institutions.

Policies can take different forms and expressions and can be directed toward different ends. Some policies take the form of legislations and regulations. Some policies take the form of directives. Some policies take the form of decisions issued by governments. Some policies take form of minister statements. Some policies take the form of programs. Some policies take form of plans and proposals.

Policy is focus on purposive or goal oriented actions or actively rather than random or chance behaviors. It refers to courses or patterns of action, rather than separate discrete decisions. Usually policy development and application involves a number of related decisions, rather than a single decision.

1.9   Institutional Perspective on Educational System

Institutions are sets of ordered relationships among people that define their rights and responsibilities. A set of relationship at one level is embedded in a set of relationship at a higher level to make up a complex system. Institutions are human relationships that structure opportunities via constraints and enablement. They structure incentives used in calculating individual advantage. They also affect beliefs and preferences and provide cues to uncalculated action. They provide order and predictability to human interaction. The mental images created by law and custom coordinate human action to one purpose or another and determine whose interests count.

Although educational institutions work as a social system, they can be analytically grouped into two distinct segments to enhance our understanding of their functions. As far as education is concerned, institutional environment is defined as a set of fundamental legal rules that establish the basis of educational activities. Institutional arrangements provide a structure within which members cooperate or compete. Institutional arrangements include the governance structure and the evolution of institutional environments.

To design educational institutions that can achieve a particular educational performance, it is useful to understand the source of human interdependence. Different kinds of goods and services create different kind of interdependencies, and thus it takes different institutions to control and direct them. Educational Institutions define the opportunity sets of interdependent transacting parties in the educational process.

Some educational institutions are formal such as laws, administrative regulations, while others are informal such as ideological, customs, and procedures. Some are public and others are private. Educational institutions are the humanly devised constraints that structure educational interaction.

1.10   Characteristics of the Educational System in China Before the Reform and Opening up to the Outside World

Soon after the formation of the People's Republic of China in 1949, the country took steps to establish a socialist system of education. This kind of educational system was mostly an adjustment to the planned socialist economic system. It was characterized by highly centralized and unitary leadership; it was dominated by the government. This kind of educational system had three features.

Firstly, schools at various levels were financed and administrated by governments. All Higher Education Institutions (HEI) were public institutions. No private HEIs existed. Though most schools were funded and managed by the governments, some schools in villages were funded by collectives and managed by communities.

Secondly, the central government had full control of the administration of education undertakings. The local governments could administer the schools under their jurisdiction, but they had to strictly go by the directives issued by the central government.

Thirdly, the structure of education was rigid and monotonous. Schools at different levels trained skilled labor force on the basis of the socialist economic model.

1.11 The Beginning of the Educational Reform Since 1978 in China

From 1978 on, China embarked on the reform of economic system. In the new situation, the shortcomings of the original educational system became increasingly glaring. The overdue centralized and unitary management by governments needed to be reformed.

Up to 1978, in terms of basic education, the system of schooling, curricula, and textbooks were all managed unitarily across the whole country.

While general education developed rapidly, vocational and technical education developed very slowly.

In terms of higher education development, the specialties were divided into narrow fields. The enrollment of students was determined by governments, HEIs were funded totally by governments. Students did not have to pay for higher education.

In 1984 the Central Government issued the *Decisions on Reform of Economic System*. The reform in urban areas and enterprises started. The reform of ownership system, management system, labor and personnel system, distribution system were introduced gradually. Under this circumstance, reform of the educational system had to be carried out systematically.

1.12 Direction of the Reform of the Educational System After the Initiation of Economic Reform

Educational system includes four subsystems. These subsystems are: decision making system, information system, regulation system, organization system. In China reform of educational system was to be directed towards the socialist educational system with a better micro-management structure with Chinese features.

In terms of decision-making, the centralized system should be changed into decentralized system which has the participation of governments, schools, teachers and students. The governments' decision making power should focus on the macro-management of education such as formulation of educational development goal, formulation of educational investment plan, setting up educational guideline and policies. Governments should care about the balance between educational supply and demand. The decision making powers of the central government and the local governments should be divided and exercised effectively. Primary education and secondary education should be administrated by local governments; higher education institutions should be administrated by central governments, provincial governments and municipal governments. Except for the Ministry of Education, other ministries under the State Council need not administrate higher education institutions directly. The central government should focus on macro-management of education. Schools should have sufficient micro decision-making powers, such as, the power of domination of personnel, materials and funds, and the power of making educational planning in schools. Teachers should have the power of being employed, power of choice of resignation, power to change jobs, power of selecting instruction contents and methods. Students should have the power of choosing vacation.

In terms of information, the information system that is built on the basis of monotonous and mainly horizontal information circulation should be changed into an information system on the basis of horizontal information transmission in conjunction with vertical information transmission. The information production and transmission process should be perfected. Decision-makers at various levels should regulate educational resource allocation on the basis of the requirement of labor forces.

In terms of regulation system, the planning regulation system should be transformed into a new system by the combination of planning regulation and market oriented regulation in which administrative means, economic means, and legal means are used.

1.13   Goals, Tasks and Measures for the Reform of Educational System in 1985

On 27 May 1985, *Decisions on Reform of Educational System* was issued by the Central Committee of the CCP. The guidelines and policies for the reform of educational system were formulated and implemented (Editorial Board of China's Education Yearbook 1984).

The reform of educational system aims at enhancing national competence and providing more and better manpower. Education should serve the socialist country, and socialist construction should rely on education.

In order to change the current situation, the educational system should be reformed systematically. In terms of educational management, better selection of staff and simpler administration should be pursued. Autonomous powers of schools should be strengthened. Educational structures should be regulated and the system of labor and personnel should be reformed.

In terms of basic educational development, the power of management should be delegated to local governments. The system of local governments taking up overall responsibilities in terms of basic education development and management at various levels should be established.

In terms of vocational education, the vocational system with various levels, in line with industrial development, with rational structures, connected with general education should be established. Enterprises' and industries' interest in and enthusiasm for educational development should be aroused.

In terms of higher education, the administrative system in which governments exercise too much power over higher education institutions should be reformed. Under the guidance of the State's educational guidelines and plans, the autonomous powers of HEIs should be increased.

1.14   Deepening the Reform of Educational System in 1990s

In 1993 *Program of China's Educational Reform and Development* was issued by the Central Committee of the CCP and the State Council (He 1998a, b). It signified the deepening of the reform of the educational system.

The goal of the reform of the educational system was to establish a new educational system that was adapted to the reform of socialist market oriented economic and political system, and to scientific and technological development. In order to achieve this goal, it was necessary to take comprehensive and coordinated measures to carry forward the reform step by step and to deepen it further. The old system in which governments took too many responsibilities and practiced a rigid style of management should be reformed further (Jin 2000, P. 491).

Reform of educational system should help the training of constructors and those who are successful and abide by socialist directions and be able to arouse the enthusiasm of governments, society, teachers and students, and be able to enhance educational qualities, research levels and the effectiveness of running schools, and be beneficial to make education serve socialist construction.

The reform of educational system should center on three aspects: First, it should bring about a change in the system of educational provision. The system of governments taking all responsibilities in education provision needed to be changed. The system of governments' taking the main responsibilities and social communities assisting in educational provision should be established. Second, the educational reform at secondary or lower levels of education should be strengthened. The system of educational provision at various levels and management at various levels should be instituted. The system of enrollment in HEIs and graduates' employment should be reformed. Third, the system of tuitions and fees should be instituted. The system of independent employment should also be instituted. The system of personnel should be reformed so as to adapt to the needs of the reform of educational system.

1.15   "National Guidelines" Enforcement and Local Educational Reform Initiation

In 2010, *National Guidelines for Medium-long-term Educational Reform and Development Program (2010–2020)* was formally promulgated, and it sets the guiding principles and goals for deepening educational reform and promoting the educational undertakings in the near future. The *National Guidelines* stipulated strategic goals of educational development, namely achieving educational modernization, constructing the learning-centered society and building a nation with strong human resources in 2020. The *National Guidelines* stipulated development tasks for education of all levels and types. As far as the reform of educational system was concerned, reform goals and measures for five kinds of educational system were identified; these five systems were the training system, the system of examination and enrollment, the system of educational provision, the system of educational administration, the system of internal management. Since 2010 the central government has tried to divide this gigantic task of educational reform into various components and to devise proper division of labor in implementation; and steps have been taken to promote cooperation between different governmental departments. The Ministry of Education ordered local authorities to conduct pilot projects on reform of education. Governments at provincial-level and county-level also made plans of educational reform and development in light of local realities and actual needs. Local governments and schools at various levels have made a great deal of innovations in educational reform.

1.16   The Outline of This Book

Except for an introduction, this book covers nine concrete educational systems. In each chapter five aspects are explored.

Firstly, the concept, kinds and functions of different systems are explained.

Secondly, the historical development of each concrete educational system is described.

Thirdly, the current situation of each educational system is described.

Fourthly, the problems facing China's educational system are discussed.

Finally, the relevant strategies and measures for tracking these difficulties and problems are put forward.

References

Editorial Board of China's Education Yearbook (Ed.). (1984). *China's education yearbook.* Beijing: Chinese Great Encyclopedia Publishing House.

Editorial Board of China's Education Yearbook (Ed.). (1991). *The great Chinese dictionary.* Beijing: Commercial Publishing House.

Gregory, P. R., & Robert, S. C. (1980). *A comparative study on economic system.* New York: Houghton Mifflin Company.

Gu, M. (Ed.). (1992). *The great dictionary of education.* Shanghai: Shanghai Education Press.

He, D. (Ed.). (1998a). *Important documents in the People's Republic of China (1949–1975).* Haikou: Hainan Press.

He, D. (Ed.). (1998b). *Important documents in the People's Republic of China (1976–1990).* Haikou: Hainan Press.

Hough, J. R. (Ed.). (1984). *Educational policies: An international survey.* New York: St. Martin's Press.

Jianguo, T. (1990). *On higher education.* Jinan: Shandong education Publishing House.

Jin, Y. (Ed.). (2000). *A history of Chinese socialist education.* Shanghai: East China Normal University Press.

Liu, H. (1999). *Massification of higher education and reform of the system of higher education.* Doctoral Dissertation.

Pan, M. Y. (1995). *Teaching Principles and Methods for Higher Edcuation.* Beijing: People's Education Press.

Procter, P. (Ed.). (1978). *The Longman dictionary of contemporary english.* Bath: Longman Group Limited.

Wan, S. (Ed.). (1989). *Economics of education.* Beijing: Beijing Normal University.

Wan, Y. (1992). *Ten articles on higher education.* Shanghai: East China Normal University.

Wang, J. (2002). *A Macro-analysis of Higher Education.* Beijing: Higher Education Press.

Xiao, H. (2004). *Educational development.* Wuhan: Wuhan University Press.

Zhao, D. (Ed.). (2003). *Rights and responsibilities: Research on relations between governments and universities.* Haerbing: Heilongjiang People's Press.

Chapter 2
Pursuing Good Governance: Educational Administration System in China

2.1 Introduction to the System of Educational Administration

2.1.1 The Concept of the System of Educational Administration

The expression 'educational administration' refers to a range of activities connected with organizing and supervising the way education is managed. The expression educational administration may be understood in a static sense or in a dynamic sense. In the static sense, it refers to the administrative organizations and institutions that manage educational affairs. In the dynamic sense, it refers to the activities of the administrative departments that manage and guide educational processes.

Educational administrative departments at various levels in a country can be classified as central and local educational administrative departments. Ordinarily, when one speaks of educational administration, it also includes educational management.

The words 'administration' and 'management' are often used to signify the same process, though they are not exactly the same. The concept of management has a broader sense than the concept of administration. School management is different from educational administration because school management concerns schools' behaviors, while educational administration concerns governmental behaviors. In a broad sense, educational management includes both educational administration and school management.

Educational administration is intimately related to the establishment of a public education system. As this kind of system was instituted in a definite period, the State's function of education was strengthened. The State began to play a much greater role in the management of educational affairs.

© Springer Nature Singapore Pte Ltd. and Higher Education Press 2018
M. Yang and H. Ni, *Educational Governance in China*,
https://doi.org/10.1007/978-981-13-0842-0_2

The system of educational administration aims at answering questions regarding decision-making powers, as well as the question of who makes decisions. Usually there are three kind of decision-making models. The first kind is the centralized decision-making model; the second kind is the decentralized decision-making model; the third kind is a combination of both centralized and decentralized decision-making models.

The system of educational administration is only a part of the total educational system in the country. It is also a part of the system of the national administration (Wu 2000). The author of *On Educational Administration* says that the system of educational administration is the basic ways of a State's guidance on education. The system of national administration refers to central government and local governments' administrative organizations and institutions.

The system of educational administration is the basic system of the State's organizing and managing education. Administratively the structure of the educational system is a partnership among the central government, local governments and schools, where each has its own specific powers and duties. The System of educational administration pertains to division of powers of managing education between central government and local governments, between governments and schools at various levels and the relationship of these social actors. The system of educational administration determines the principles, methods and procedures in organizing educational administration. The central government defines national objectives, while the task of implementing them falls on the local governments and schools. The ministers of department of education can use legislation and regulations to lay down objectives, impose standards and to confer powers. The increase in public educational expenditures has meant that there has been a close involvement of the central government which exercises control by means of appropriation. It is incumbent on each local government to establish an educational commission and take responsibility for primary educational development and secondary educational development.

2.1.2 Classification of the System of Educational Administration

Educational administration is classified according to the different levels of education existing in the country, such as primary, secondary, and higher education.

In the People's Republic of China, both primary and secondary education are administrated by local governments, under the direction of the State Council and the leadership of governments of provinces. Higher education is administrated by the State Council and the people's governments of the provinces, autonomous regions, and municipalities directly under the State Council.

From the point of view of management, educational administration may be classified as both macro and micro level management of educational affairs. Macro

-management refers to the relationships between governments and the educational institutions. Micro-management refers to decision-making conducted by social actors within schools.

In terms of the degree of independence enjoyed by educational institutions, we may classify educational administration into affiliated systems of educational administration and indepengdent system of educational administration.

In the affiliated system of administration, the educational institutions or departments at various levels are affiliated to the government's Ministry or Board of Education. The individual educational institution, school or college is guided by the directives of the governments.

In the independent system of administration, the local educational institutions or departments are not functioning departments of local governments. They have autonomous power in administering educational affairs.

As far as government's control is concerned, the system of educational administration can be classified as centralized and decentralized system.

The centralized system is a kind of system in which power is concentrated in the central government, while the local governments and lower administrative institutions have little power; in this koind of system, most measures are based on central government's directives.

There are four features concerning the centralized system: (1) the educational power is concentrated on the Ministry of Education; (2) the State has unitary educational goals, instructional programs, curricula, criteria of evaluation; (3) the laws and regulations are determined by law-makers and central government and they have absolute power of constraints; (4) the State provides most educational funds for various schools.

The centralized system has five shortcomings. Firstly, the efficiency may be low becaus educational administrative departments cannot adapt to new changes easily. Secondly, institutions are not easy to be changed so many opportunities will be lost in the process of development. Thirdly, local social actors' involvement is not enough and localities' enthusiasm cannot be aroused. Fourthly, schools have little autonomous power in the running of educational institutions. Fifthly, the cost of management is too high because of the inflexibility of decision-making and implementation of decisions.

The decentralized system is a system whereby lower administrative institutions and local governments have sufficient autonomy; central government does not interfere with internal affairs of lower administrative institutions and local governments. Decentralization of power includes delegation of tasks, empowerment and devolution. Decentralized system has three features. The Ministry of Education has limited power. Curricula and choice of textbook are determined by local educational administrative departments, some laws are formulated by localities. Localities provide educational funds. There are several strengths in the decentralized system. Educational administration is flexible and local situations can be considered completely. Enthusiasm of localities and lower administrative departments can be aroused effectively. Decentralized system can help enhance educational efficiency. Decentralized system helps improve democratic management.

Educational resources may be increased under decentralized system. There are some shortcomings with the decentralized system. Firstly, there may not be unitary guidance and management across the whole country and between different regions. Secondly, educational development can be separated from the needs of the total State, and coordination may be difficult.

2.1.3 The Functions of the System of Educational Administration

The system of educational administration pertains to the relationship between governments, markets, society and schools. The ideal system of educational administration is a system where the governments take care of macro-management, the society ensures a broad involvement in educational activities, and schools have autonomous power of operations. Generally speaking, the system of educational administration has four functions: the function of guiding and directing education; distribution of power; improvement in labor division and coordination; enhancement of efficiency.

The responsibilities of government in educational reform and development include eight aspects: (1) to guide and supervise educational undertakings and guarantee directions of educational development by formulating educational guidelines, laws, policies; (2) to make educational development scale in line with the comprehensive powers of the state; (3) to formulate the criteria of educational quality; (4) to coordinate and control educational structures; (5) to manage and optimize educational resource allocation; (6) to supervise instruction and make monitoring of educational qualities; (7) to facilitate liaison between governments, markets, society and schools; and (8) to establish service systems for educational development and reform.

The historical development of educational administration system in China since 1949 can be divided into five stages.

2.2 The System of Educational Administration at the Stage of Completing Socialist Restructuring (1949–1956)

In this period, the new system of educational administration was established. In order to adapt to the centralized and unitary planning economic system, the system of educational administrati on was also centralized and unitary.

2.2.1   The Context, Tasks, Guideline and Achievements in Educational Reform and Development in This Period

2.2.1.1   The State of Education Before the Founding of the People's Republic of China

Before the liberation, the educational level of the people in China was very low. Most persons could not receive an education at all. Among the adults aged above 18 years, 80% were illiterate; the literacy rate in rural areas was much lower than it was in the urban areas. In 1947, there were 205 Higher Education Institutions (HEI) in China. The enrollment was 0.15 million in HEIs, 22.85 million in primary schools and 1.798 million in secondary schools (Editorial Board of China's Education Yearbook 1986).

2.2.1.2   Arduous Tasks in the Reform and Development of Education in This Period

Since the Chinese Communist Party took control of the new national power, how to cope with the old educational system and maintain the operation of various schools under new circumstances and how to construct a new educational system serving the new national construction goal and task, was a great challenge for the new Chinese governments. Great transformation was taken place in China hereafter.

On 21 September, 1949, the First Plenary Session of the Chinese People's Political Consultative Conference (CPPCC) was held in Beijing. At this meeting the Common Program of CPPCC was issued. The Common Program stipulated that the State should popularize education with well planned and effective measures, strengthen secondary and higher education, lay emphasis on vocational and technical education, promote spare time education of workers and peasants as well as on-the-job training of cadres, and educate the youth and the intellectuals of the old society (He 1998).

In 1949, during the First National Conference on Education, the vice minister, Qian Junrui, pointed out the seven challenges facing the reform and development of education in PRC, namely: (1) building a new democratic system of education by absorbing the useful experiences of the old society and borrowing from the Soviet Union experience; (2) establishing the People's Universities to cultivate professionals and fast middle schools to cultivate intellectuals; (3) conducting literacy movements across whole country; (4) improving the quality of education in the old liberated areas; (5) uniting and reforming the thinking of intellectuals in the old liberated areas; (6) reforming the old educational system gradually and accumulating experiences; (7) preserving and restructuring private schools administrated by Chinese governments (Editorial Board of China's Education Yearbook 1986).

2.2.1.3   New Guideline for the Education Development in the Early 1950s

In an article entitled *On New Democracy*, published in 1940, Mao Zedong pointed out that the revolution in China would be carried out in two steps. One step was to establish a country characterized by a new kind of democracy, and the other step was to build a socialist country. The nature of the culture and education inculcated in this new democracy was to be national, scientific and people-oriented (Mao 1991).

On 1 October, 1949, the People's Republic of China was formally founded. On this day, Chairmen Mao released a Government Circular which stated that the Common Program of the People's Political Consultative Conference (PPCC) would be the guiding principles for the Central Government in China. So the national policies of education would be in accordance with the guidelines of the PPCC.

The Common Program was considered as a temporary Constitution. The fifth chapter of the Common Program stipulated that culture and education in this new democracy would have strong national features, a scientific temper, and would be directed to the needs of the people. The task of the Central Government and the local governments would be to enhance the cultural levels of the people and provide manpower for building up a socialist nation.

On 20 September, 1954, the First Session of the National Congress issued *the Constitution of the People's Republic of China* (He 1998). The Constitution stipulated that citizens of the People's Republic of China had a right to receive education; that the State would establish and expand schools and other educational institutions so as to guarantee the educational rights of the citizens.; that the State was concerned about the physical and mental development of children and youth.; that the People's Republic of China guarantees the freedom of its citizens to pursue scientific research, literature, art and other cultural activities.

In order to facilitate educational reform and development, it was necessary to set up new educational management systems and administrative agencies, restructuring the old system and creating a new system of educational administration.

2.2.1.4   Main Achievements in This Period

From the founding of the People's Republic of China in 1949 to completing socialist restructuring in 1956, under the guidance and the administration of CPC, China completed the process of transforming itself into a true socialist country, putting the country on the road to development through large-scale planned economic construction. Thus in a very short time China had completed its socialist transformation from private ownership of means of production and established public ownership of means of production.

This period included two stages. The period from 1949 to 1952 was called transitional period. In this period China established governments at various levels, confiscated enterprises dominated by former bureaucratic capitalists and transformed them into state-owned enterprises, finished the land reforms, launched a movement against corruption, wastage, bureaucracy, bribery, tax evasion, theft of state property, cheating in work, stealing state economic information. In 1952, the Central Committee of the CCP put forward the Total Guideline. According to the Total Guideline, over a long period the socialist industrialization was to be realized, and the restructuring of agriculture, manual industry, capitalist industry and commerce were to be accomplished.

From 1953 to 1957 was the period of implementation of the First Five-year Plan. In the First Five Year Plan period, the Chinese economy developed quickly. Some basic industries were established, markets began to pick up, and people's living standards started improving gradually.

2.2.2 Establishment of Educational Administrative Institutions at Various Levels

2.2.2.1 The Setting up of Educational Administrative Institutions

The setting up of new administrative organization was important for educational reform and development.

On 27 September, 1949, the First Plenary of the People' Political Consultative Conference issued *Central Government Organization Law in China*. According to the Organization Law, the Administrative Council was the highest executive functioning institution in terms of state affairs in China. Under the jurisdiction of the Administrative Council there were 35 departments and four high-level commissions. The Commissions were the Political and Law Commission, the Finance and Economy Commission, the Culture and Education Commission, the People's Supervision Commission.

From 1949 to 1953, a special administrative level known as the Great Administrative Regions (GAR) was set up. There were six such Regions. For each GAR, there was the Government of the great administrative regions; they were representative organs of the Central Government in each great administrative region.

Under the level of the great administrative regions, there was the next administrative level called Governments of Provinces or Provincial Governments. Under every Provincial Government there were about 20 departments.

The cities had a special administrative arrangement in which the governments of the cities were under the jurisdiction of the central governments, the GAR, and the provinces. There were 150 cities in China in 1949.

Under the provincial governments were the governments of counties. In 1952 there were 2149 counties. The governments of counties were supervised by governments of provinces and governments of prefectures.

Under the Government of the Counties were the governments of districts. The lowest level of government was the government of towns.

By the end of 1951 there were 35 departments and commissions under the Administrative Council. In 1952 as the large construction across the whole country began, the number of departments in the Administrative Council increased to 45.

The Central Government Organization Law in China also stipulated that the Ministry of Education was an integral part of Administrative Council.

On 19 October, 1949, the Central Committee of the CCP appointed the famous historian Guo Moluo as the Director of the Culture and Education Commission. The Commission was in charge of three ministries—the Ministry of Culture, the Ministry of Education, and the Ministry of Hygiene. Also on the same day, Ma Xulun, a very famous scholar and educator, was appointed the first minister of the Ministry of Education.

On 31 October, 1949, according to the directive issued by the central government, the former Ministry of Education and the Ministry of Higher Education affiliated to the Huabei People's Government became the basis of setting up the new Ministry of Education in China (Mao and Sheng 1989).

The Ministry of Education was formally established on 1st November 1949.

The founding of the Chinese Culture and Education Commission as well as the Ministry of Education, was a very important step for implementing guidelines and policies set by the Chinese Communist Party and the central government, for restructuring the old educational system and launching the new educational initiatives.

In 1952, the Ministry of Higher Education was instituted. Its responsibilities were directed to higher education, while the Ministry of Education was in charge of regular primary and secondary education, normal education, nationality education and spare time education of workers and peasants.

The year 1954 saw many changes in the People's Republic of China—the First National Congress was convened and the first *Constitution of PRC* approved. The Chairman of the People's Republic of China was elected. The Administrative Council was changed into State Council. Also in 1954, the administrative institutions of the Great Administrative Regions were revoked.

On 23 December, 1949, the Ministry of Education organized the first national conference on education in Beijing. In this conference some guidelines and policies of education were set up. It was suggested that education must serve to build up a socialist country, and schools should be open to workers and peasants. The main task of governments should be to look after the following five aspects: (1) establishing a democratic educational system by using the educational experience of the former liberated area and the Soviet Union; (2) creating the People's University and the Haerbing Industrial University and a number of Fast Schools for workers and peasants; (3) carrying out Massive Literacy Movements; (4) enhancing the quality of educational in the old liberated area; (5) continuing the operation of educational institutions in new liberated area; (6) reconstructing the old educational system; (7) maintaining status quo, strengthening leadership and reconstructing gradually for the development of private schools.

In this period the central government and local governments made great efforts to reform private schools at various levels.

2.2.2.2   Educational Administration in Primary Schools and Secondary Schools (1949–1956)

A. Educational Administration in Primary Schools in the 1950s

Concerned with the system of administration of primary education, the Ministry of Education issued the Provisional Regulations on Primary Schools. The Regulations stipulated the following tasks for the various levels of administration:

The Ministry of Education should draw up the syllabus for every subject in primary schools, edit textbooks, specify the facilities required in primary schools, establish criteria for constructing school buildings and establish life guidance criteria.

The educational administrative departments of the provincial level shall establish the criteria as regards the size of the teaching staff, administrative staff and workers as well as criteria of educational expenditure.

The educational administrative departments of the county-level governments shall determine the establishment, modification or dissolution of primary schools. The educational administrative departments of the county-level governments shall administrate public and private schools uniformly.

On 26 November, 1953, the Administrative Council issued *Directives on Improvement and Development of Primary Education.* The *Directives* pointed out that localities should strengthen the administration of schools under the governments of counties (Editorial Board of China's Education Yearbook 1986).

B. Educational administration in secondary schools in 1950s

In the 1950s, great changes were taking place also in the administrative system of secondary education.

The Ministry of Education issued *Provisional Regulations on Secondary Schools.* The *Regulations* stipulated that secondary schools were to be administrated unitarily by departments of culture and education under provincial governments in accord with the regulations of the central government and the governments in great administrative regions.

The establishment, modification or dissolution of secondary schools had to be examined and ratified by provincial governments, and the relevant documents filed the department of culture and education of the Great Administrative Region.

The department of culture and education under the provincial governments were to entrust the administration of secondary schools to the governments of prefectures or governments of counties.

In the case of secondary schools established by the ministries under the Central Government or the departments under the Government of the great administrative regions, their establishment, modification or dissolution were to be examined by the concerned ministries or departments and the relevant papers filed with the ministry of education or the department of education of the great administrative regions.

The establishment, modification or dissolution of secondary schools established by departments under the provincial governments had to be examined and approved by provincial governments. The administrative affairs were to be managed by departments concerned.

The guidelines, policies, system of schooling, educational plans and instruction were to be administrated by departments of education under the province-level governments.

On 8 April, 1954, the Administrative Council issued *Directives on Improvement and Development of Secondary Education*. The *Directives* stipulated that the education departments of provinces should improve the administrative system of secondary schools. According to the principle of "unitary guidance with management at different levels", the secondary schools under the jurisdiction of provincial governments should be administrated by provincial governments, and those under the jurisdiction of county governments should be administrated by the governments of prefectures. Every province should have at least some secondary schools and run them efficiently (Editorial Board of China's Education Yearbook 1986).

2.2.2.3 Educational Administration in Higher Education Institutions (1949–1956)

A. Educational administration in higher education institutions from 1949 to 1952

The unitary system of administration of higher education institutions (HEI) was in force from 1948 to 1952.

In the early 1950s, the system of administration of higher education underwent two stages of development. From 1949 to 1952, higher education was administrated by the Ministry of Education and the Department of Education within the great administrative regions, but most HEIs were administrated by the department of education within the great administrative regions.

On 1 June, 1950, the Ffst national conference on higher education was convened in Beijing, the conference emphasized the need for teaching basic science and introducing research initiatives, and stressed unitary and centralized leadership by government.

On 5 May, 1950, the Administrative Council issued Provisional Regulations on the Administration of Higher Education Institutions in each Great Administrative Regions (Editorial Board of China's Education Yearbook 1986, p. 776). In this period, there were six great administrative regions, and they were called Huabei, Dongbei, Xibei, Xinan, Zhongnan, Huadong. The Provisional Regulations stipulated that the Ministry of Education administer HEIs in Huabei Region, while HEIs in the other great administrative regions were to be administered by the departments of education under the Great Administrative Regions on behalf on the Ministry of Education. The presidents of HEIs were nominated by the Ministry of Education and ratified by the Administrative Council. The great administrative regions should issue regulations adapting adapted to local situations in addition to the general regulations issued by the Administrative Council. The budgets of HEIs in great administrative regions were examined and approved by the department of education and sent to the Ministry of Education for preliminary registration.

On August 2, 1950, the Administrative Council issued *Decision on Problems of Administrative Affairs in Higher Education Institutions*. It addressed the issue of the control of the Ministry of Education over all higher education institutions across the country; while the major regional departments of education were having control over colleges and universities under their jurisdiction (Editing Board of China's Education Yearbook 1986).

According to the Decision, the Ministry of Education would take measures to take direct control over HEIs in each region. The comprehensive universities should be under leadership of the Ministry of Education or other Departments of Education under the Great Administrative Regions.

On 14 August, 1950, the Ministry of Education issued Provisional Regulations for Universities and Colleges as well as for Specialized Higher Education Schools (Editorial Board of China's Education Yearbook 1986).

The *Regulations* specified the basic relationships between the governments and the universities and colleges. The regulation stipulated that higher education institutions included universities and colleges; that the establishment and dissolution of universities and colleges would be ratified by the Administrative Council; that the establishment and dissolution of departments should be approved by the Ministry of Education; that the establishment of colleges within a university would be determined by the Ministry of Education; that the length of schooling for universities and colleges should be 3–5 years.

Regulations on Specialized Higher Education Schools stipulated the establishment and dissolution of specialized higher education schools should be approved by the Ministry of Education or other ministries under the Administrative Council. The establishment and dissolution of subjects and disciplines should be determined by the Ministry of Education or other Ministries under the Administrative Council.

On 16 July, 1952, the Ministry of Education issued *Regulations for the Higher Normal Universities and Colleges* (He 1998, p. 79). The *Regulations* stipulated that normal HEIs include normal universities and colleges as well as higher specialized schools. The normal universities and colleges under the jurisdiction of the Great Administrative Regions should be administered by the department of education under the Great Administrative Regions.

B. System of educational administration in higher education institutions by the ministry of higher education (1952–1956)

In order to adapt to the needs of lage-scale planned construction and to strengthen the leadership in educational institutions, on 15 December, 1952, the 19th Plenary Session of the Central Government passed a Resolution (Editorial Board of China's Education Yearbook 1986). The Resolution decided to set up the Ministry of Higher Education. The Ministry of Higher Education was to be in charge of higher education affairs, and the Ministry of Education in charge of general education, normal education, minority education and spare-time education of workers and peasants. This was the first time that two different Ministries together controlled educational affairs, although each had its own functions and responsibilities.

On 11 October, 1953, the Administrative Council issued *Revised Decisions on Control over Higher Education Institutions.* According to the *Decisions*, the Ministry of Higher Education would exercise unitary leadership on all higher education institutions, except those belonging to the military. The HEIs should abide by the construction plans, financial plans, financial systems, personnel systems, instruction plans, instruction programs and other regulations regarding higher education that are issued by the Ministry of Higher Education. The direct administration of higher education institutions was taken by the Ministry of Higher Education and other Ministries concerned. The comprehensive universities and polytechnic colleges were directly administrated by the Ministry of Higher education. The multi-disciplinary industrial colleges were administrated by the Ministry of Higher Education. If necessary, they could be delegated to ministries under the Administrative Council. Those colleges or universities with single purpose were mainly administrated by the respective ministries. The management of some other colleges or universities could be given to the governments of provinces, municipalities or autonomous regions of ethnic minorities if the Ministry of Higher Education and other Ministries were finding it not easy to administer them. The ministries under the Administrative Council and local governments should abide by the regulations issued by the Administrative Council and the Ministry of Higher education and consult them. In matters concerning textbooks, facilities, production fieldwork and scientific research, the Ministry of Higher Education should consult other ministries. Higher education institutions should receive guidance and help from the Great Administrative Regions and provincial governments (He 1998).

In comparison with the *Regulations* on administrative system of higher education issued in 1950, the *Regulations* issued in 1953 stressed the unitary leadership of the Ministry of Higher Education. Most HEIs were under the direct guidance of the Ministry of Higher Education and other ministries under the Administrative Council. The central governments controlled higher education tightly. Under this

Regulation, a new administrative tier was added, namely, the provincial governments. From 1953 on China's system of unified control and management at two levels for higher education had a new starting point.

2.2.3   Measures Taken by the New Educational Administrative Departments to Reform Public and Private Education

Earlier on 28 October, 1949, the Third Plenary Session of the Administrative Council passed *Decree on the Taking over of Commission under the Administrative Council*. The *Decree* set up the guidelines for taking over schools (He 1998).

On 1 October, 1949, the Military Regulation Commission sent delegates to take control over Tsinghua University. The takeover meant two things: one task was taking possession of these schools; the other task was taking charge of the administration of these schools. While taking control of it, the Military Regulation Commission assured the safety of the teachers and students and promised to bear the cost of maintenance and other expenses of these schools.

In June 1949, the Military Regulation Commission took control of Shanghai Jiaotong University, Fudan University and Tongji University. In the latter half of the year, the administration of these schools was streamlined; the Commission for School Affairs was set up; the People's Grants for students were established; some schools and departments were merged and the curricula restructured.

2.3   Educational Administration at the Stage of the Socialist Construction (1957–1965)

After the completion of socialist restructuring, China launched socialism on a large-scale. From 1957 to 1965, a great deal of new industries were established, the structure of industries improved, and the capital construction and technological transformation were carried out on a large-scale. Educational undertakings developed rapidly.

As social and economic development accelerated, the system of educational administration showed its strengths and shortcomings. The strengths were manifested in the concentration of forces in the State to facilitate educational development. The shortcomings were manifested in the diminishing enthusiasm of local bodies and social groups in running schools. So in the late 1950s and early 1960s the reform of educational administration centered on devolution.

2.3.1 The Organization and Policy Changes in This Period

2.3.1.1 Organizational Changes in Educational Administrative System from 1957 to 1965

As the development indicators of the first Five Year Plan were fulfilled and the socialist restructuring accomplished ahead of time, the ownership of the means of production was changed into a kind of public ownership. The economic and cultural developments were taken care of by making and implementing the plans. The scale of construction expanded rapidly; the socialization and 'professionalization' of production developed rapidly. Under these circumstances, the economic system was excessively centralized.

The increase in the administrative institutions led to high centralization of power and a reduction in the autonomy of local bodies. As a consequence, they began to ask the central government to devolve powers. Hence from 1958, the central government began to devolve powers to localities. Many enterprises and public institutions were delegated to localities.

A. Educational administration in higher education institutions (1957–1962)

In February, 1958, the Ministry of Higher education and the Ministry of Education were merged; the new ministry was called the Ministry of Education. The responsibilities of the ministry included making greater efforts to improve research and implementing the guideline and policies of the Chinese Communist Party; making a comprehensive plan for national education; helping local governments to conduct ideological education; guiding instruction and research; organizing the editing of textbooks; formulating regulations and rules; allocating teachers; communicating experiences of running of schools; running schools under their jurisdiction (Editorial Board of China's Education Yearbook 1986).

B. Administration in higher education institutions (1963–1965)

On 23 October, 1963, Premier Zhou Enlai announced in the 137th Plenary of the State Council that the Ministry of Education was divided into two ministries, one called the Ministry of Education, and the other the Ministry of Higher Education. These new ministry was in operation from March 1964. This was the first time that the reunited Ministry of Education was divided again. We should keep in mind that in five years the chief administrative authority of education was restructured again.

2.3.1.2 Policy Changes in Educational Administration

In the period of implementation of the first five year plan, China established a centralized and unitary system of educational administration. This system was helpful in establishing regular educational directives and instruction orders, enhancing the quality of education, assuring proportional and planned development of education. The educational development played an important part in directing technological forces for the construction of key projects and in supplying specialists for the development of economy.

But the system of educational administration had its own historical limits. As the time lapsed, the malady of excessive concentration and excessive unity became evident. In the first five year plan, the Central Committee of the CCP was aware of this phenomenon.

Earlier in 1956, Chairman Mao Zedong published the famous article *On Ten Relationship*. Mao Zedong pointed out that while strengthening the central unitary leadership, it was necessary to enlarge powers of local bodies. Mao Zedong also stressed that China should learn from the strengths of other nations, but we should look at them with critical eyes, and not imitate them mechanically. This should be the case even in our relationship with the Soviet Union.

On 4 August, 1958, the Central Committee of the CCP and the State Council issued *Regulations for Decentralizing Authorities of Educational Management at Local Level*. The *Regulations* stipulated that the old system of educational administration which was industry-led model should be reformed, and the local governments should be given more power and responsibilities in the management of education. Henceforth, the Ministry of Education and other ministries under the State Council should concentrate on the following aspects: (1) research and implementation of the central government's guidelines and policies regarding education; (2) making of a comprehensive plan for the development of education; (3) assisting the local governments in political education; (4) guiding instruction and scientific research; (5) editing and publishing textbooks; (6) specifying the necessary regulations and systems; (7) making allocation of teachers in HEIs; (8) administrating the schools under its jurisdiction (Editorial Board of China's Education Yearbook 1986).

2.3.2 The Administrative System of Education in Primary and Secondary Education (1957–1965)

2.3.2.1 Educational Administration in Primary Schools

A. The devolution of administrative power in primary schools in 1958

On 4 August, 1958, the Central Committee of the CCP and the State Council issued *Regulations for Decentralizing Authorities of Educational Management at Local Levels*. The *Regulations* stipulated that the establishment and development of primary schools, regular secondary schools, vocational schools, regular secondary specialized schools, spare time schools at various levels and public or private schools should be administered by local governments (Editorial Board of China's Education Yearbook 1986); that local governments could revise instruction programs, syllabi, textbooks issued by the Ministry of Education and other ministries under the State Council; that cadres and teachers in schools administrated by local governments should be appointed by the local governments.

B. Emphasis of Party's guidance of education (1958–1962)

On 19 September, 1958, the Central Committee and the State Council issued the *Directives on Educational Undertakings* (Editorial Board of China's Education Yearbook, 1986) leading to two important changes in educational administration. Firstly, the directives stressed the Party's leadership in educational undertakings. The party's educational guideline was "education should serve proletarian politics; education should be combined with the production labor."

The *Directives* also stressed the importance of delegating the power of education management. The *Directives* pointed out that it was necessary to mobilize all active factors so as to develop education quickly. The enthusiasm of both the central government and the government of the localities, as well as various enterprises, companies, communes, schools were mobilized.

The *Directives* stipulated that all primary and secondary schools and most universities and colleges were to be delegated to and administrated by the governments of provinces, municipalities and autonomous regions. The specialized secondary schools and technical schools that were formerly administered by the respective ministries were also regulated and were to be administered by factories, enterprises and farms under the jurisdiction of the respective ministries. The Great Cooperation Region was required to establish a complete educational system suited to the actual needs of the people. In brief, the *Directives* wanted to see a comprehensive education system in every province, municipality and autonomous region.

On 17 July, 1959, the Department of Propaganda under the Central Government approved *Regulations on Strengthening Guidance and Management of Education Undertakings in People's Communes* submitted by the Chinese Communist Party Commission and the government of Guangdong Province. The *Regulation* stipulated that the general, public, and full-time primary schools were to be directly administrated by the communes, and the private primary schools directly administrated by the production units (Mao and Sh 1989).

C. Working regulations on full-time primary schools and normalization of administration of primary education

On 18 March, 1963, the Central Commission of the CCP issued *Working Regulations on Full-time Primary Schools*. The *Working Regulations* stipulated that the State-run full-time primary schools were to be administered by governments of counties or districts affiliated to prefectures. Schools in counties far from the towns could be delegated to and administered by districts or communes. The full-time primary schools were obliged to carry out the instruction in accordance with the plans, syllabus and textbooks stipulated by the Ministry of Education of the People's Republic of China (Editorial Board of China's Education Yearbook 1986).

2.3.2.2   Educational Administration in Secondary Schools

The system of educational administration in secondary schools was reformed in 1958. In August 1958, the Central Committee of the CCP and the State Council issued *Regulations on the Delegation of Administrative Power of Educational Undertakings*. The Regulations pointed out that the establishment and development of general and vocational secondary schools, public or private, were to be decided by local governments on their own. The local governments could revise and improve instruction plans, syllabus and textbooks and edit textbooks and learning materials on their own (He 1998).

In March 1963, the Central Commission of the CCP issued *Working Regulations on Full-time Secondary Schools*. The *Workiong Regulations* stipulated that the State-run full-time secondary schools were to be managed according to the levels they belong to. Accordingly, the full-time junior secondary schools were to be administered by the educational administrative departments of the counties and cities while the full-time senior secondary schools and complete schools were to be administered by the government's department of education or delegated to and administered by the department of education under government of prefectures or counties (He 1998).

It could be seen that the Regulations issued in 1963 stressed the macro-management.

2.3.3   *Educational Administration in Higher Education Institutions (1957–1965)*

The reform of the system of educational administration in the late 1950s had its strength and weakness. The reform was a challenging task.

On 2 February, 1958, the Fifth Plenary of the National Congress issued *Decisions on Adjustment of the Institutions Affiliated to State Council*. The *Decisions* stipulated that the Ministry of Higher Education and the Ministry of Education would be merged into a single Ministry, called as the Ministry of Education, which would be in operation from 1 March 1958.

2.3.3.1   Devolution of the Administrative Powers of Higher Education Institutions

With a view to give more powers to local governments to train personnel suited to local needs, the Administrative Council issued *Regulations for Decentralizing Powers of Educational Management at Local Level* in August 1958.

According to these Regulations, 187 colleges and universities out of 229 were transferred to local control at the level of provinces, municipalities and autonomous regions. But new problems arose soon after—colleges and universities were developed too rapidly and without proper planning.

2.3.3.2 Normalization of Educational Administration in Higher Education Institutions

In September 1961, the Central Committee of the CCP issued *Working Regulation on Higher Education Institutions Affiliated to the Ministry of Education*. The Regulations stipulated that higher education institutions affiliated to the Ministry of Education were to be administered by the Ministry of Education in terms of administrative affairs, but administered by the governments of provinces, municipalities, or autonomous regions in terms of Partys' construction affairs. The party commissions in provinces, municipalities, autonomous regions and higher education institutions were obliged to abide by the guidelines and policies of the Central Committee of the CCP and the State Council and the regulations issued by the Ministry of Education (He 1998).

On the basis of the experiences of the past, on May 21, 1963, the Central Committee of the Chinese Communist Party and the State Council issued the *Decisions on Strengthening the Unitary Leadership and Management at Different Levels*. The *Decisions* stipulated that the Central Committee of the Chinese Communist Party and the State Council would take responsibility for the unitary central leadership in higher education institutions. It further stated that the central government and governments of provinces, Municipalities and Autonomous Regions were two different management levels. The division of management at these two levels was also concretely specified in the *Decision*.

2.4 Educational Administration During the "Cultural Revolution" (1966–1976)

2.4.1 Organization and Policy Changes in Educational Administration (1966–1976)

During the "Cultural Revolution", the ministries which were in charge of education had changed three times.

2.4.1.1 The Administration of Education by the Ministry of Education

On 23 July, 1966, the Central Committee of the CCP approved the suggestion put forward by the Ministry of Propaganda that the Ministry of Higher Education and the Ministry of Education should be merged into one, namely, the Ministry of Education (Editing Board of China Education Yearbook 1986).

2.4.1.2   Administration of Education by the Office of Science and Education (1970–1974)

In 1970, the Office of Science and Education was established to administrate education affairs. This institution, directed by the famous geologist Li Siguang, took responsibilities for the administration of science and education.

2.4.1.3   Administration of Education by the Ministry of Education (1975–1976)

On 17 January, 1975, the First Plenary of National Congress took a decision to revoke the Office of Science and Education and bring back the Ministry of Education.

In 1975, when Premier Zhou Enlai fell ill, Vice Premier Deng Xiaoping took over the responsibilities of the Central Commission under the guidance of Mao Zedong. Deng Xiaoping convened a series of meetings of the military force, industry, agriculture, transportation, and technology. Under the leadership of Deng Xiaoping, the economic order was stabilized and the situation improved greatly. (Deng 1983).

2.4.2   Administration of Primary Education and Secondary Education (1966–1976)

2.4.2.1   New Tasks Facing Pupils

On 7 May, 1991, Mao Zedong wrote a letter to Lin Biao. In that letter, Mao said that students should not only acquire knowledge, but should also learn other things: they should have knowledge and skills of industry, agriculture and military affairs. They should have knowledge and skills of industry, agriculture and military affairs. The length of schooling should be shorter (Mao 1991).

Mao Zedong advocated that students should not only be concerned with science and technology, but also learn many other things. At school the students should not only focus on the mastery of basic knowledge and skills. Mao Zedong stressed the need for an educational revolution. This meant the system of administration had to be transformed.

2.4.2.2   Educational Administration in Primary Schools

As far as primary education was concerned, the Ministry of Education and educational administrative departments at various levels were only responsible for allocation of educational expenditures to some extent, but not guide or give instruction on administrative affairs. There was not a unitary system of schooling, instruction plans, syllabus and textbooks. There were no unitary rules governing schools; the schools could suspend the classes and stop educational activities at random.

On 15 November, 1968, the People's Daily established a column to discuss about delegating public schools in rural areas to the production units. The governments did not invest in the schools. According to the proposal, the teachers went back to production units. The governments did not give salaries. Teachers got work record as peasants did. After discussion some local governments made pilot experiments. For example, in Hebei Province thousands of teachers were sent back to production units.

2.4.2.3   The System of Educational Administration in Secondary Schools

During the Cultural Revolution, most secondary schools in rural areas were administered by the administrative institutions of counties and communes. Senior high schools were administered by the administrative institutions of counties. Junior high schools were administrated by the administrative institutions within communes.

2.4.3   Educational Administration in Higher Education Institutions (1966–1976)

During the "Cultural Revolution", the relationship between government and higher education institutions (HEIs) changed greatly.

Governments changed the legal relationship between governments and HEIs. HEIs were educational institutions that needed autonomy. If they had no such autonomy, they could not perform their tasks well. As far as financing of higher education was concerned, the central government and local governments provided recurrent expenditure for regular HEIs. During the "Cultural Revolution", the appointment and removal of administrators were mainly controlled by governments.

2.5 Educational Administration at the Stage of Building the Socialist Commodity Markets (1977–1991)

2.5.1 Organization and Policy Changes in Terms of Educational Administration (1977–1991)

Educational system in China before 1978 was characterized by four features. The first feature was the highly centralized decision making mechanism; the second was the horizontal and closed information transmission; the third was the planning resources allocation mechanism; and the fourth was the segmented organization.

In the period of 1949–1976, the system of educational administration in China was centralized and unitary. This kind of system had three shortcomings: first, the localities had not so much motivation of involvement in education; secondly, schools had no autonomy and lacked vigor; thirdly, the central government had no resources to establish enough schools. So from 1978 on, China embarked on a reform of the system of educational administration.

2.5.1.1 Organizational Changes in Terms of Educational Administration

In 1978 the 5th National People's Congress stipulated that the State Council included 37 ministries, 32 affiliated institutions, 7 general offices.

As the main national work centered on economic construction, the governments and the masses were eager to push up the economic development. They urged the rehabilitation of the revoked ministries. So in 1981 there were 52 ministries, 43 affiliated institutions and 5 general offices under the State Council.

In 1985, the 11th Plenary Session of the Standing Committee of the People's Congress passed a resolution and accepted the establishment of the State Education Commission (SEC), a multi-functional executive branch of the State council. The SEC is the supreme administrative authority for turning out personnel that are well educated and trained in various subjects and fields. The SEC formulates major educational policies, designs overall strategies for promoting education, coordinates educational undertakings supervised by various ministries, and directs educational reforms. After the National Education Commission was set up, the original Ministry of Education was revoked.

2.5.1.2 Policy Changes in Terms of Educational Administration

In December 1978, the Third Plenary Session of Central Committee of the CCP was held in Beijing. The new guideline was put forward, namely "Liberating Thoughts, Using One's Brains, Seeking truth from Facts, Looking forward" (Deng 1992).

In 1982 the Constitution was revised. From then on educational development in China entered a route of management and reform of education on the basis of law.

The revised *Constitution* stipulated the basic system framework of China. The National People's Congress holds the highest authority of state power. The standing committee of the National People's Congress exercises the functions of the Congress between its annual sessions. According to the decisions made by the national People's Congress and its standing committee, the chairman of the state promulgates laws, appoints and removes the premier and other senior officials, and represents the state in foreign countries.

The State Council is the highest administrative organ of the state. The Ministry of Education is in charge of educational affairs across the whole country.

2.5.1.3 Restoration of Educational Orders

From 1978 on, Vice President of Central Committee of the CCP, Deng Xiaoping, was in charge of the affairs of education and science. He called upon the Party Commission of the CCP and governments at various levels to focus on education; all ranks and files to support education. He stressed that the modernization of the whole country could not go without educational development (Zhuo 1992).

After eight years of rehabilitation, adjustment and reform, the basic education went into a new stage of wholesome and deep level reform.

2.5.1.4 Local Governments Taking Responsibilities and Managing at Various Levels

On 27 May, 1985, the Central Committee of the CCP issued *Decision on the Reform of Educational System*. The *Decision* stipulated that the state would implement the system of "local governments taking overall responsibilities and managing at various levels" in basic education. The administration of basic education was entrusted to the local governments and other stakeholders. In the process of developing basic education, except for the main policies and macro-planning determined by the Central Committee of the CCP—the formulation and implementation of policies, program and plan, guidance, administration, all these responsibilities and powers were given to localities. The government of provinces, municipalities and autonomous regions would decide the division of responsibilities between governments of provinces, counties, towns.

The *Decision* pointed out that nine-year compulsory education was an important part of the development of Chinese education and the reform of its educational system. As China has a vast territory, and the development of economy and culture was extremely unbalanced, it was necessary to make development of education suitable to local situations.

The management power of basic education belonged to local governments. The important policies and macro-planning were made by the Central Committee of the CCP. But the concrete policies, making and implementing of plans, the leadership, and management of schools were within the scope of the responsibilities and powers of local governments. The province, municipality, and autonomous regions would make policies to divide management responsibilities between governments at the levels of province, prefecture, county and town.

On 15 June, 1987, the State Education Commission issued *Opinions on Certain Questions regarding the Reform of the Management System of Rural Basic Education.* The Opinions pointed out that a scientific division of power and responsibilities between the governments at various levels was the key to the reform of the administration of rural basic education system. The reform should be based on economic levels, level of popularization of education, scale of educational development, and political organization at the grassroots level. After the implementation of the system where local governments take the responsibilities, the powers and responsibilities of governments of provinces, prefectures, counties, and towns should be clearly defined. Each county should integrate educational development into its total planning, formulate concrete methods of activating the governments at various levels and train managers and teachers, improve educational conditions, strengthen instruction guidance, facilitate planning and coordination of educational structures.

The town is the grassroots level base of political power in China. Increasing the responsibilities of governments of towns in the administration of basic education was the key to basic education reform. The governments of towns should establish the administrative department with personnel from officials of governments, enterprise managers and school managers. The administrative departments should coordinate with the educational administrative departments under the government of the counties. They should focus on educational planning, training of cadres and teachers, raising funds, solving problems of privately-supported teachers, keep in touch with the society, and improve education conditions.

2.5.1.5   Establishment of a System of Educational Supervision

In the late 1980s, China established an educational supervision system. On 14 September, 1988, the State Education Commission and the Ministry of Personnel issued *Notice on Setting-up Education Supervision Institutions.*

On 6 November, 1988, the State Education Commission issued *the Report on Five Examinations of Primary and Secondary Education.* On 26 April, 1991, it issued the *Provisional Regulations on Educational Supervision.* According to the Regulations, Each government of county should establish educational supervision institution.

2.5.2 Reform of the System of Administration of Primary and Secondary Education (1977–1997)

2.5.2.1 Reform of System of Administration in Primary Education

On 3 December, 1980, the Central Committee of the CCP and the State Council issued *Decisions on Problems in Popularization of Primary Education*. The *Decisions* pointed out that as the reform of financial and economic management systems was deepening, the local governments should take greater responsibilities for education development. The formulation and implementation of educational development plan, the fixing of educational expenditures, and the establishment of personnel size of scale were arranged by the Party Commission and governments at province levels. The governments of provinces, prefectures and counties should take popularization of respective primary schools as an important task. The leaders of government of provinces, prefectures, counties and the leaders of the Party Commissions should themselves take care of educational development. The administrative institutions of counties and communes should take responsibilities for the reform and development of primary education. In order to strengthen the guidance of educational undertakings, the Ministry of Education should study the problems of popularization of primary education, make investigation on the educational situation, formulate educational development plans, determine instruction programs and draw up regulations and rules.

2.5.2.2 Reform of Educational Administration in Secondary Schools

In September 1978, the Ministry of Education issued *Scheme on Running of Key Primary Schools and Secondary Schools*. The Scheme stipulated that full-time secondary schools were to be guided and administrated by the administrative departments at the level of the county or above. The commune-run schools could be administrated by the communes under the unitary guidance of government of counties.

A. System of educational administration in key secondary schools

Since 1978, the party commissions and educational administrative departments in each province implemented the directives for running key secondary schools seriously and specified a number of key schools. There were more than 5000 key secondary schools. But there were some problems in running these schools. Firstly, localities did not concentrate their forces to run key secondary schools; the inputs of key schools were not as much as anticipated. So some key schools were actually not key schools. Secondly, key schools increase learning load of students and neglect students' moral, intellectual and physical development to a certain extent.

The running of key secondary schools was a strategic measure to enhance the quality of education. The educational administrative departments should specify measures for running key secondary schools. The key secondary schools should be run by governments of provinces, prefectures counties.

On 14 October, 1980, the Ministry of education issued *Decision on Running of Key Secondary Schools.*

B. Structural reform in secondary education

On 7 October 1980, the State Council ratified *Report on Reform of Secondary Education Structure* submitted by the Ministry of Education. The Report pointed out that vocational and technical education was an important part of the socialist educational system. Reforming secondary education structure was an important part of the construction of a socialist educational system. In order to make the reform more effective, it was not enough to rely on educational departments only. It was suggested that each province, municipality and autonomous region set up a leadership group and absorb members from other units, to create a unitary management body for the reform of secondary education. The local governments should combine reform of education structure with reform of economic structure, organize relevant departments to take concrete measures and meet the needs of economic development and employment.

2.5.3   Reform of Educational Administration in Higher Education Institutions (1977–1991)

2.5.3.1   Resumption of the Central Unitary Leadership and Management at the Central and Provincial Levels of Governments

On 18 September, 1979, the Central Government of the CCP dispatched the report of the Ministry of Education, reaffirming the *Decision* made in 1963 on the system of unified control and management at two different levels.

The *Decision* pointed out that in the development of higher education, each region, each department, each higher education institution should carry out the guideline and policy made by the Central Committee of the CCP, abide by instructions and do things according to the national plan of higher education. The decision also stressed that, under the unitary leadership of the Central Committee of the CCP and the State Council, the Ministry of Education, other Ministries under the State Council, governments at provinces, municipalities and autonomous regions should have a suitable work division and collaborate so as to run higher education institutions well.

2.5.3.2   Enlargement of Autonomy in HEIs and Strengthening Macro-Management

On 6 September, 1979, four famous presidents in Shanghai, Su Buqing, Li Guohao, Liu Funian, Deng Xiaochu, published an article in the People's Daily, asking governments to give some autonomy to higher education institutions. This article heralded the reform of the higher education administrative system. Immediately after this, some provinces made efforts to enlarge the autonomy of higher education institutions (Zhuo 1992).

In the 1980s, there existed two problems in educational reform and development. Firstly, the strategic position of educational development was not fully established. The old tendency of laying emphasis on material input, disregarding human resource input had not changed. Educational development was seen as a 'soft task' in comparison with the 'hard task' of economic development. Secondly, the reform of educational system lagged behind the reform of economic system. Schools did not have sufficient powers.

On 27 May, 1985, the Central Committee of the CCP issued *Decision on the Reform of Educational System*. The Decision pointed out that although educational undertakings had recovered and developed rapidly, some problems still existed, for example, the mistaken attitude of despising education and disregarding talents was taken by some managers. Educational undertakings were not adjusting to the needs of socialist modernization construction.

The *Decision* stipulated that the key to the reform of higher education lay in changing the system of excessive governmental control over higher education institutions. It further pointed out that in order to reform higher education system, it was necessary to assure the autonomy of higher education institutions under the guidance of the national unitary guideline and polices, strengthen the liaison between higher education institutions and production units, research institutes and other organizations. The main task was to assure the autonomy of higher education institutions.

The main problems confronting the reform of Chinese education system were as follows: the governments controlled the schools, especially higher education institutions, too tightly to the extent of depriving the schools and higher education institutions of their vigor. At the same times, the government could not manage things that it needed to manage well.

The *Decision* made two important reforms with regard to educational administration. One was the relegation of powers to local governments and the setting up of a system in which local governments would take the main responsibility to manage the concerned educational affairs at different levels.

The *Decisions* stipulated that the State and the administrative departments should strengthen the macro-guidance and management of higher education. In this arrangement, the administrative departments of education would have to organize educational fields and intellectual fields, while the employment department would assess the education levels of higher education institutions. Higher education institutions with exceptional achievement records would be supported with material and spiritual incentives. Higher education institutions with poor achievements would be warned.

2.5.3.3   Responsibilities System in Higher Education Management

On 3 March, 1986, the State Council issued *Provisional Regulations for the Management of Higher Education*. The Regulations stated that the State Education Commission was in charge of the national educational affairs, under the leadership of the State Council. Its responsibilities included organizing national manpower forecast; formulating educational planning; regulating higher educational structures; making adjustments of locations of schools; formulating criteria for establishing HEIs and postgraduate colleges; formulating the list of specialties of HEIs; examining and approving specialties; formulating management rules for capital construction, operational funds, size of staff, labor management and distribution of facilities; forming institutions for teachers and cadre management; guiding various work in HEIs; guiding scientific research in HEIs; guiding enrollment and training of postgraduates; guiding education of overseas students; guiding educational information processing and examinations in HEIs. In the provisional regulations the responsibilities for other ministries and provincial governments were specified.

It was necessary to increase the management power of higher education institutions so as to increase the higher education institutions' capabilities of adapting to economic and social development.

On 12 December, 1986, the State Council issued *Notice on the Setting-up of Higher Education Institutions*. The *Notice* stipulated that regular higher education institutions assumed responsibilities for training high level professionals and development of science, technology and culture. The *Notice* stipulated that the setting-up of regular higher education institutions should be ratified by the State Education Commission. The Notice also specified that the criterion of setting-up regular higher education institutions included the following aspects: (1) suitable president and vice presidents, the deans of departments and specializations; (2) sufficient qualified teachers with a minimum number of professors, associate professors and lecturers in each public mandatory curricula, basic mandatory specialty curricula, basic mandatory curricula; (3) necessary buildings and facilities; (4) a certain number of books and production training bases; (5) basic construction expenses and operational expenses. The *Notice* also stipulated that a higher education institution could be called a university, a college or a higher vocational college, according to the level of the undergraduates or graduates in the higher education institution, the disciplines it covered, and the scale of HEIs (State Education Commission 1992).

2.6   The System of Educational Administration at the Stage of Building Socialist Market Economy (1992–2016)

In 1992, Deng Xiaoping went to Wunhan, Shanghai, Shenzhen, Guangzhou and made several very important speeches. In the same year, the Fourteenth Plenary Session of the Central Committee of the CCP issued its *Report*. The *Report* pointed out that the most important task China faced was to make the transition from socialist planned economy to socialist market economy (Deng 1993).

2.6.1   Organizational and Policy Changes in Terms of Educational Administration (1992–2016)

2.6.1.1   Organizational and Policy Changes in Terms of System of Educational Administration

In 1998, the State Education Commission was renamed the Ministry of Education. In the same year, the new administration led by Hu Jiantao was set up. Premier Zhu Rongji said that this administration would regard educational development and scientific development as the first and foremost task. The leadership group of education and science under the State Council was instituted and Premier Zhu was its director.

2.6.1.2   Policy Changes in Terms of the System of Educational Administration

On 2 February 1993, the Central Committee of the Chinese Communist Party and the State Council issued *Program of China's Educational Reform and Development*.

The *Program* pointed out that the education system and operation mechanism of education was not adjusted to the needs of deepening the reform of the economic system, political system, scientific and technological system. As economic development and reform was deepening, it was important to tackle the problems of educational reform.

At this stage, it was necessary that the reform of the education system should adopt the comprehensive scheme to improve the current system that tended to take up too many responsibilities and exercised too much control.

The *Program* stipulated that the deepening of reform of education at secondary and lower levels was necessary. The practice of running schools at different levels with management at various levels was to be continued. For secondary and lower levels, education was coordinated and administrated by local governments, under the guidance of the central government. The central government formulated the basic system of schooling and set the criteria for curricula, personnel size of scale, qualification of teachers and basic salary of teachers. The governments at province level determined the regional system of schooling, the yearly enrollment scale, instruction plan, the choice of textbooks, examination and approval of textbooks, the quota of teachers' title and the level of teachers' salary.

The reform of higher education system aimed at dealing with the relationship between governments and higher education institutions, the central government and local governments, the State Education Commission and the Ministries under the State Council, and established the system characterized by macro-management of governments and the autonomy of running of schools by the higher education institutions.

On 3 July, 1994, the State Council issued *Implementation Opinions on the Program of China's Education Reform and Development*. The *Implementation Opinions* gave more detailed stipulations on the Program. As for reform of secondary and lower level education, except for the functions of central government and governments at province level, the governments of prefectures and governments of cities coordinated and guided compulsory education in compliance with the laws, guidelines and policies set by the central government and governments of provinces. The governments of counties took the main responsibility for implementing compulsory education. The responsibility covered making of overall plans and administrating educational expenditures, allocating and administrating principals and teachers, guiding educational and instructional work in primary schools and secondary schools.

On 29 July, 2010, the Central Committee of the Chinese Communist Party and the State Council issued *National Guidelines for Medium and Long-term Educational Reform and Development Program (2010–2020)*. The *National Guidelines* took the reform of educational system as the fundamental means to achieve the ambitious goal of educational modernization. As far as the reform of educational administration was concerned, the main goals were specified as perfecting the system of educational administration, strengthening powers at provincial level, changing the functions of governmental management.

2.6.2   Reform of Educational Administration in Primary Schools and Secondary Schools (1992–2016)

2.6.2.1   Reform of Educational Administration in Primary Schools

The system of local governments' taking overall responsibilities of educational management at various levels has made great progress since 2001.

On 29 May, 2001, the State Council issued *Decision on Reform and Development of Basic Education*. The *Decision* stipulated that it was necessary to reform the system of administration of compulsory education in rural areas. China implemented the system of compulsory education by making local governments take responsibility at various levels. The governments of counties took the main responsibility under the guidance of the State Council. Under this new system, governments at various levels had different responsibilities. The State formulated the system of instruction, set up the curricula, the criteria for curricula and examination of textbooks in compulsory education. The central government and provincial governments facilitated the transfer of funds and increased the financial support for the poor areas and areas of minorities. The provincial governments and governments of prefectures took care of the comprehensive planning and coordination of education, and guaranteed the requirements of compulsory education in rural areas when making arrangement for transfer of funds. The government of counties took the main responsibility for the compulsory education in rural areas. They had to plan everything carefully—the geographical distribution of schools, dispersal of teachers' remuneration unitarily, management of principals and teachers and the follow-up of the instruction and teaching in the schools. The government of towns had to do the same in schools under their jurisdiction. They had to raise funds according to the state regulations, improve educational conditions and enhance the remuneration of teachers. The function of autonomous organizations should be fulfilled. The towns and villages had the responsibility of sending children to schools and making sure the schools are safe places (He 2003).

On 14 April, 2002, the Office of General Affairs under the State Council issued *Circular on Improvement of the Management System of Compulsory Education in Rural Areas*. The *Circular* stipulated that, as concerned with system of compulsory education, the State implement the system where the government of counties would take the responsibility and manage at various levels under the guidance of the State Council. The provincial governments would take the responsibility of making a comprehensive plan of compulsory education in rural areas, formulate concrete measures with regard to the number of teachers, examine and approve the number of teachers in schools in rural areas, examine the financial competence of various counties, make comprehensive distribution plans of funds in the provinces, help and encourage governments of counties to ensure the delivery of remuneration of teachers through appropriate structures for the transfer of central government funds. The provincial governments would determine the criteria and the quota of public expenditure for primary and secondary schools in rural areas, determine the criteria of fees to be paid by students in rural areas. The government of provinces would also increase the special funds for demolishing dangerous school buildings and constructing new ones and setting in place a working mechanism for eliminating dangerous buildings. The government of provinces would also set up student support systems and strengthen the supervision and assessment of education.

In implementing compulsory education in rural areas, the governments of counties had nine tasks (1) formulating and implementing a plan for compulsory education in rural areas; (2) making plans according to the actual geographical distribution of schools; (3) ensuring the number of teachers required in rural schools on the basis of national criteria and stipulations issued by the provincial governments; (4) taking responsibility for the management of principals and teachers; (5) regulating the structure of educational expenditures, enhancing educational expenditures, ensuring that the remunerations of teachers are delivered in time; (6) making arrangements for public funds, arranging funds for demolishing dangerous school buildings and constructing new ones, (7) following up the course of instruction in the schools, (8) ensuring schools are kept safe and that teaching and instruction are regularly conducted (9) carrying out supervision and assessment of education in the rural schools.

2.6.2.2   The Reform of Educational Administration in Secondary Schools

On 27 February, 1997, the State Education Commission issued *Guideline for Educational Supervision in Primary School and Secondary Schools*. The *Guideline* pointed out that supervisory evaluation should be made in all primary schools and secondary schools This evaluation covers directives on running of schools, system of management, teachers' management and professional development, education and instruction, administrative work, conditions of running of schools, educational qualities.

On 13 June, 1999, the Central Committee of the CCP and the State Council issued the *Decisions on Deepening Education Reform and Promoting Competence Education*. The *Decisions* stipulated that the system of fundamental education management at the different levels with the local governments taking the main responsibility in accordance with laws should be conducted. The powers of the county governments to make overall plans for education expenses, for management of teachers and for appointment and removal of principals, were enlarged. The governments at various local levels should strengthen the overall planning for vocational education and adult education.

On 2 July, 2016, the State Council issued *Opinions on Reform and Development of Compulsory Education between Rural Areas and Urban Areas at the Level of County*. The *Opinions* stipulated that the governance of compulsory education, teachers management and assurance mechanism should be reformed, monitoring system and supervisional evaluation should be stressed; the power at provincial level should be strengthened.

2.6.3   Reform of Administration in Higher Education Institutions (1992–2016)

On 2 February, 1993, the Central Committee of the Chinese Communist Party and the State Council issued the *Program of China's Educational Reform and Development*. As concerned with higher education, the key points of the reform were the relationships between governments and higher education institutions, the central government and local governments, the Ministry of Education and other Ministries under the State Council so as to construct a system wherein Higher Education Institutions (HEIs) would have their autonomy while the government would have an effective control at the macro-level.

In dealing with the relationship between governments and higher education institutions, it was necessary to make HEIs become a legal entity of school-runners orientated to the society's need.

The governments should transform their functions and reinforce their macro-management through lawmaking, appropriations, planning, information service, policy guidance and other necessary administrative means.

In dealing with the relationship between the central government and local governments, it was necessary to further improve the system of management at the level of the central government and local government, giving each level of government its own responsibilities and functions.

In dealing the relationship between the Ministry of Education and other Ministries under the State Council, it was necessary to let the Ministry of Education take responsibility for comprehensive planning, policy guidance, organizational coordination, examination and supervision, service provisions; the Ministries under the State Council would strengthen forecasting and planning manpower for own department, help the Ministry of Education to guide the training of professionals in own department, take responsibility for managing affiliated higher education institutions.

On 3 July, 1994, the State Council issued *Implementation Opinions on Program of China's Educational Reform and Development*. As for the reform of higher education, the *Implementation Opinions* pointed out that the provincial governments' powers of decision-making and overall planning were enlarged. These powers included: (1) Provincial governments would make the overall planning for all HEIs within their jurisdiction and bring about the necessary adjustments of HEIs and Specialties on a voluntary basis through negotiation. (2) In the economically developed regions, the HEIs would be administrated by governments of cities on the basis of plans made by the governments. (3) The establishment of higher education institutions would be examined and approved by the State Education Commission.

On 13 June, 1999, the Central Committee of the CCP and the State Council issued *Decisions on Deepening Education Reform and Promoting Competence Education*. The *Decisions* stipulated that the adjustment of the system of higher education administration would be completed between 1999 and 2002. From then on, there would be a new system of management by the central and provincial governments, where provincial governments would take the main responsibilities. Authorized by the State Council, the power and responsibilities for the development of higher vocational education and higher specialized education were delegated to the provincial governments. The Provincial governments administrated the vocational technical colleges and higher specialized colleges.

In the early 1990s, some localities consolidated local universities on the principle of synergizing their mutually complementary strengths and resources. Nanchang, Shanghai, Yangzhou, Guangxi, and Yanbian Universities emerged successful in this merger experiment. The Ministry of Education assessed their experience and endorsed it before introducing it to other places. At the same time, many universities began different forms of cooperation in their management and

administration. The basic guideline of "joint construction, readjustment, cooperation and consolidation" was derived from their practice of reform.

"Joint construction" meant that central government departments and localities
would have to stop going it alone and start running schools in cooperation.
Accordingly, some universities were set up by the central ministry or commission in
cooperation with localities; others have been established locally but with central
government support. For these universities new recruits are chosen mainly from
among students in the localities, and the teaching and research in them are geared to
local economic and social development. In this way both central ministries and
localities are motivated to work together and run universities well.

"Readjustment" means remedying any injudicious geographical distribution of
higher education and rationalizing the course set-up by adjusting the administrative
system and regrouping universities and faculties.

"Cooperation" meant that universities should support each other with their
strengths and resources, foster interdisciplinary cooperation in teaching and
research, do their best to run schools in an open manner, and avoid building
"copycat" universities and overlapping faculties.

"Consolidation" meant merging certain universities, in the light of local circumstances, so as to improve their teaching quality and administrative efficiency. It
allowed faculties to make their resources mutually complementary, delivering
efficiency benefits from the expanded cooperation and connecting with others.

The General Office of the State Council held four meetings to discuss the reform
of the higher education administrative system. These meetings were held in
Shanghai in 1994, in Nangchang in 1995, in Beidaihe in 1996 and in Yangzhou in
1998. These meetings served to summarize and exchange experiences, to seek
further consensus among various stakeholders, to push the reform from a few pilot
cases to the entire field of higher education, and to lay a solid foundation for
revamping the system of higher education administration on a large scale.

After the 15th Plenary Session of the Central Comittee of the CPC in 1997,
educational reform entered a new stage of all-round development, with redoubled
efforts and on an accelerated pace.

In 1998, seizing the opportunity of government organization reform, 72 adult
education universities and many specialized secondary schools and technical
schools affiliated to the nine ministries under the State Council were detached as
these nine ministries were canceled in this year.

Early in 1999, there took place the rectification of administrative systems in 25
universities, 34 adult education institutions and several hundred specialized secondary and technical schools affiliated with five national defense industrial cor-
porations. From 2001 to 2002 more higher education institutions and other schools
were merged.

On 29 July, 2010, the Central Committee of the Chinese Communist Party and
the State Council issued *National Guidelines for Medium and Long-term
Educational Reform and Development Program (2010–2020)*.The *National
Guidelines* stipulated that the reform of separation of governmental management
from HEIs' management, and separation of management from running of HEIs

should be pushed up.The modern higher education system is characterized by governmental management according to laws and regulations, HEIs' automomous management, stakeholders' democratic monitoring, social active participation.

2.6.4 The Historical Experiences of Reform of the System of Educational Administration

In the past sixty years, great changes have taken place in the system of educational administration in China. Four conclusions can be drawn from this experience of reform of the system of educational administration.

First, the establishment of the system of educational administration in China was based on the principles of Marxism-Leninism and Mao Zedong's Thoughts; and the Party' influence on education was strengthened. The establishment of socialist educational system was driven by Marxism. The learning of Marxism-Leninism and Mao Zedong's thoughts were basic curricula in schools at various levels. The Party takes complete responsibility for guiding educational undertakings.

Second, top-down organizational systems have been established, educational management institutions have been instituted. The four levels of governments and their respective educational administrative departments have been established. The central educational administrative departments mainly included the Ministry of Education and other ministries under the State Council. Local educational administrative departments included educational administrative departments at provincial, prefecture, county and town levels.

Third, the system of leadership and management has been established. Governments and educational administrative departments at various levels have strengthened unitary leadership and management of education so as to guarantee a healthy and sustainable educational development.

Fourth, educational undertakings have been developing by formulating and implementing plans which fulfill the functions of education in social and economic development and carry forward coordinated social and economic development.

2.7 Current Situation of Reform of the System of Educational Administration

2.7.1 Current Situation of the System of Educational Leadership and Administration

As far as the relationship between governments and schools is concerned, the functions of governments have changed, the macro-level decision-making power belongs to governments, and the micro-level decision-making power belongs to schools of all types and levels.

As far as the relationship between the central government and local governments is concerned, the national level decision-making powers belong to the central government, and the local level decision-making powers belong to local governments. Governments make macro-management of education through lawmaking, appropriations and administrative measures. Recently great efforts have been made to strengthen the powers of provincial governments.

As far as the relationship between governments and markets is concerned, in the context of the development of market economy, the centralized decision-makers are rejected by market economy; different decision-makers emerge and they all have their own respective powers of decision-making; the governments are no longer the only main decision-makers.

As far as relationship between governments and society is concerned, social intermediary organizations have been instituted; they have been playing a role in educational decision-making. These social intermediary organizations include counseling organizations, information organizations and educational evaluation organizations (Xu 1999).

Five changes have taken place in China since the 1990s.

First, there has been a steady tendency of devolution of powers. Powers concerning school construction, establishment of curricula, examination of instruction program and syllabus, resource allocation, have been devoluted to local governments and local educational administrative departments.

Second, sponsors of schools have multiplied. The monotypic sponsorship of schools by governments has been changed. Social groups and individuals have been participating in running of schools.

Third, schools have more autonomy. Schools, especially HEIs, have powers with regard to the establishment of specialties, students' enrollment and employment, and the examination and approval of teachers' titles.

Fourth, the principals take overall responsibility for school affairs. Principals are representatives of legal entities.

Fifth, educational inputs have been diversified. Local governments have delivered much more input in education.

Nowadays the State Council and local governments at all levels guide and administer educational work according to the principle of management at different levels with suitable division of responsibilities. Educational institutions at the secondary or lower levels are administered by local governments under the guidance of the State Council. Higher education institutions are administered by the State Council and governments at the level of the provinces, autonomous regions and municipalities directly under the central government. The educational administrative departments under the State Council are in charge of educational work throughout the country, and undertake overall planning, coordination and management of educational undertakings. The educational administrative departments under governments at or above the county level are in charge of educational work in their respective administrative regions. Other administrative departments of governments at or above county level are responsible for the relevant educational work within their jurisdiction.

The 31 governments of provinces, municipalities, autonomous regions have their administrative organizations. Usually they are called the provincial education departments.

As subordinate institutions of the provincial government, or as independent administrative organizations, the prefectures have their management functions.

The county governments are an important level of government. Basic education was chiefly the responsibility of governments at this level. Usually, the governments of counties have education bureaus as their administrative organizations.

The towns also have their administrative organizations, and they usually call them educational offices.

The reform of the system of educational administration in China was oriented to strengthening macro-management and increasing the dynamism of the schools. At the macro levels, the subjects are the governments at various levels. At the micro level the subjects are the schools at various levels.

2.7.2 Current Situation of Educational Administration in Primary Schools and Secondary Schools

In the field of basic education, the system of "running of schools at different levels and managing education at different levels" has been set up.

The power of the governments of counties to make the overall plan for basic education was strengthened. Administration mainly by governments of counties was established.

The development of basic education was oriented to local development. The task of running of schools was given to localities and the management of schools too was given to the localities.

With regard to vocational and technical education development, the main policy was to introduce enterprise-based management.

2.7.3 Current Situation of Educational Administration in Higher Education Institutions

According to *Higher Education Law*, the State Council should provide unified guidance and administration for higher education throughout the country. The governments of provinces, autonomous regions and municipalities which are directly under the central government should make the overall coordination of higher education in their own administrative regions; administer higher education institutions that mainly train local people and administer higher education institutions that they are authorized by the State Council. The administrative department for higher education under the State Council should be in charge of the work of higher education throughout the country and administer affairs of higher education institutions designated by the State Council as schools that mainly train people for the country as a whole. Other administrative departments under the State council should be responsible for the work related to higher education within the limits of their duties defined by the State Council (Tian 1990).

In recent times, the new system of management at the level of central and provincial governments, with the provincial governments' taking the main responsibility in running of HEIs is established.

2.8   Problems Facing China in the Reform of Educational Administration

2.8.1   Problems Facing China Due to Governments' Position in Educational Development

Four problems exist in terms of governments' functions in educational development. First, Governments may not fulfill the function of social management as well as people anticipated. As far as g positiong ia concerned, governments may not manage what they should manage, and manage too many things that are beyond their scope. Governments' main functions in the field of education are formulation and implementation of educational laws. In China some educational laws, regulations and policies have been formulated, but the implementation of these laws and polices need to be strengthened.

Second, governments have not been good providers of educational expenditure as most people anticipated. Governments should be important providers of educational expenditures. At present, governments have not made enough appropriations on education.

Third, governments do not fulfill the function of education producers very well. The ways of education provision by governments are monotonous.

Fourth, the allotment of responsibilities at various levels of governments is not clear enough. The Ministry of Education and other ministries under the State Council all establish HEIs; their responsibilities may overlap.

2.8.2   Problems Facing China Due to Governments' Macro-management of Education

In the process of educational development, there exist problems arising from the way the system of educational administration operates. They are manifested in the relationships between governments and the markets, the central government and local governments, the governments and the schools at various levels, the governments and the society.

2.8.2.1 Misunderstanding of Markets' Main Responsibilities in Educational Resource Allocation

In recent times, the government did not take the leading role in the provision of education as there were some misunderstandings about the markets' role in educational resources allocation. With regard to the relationship between governments and markets, the main problem was that governments did not take the leading role in education resource allocation.

In the late 1980s, some Chinese scholars suggested that the 'commoditization' of education could be the new direction for reform of the educational system. In the 1990s there were fierce debates on this issue. In the early 21st century the policy of industrialization of education was put forward by some scholars. They thought market should play a basic role in the provision of education.

Education cannot be industrialized or 'commoditized' in the strict sense. The 'marketization' of education is feasible in technical logic. But the 'industralization' of education cannot be rationally justified. Even in the United States and England, education resources are not mainly allocated through markets. Lao Kaisheng pointed out that educational markets were not normalized. As the national financial capacity-building speeded up, more educational goods would like to be provided by the governments.

2.8.2.2 Division of Responsibilities Between the Central and Provincial Governments

With regard to the relationship between the different levels of governments, the central government and the provincial governments have a lot of powers and funds, but they do not take responsibilities commensurate with their powers.

Lao Kaisheng pointed out that the process of reallocation of powers between the central government and local governments was slow and lagged behind other areas. A new power relationship with a clear division of responsibilities needs to be set up.

2.8.2.3 Governments' Emphasis on Macro-Management and Assurance of Autonomy of Schools at Various Levels

As regards the relationship between the governments and schools at various levels, governments' powers of educational management are centralized; governments interfere with the internal affairs of schools at various levels.

Lao Kaisheng pointed out that power sharing between governments and schools at various levels was not clear. So the exercise of public powers has not been normalized. Governments still are the direct investors, managers and runners of the schools.

2.8.3 Problems in the System of Educational Administration in Primary and Secondary Schools in China

One problem is that the division of responsibilities among the localities is not very clear and the power division among localities is also not very clear. As the divisions of powers are ambiguous, responsibilities are given to the towns and villages. Although the system of the governments taking the main responsibilities is in operation, some governments of counties are weak in financial capacities; they cannot support the schools under their jurisdiction. Many finance systems in government of counties are only capable of supporting the personnel's salaries. The central government and provincial governments are strong in financial power but they do not take enough responsibilities in the implementation of compulsory education.

The second problem is the widening gap between the various regions and between urban areas and rural areas. In the reform of basic education administrative system, the financial support for basic education development depends on the economic development levels at localities. China is a very large country. There are vast regions with different natural and cultural conditions. The responsibilities of financing of basic education are entrusted to the localities. The difference of localities can bring about great difference of educational resource allocation between localities.

2.8.4 Problems in the System of Educational Administration in Higher Education Institutions in China

As regards the relationship between HEIs and governments, China is in the middle of a process of moving from a state control model to a state supervision model. In this process there are difficult questions to be answered about the respective roles and powers of the Ministry of Education, the other ministries and provincial governments. What powers and controls would allow the State to fulfill its micromanagement functions and unleash the latent energy and enthusiasm within institutions? What kind of regulatory approach should be adopted by governmets? Should it be based on "command and control model" or on financing incentives t?

Nowadays many HEIs that were formerly sponsored and administered by central industrial ministries have been delegated to provinces or municipalities after the merger of HEIs. But there are more than 60 HEIs under the jurisdiction of central industrial ministries. The current state where many HEIs are sponsored and administered by industrial ministries is not beneficial to the unitary planning and effective management by the Ministry of Education. The ideal model of administration of higher education is the two level system of administration: one level is the Ministry of Education, and the other level is the provincial governments. So in the near future, HIEs that were formerly under the jurisdiction of industrial ministries should be brought under the jurisdiction of provincial governments (Cai 1996).

As far as the division of powers and responsibilities between central government and provincial governments is concerned, provincial governments' powers of decision making is constrained.

At present the educational administrative departments have tight control on HEIs. Although HEIs are regarded as legal entities by educational law and the expansion of HEIs' autonomy is advocated, many powers concerning management of HEIs have not been completely delegated to HEIs. So, practical and effective ways of empowerment of HEIs should be sought.

2.9   Strategies and Measures for Further Reforms of the System of Educational Administration

In order to deepen the reform of the system of educational administration, five principles should be adhered to. Firstly, educational reform and development should be combined so as to bring about the coordination of reform and development. Educational development scale should be adapted to national economic development. Educational development should meet the present need and long-term need of national economic and social development. Secondly, reform of the system of educational administration should go in conjunction with various social reforms. Reform of educational system is linked to other social system reforms. Without reforms in other areas educational reform cannot go ahead smoothly. Thirdly, implementation of reform and openness to the outside world should be combined with macro-management. Fourthly, abolishing the old system should go along with establishing the new system. The relations between reform, stability and development should be rationalized. Fifthly, reform of educational system should go hand in hand with lawmaking on education.

2.9.1   Addressing Problems of Governmental Functions in Educational Administration

In order to urge governments to fulfill their functions in educational administration effectively, four measures should be taken. Firstly, in order to guarantee that educational laws will be implemented effectively, the system of supervision of educational administrative departments and schools' behavior should be conducted by the people's congress. Secondly, governments at various levels, especially the central government and provincial governments, should make more appropriations on education. Compulsory education should be completely free and governments should provide enough educational funds for compulsory education as well as other kinds of education. Thirdly, at the stage of non-compulsory education, governments only need to sponsor the main part of the school. Many schools can be sponsored by social forces. The government needs to subsidize private schools, but social forces' involvement in schools can reduce the governments' burden in educational provision and pave the way for rapid educational development. Fourthly, allocation of educational responsibilities among different levels of governments should be made clearly.

2.9.2   Strengthening Governments' Macro-management

The most important task facing governments is to build normative governance structure in educational management. The key is to make clear the positioning of governments' powers and responsibilities in education development. It is necessary to determine the principles, scope, powers, responsibilities and procedures. For educational development to progress it is necessary to set up guidelines and policies, a rational structure and provide increased input; also, macro-management is crucial for the success of educational development. Education should be the first and foremost responsibility of governments. The main responsibilities of the government lie in the creation of a benign environment for the healthy development of education; ensuring the implementation of the State's educational polices; assuring the correct orientation of school operation; formulating norms and standards for equipment and facilities.

A good system of educational laws should have several features. It should guarantee the effective implementation of state's guidance and policies on education, guarantee citizen's educational rights and all-round development rights, and guarantee good instruction. It also should include complete educational laws, monitoring system, and have a suitable legal culture.

In order to address the problems of strengthening governmental macro-management, it is necessary to keep in mind the following four aspects. Firstly, education is neither a production industry nor an economic industry. Although education has characteristics of production and educational investment is a productive investment, the nature of educational production and the economic benefits of education are indirect and potential. Only after the educated manpower and professionals take part in production activities can education bring about actual productive and economic benefits. Education is a kind of non-profit public industry. In most cases, education is a kind of public goods and a kind of quasi-public goods; it is not a kind of private goods. So education does not have the necessary conditions for marketization. Under these circumstances most part of education products or service should be provided by governments. So governments should take much more responsibilities in educational development.

Governments should delegate most of the powers in internal management of school affairs back to schools. And schools should have management autonomy. For instance higher education institutions should have powers of determining the number of enrollments, number of specialties, number of internal institutions, use and removal of employees, allocation and use of resources. The relationship between governments and society should be restructured. Modern education is public service concerned with every member in society, concerned with the benefits of every citizen, concerned with the self-fulfillment of every citizen. So, educational development needs the active involvement of the whole society. Scientific research on macro-level decision making in education should be strengthened so as to make decision making in education more scientific and democratic. The decision making process in educational administration and the system of management should be improved, and a contingent of high quality educational administrators and managerial personnel should be developed so as to enhance the level of administration and governance by law.

2.9.3 Strategies and Measures for Reform of the System of Educational Administ-Ration in Primary Schools and Secondary Schools

In order to prefect the system of educational administration in primary and secondary schools, three measures should be taken. Firstly, the unitary guidance of the central government should be maintained. The unitary guidance of the central government does not mean that central government should determine everything; it does not mean that educational administrative departments should take direct control over the management of schools. The unitary guidance means that the main guidelines and policies should be formulated by the central government. Secondly, management at local levels should be maintained. The responsibilities and powers should be matched. Thirdly, we must arouse the enthusiasms of everyone concerning basic education. The effective running of schools needs the cooperation of different stakeholders. The enthusiasm of central government, local governments, schools and parents should be aroused.

In order to differentiate the responsibilities of governments at various levels, the following measures should be taken. The main responsibilities of compulsory education development in rural areas should be transferred from peasants to governments. The governmental responsibilities in compulsory education should be changed. There should be a transformation from relying on governments of towns to that of mainly relying on governments of counties. The responsibilities of government of counties in educational development should be specified. The responsibilities of Governments above county level should be increased.

Governments of counties should deliver the salaries of teachers. Governments of town should continue to support educational development.

To make sure governments of counties to take main responsibilities, two measures need to be taken. Firstly, specify more concisely and clearly the laws and regulations with clear divisions between governments at the center province, prefecture, county, and town levels. Secondly, a balanced educational development policy should be formulated and carried out effectively.

2.9.4 Strategies and Measures for the Reform of the System of Educational Administration in Higher Education Institutions

In order to deepen the reform of the system of educational administration in higher education institutions, two measures can be taken up. Firstly, most higher education institutions that are under the jurisdiction of industrial ministries should be reformed; they should be placed under the jurisdiction of provincial governments. Secondly, some HEIs that are now under the jurisdiction of the Ministry of Education should also be reformed; they should be brought under the jurisdiction of provincial governments. The Ministry of Education should only administer some key HEIs, and the number of HEIs under their jurisdiction should be lessened. In the process of this reform, the system of financing higher education should be reformed. Generally speaking, HEIs that are under the jurisdiction of provincial governments can also receive research funds and students subsidies from the central government on the basis of fair competition.

The ideal system of educational administration is one where there will be central unitary guidance and local governments take up all other responsibilities. The relationship between central government and local governments is both complementary and competitive. The benefits accruing to both sides may be in harmony at some times, but in conflict at other times. In order to reduce friction and increase coordination, the limits of powers of both sides should be specified in laws and regulations. The clear division of powers and responsibilities will be beneficial to both sides. The future system of higher education administration should be centered on local administration. Most concrete educational affairs should be delegated to local governments and other social actors. The central government should retain only the powers of giving guidelines and making educational plans.

In order to enlarge HIEs' autonomy, the governments should change their style of functioning; the direct command and control model should be changed into an indirect supervision model. Meanwhile a social supervision mechanism conducted by society should be instituted. The fair competition mechanism between different kinds of HEIs should be established. The monopoly of HEIs can harm both the equity and efficiency of higher education. The democratic management, democratic supervision and scientific decision making mechanism within HEIs should be established and perfected.

References

Cai, K. (1996). *An introduction to research on higher education.* Beijing: The Capital Normal University.

Deng, X. (1983). *Deng Xiaoping' selected works.* Beijing: People's Press.

Deng, X. (1993). *Deng Xiaoping' selected works.* Beijing: People's Press.

Editorial Board of China's Education Yearbook. (1986). *China Education Yearbook.* Beijing: People's Education Press.

He, D. (Ed.). (1998). *Important documents in the People's Republic of China (1949–1975).* Haikou: Hainan Press.

He, D. (Ed.). (2003). *Important documents in the People's Republic of China (1998–2002).* Haikou: Hainan Press.

Jianguo, Tian. (1990). *On higher education.* Jinan: Shandong ducation Publishing House.

Mao, L., & Sheng, G. (Eds.). (1989). *A history of education in China.* Jinang: Shangdong Education Publishing House.

The State Education Commission. (1992). *Important documents since the third plenary session of the 11th national congress of the central committee of the CCP.* Beijing: Educational Science Press.

Wu, Z. (2000). *On educational administration.* Beijing: People's Education Press.

Xu, H. (1999). *Mission in an Era of change.* Hangzhou: Zhejiang University Press.

Zedong, M. (1991). *Mao Zedong's selected work.* Beijing: People's Press.

Zhuo, Q. (1992). *Education reform.* Dalin: Dalin Press.

Chapter 3
Increasing Education Vigor: Internal Management System in Schools in China

3.1 Introduction to the System of Internal Management

3.1.1 The Concept of the System of Internal Management

Management is a difficult term to define, just as managers' jobs are difficult to identify with precision. Managers are people who are responsible for achieving the organization' objectives. They would like to be responsible for other people's work or for their own as specialists at the same level. Management means the process and outcome based on managers' use of specific procedures and methods (Hills 1982).

The system of internal management is an important part of the educational system. The system of internal management covers the system of leadership and management, system of personnel management and system of salary distribution (Wu 1999).

Modern system of leadership and management is the fundamental system for guiding and administering schools. A good and prefect system of internal management within schools is likely to arouse the enthusiasm of teachers and students. The system of internal management includes leadership and administration within schools, the system of leadership and management of teachers, the system of distribution of benefits among teachers and the system of management institutions and the relevant rules of these institutions.

The system of leadership and management is the basic system of guiding and managing school affairs, and it actually dominates all managerial work in schools. The system of internal management concerns questions of who are chosen as leaders, how institutions are set up, how the power and responsibilities are allocated among administrators.

Organization is an important tool for management. Since educational activities cover a vast range of interests, ages and subjects, and since the processes of education are dependent on the interchange of information and opinions among people, it is inevitable that a great many organizations are formed which play a part in the

© Springer Nature Singapore Pte Ltd. and Higher Education Press 2018
M. Yang and H. Ni, *Educational Governance in China*,
https://doi.org/10.1007/978-981-13-0842-0_3

educational system. One can distinguish several types of organizations: administrative organization, professional organization, research organization, supportive organization. The educational administrative organization is hence carried out through a tiered structure of regional and local organizations dealing with all the necessary aspects of finance, buildings, staffing, material provision and educational policies and practice.

Administrative positions are important in the management of education. Administrative positions are those posts held by staff members who carry out the functions of procurement, coordination and allocation of the resources necessary for the survival of the school organization.

The single-school staffs are key factors of education production. The individual school is generally the smallest school. In China, most single-school administrators are promoted from the teaching ranks, with the promotion often determined largely on assessed success in teaching. Principals in schools are promoted from the primary teaching ranks.

The principals would teach only a part of the day. The principals' role varies from senior teacher to that of manager. The management function includes responsibilities for curriculum and finance; the selection, promotion and assessment of teachers and the relationship with the authorities and communities.

The reform of the system of personnel management and reform of the system of salary and fringe benefits distribution are the key areas for the reform of the system of internal management. For school development, teachers are a very important force.

The management of teachers is at the core of internal management of schools. So in this chapter the system of teacher management will be explored in conjunction with the system of leadership and management.

Great changes have taken place in the system of management of teacher since 1978. In the era of state planned economy, China implemented the system of unitary assignment of professionals who have received specialized secondary education and higher education. The management of professionals is a kind of system of departments' ownership and system of localities' ownership. The model of management of professionals is monotonous. The State controls the allocation and use of professionals. Generally speaking, the managers in schools can be promoted, but they cannot be demoted. Personnel can be employed by schools, but they cannot be dismissed from schools unless they break laws. Teachers' salaries can be increased, but they cannot be lowered. Professionals cannot be transferred freely between schools. So the system of lifelong employment of professionals was established. This kind of system is not beneficial to achieving the policy goal of equity and efficiency. So reform of this system is urgent for school development.

As far as the system of work management was concerned, the system of accountability and evaluation was lacking before 1978. The responsibilities of teachers were not clearly specified. The scale of school was increasing rapidly. The effectiveness of instruction and research were going down to some extent. Teachers' workload was decreasing. In some schools in urban areas the teachers' weekly workload was less than 8 lessons.

In terms of teachers' salaries, lack of equity in the distribution of salaries welfare benefits among members was prevalent. The remuneration was to a certain extent the same for people who work and who do not work, who do much work and who do little work, who work hard and who are lazy. In this situation the teachers' enthusiasm for work was weakened. The efficiency of instruction, research and service could not be enhanced.

Since 1978 the situations mentioned above have changed a great deal.

3.1.2 Classification of the System of Internal Management

According to the number of highest level decision makers, the system of internal management can be classified as system of unit's head taking overall responsibilities and system of the collective's taking overall responsibilities. The system of unit's head's taking overall responsibilities means that the power of making the final decision is concentrated on the head of a unit. The system of a collective taking overall responsibilities means that the power of making the final decision is given to the collective (Xiao 1988).

Under the system of unit's head's taking the overall responsibility of management of school, the power of the head of a unit and other leaders in the unit all have the same power, but the head in unit has powers to make the final decision. For instance, when there is one principal and some vice-principals, their power is not the same when they are making decisions. The principal has the power of making final decisions.

Under the system where the collective takes overall responsibilities, the power of making decisions is relatively the same for all members when they make decisions simultaneously. For example, the chairman or general secretary convenes and presides over the meeting and deals with regular affairs, but the members participating in the meeting do not have the power of making the final decisions. The power of making the final decision is delegated to the collective. In the case of Party Commission's taking overall responsibilities in HEIs, Party commission is a collective; this collective consists of some members. In the meeting of the Party Commission, the power of each member is the same. When conflicts take place in the meeting, the principle "the smaller group follows the opinion of the majority group" is used. Each member has only one vote. In this respect they are all the same.

Under the system of unit's head taking overall responsibilities, the head in a unit takes personal responsibility for the final decision made in the unit.

Under the system of collective's taking overall responsibilities, each member is responsible for the final decision made in the unit. Each member contributes to the final decision and fulfills his functions, but all members do not take personal responsibility for the collective decision. For instance, if a member put forward a suggestion and this suggestion is accepted in the meeting participated by all members, no one individual is responsible for the final decision.

The system of unit's head's taking overall responsibilities has both strengths and weaknesses. This system lays emphasis on system of responsibilities and experts' leadership. The strengths of this system are manifested in the concentration of power, clarity of responsibilities, rapid movement and high efficiency. The weakness of this system is manifested in the difficulty in making well-elaborated decisions for limitations of personal wisdom, competence and experience.

In the case of the system of the collective's taking overall responsibilities, the power of making decisions has both strengths and weakness. The strengths of this system are the democratic nature of the decision-making process, pooling of the wisdom of the entire group, making complete consideration of affairs and avoidance of personal dictatorship. The weakness of this system is the scattering of power, ambiguity of responsibilities, and slowness in making decisions, low efficiency and difficulties in making final decisions.

Under which circumstance should the system of unit's head]s taking overall responsibilities be implemented? Under which circumstance should the system of collective taking overall responsibilities be implemented? Generally speaking, in administrative affairs, business affairs, executive affairs, technological affairs, and disciplinary affairs, where things have to be decided quickly, the system of unit's heads taking overall responsibilities should be used.

In affairs such as guideline affairs, policy affairs, long run planning affairs, lawmaking affairs, counseling affairs, coordinative affairs, academic affairs, the system of collectives taking overall responsibilities should be used.

In order to conduct general guidelines, collective's taking overall responsibilities should be used. The administration, instruction and research ask for managers who can make unitary, effective and instantaneous decisions and most affairs in schools are administrative, executive and business-like affairs, so the system of head's taking overall responsibilities should be used.

3.1.3   Functions of the System of Internal Management

Reform of the system of internal management is an important part of the reform of the educational system. The final goal of reform of the educational system is to make sure that schools have sufficient vigor.

The reform of the system of internal management pertains to the quality of reform of educational system and decides whether the reform of educational system is a success or not. Without a deepening of the reform of the system of internal management, the reform of educational system cannot be successful.

In the process of the reform of the system of internal management, it is necessary to establish a new system that adjusts itself to social and economic development and facilitates healthy educational development.

The historical development of the system of Internal Management in schools in China can be classified into five periods.

3.2   The System of Internal Management in Primary and Secondary Schools at the Stage of Completing Socialist Restructuring (1949–1956)

In the period of 1949–1956, schools of all levels and types were restructured, As far as system of leadership and management was concerned, three system were established, the first system focused on collective leadership, the second system focused on principal's role, the third focused on Party's functions.

3.2.1   The System of Internal Management in Primary Schools and Secondary Schools (1949–1956)

3.2.1.1   The System of Leadership and Management in Primary Schools and Secondary Schools (1949–1956)

A.   Establishment of the school administrative affairs committee (1949–1951)

The first system of leadership and management that was implemented in primary and secondary schools universally was the system of school administrative affairs committee.

After the founding of the People's Republic of China, the committees of school affairs were established in most primary and secondary schools.

The members of these committees were chosen from the representatives of teachers with progressive thoughts and good deal of experience. They were appointed by the local educational administrative departments. They engaged in management of school collectively and used democratic ways to run schools.

From 1949 on, it was urgent to rehabilitate the educational order. This system was beneficial to keeping order in schools and making initial reforms in schools. But the system was inclined to produce excessive democratic way of management and cause the phenomenon of nobody taking responsibility for the concerned affairs in some cases.

B.   The system of principals taking overall responsibilities (1952–1955)

On 18 March, 1952, the Ministry of Education issued *Provisional Regulations on Primary Schools*. The *Regulations* stipulated that the system of internal management whereby the principals should take overall responsibilities of the management of school should be established in schools. The principal was appointed by the government and was responsible to the government (Editorial Board of China's Education Yearbook 1984).

The *Regulations* clarified out the administrative organization in schools and defined the relevant responsibilities. A principal was in charge of the internal affairs in school.

The *Regulations* also made decisions on the management of classes within schools. If a school had more than five classes, a director, responsible for the general instruction affairs and students in each class, was needed.

The principal and the directors of instruction needed to take lessons for students, besides spending time in management affairs. The classes used the system of teachers taking overall responsibilities. Every class should set up the post of the main teacher who was in charge of the ideological matters and group activities of a class.

In order to implement the principle of democratic management, it was necessary to set up institutions for holding meeting by concerned individuals. The schools should hold the meeting of school affairs, with the participation of the principal and all teachers and staff. The principals would preside over the meetings. The meetings regarding instruction research should be attended by all the teachers. The delegates of parents of students and administrators in local education administrative departments could be invited to take part in such meetings.

On 18 March, 1952, the Ministry of Education issued *Provisional Regulation on Secondary Schools*. The *Regulations* stipulated that the middle schools should implement the system of principal's taking overall responsibilities in the management of schools. A principal was in charge of the general affairs in school. The post of vice-principal was set up in schools if necessary. The principals in middle schools under the jurisdiction of the provincial governments would be appointed by the provincial government. The principals in middle schools under the jurisdiction of governments of cities would be appointed by the governments of cities. The principals in middle schools under the jurisdiction of the department of government would be appointed by department of government (Editorial Board of China's Education Yearbook 1984).

The *Regulation* stipulated the administrative institutions and organization in schools. Accordingly, the middle schools would set up the office of instruction affairs and the office of general affairs. The school would set up the post of director for office of instruction affairs, and the director would be in charge of the organization, examination of instruction affairs and the daily life affairs of students.

The office of instructional research based on subject classification should establish in the secondary schools.

The *Regulations* stipulated the system of concerned meeting. The managers in the middle schools should hold the meeting of school affairs, the meeting of instruction research, and the meeting of main teachers in classes, of the directors, and of the parents.

On 8 April, the Administrative Council issued *Directives on Improvement and Development of Secondary Education*. The *Directives* stipulated that it was necessary to improve the leadership of secondary schools with a view to establish leadership cores and to fulfill the role of collective leadership. The principals would have to take over-all responsibilities for schools; the leader should focus on the instruction.

The principals were appointed by governments and were responsible to the government. The solving of problems within the schools would be decided by the principals. Such a system would be useful for implementing the guidelines and policies of Chinese Communist Party and governments at various levels and would change the situation whereby nobody was responsible for the work in schools. But the shortcoming of this system was the possibility of principals acting arbitrarily if there were no institutions and system of supervisions.

C. Principals taking responsibilities under the guidance of the chinese communist party's branch (1956–1957)

In 1956, the Chinese Communist Party Constitution, which was passed in the Eighth Plenary Session of the Central Committee of CPP, stipulated that the basic organization in enterprises, villages, and schools at various levels and army forces, should guide and supervise the administrative units and the workers and staffs should implement the resolutions made in the *Constitution*. So the system of internal management changed into the principal's taking responsibilities under the guidance of the branch of the Chinese Communist Party (He 1998a).

In 1956, the system of principal's taking responsibilities under the guidance of the Chinese Communist Party's branch was established. As the political situation was good, the system was helpful in bringing about a balance of the administrative power and the Chinese Communist Party's branch's power.

The *Regulations* stressed the importance of the leadership of the Chinese Communist Party. The leadership of the Chinese Communist Party is the fundamental guarantee for effective running of schools. Every Chinese Communist Party Commission at various levels should strengthen the leadership of the primary education. The responsibilities of the Chinese Communist Party's branch was to implement the resolution of the upper-level Chinese Communist Party Commission, assure the fulfillment of the directives made by the upper-level administrative departments, guide the political education in schools and facilitate the construction of the Chinese Communist Party; and guide the Chinese Communist Youth League.

3.2.1.2   Management of Teachers in Primary Schools and Secondary Schools (1949–1956)

A. The recruitment of teachers

At this stage, the State exercised centralized and unitary administration on educational affairs, and the recruitment of teachers was mainly through the way of dispatch and reallocation. Dispatch meant that the teachers should follow the State's job allocation plans. The reallocation meant that teachers could be transferred to other schools on the basis of national plans. The educational administrative department would like to dispatch teachers to the schools and reallocate teachers among the schools. The administrative department of personnel would reallocate teachers to the concerned schools. This way of choice of teachers had some advantages such as the convenience of procedure, easy for the administrative department to make overall plan and to do coordination work, stability of teacher's group. But it had some disadvantages such as little maneuvers for schools, the separation of dispatch from use (Editing Board of China Education Yearbook 1984).

B. The system of teachers' salaries

In 1952, the Ministry of Education issued the *Circular on Adjustment of Salaries for Teachers in Schools of Various Types and Levels*. The salaries were calculated into monetary salaries on basis of the price of foods, clothing, oil, salt and coal (Liu 1993).

In November 1952, the Ministry of Education issued the Circular on the Revision of Criteria of Salaries for Teachers in Secondary Schools and Circular on the Revision of Criteria of Salaries for Teachers in primary Schools. The criteria of salaries of 1952 were revoked. The Circular established a national unitary system of salaries for teachers.

In October 1955, the Ministry of Education issued a *Notice*. The *Notice* stipulated that the salaries criteria for teachers were transformed to the monetary salary criteria for teachers and the subsidies for compensation for price increase were delivered from 1955 on (Editing Board of China Education Yearbook 1984).

In 1956, the Ministry of Education issued *Directives on Adjustment of Salaries for Teachers Engagement in General Education and Normal Education*. The *Directives* stipulated that there were two criteria of salaries for teachers and administrative staff. The criteria of salaries had eight grades. From then on, the eight-grade system was the basic salary system for the next 20 years (Liu 1993).

3.2.2 The System of Internal Management in Higher Education Institutions (1949–1956)

3.2.2.1 Leadership and Management System in Higher Education Institutions (1949–1956)

At this stage there were three systems of leadership and management adopted by higher education institutions.

A. System of principals taking overall responsibilities in 1950

On April 1950, the central government ordered that higher education institutions whose presidents were appointed by the Central Government were implementing the system of the presidents taking overall responsibility.

On 14 August, 1950, the Administrative Council issued Provisional Regulations on Higher Education Institutions. The *Regulations* stipulated that universities and colleges were institutions in which the presidents took overall responsibilities of management of universities and colleges.

B. The system of HEIs' Committee of Affairs under guidance of the communist party's commission in 1951

In September 1951, the Ministry of Education issued *Regulations on Higher Education Institutions Affiliated with the Ministry of Education*. The *Regulations* stipulated that the system of leadership in higher education institutions should be the system of HEIs' Commission of Affairs under guidance of the Chinese Communist Party Committee. The presidents of HEIs were the administrative leaders appointed by government; they would represent HEIs externally and preside over HEIs's affairs committee and manage the regular operation of higher education institution.

C. System of university council or college council in 1956

In 1956, the *Constitution of Chinese Communist Party* stipulated that the system of internal management in higher education institutions should be the system of university council or college council.

3.2.2.2   The System of to Management of Teachers in Higher Education Institutions (1949–1956)

In 1952, the Ministry of Education issued Circular on *Adjustment of Salaries of Teachers in Schools of Various Types and Levels*. The salaries were calculated into monetary salaries on the basis of the price of foods, clothing, oil, salt and coal.

In November 1952, the Ministry of Higher Education issued the *Circular on Revision of Criteria of Salaries for Teachers in Higher Education Institutions*. The *Circular* established new salary criteria for teachers in HEIs. The salaries of teachers were increased widely.

In October 1955, the Ministry of Higher Education issued a Notice. The *Notice* stipulated that the salary criteria for teachers were transformed to the monetary salary criteria for teachers.

In 1956, the Ministry of Higher Education issued *Directives on the Adjustment of the Salaries for Teachers Engagement in Higher Education*. The *Directives* stipulated that there were three salary criteria for teachers, auxiliary teachers and administrative staff. The salary criteria had eight grades.

3.3   The System of Internal Management in Primary Schools and Secondary Schools at the Stage of Completing the Socialist Construction (1957–1965)

3.3.1   The System of Internal Management in Primary Schools and Secondary Schools (1957–1965)

3.3.1.1   The System of Leadership and Management in Primary Schools and Secondary Schools (1957–1965)

At this stage there were two systems of leadership and management in schools. One system was the system of the principals' accountability under the guidance of Chinese Communist Party's branch, and the other system was the system of the principals' accountability under the guidance of the local Communist Party Committee and educational administrative departments.

A. The system of the principals' accountability under the guidance of communist party's branch from 1958 to 1962

In 1958, the Central Committee of the CCP and the State Council issued *Directives on Educational Undertakings*. The *Directives* pointed out that the one-head system in schools was inclined to alienate from the leadership of the Communist Party, so it was not a suitable system.

The *Directives* stipulated that all educational administrative units and schools at various levels should be under the leadership of the Chinese Communist Party. In the schools, school affairs committees under the leadership of the Chinese Communist Party's branch were set up and the committees took responsibility for the management of schools.

From 1957 on, primary schools and secondary schools established communist party's branches. The Chinese Communist Party's branch took overall responsibilities; actually the secretary of Chinese Communist Party's branch decided all matters. As there was not any distinction between the responsibilities of the secretary of Chinese Communist Party's branch and the responsibilities of Administrators, the functions of administrative institutes and administrators were not realized in some cases.

B. System of principals' accountabilities (1963–1965)

In the early 1960s, the Central Committee of the CCP summarized the lessons and experiences of the past twelve years and made a wise decision about the system of internal management.

In March 1963, the Central Committee of the Chinese Communist Party issued *Regulations on Full-time Primary Schools and Regulations on Full-time Secondary Schools*. The *Regulations* stipulated that the principal is the administrative leader of the school. Under the leadership of the local Chinese Communist Party Committee and administrative departments, the principals were in charge of the whole operation of schools so as to fulfill the instruction plan.

The responsibilities of principals were to implement the educational guidelines and policy made by the Central Committee of the CCP and the State Council; to implement directives issued by the local educational administrative departments; to guide instruction affairs and political education; guide and organize teachers and students to take part in labor; to take care of the life of teachers, students and workers within the school so as to take care of their health; to manage the personnel affairs; to manage the facilities, buildings.

After the implementation of this system, the conflicts between the Chinese Communist Party's branch and the administrative institutions were reduced by clearly differentiating their responsibilities. The administrative institutions and administrators could fulfill their functions well. Under this system the main work of schools usually focused on instruction.

3.3.1.2   The System of Management of Teachers in Primary Schools and Secondary Schools (1957–1965)

In 1959 and 1960, the salaries of teachers who were on very low grades of salaries were increased. In 1959, 5 percent of the teachers in primary schools and 4% of the teachers in regular secondary schools had an increase in their salaries.

In 1963, the Central Committee of the CCP and the State Council made some decisions regarding the adjustment of salaries for teachers at various levels. The salaries of many teachers were increased (Liu 1993).

3.3.2   The System of Internal Management in Higher Education Institutions (1957–1965)

3.3.2.1   The System of Leadership and Management in HEIs (1957–1965)

A. System of HEIs' Committee of Affairs under the leader of the Chinese Communist Party Committee (1957–1965)

The system of HEIs' Affairs Committee under the leadership of the Chinese Communist Party Committee was established in this period.

The Central Commission of the CCP and the State Council issued *Directives on Educational Undertakings* in 1958. The *Directives* stipulated that in higher education institutions the system of HEIs' Affairs Committee under the leadership of the Chinese Communist Party Committee be set up. This system strengthened the Party's guidance on schools at various levels.

3.3.2.2   System of Management of Teachers in Higher Education Institutions from 1957 to 1965

In 1959, 1960 and 1963, the Central Committee of the CCP and the State Council made adjustment of the salaries for teachers.

3.4   The System of Internal Management in Schools at Various Levels at the Stage of the "Cultural Revolution" (1966–1976)

3.4.1   The System of Internal Management in Primary Schools and Secondary Schools (1966–1976)

3.4.1.1   The System of Leadership and Management in Primary Schools and Secondary Schools (1966–1976)

A. The System of "Cultural Revolution Commission" (1966–1967)

On 8 August, 1966, the Central Committee of the CCP issued the *Decisions on Proletarian "Cultural Revolution*. The *Decisions* stipulated "Cultural Revolution Commissions" and "Cultural Revolution Groups" were introduced in primary and secondary schools. They were new-born things. "Cultural Revolution Commission", "Cultural Revolution Group" were the best organizations for the masses to educate themselves under the leadership of Party.

On 4 April, 1967, the Central Committee of the CCP issued the Circulars on Proletarian Cultural Revolution in Primary Schools and Circulars on Proletarian Cultural Revolution in Secondary Schools. The Circulars stipulated that during Proletarian Cultural Revolution, "Cultural Revolution Commission" and "Cultural Revolution Group" should be elected democratically by teachers and high-grade students.

3.4.2   The System of Internal Management in HEIs (1966–1976)

The System of leadership and management in HEIs was implemented in this period.

On 7 March, 1967, the Central Committee issued the *Decisions on Proletarian "Culture Revolution" in Universities and Colleges*. The *Decision* stipulated that in universities and colleges should establish temporary administrative institutions, the Cultural Revolution groups or Cultural Revolution Commissions were set up through election.

3.5   The System of Internal Management in Schools at Various Levels at the Stage of Building Socialist Commodity Markets (1977–1991)

The necessity of the reform of the system of internal management was very clear in the late 1970s. As the social and economic development speeded up, the old system was becoming increasingly unable to adjust to the new situations.

3.5.1   The System of Internal Management in Primary Schools and Secondary Schools (1977–1991)

3.5.1.1   The System of Leadership and Management in Primary and Secondary Schools (1977–1991)

A. Principals taking overall responsibilities under the guidance of communist party branch

In September 1978, the Ministry of Education issued the *Provisional Regulations on Full-time Primary School* and the *Provisional Regulations on Full-time Secondary School*. These two regulations were the revised edition of the respective Regulations issued in 1963.

Compared with *Regulations* issued in 1963, the most important changes concerning the system of internal management in these Regulations was regarding the system of internal management in primary schools and secondary schools, namely, the principals taking responsibilities in management of schools collectively under guidance of communist party's branch.

A new task for the principal was added. The principal had to guide and organize the political, cultural, professional learning of teachers and students and guide the running of factories and farms affiliated to schools.

In 1984, the Ministry of Education issued the *Opinions on Adjustment of Leader Group in Regular Secondary Schools*. The Opinions stipulated that the system of internal management in regular secondary schools was the System of Principals' Accountabilities under the guidance of the Chinese Communist Party's branch.

The Chinese Communist Party's branch and the administrators should divide the responsibilities and coordinate their activities so as to work more effectively.

B. System of principals' accountabilities (1985–1989)

In 1985, *Decision on Reform of Educational System* was issued. The *Decision* stipulated that schools at various levels should implement the system of principals' accountabilities. The schools with contingent conditions should establish commissions of general administrative affairs. The Chinese Communist Party's branch should free itself from the state of managing everything, concentrate on the construction of the Chinese Communist Party and strengthen the political education. The Chinese Communist Party's organizations should make efforts to unite all teachers and students, and make sure that the guidelines, policies and plans of the Party are implemented.

In 1987, the 13th Plenary Session of the Central Committee of the CCP issued a *Report*. The *Report* stipulated that the key factor for the reform of political system was the division of the Chinese Communist Party's leadership and governmental administrative leadership.

3.5.1.2   The System of Management of Teachers in Primary Schools and Secondary Schools (1977–1991)

A. The system of professional titles for teachers

On 6 May, 1983, the Central Committee of the CCP and the State Council issued *Circular on Strengthening and Reforming Schooling in Rural Areas* (State Education Commission 1991). The *Circula*r stipulated that the Ministry of Education should formulate a system of titles for teachers as soon as possible. After a pilot experiment, the system was to be instituted widely.

On 19 May, 1986, the Leading Group of the Central Committee for Reform of Professional Titles approved the Provisional Regulations on Teachers in Secondary Schools and Provisional Regulations on Teachers in Primary Schools submitted by the State Education Commission (He 1998b). The *Regulations* stipulated that the professional titles in secondary schools and primary schools include the high-grade teachers, first-grade teachers, second-grade teachers, third-grade teachers. The regulations stipulated the responsibilities for teachers and the application requirement for teachers.

B. The system of appointment of teachers

In 1985, Decision *on the Reform of Educational System* was issued. It stressed that in five years those who had the qualified academic records and had the necessary certificate for teacher's post could be recruited as teachers.

C. The system of salaries of teachers

In order to overcome the general ways of equalitarianism with respect to salaries and in order to fire teacher's enthusiasm, many schools implemented the system of determining necessary posts and size of posts, limiting the total salaries and distributing salaries according to one's contribution, instituting a system of appointment. Many schools implemented the system of structural salaries. Under this new system the earnings of teachers would depend on his or her work quantities and qualities as well as achievements. If one works more, one would like to earn more. The structural salaries consisted of four parts.

(1) The basic salaries on the basis of one's professional titles;
(2) The salaries from subsidies such as the subsidies for price adjustment, subsidies for one-child practice, subsidies for commuting, subsidies for housing, subsidies for buying books;
(3) The salaries from fulfilling the necessary workload;
(4) The salaries for rewarding good performance.

Each school may have its own ways of determining structural salaries. The structural salary made a difference in teachers' salaries; it activated teacher's enthusiasm.

3.5.2 The System of Internal Management in Higher Education Institutions (1977–1991)

3.5.2.1 The System of Leadership and Management (1977–1991)

A. Presidents taking responsibilities under the leadership of communist party committee (1978–1984)

According to *Provisional Regulations for Key Colleges or Universities* notified by the Ministry of Education on 4 October, 1978, the system of management of colleges or universities is a system for which the president takes responsibilities under leadership of the Communist Party's Committee. The presidents of colleges or universities are the top administrators appointed by the state. They took the leading positions in representing colleges or universities externally and managed college or university internally (Editing Board of China's Education Yearbook 1984).

The Staff Representative Conference is to be held periodically to discuss, examine, criticize and make suggestions on the important issues regarding teaching, research and general affairs in colleges or universities.

Academic committees are to be set up at all colleges and universities for dealing with the examination and approval for research projects and post-graduate programs, as well as examination and promotion for professorships and associate professorships.

B. Establishment of system of presidents' accountabilities (1985–1988)

In 1985, the Central Committee of the CCP issued *Decisions on the Reform of Educational System*. The *Decision* stipulated that schools at various levels should implement the system of principals' accountabilities. The schools at various levels should set up school affair committees and the staff representative committees so as to strengthen the democratic management and democratic supervision.

On 27 April, 1988, the State Education Commission issued *Opinions on the Implementation of the Presidents' taking responsibilities of Management of HEIs* (He 1998a). The *Opinions* stipulated that higher education institutions should implement the system of presidents' taking responsibilities according to the principle of division between the party's leadership and administrators' leadership. The direction of implementation of presidents' taking overall responsibilities should be clear, the attitudes should be firm, the step should be reasonable.

The President's responsibilities were: to formulate and implement comprehensive plans and yearly plans in higher education institutions in accordance to requirements of national construction; to lead teachers and students to enhance educational qualities and research qualities and assure the fulfillment of tasks in training of professionals and conduct of scientific research; to conduct ideological education and moral education; to do scientific research and service so as to foster students' all-around development; to strengthen the capacity-building of teachers and improve their political, ideological and professional competence; to improve the living and working conditions for teachers and students.

C. Presidents taking main responsibilities under the leadership of the communist party's committee (1989–1991)

In July 1989, the National Conference on Higher Education stressed that the Chinese Communist Party should play a more important role in the management of higher education.

In 15 July, 1989, the minister of the State Education Commission, Li Tieying, pointed out that higher education institutions should maintain socialist directions. It was necessary to maintain and support the Party's guidance on schools at various levels and assure the Party organization's function of guidance in educational undertakings. There were some higher education institutions implementing the system of presidents' taking overall responsibilities. If they achieved good results, they should continue to explore and summarize their experiences. But from hereafter the higher education institutions that took part in the experiment should not be increased. No matter which system the universities and colleges chose, they should care about the Chinese Communist Party's guidance.

3.5.2.2 The System of Management of Teachers in Higher Educational Institutions (1977–1991)

A. The system of professional titles for teachers in HEIs

On 7 March, 1978, the State Council approved the *Report on Rehabilitation and Promotion of Professional Titles for Teachers in HEIs* submitted by the Ministry of Education (He 1998a). The *Report* stipulated that the system of professional titles for teachers who were promoted as professors, associate professors, lecturers and assistant instructors should be rehabilitated. The Chinese Communist Party Commission of HEIs would examine and approve the professional titles of the teachers. The power of final approval of professional titles for teachers was transferred to provincial governments.

On 3 March, 1986, the Group on Reform of Professional Titles under the Central Committee of the CCP issued *Provisional Regulations on Professional Titles for Teachers in HEIs*. The *Regulations* stipulated the responsibilities for teachers with the respective titles. The *Regulations* specified the application requirement for professional titles, the examination and approval procedure for determining teachers' professional titles (He 1998a).

B. System of teachers' responsibilities

On 27 November, 1979, the Ministry of Education issued the *Provisional Regulations on Teacher's Responsibilities*. The Regulations stipulated that assistant instructors, lecturers, associate professors, and professors should take definite responsibilities. The evaluation of teachers should center on professional competences and achievements of work on the basis of responsibilities (He 1998a).

C. System of salaries of teachers

On 20 April, 1981, the Ministry of Education issued *Circular on the System of Work Quantities for Teachers in HEIs* (The Ministry of Finance 1990). The *Circular* stipulated that the establishment and perfection of the system of work quantities for teachers in HEIs was an important measure to manage HEIs. The system was beneficial to create enthusiasm among teachers, enhance the quality of education, and facilitate teachers' professional development.

3.6   The System of Internal Management at Various Levels at the Stage of Building Socialist Market Economy (1992–2016)

3.6.1   The System of Internal Management in Primary Schools and Secondary Schools (1992–2016)

3.6.1.1   The System of Leadership and Management (1992–2016)

The system of Principals' taking responsibilities in management of schools was implemented in this period.

On 18 March, 1995, Education Law of the People's Republic of China was adopted by the Third Session of the Eighth National People's Congress. The *Education Law* stipulated that sponsors of schools or other types of educational institutions should, in accordance with the relevant regulations of the State, determine the system of internal management of schools or other educational institutions under the sponsorship (He 2003).

On 29 July, 2010, the Central Committee of the Chinese Communist Party and the State Council issued *National Guidelines for Medium and Long-term Educational Reform and Development Program (2010–2020)*. The *National Guidelines* stipulated that in regular primary schools, secondary schools and secondary vocational schools the system of principals' taking responsibilities in management of schools should be perfected. The terms and ways of appointment and employment should be perfected. The system of schools' general meeting should be instituted. The commission of students' parents should be instituted. The communities and professionals should be invited to take part in the management of schools.

3.6.1.2   Management of Teachers in Primary and Secondary Schools

A. The system of qualification of teachers

On 31 October, 1993, *Teachers Law of the People's Republic of China* was issued by the Fourth Plenary Session of the Eighth National Congress. The *Teachers Law* stipulated that the State should institute a system of qualifications for teachers (He 1998a, b).

The qualifications for teachers in primary schools and secondary schools should be evaluated and approved by educational administrative departments under the local governments at or above county level. The qualifications for teachers in secondary schools should be evaluated and approved by the relevant competent departments, under the auspices of the educational administrative departments under the local governments at or above county level.

On 12 December, 1995, the State Council issued *Regulations on Qualification for Teachers*. The implementation of the system of qualification for teachers was a significant step for the construction of contingents of teachers. It facilitated the rule of law of construction of contingents of teachers.

In 1998, the State Education Committee issued *Decision on Principal' Taking up Posts with Certificate*. This *Decision* stipulated that principals in schools should take part in the in-service training so as to get certificates.

On 29 June, 2006, the Twelfth Plenary Session of the National People's Congress revised Compulsory Education Law of the People's Republic of China. The revised *Law* stipulated that teachers should obtain teacher's qualification in accord with the state's requirements.

B. The system of professional titles for teachers

In 1993, *Teachers Law of the People's Republic of China* stipulated that the State implement the system of professional titles for teachers.

The revised *Compulsory Education Law of the People's Republic of China* stipulated that the State establish the unitary system of professional titles for teachers in compulsory education.

Education Law of the People's Republic of China stipulated that the State implement the system of titles for teachers.

C. The system of appointment of teachers

In 1993, *Teachers Law of the People's Republic of China* stipulated that the appointment of teachers should be based on the principle of equality between both parties—the school and the teachers. The school and the teachers should sign an appointment contract, defining each other's rights, obligations and responsibilities. Steps and measures for implementing the system of appointment for teachers should be formulated by educational administrative departments under the State Council.

The *Education Law in the People's Republic of China* stipulates that the State should implement the system of appointment of teachers.

D. The system of salaries of teachers

On 1 October, 1993, the new system of salaries of teachers, named the System of Salaries Based on Professional Titles, was established. The new system divided the salaries of teachers into two parts. One part was on the basis of the professional titles, and the other part consisted of subsidies for teachers on the basis of the performance of work.

On 20 August, 2012, the State Council issued *Opinions on Strengthening the Teachers' Team Construction*, the Opinions stipulated that the criterion of teachers' authorized structure should be unitary for all schools in rural areas and urban areas, the system of qualification and recruitment of teachers should be implemented according to laws and regulations, the system of teachers' post and titles should be reformed. The system of contracted employment and management should be implemented systematically. The evaluation of teachers should be perfected.

3.6.2 The System of Internal Management in HEIs (1992–2016)

3.6.2.1 The System of Leadership and Management in HEIs (1992–2016)

A. The system of Presidents' taking responsibilities under the leadership of the Communist Party Committee (1996–2016)

In March 1996, *Regulations on Basic Organization of CPP in Regular Higher Education Institutions* were issued (He 1998b). The *Regulation* stipulated that HEIs should implement the rule of the 'President's taking responsibilities under leadership of the Communist Party Committee'.

The Higher Education Law of the People's Republic of China stipulated that in higher education institutions run by the State, the system should be applied whereby the president's take overall responsibilities under the leadership of primary committees of the Chinese Communist Party in higher education institutions. Such committees should, in accordance with the Constitution of the Chinese Communist Party and the relevant regulations, exercise unified leadership over the work of the institutions and support presidents in exercising their functions and powers independently and responsibility.

On 21 August, 1992, the State Education Commission issued *Suggestions on Internal Management Reform in Higher Education Institutions Affiliated with the SEC*. The *Suggestions* pointed out that it was necessary to reform the internal management system.

The reform of the system of personnel management was the key point of reform. HEIs should implement various ways to use personnel and combining the fixed posts of institutions with fluid posts of institutions, combining posts of public institutions with posts of enterprise institutions. HEIs should strengthen leadership on discipline. HEIs should improve the setting of posts and determine teachers' and other kinds of professionals' titles. The industrial workers and logistics workers should be taken as contract workers.

On 28 May, 2014, the Office of General Affairs under the Ministry of Education issued the Notice on Writing, Approval and Implementation of HEIs' Regulations. The Notice stipulated that by the end of 2015 all HEIs' Regulations in China should be examined and approved by the Ministry of Education. In order to make HEIs' regulations effective, it is necessary to share the responsibilities by the administrators in HEIs, to perfect the examination and approval procedure, to perfect the implementation mechanism.

On 31 March, 2016, the Commission of the CCP of the Ministry of Education issued Notice on Implementation of the System of Presidents' Taking Responsibilities under the Leadership of the Communist Party Committee. The Notice stipulated that the system of HEIs' administrators' hold meetings and regulations of discussing affairs should be perfected, the report system of implementation of the system of presidents' taking responsibilities under the leadership of the Communist Party Committee should be perfected, and the system of reporting of performance should be instituted.

3.6.2.2   The System of Management of Teachers (1992–2009)

A. The system of qualification for teachers in HEIs

In 1998, Higher Education Law of the People's Republic of China stipulated that higher education institutions should implement the system of qualification for teachers. Chinese citizens, who abided by the Constitution and laws, love education as a cause, have sound ideology and moral character, have completed undergraduate or graduate program, have the necessary competence in education and teaching, and are considered qualified, may serve as teachers in higher education institutions.

B. System of professional titles for teachers

In 1998, Higher Education Law of the People's Republic of China stipulated that the State implement the system of qualification titles. The number of such titles in higher education institutions should be determined on the basis of the need of teaching, research and other tasks which are shouldered by the institutions. The professional titles of teachers included teaching assistant, lecturer, associate professors and professors.

C. The system of appointment of teachers

In 1998, Higher Education Law of the People's Republic of China stipulated that higher education institutions should implement the system of appointment. A person, having been evaluated as being qualified for holding a teaching post, should be appointed by higher education institutions according to the duties, requirements and tenure of office for the post. Appointment of teachers of higher education institutions should be based on the principle of equality and willingness on both sides, and contracts of appointment should be signed by presidents of higher education institutions and the teachers appointed.

D. The system of salaries for teachers

On 21 August, 1992, the State Education Commission issued *Suggestions on Internal Management Reform in Higher Education Institutions Affiliated with the SEC* (He 1998b). The *Suggestions* stipulated that the system of internal benefits assignment should be reformed. In accompanying national salary reform and increase the actual salary, the system of allowance should be set up in higher education institutions. It was necessary to rationalize salary structure, normalize bonus allocation, let some part of the hidden income become transparent, form the internal assignment model that adapt to the national salary and system of internal allowance.

3.6.3 Historical Experiences in the Reform and Development of the System of Internal Management in China

There are some experiences that can be summarized from the point of their historical development.

Firstly, the difference between the system of internal management in primary schools and secondary schools and the system of internal management in HEIs is obvious.

Secondly, the connection of national development orientation and the system of internal management should be strengthened. Thirdly, the strength of the three kinds of systems of internal management should be promoted and the weaknesses should be overcome.

In the past several decades, there were three types of internal management systems. The first type is the system of commissions. This system stresses the collective leadership and democratic management. The system of principal's taking overall responsibilities is a kind of one-head system in nature. The essence of one-head system is the accountability and leadership of expert. The system of leadership by Chinese Communist Party's branch is another from of commissions. Here the member was the member of the Chinese Communist Party's branch. The Party's leadership is a kind of collective leadership.

3.7 Current Situation of the System of Internal Management in China

Nowadays the system of internal management in terms of educational institutions in China is adapting to the changes of national political system, economic system and scientific and technological system.

The present main task of our country is to set up the socialist market economic system and realize the socialist modernization. To sum up, the internal management systems in schools at various levels have gone along the road of scientific development.

3.7.1 Current Situation of the System of Internal Management in Primary and Secondary Schools

3.7.1.1 The System of Leadership and Management in Primary and Secondary Schools

A. Regulations on the system of internal management in primary and secondary schools

At present all types of schools at levels of secondary education and below are implementing the system of principals' accountabilities.

According to the Education Law, principals in schools should be responsible for conducting of instruction and other administrative matters in their schools.

The schools should observe laws and regulations, implement the State's educational policies, comply with the State's educational standards and guarantee educational quality, safeguard lawful rights and interests of students, teachers and other staff and workers; let the students and their guardians be informed of the scholastic record and other relevant matters of the students through suitable ways. To meet the requirement of the State and fulfill the functions of schools, the principals should get to know what they need to do and how they can do these things well.

B. Responsibilities of principals in primary and secondary schools

The principals should implement educational guidance and policies made out by the Communist Party and the governments at various levels.

The principals should take responsibilities of management of instruction and other administrative affairs.

C. The Conference of Representatives of Teachers

According to Education Law, schools, in accordance with the relevant regulations of the State, guarantee that teachers and staff are to be involved in the democratic management and supervision of school through the conference of representatives of teachers, other staff and workers with teachers as its main body.

The representatives of teachers, staffs and workers would convene once in a year. The principal will make a report. The delegates will discuss the report and criticize it and offer suggestions on the working of the school.

D. System of meetings in schools

The schools establish some important system of meetings, including the meeting of the school council, the meeting of staff representatives and the meeting of administrative affairs.

The principal's working meeting is convened once a week. It aims at researching on the daily work and examining the work of the past.

The meeting of the director of teaching and research group would be convened regular. The principal should preside over this meeting.

3.7.1.2   The System of Management of Teachers in Primary and Secondary Schools

A. The system of qualification for teachers.

The system of qualification for teachers is an important assurance system of high quality of education. The qualifications for teachers is examined and approved by governments at county or higher levels.

A citizen who, without the record of formal schooling for teachers' qualifications as stipulated in this Law, apply for teachers' qualifications must pass the national teachers' qualification examinations.

As a result of the implementation of system of qualification for teachers, the rates of qualified teachers were increasing.

B. System of fulfillment of responsibilities by teachers

Schools should implement the system of fulfillment of responsibilities by teachers. The school and the teachers should sign an appointment contract defining each other' rights, obligations and responsibilities. The appointment procedure includes three steps. Firstly, the school determines the number of posts according to the scope of the power and responsibilities for each department. Secondly, the responsibilities and requirements for each post are specified clearly. After a period of time the teacher's performance is assessed, and the new period of appointment may be prolonged. If teacher's performance is satisfactory, he or she will receive reward and his or her post in the next period will be probably assured.

C. The system of appointment for teachers

The schools of various types and levels have been instituting the system of appointment for teachers. The following principle should be followed by principals in the process of appointment. Firstly, principals should appoint teachers on the basis of professional level and work performance. Secondly, principals should make a rational organization of teachers and optimize the use of teachers. Thirdly, principals should facilitate the mobility of teachers. Fourthly, the principle of mutual choice should be observed.

D. The system of professional titles for teachers

From 1986 on, the State Education Commission decided that the system of professional titles for teachers should be instituted. In the same year *Provisional Regulations on Professional Titles for Teachers in Primary Schools and Provisional Regulations on Professional Titles for Teachers in Secondary Schools* were formulated. In primary schools there are four kinds of professional titles for teachers; they are advanced teachers, the first level teachers, the second level teachers, and the third level teachers, in a descending order.

Every year, educational administrative departments conduct examination and approval of professional titles of teachers in schools. The qualification and quotas are published, teachers apply, schools and educational administrations conduct examinations and approval.

3.7.2 Current Situation of the System of Internal Management in Higher Education Institutions

3.7.2.1 The System of Leadership and Management in Higher Education Institutions

A. The system of leadership and management in higher education institutions on the basis of laws and regulations

At present the State-run higher education institutions implement the system of presidents' taking responsibilities of management in HEI under leadership of the grassroots communist commission. The grassroots communist commission exercises unitary leadership over HEIs, support the presidents taking responsibilities independently.

The responsibilities of the grassroots communist commissions were to adhere to the lines, principles and policies of the Chinese Communist Party, to keep to the socialist orientation in running schools, to provide guidance to ideological and political works and moral education in institutions, to discuss and decide on internal structure and directors of department on the institutions and other matters, to ensure fulfillment of all tasks centering on the training of students.

B. Responsibilities of presidents in HEIs

The post of the president of a higher education institution is held by a citizen who meets the qualification for the post as provided in Education Law. The president and vice-presidents should be appointed and removed according to the relevant regulations of the State.

Under the president, several vice presidents are in charge of academic, student, personnel, business, and other affairs. Below the level of the vice president, the administrative structures differ from institution to institution.

C. The academic organizations in HEIs

HEIs establish academic commissions. The responsibilities of this kind of commission include deliberating on the disciplines and specialties to be offered, teaching and research plans, and evaluate the academic matters relating to the success achieved in teaching and research.

D. System of meetings in higher education institutions

HEIs often establish some necessary management organizations and institutions. HEIs should convene presidents' working meetings. HEIs should convene meetings on administrative affairs, and these meetings are presided over by the presidents.

Higher education institutions should be in accordance with law and, through the conference of representatives of teachers and administrative staff workers, with teachers as its main body, or through other forms, guarantee that teachers and staff workers are involved in the democratic management and supervision of the institutions and safeguard their lawful rights and interests.

3.7.2.2 The System of Management of Teachers in Higher Education Institutions

A. The system of appointment of teachers

The system of appointment of teachers should be institutes in Higher education institutions. A person who has been evaluated as being qualified for a teaching post should be appointed by a higher education institutions according to the duties, requirements.

B. The System of professional titles for teachers

The system of professional titles for teachers should be institutes in Higher education institutions. The number of such titles should be determined on the basis of the need of teaching, research and other tasks which are shouldered by the institutions. The professional titles for teachers include the assistant, lecturer, associate professor, professor.

3.8 The Problems Facing China in the System of Internal Management

3.8.1 The Problems Facing China in the System of Internal Management in Primary and Secondary Schools

The problems facing China in the system of internal management in basic education concern the principal's exercising power and the improvement of management of leaders.

3.8.1.1 The Problems Facing China in the System of Leadership and Management in Primary and Secondary Schools

There exist three problems in the system of leadership and management in primary schools and secondary schools.

Firstly, one of most hotly debated problems is the relation between guidance of the Party's Branch and the administrative institutions. There were disputes about the function of principals and secretaries of the communist party's branches. Some think that the principals should take responsibilities on affairs of personnel management and political and moral education. They reckon that only after principals are given the necessary powers of management of personnel, can they make effective leadership on instruction, research and administration affairs. The management of personnel and management of affairs should be connected. Some think that the secretaries of the communist party's branches should take responsibilities for the affairs of personnel management and political and moral education. They think that the secretary of the party's branch should manage political education, and the principals should take responsibility of management of instruction, research and administrative affairs. If the schools in one region had different management models, they would conflict with the others. Most persons think that the principals should take overall responsibilities. If the secretary of the Party's branch and the principals take overall responsibility mutually, there will not be a clear differentiation of functions between them, and finally nobody will really take responsibility.

Secondly, the principals do not have too much autonomy in the management of schools. Nearly all schools have implemented the system of principal's accountabilities, but the effects of implementation were not very satisfactory as many anticipated. The problems not only arise from the incompleteness of macro-management, but also from the incompleteness of internal management reform. In order to implement the system of principal's accountabilities effectively, the system of appointment of principals, the system of setting up and fulfillment of the system of goal attainment, the system of appointment of teachers, the system of teachers' responsibilities, need to be established and carried out smoothly.

Thirdly, one of the problems facing China in conducting of principal's accountabilities is that some principals will act willfully on their own in schools. The great challenge facing schools is how to take the effective supervision over the fulfillment of functions by principals and facilitate democratic involvement of teachers, administrative persons, students, parents and society.

3.8.1.2 Problems Facing China in the System of Management of Teachers in Primary and Secondary Schools

Firstly, as far as the management of teachers was concerned, it was not as effective as many people expected. The use and management of teachers still have a lot of things to do. Although our country has passed the Teacher's Law, there was not sufficient implementation rules, such as how to determine concrete qualifications for teachers, how to select the teachers and use them, how to determine the professional titles of teachers, how to train teachers, how to allocate teachers, how to appraise teachers, how to determine salary and allowances for teachers. These are still short of implementation rules.

Secondly, the system of appointments of teachers had some shortcomings. In the process of implementation of this system the principals may misuse their power to appoint teachers. The misuse of power can instigate uneasiness among teachers.

Thirdly, the system of internal management was based on the governmental management model. So it was inclined to ignore the educational law and regulations. For a long period of time, our internal management institutions were based on government's administrative model. If the government establishes a kind of department, the schools also designate some functioning posts, and take the same or similar operation mechanism. Under this system the efficiency of management was not assured. On the one side, the administrative staff's desire and department workers' desire would surpass the general stakeholders' benefits. The administrators would ignore the academic characteristics of schools at various levels. On the other side, the management was centered on the administrative side, the administration and department' role was emphasized excessively.

Concerned with the reform of the system of salaries of teachers, the most serious problem was the excessive percentage of the subsidies for teachers. According to the new system of salaries, the salaries calculated on the basis of the professional titles were no more than 70% of the total salaries. This causes the salaries calculated on the basis of the professional titles to lose the potentiality of actualizing the enthusiasm for teachers.

3.8.2   The Problems Facing China in the System of Internal Management in Higher Education Institutions

3.8.2.1   The Problems Facing China in the Leadership and Management in Higher Education Institutions

A. The problems facing in terms of leadership and administration within higher education institutions

There were some problems with the leadership and management system.

Firstly, the imbalance of administrative power and academic power is evident. China's universities and colleges are using power model based on the administrative powers. The distribution of powers is tilted toward powers at upper levels; the academic power is affiliated with the administrative power. The power model in China is influenced by the long lasting state planned economic system. The model of power in universities and colleges was on the basis of general administrative model.

B. Problems facing china in the relationship between academic powers and
   administrative powers

There are some problems facing China in the relationship between academic
powers and administrative powers in management of HEIs.

Firstly, the current decision-making model is centered on the use of administrative models; many things are decided by the administrative institutions without
consulting academic members. The management model in HEIs is similar to the
model of functioning departments in governments. The management using of
administrative power is imitated by many units in HEIs and this causes problems
beyond the control of academic members.

Secondly, there are no clear differentiation of administrative affairs and academic
affairs; also no clear differentiation of general affairs and administrative affairs.

Thirdly, there no clear regulations on the scope, function and degree of functioning of academic powers and administrative powers. In many cases the administrative powers are substituting for the academic powers. The power structure in
higher education institutions is ambiguous.

Fourthly, academic powers in higher education institution are weak in comparison with administrative powers (Zhang 2002).

C. The problems facing china in the organization structure in HEIs

Since the 1980s, the system of colleges was established in some universities.
The internal college is the substratum of the university. And the department is the
lower stratum in a university that has administrative power.

In terms of the system of internal colleges, there are four problems:

Firstly, in many cases, an individual college covers too few of disciplines. In the
United States, a university usually has more than ten colleges; among them the
undergraduate college is the basis of the university and there are some graduate
colleges. In China, there are more than twenty or thirty colleges in one university.
In some cases, individual college is transformed into one department or several
small departments. Individual colleges cover very few disciplines. The system of
internal colleges imitates system of departments.

Secondly, the definite responsibilities, rights, power relation between university,
internal colleges and departments in a university do not coordinate with each other,
and the administrator's power in a college is not strong enough as many anticipated.
As the colleges established, the powers at the university level do not devolve
sufficiently; the power in a college is the same as the power in a department. But the
college is a bigger unit than a department; its work scope is wider, its regular affairs
are more, its tasks are more arduous. The power in colleges do not increase, the
college cannot use necessary resources to fulfill their functions.

Thirdly, the increase in levels of management may reduce the efficiency of
management. A university has several dozens of colleges, a college has several
departments. And a department has more divisions. There are too many management levels that administrators at each level feel that the management is too
burdensome.

Fourthly, the linear organizing form of system of internal colleges is not beneficial to the cross-disciplinary development in a university. The linear organizing form of system of college means that the leadership in university is vertical or top-bottom type of leadership. The topmost power source is president's power. From presidents to directors, deans, the leadership is unitary and linear. This form of leadership is characterized by concentration of power, fast decision-making, detailed division of labor. This leadership is beneficial to the unitary leadership and the implementation of policies, but it is not suitable for the complicated environment with many difficult tasks especially exploring tasks.

3.8.2.2 Main Problems Facing China in Management of Teachers in Higher Education Institutions

Firstly, the main problems in the evaluation of teachers were manifested in that the evaluation items were too general without considering the practical work of teachers, especially without considering the difference between the instruction and research, so all teachers were evaluated by the same yardsticks.

Secondly, HEIs have not established self-initiation, self-development and self-constraint mechanisms. The reform of educational system aims at establishing the system of governmental micro-management and assurance of autonomy in the running of schools.

3.9 The Strategies and Measures for Reform of System of Internal Management in China

3.9.1 The Strategies and Measures for the Reform of the System of Internal Management in Primary and Secondary Schools in China

3.9.1.1 The Strategies and Measures for Reform and Improvement of Leadership in Schools

The strategies and measures for reform and improvement of leadership in schools should be seen as follows.

Firstly, in order to increase the autonomy of schools, schools should carry out a number of reforms. Only through this kind of reform can schools combine goal with process and result, combine work quantity with work quality, combine powers with the responsibilities and benefits.

Secondly, principals should strengthen the autonomy of their roles. The principals should deal with the relationship between themselves and the leaders at higher levels. Principals should function under the guidance of higher level leaders, and should not stick to their own ways of doing things. The principals should deal with relations between them and the members of the staff representative meetings. Principals should report to the representatives and listen to opinions of delegates.

For educational administrative departments, they should make prudent choice of principals. The criteria of choosing principals should be established and publicized. The choice procedures should be open and equitable. The public opinion about candidates should be observed. Moreover, internal and external supervision and assessment of principals is very important.

Within schools, the institutions and rules of management should be established and perfected. The important things should be decided through collective choice mechanism.

3.9.1.2   Strategies and Measures for Reform of Management of Teachers in Primary and Secondary Schools in China

In order to implement Teachers Law effectively, it is necessary to formulate relevant detailed regulations by the State Council and provincial governments. Each main system of teacher management should have matching regulations.

The principals should take overall responsibility of management of schools. So they may have great powers of distribution of tasks in schools. The powers of principals and general teachers are not symmetrical. To guarantee teachers' rights, three measures should be taken. Firstly, the appointment of principals should be based on the public opinions of teachers. If principals fail in the survey of teachers' opinions, they could be removed from their posts. Secondly, the appointments of teachers should be based on laws and regulations, and teachers cannot be removed on the basis of some person's opinion or subjective judgment. Thirdly, Party's branch and labor union should take supervision responsibilities of principals.

The managers-based culture should be changed. Schools are educational institutions that aim at training students and conducting instruction and research. They are not the same as enterprises; they are not public administrative institutions. Teachers are persons with high level of learning experience. So academic freedom and institutional autonomy is very precious for schools. Models of management of schools should be based on teachers, staffs and workers' self-discipline, self-consciousness and self-internal reflection. The management of schools should be more humanized.

The salary determination mechanism should be reformed. The professional titles should be the main determinant of teacher salaries. The part of subsidies that are based on fulfilling of functions should be lessened to some extent. The system of salaries should be reformed. The part of basic salaries for teachers should be increased. The structure of salaries should be optimized.

3.9.2 The Strategies and Measures for Reform of System of Internal Management Reform in HEIs in China

3.9.2.1 The Strategies and Measures for Reform in Leadership and Management in HEIs in China

A. The strategies and measures for redressing problems in the relation between academic powers and administrative powers

The functioning of institutions should be perfected. Simple administration should be the basic principle of management. Reform of management should help to differentiate between the Chinese Communist Party's leadership and the administrator's functioning.

Firstly, in order to redress problems of great influence of the cadres-centered culture in management of education and the government control model of educational management, one should study the educational laws. The educational work has its internal logic. Education is a profession. The educational management should have great independence.

Secondly, in order to redress problem of shortage of rules and regulations for implementation of *Teachers Law of People's Republic of China* and other Laws concerned with education, it is necessary to speed up educational lawmaking progress. More regulations should be issued by the State Council. Besides, the local governments and educational administrative departments should take responsibilities for perfecting the administrative system.

B. Strategies and measures for redressing problems in the relationship between academic power and administrative power

For many reasons, higher education in China is being carried out according to the unitary and centralized management model for a long period of time. Higher education institutions look like a "production unit", the production process is directed by directives issued by educational administrative departments. The ideal of academic autonomy and academic freedom is cherished by the academic community. Concerning the academic exploration, the academic professionals should have more say in the academic affairs.

The management of higher education institutions should stress the value of academic persons, encourage innovation, pursue excellence, and increase powers of academic decisions. Effective academic management mechanism should be set up.

To establish the differentiation of academic affairs, general affairs and administrative affairs, special institutions for dealing with these things should be established. Usually the academic affairs concerning instruction and research belong to academic affairs. The administrative work concerning persons, materials, and funds belong to the administrative affairs. And the administrative affairs should be differentiated further. The general affairs and administrative affairs are different. The academic administrative department should take responsibility for academic affairs.

The general administrative department should take responsibilities for administrative affairs. The academic affairs should be administrated according to the law of academic development; they cannot be administrated in general administrative ways. The academic management is the main task of HEIs. The use of academic power aims at facilitating academic development. The use of academic powers is serving the academic development.

There are three types of powers. The party commission exercises political powers. The presidents exercise administrative powers. The professors exercise academic powers. These three kinds of powers have different sources and functions.

The policy making process is relying on administrative forces and academic forces. The policy making in HEIs depend very much on administrative powers. The administrative power is the main power in policy making in HEIs across the world, but each country has a different situation. In the past, higher education institutions relied on administrative powers in decision making in China. After the implementation of reform and the policy of opening up to the outside world, the management models of HEIs in China have changed a great deal. The academic powers in HEIs are increasing, but they are weak compared with the administrative powers.

HEIs should make greater efforts to establish self-initiation, self-development, and self-constraints mechanism. HEIs are not only an organization, but also a self-organization. Self-organization is an important characteristic of the open system. The self-organization factors bring about self-steering and self-regulation competence for open system. HEIs should increase coordination competence in self-adaptation. HEIs are relatively benefit subjects. They should adapt to development of socialist market economy. In order to establish the new mechanism, HEIs should deal with the six relationships well, namely: the relationship between self-development and self- constraints, the relationship between internal and external constraints, the relationship between economic and social benefits, the relationship between unit benefit and social benefits, the relationship between management mechanism and education laws, the relationship between thought stimulus and benefits stimulus. In order to establish this system, the six steps should be followed, namely, construction of scientific management system, perfection of internal management system, implementation of normalized management, formation of pressure and motivations, use of benefits stimulus and development of grassroots organizations.

C. The strategies and measures for redressing problems of organizational structure in HEI

Four strategies and measures should be taken to optimize the organizational structure in HEIs. Firstly, it is necessary to strengthen the integration of disciplines and to enlarge coverage of disciplines in colleges. The construction of disciplines is the eternal topic for universities and the key for the development of universities. Scientific research and training of professionals should be based on development of disciplines. In future, China's universities and colleges should strengthen development of high-tech disciplines and disciplines related to national economy. These disciplines include life science and technology, information sciences and technology, materials sciences and technology, environment sciences and technology, agricultural sciences and technology, oceanology sciences and technology, engineering sciences and technology. China should strengthen cross-disciplines development. In the case of China, usually establishment of disciplines or specialties is based on mono-discipline. In the process of perfecting the system of internal colleges, China's universities should transform from the system of colleges based on the mono-discipline to system of internal colleges based on the multi-disciplines.

Secondly, it is beneficial to increase the power of colleges. The internal colleges should become a kind of entity with sufficient powers. Many important powers should be devolved to internal colleges. The regulations and rules should be established to make the devolution of power easier.

Thirdly, China's universities should respect the nature of loosely coupled systems concerning universities and enlarge the autonomy of grassroots disciplinary organization. Tony Bush maintains that the loosely coupled system is characterized by the implicit goal, unclearness of means and procedures, dismantled organization, unclear organization structure. In order to increase the power of internal colleges, it was necessary to make clear differentiation of powers between universities and colleges, to establish the system of internal management concerning devolution, and to establish the distribution model of powers.

Fourthly, it is necessary to establish the nonlinear management model. Universities are loosely coupled systems. If the university management follows the identical and linear management models, universities would be in a difficult position. A culture of disciplinary organization and optimization of the multi-disciplinary development environment should be created. The multi-disciplinary development environment includes material culture, institutional culture, and ideological culture. The universities should internalize the cultures.

3.9.2.2 Strategies and Measures for Redressing Problems in the Management of Teachers

The teachers are subjects of higher education institutions. They have characteristics other than that of the general workers. They have high academic records and high level of consciousness of independence. Higher education institutions should make out the scientific, all-round, practical evaluation criteria by considering the specialties of instruction and research. The evaluation criteria should have many dimensions. Different kinds of personnel need different criteria.

The educational work is a normalized, institutionalized work. The teachers should do their own jobs. Only if they do their own duties, they will receive the best salaries. If most or a very large part of the salary is from extra work, the teachers will be inclined to care less about the necessary work and seek more extra work that could bring them more benefits. So the distribution of work and the salaries structure should be rationalized.

References

Editorial Board of China's Education Yearbook (Ed.). (1984). *China's education yearbook.* Beijing: Chinese Great Encyclopedia Publishing House.

He, D. (Ed.). (1998a). *Important documents in the People's Republic of China (1949–1975).* Haikou: Hainan Press.

He, D. (Ed.). (1998b). *Important documents in the People's Republic of China (1976–1990).* Haikou: Hainan Press.

He, D. (Ed.). (2003). *Important documents in the People's Republic of China (1998–2002).* Haikou: Hainan Press.

Hills, P. J. (Ed.). (1982). *A dictionary of education.* London: Routledge and Kogan Paul Limited.

Liu, Y. J. (Ed.). (1993). *A book of major educational events in China.* Hangzhou: Zhejiang Education Press.

Ministry of Finance. (1990). *Selected data on system of financial management.* Beijing: China's Economy and Finance Press.

The State Education Commission. (1991). *Collections of educational laws and regulations in China.* Beijing: People's Education Press.

Wu, D. (1999). *A study on education reform in China.* Beijing: The Central Party's College Press.

Xiao, Z. (1988). *On management of school.* Beijing: People's Education Press.

Zhang, D. X. (2002). *Academic Power and Administrative Power in HEIs.* Nanjing: Nanjing Normal University.

Chapter 4
Engaging Social Actors: Educational Provision System in China

4.1 Introduction to the System of Educational Provision

4.1.1 The Concept of the System of Educational Provision

Here the concept of the system of educational provision is used instead of the system of running of schools. There are two reasons for this change.

The first reason lies in the fact that there is a difference between production and provision. Education is a process of input, production and output. Provision means the supply of all products that are produced by all kinds of subjects or social actors. Production means direct production and management; the subjects use human resources, and materials to make products. Provision includes direct production and indirect purchasing of products. For instance, the government can make production by instituting public schools, or buy products from private schools or other educational institutions.

The second reason is the difference between sponsors, managers and administrators. For a school there are three kinds of social actors pertaining to the running of schools. The first kind of social actors are sponsors. The function of sponsors is to provide funds, facilities and other necessary conditions for instituting schools. For public schools the sponsors are governments at various levels. For private schools the sponsors are individuals or social groups. The second kind of social actors are managers. The mangers are principals and related administrative institutions in schools. The schools are legal entities, and they may exercise powers of running of schools. The third kind of social actors are the administrators of educational undertakings. Schools are part of the national education system. They must work under the constraints of national education laws, regulations, policies and other social institutions.

From 1952 to 1976, the powers and responsibilities of governments in education were misunderstood. Some people thought that schools were sponsored by governments, so governments had powers to manage education and run schools directly.

© Springer Nature Singapore Pte Ltd. and Higher Education Press 2018
M. Yang and H. Ni, *Educational Governance in China*,
https://doi.org/10.1007/978-981-13-0842-0_4

Governments should play a leading role in resource allocation for educational development. It does not mean that individuals should not bear educational cost. The governments provide free compulsory education on consideration of educational equity and efficiency. Even if governments play the roles of social administrators and providers of funds, they are not necessarily the only providers of educational products.

Viewing from efficiency criteria, educational products can be provided by government and other social groups or individuals. Educational products are of positive externalities.

The research on the system of educational provision aims to answer questions about who runs schools and how people run the schools.

The system of educational provision is an important part of the educational system. It denotes the organization systems and the relevant rules pertaining to running of schools. The main factors included in the system of education provision include planning for running of schools, subjects of running of schools, financing of schools, examination and approval of qualification in running of schools. The set-up of the system of educational provision and normalization of the running of schools are important measures for State's macro-management of schools.

In the usual sense there are two meanings for the concept of running of schools. Firstly, it denotes the establishment of schools and provision of facilities and funds; it equals to setting up a school. Secondly, it denotes the operation and management of schools, and in this case it is equal to the conducting of instruction and educational activities and the relevant management activities. The subjects of creating schools and manager of schools can be the same. In the case of traditional Chinese educational system the governments are both the owners of school organizations and the direct managers of school affairs. In the case of private schools, they are schools both owned by the individual citizens and managed by citizens. The subjects of setting schools and managers of schools can be separated, and they are two different kinds of subjects. Since the implementation of the reform and the policy of opening up to outside and with the deepening of reform of economic system, the relationship between governmental organization and school organization has changed dramatically. The schools have become independent legal entities. The power of conducting of instruction and education has been delegated to schools, and schools have civic rights in civic activities according to laws. Under these circumstances, the subjects who set up schools and managers of schools have been separated already; they are two different subjects. In the case of private schools that have established the board of trustees, the subjects of creating schools and managers of schools have been separated. In some provinces the State-owned schools are established with social community assistance; in these cases the subjects of setting up schools and managers of schools have been separated.

The system of educational provision includes two aspects. One aspect focuses on the subjects of running of schools. It is necessary to know who run schools and who owns the schools. The other aspect focuses on management of schools. It is necessary to know how these subjects carry out the management of these funds and assets within schools.

4.1.2   Classification of the System of Educational Provision

There are two kinds of systems of educational provision. One kind of system of educational provision is the system of educational provision whereby the governments provides all education products. This system once existed in countries such as the Soviet Union, Eastern European countries and China. The other kind of system of educational provision is the system of educational provision whereby the educational products are provided by many subjects including governments, social groups, enterprises and individuals.

There are two types of public schools. Among the first type of public school are schools instituted by the central governments. The second type of public school is instituted by local governments. These schools are called local public schools. Local governments include governments of provinces, governments of prefectures, governments of municipalities, governments of counties, and governments of town. In the case of public schools at the stage of compulsory schools, the governments are responsible for raising and distributing all the funds needed for setting up and operating the schools.

There is also a kind of classification of schools on the basis of the way of financing. Some public schools are "pure" public schools while some private schools are "pure" private schools. Here "pure" means that most or even all funds are coming from public sources or private sources.

The State-owed school with assistance from social forces is a special case. Originally these schools were public schools. But they meet with difficulties in raising funds and exercising effective management. So governments introduce the market-like type of management mechanism to run these schools. The schools could collect fees from students so as to compensate for the insufficiency of funds from governments. The powers of ownership and powers of management were separated. These schools can be called public schools as well.

There are two types of private schools. The first kind of private schools are schools set up owned by individuals or social groups, and have not received governmental financial aids. The second kind of private schools are schools run by individuals and social groups and may be assisted by the government's financial aids. The governments and educational administrative departments support the establishment of schools by providing land with favorable conditions and give approval for the establishment of schools. Some social groups establish schools with their own funds and run schools by themselves.

4.1.3   The Factors Affecting the System of Educational Provision

The reform of system of educational provision depends on the political system, economic system, and science and technology system. Before the implementation of the policy of reform and opening to the outside world, in China, there existed a system of unique public ownership. The system of national ownership and collective ownship dominated the national economy; the State controlled national economy with planning and directives. So the system of educational provision was adjusted to this economic system. Most schools were run by governments.

From 1978 on, the commodity economic system and eventually the market economic system were introduced in the process of the reform of the economic system. The system of ownership of production means was diversified. The running of schools should mainly be based on instituting schools by governments, but non-governmental subjects can also institute schools at various levels. The reform of the system of educational provision reflects the changes in economic system.

4.2   The System of Educational Provision at the Stage of Completing Socialist Restructuring (1949–1956)

4.2.1   The Reform of the System of Provision of Public Education and Private Education in Primary and Secondary Schools (1949–1956)

4.2.1.1   The Development of Public Primary Schools and Secondary Schools

Education in New China developed quickly. The reform of system of schooling was conducted mainly in 1952 and many new kinds of schools were encouraged to be set up.

A. Reforms of the system of schooling

In October 1951, the Administrative Council issued *Decision on Reform of System of Schooling*. The *Decision* stipulated that in the stage of the preschool educational institutions were kindergartens and it recruited children whose ages were from 3 to 7 years old.

The primary education included the primary education both for children and for youth and adults. The primary schools gave all-round education for children. The length of schooling in primary schools was five years. The division of junior primary schools and senior primary schools were revoked and the unitary five-year school system was implemented. The age of enrollment in primary schools was seven. The students had to pass the entrance examination to enter secondary schools.

The primary schools for youth and adults included fast primary schools for adult with two to three years of schooling. These schools recruited adults who had been mangers, workers and peasants.

The spare time primary schools for workers, youth and adult were with indefinite length of schooling, while the literacy schools for workers and peasants aimed at eliminating illiteracy.

The secondary schools included four types. The first type was regular secondary schools that included regular junior secondary schools and regular senior secondary schools. The length of schooling for each kind of schools was three years. The students who graduated from primary schools and who were over 12 years old could enroll in this kind of schools. The students who graduated from junior secondary schools and were over 15 years old had to enroll in senior secondary schools.

The second type was fast secondary schools for workers and mangers with three to four years of schooling. Workers and managers with the degree of graduation from primary schools could enroll in this kind of schools.

The third type was spare time schools including spare time junior secondary schools and spare time senior secondary schools.

The fourth type was the secondary specialized schools. This kind of schools contained technical schools, normal schools and other specialized secondary schools. Technical schools enrolled students who graduated from junior secondary schools. The length of schooling was two to four years. The age of enrollment was not specified. Junior technical schools enrolled students who graduated from primary schools. The length of schooling was two, three or four years. The age of enrollment was not specified. The normal schools were secondary schools. The length of schooling was three years. Normal schools recruited students who graduated from junior secondary schools. Junior normal schools were secondary schools. The length of schooling was three years. Junior normal schools recruited students who graduated from junior secondary schools.

To sum up, full-time primary and secondary schools were the main part of schools in basic education. For these schools, instruction plans, instruction programs, textbooks were formulated and edited by the Ministry of Education. Provincial governments could make the necessary adjustments. If schools brought about great reforms on the system of schooling, they could submit the scheme and the provincial governments would check and approve these schemes.

B.   The type of primary schools and secondary Schools

According to the time of instruction, schools can be classified as the full time schools and part time schools.

On 18 March, 1952, the Ministry of education issued *Provisional Regulations on Primary Schools*. The *Regulations* stipulated that, to meet the special needs of localities, schools were to be established where half the students would attend classes in the morning and the other half in the afternoon; there were to be schools where students would attend only in the special seasons and some schools with students studying in the morning or in the evening. Half-day schools and tour schools were also to be established. The length of schooling could be flexible.

In 1953, the Political Bureau of the Central Committee of the CCP held a meeting on education. In the meeting, a decision was made about the way of running schools. Accordingly, the primary schools and secondary schools should not run in the same mode. In rural areas there were three kinds of schools, namely central primary schools, non-formal schools, fast schools. The primary schools in rural areas should be convenient for children from families of peasants to enroll.

On 26 November, 1953, the Administrative Council issued *Directives on Regulation and Improvement of Primary Education*. The *Directives* stipulated that as the economic development in China was not balanced, the educational development was also not balanced. The running of primary schools should be based on the situations in localities; various way and forms of providing education should be used.

The type of secondary schools included junior secondary school and senior secondary schools, fast secondary schools, secondary specialized schools, normal secondary schools.

C. The change of length of schooling

Before 1950, the length of schooling in primary schools was six years. The primary education was divided into two stages, one stage was of junior primary of four years' duration; the other stage was senior primary, of two years' duration.

In June 1950, the department of primary education under the Ministry of Education chose six primary schools to carry out reform on the five-year curricula.

On 15 November, 1952, the Ministry of Education issued *Directives on Implementation of Five-year System in Primary Schools* (He 1998). The *Directives* stipulated that from 1952 on, the length of schooling in primary schools should be five years. A part of the minority areas, remote areas, backward areas could postpone the implementation of five-year system in primary schools. All areas were asked to accumulate experiences and make propaganda of these experiences. In rural areas, classes with several grades could be established for want of teachers and classrooms.

D. The establishment of fast secondary schools

On 10 February, 1951, the Ministry of Education issued *Provisional Regulations on Fast Secondary Schools for Workers and Peasants* (He 1998). The *Regulations* stipulated that the task of fast secondary schools was to recruit good students from workers and managers and to provide basic education so as make them have potentials to enroll in higher education institutions in the future. The ages of students in fast schools should be over 18 years old, graduated from primary schools, recommended by others and passed in the entrance examination. The length of schooling was three years. The subjects of instruction were Chinese, mathematics, natural sciences, chemistry, physics, geography, politics, physical training, music. The fast secondary schools took the system of principals' accountabilities and were administrated by the Ministry of Education and Administrative Department in the great administrative region.

On 19 November, 1951, the Ministry of Education issued *Decisions on Fast Secondary Schools Affiliated with HEIs* (He 1998). The *Decisions* stipulated that fast secondary schools could be established by affiliating them with HEIs. From 1952 on, the fast secondary schools had to be affiliated with HEIs. The length of schooling, instruction plans, instruction programs, and the system of internal management would be according to *Directives* issued in 1951, but HEIs would have to take responsibilities for financial management and personnel management.

From 1950 to 1954, 87 fast secondary schools were established; the total enrollment was 64700. In 1953 there were 1680 graduates, among them 1622 enrolled in higher education institutions. Among 28,000 students, 56.3% were from managers; 25.5% were from industrial workers; 18.2 percent were from soldiers (Mao and Sheng 1989).

The students of fast secondary schools were released from work to receive a period of learning, and they were excellent managers and workers, but the actual work and production were affected in units where they worked. It was difficult for them to finish study in three years. So in 1955 the fast secondary schools were suspended. The students already studying in schools would continue to finish the academic learning within three years. In 1958 all students in secondary schools finished study and graduated.

E. The transition from winter schools to spare time education for peasants

On 5 December 1949, the Ministry of Education issued *Directives on the Winter Schools Movement*. The *Directives* stipulated that education in winter schools should include political education and cultural education; peasants need to have common knowledge of political affairs; political education should combine with work in rural areas; cultural education should center on literacy. The textbooks for political education should be the Common Program. New outlines for instruction should be written down. The textbooks for literacy should be concise. Teachers should be trained so as to use the new textbooks effectively.

In May 1950, the First Conference on Workers' and Peasants' Education was convened in Beijing. The main topic of discussion was on how to conduct education for workers and peasants. The conference discussed guidelines of education for workers and peasants. The education of workers and peasants should center on cultural education.

On 15 May, 1952, the Ministry of Education issued *Notice on Carrying on Experiments on Use of "Fast Literacy Methods"*. The *Notice* demanded that "Fast Literacy Methods" should be used by workers and peasants across the whole nation. In 1953, 20 million peasants took part in the literacy movement. By the end of 1954, 1.3 million workers became literate, 8.5 millions peasants became literate.

On 21 December, 1951, the Ministry of Education issued *Directives on Spare time Education for Peasants*. The *Directives* stipulated that spare time education for peasants should be centered on literacy and should cared about knowledge and skills. Winter schools should continue to develop. If learning conditions were improved, they could be transformed into spare time schools for peasants. Learning in special seasons should be changed into regular learning. The spare time schools for peasants should be divided into junior classes and senior classes. Within three years, students in junior classes could learn 1000 words. The governments at various levels should train teachers and edit and publish textbooks for these schools.

The spare time education for workers and peasants developed quickly. By the end of 1954 the enrollment of spare time primary and secondary schools for workers was 2.9 million (Mao and Sheng 1989).

F. The structural reform in secondary education

At the beginning of the founding of the People's Republic of China, the structure of secondary education was centered on regular secondary education. In 1949, there were 0.95 million students in junior secondary schools; among them 87.4% were in junior secondary schools and 12.6% were in junior specialized secondary school. There were 0.31 million students in senior secondary schools; among them 65% were studying in regular senior secondary schools, and 35% were in specialized secondary schools and technical schools.

On 23 December, 1949, the first conference on education was held by the Ministry of Education. It was pointed out that in secondary schools there were too many regular secondary schools and too few technical secondary schools. The current situation could not meet the demand of economic development.

On 19 March, 1953, the First Conference on National Secondary Education was held by the Ministry of Education in Beijing. In the conference it was pointed out that the national defense, economic construction, cultural construction needed a lot of professionals. So in the future, policies about regulation of secondary technical education should be implemented. The regular secondary schools should be regulated, consolidated and improved.

In 1952, there were 2.55 million students in junior secondary schools; 87.1% of them were in junior secondary schools, 12.69% in junior specialized secondary school. There were 0.58 million students in senior secondary schools; among them 44% were studying in regular senior secondary schools and 56% in specialized secondary schools and technical schools.

In 1953, a meeting on education was held by the Culture and Education Commission under the Administrative Council. It was pointed out that the secondary technical schools should be regulated so as to train professionals for the State. The junior and senior normal schools should be run to train on-the-job teachers and enhance educational qualities.

In 1957, there were 5.43 million students in junior secondary schools; 99% of them were in junior secondary schools and 1% in junior specialized secondary school. There were 1.69 million students in senior secondary schools; among them, 53% were studying in regular senior secondary schools and 46% in specialized secondary schools and technical schools. Compared with the figures of 1952, secondary technical education was gaining priority rapidly. It could be seen that this phenomenon was caused by the more rapid development of junior regular secondary schools and senior secondary schools.

4.2.1.2   The Development of Private Primary Schools and Secondary Schools

Private education was an important part of the educational system. On 30 December, 1949, the vice minister of the Ministry of Education, Qian Junrui, pointed out that, except for some bad private schools which should be taken over, most private schools should be protected. Good private schools should be supported. The for-profit private schools should be regulated and restructured. Private schools that suffered from shortage of expenses should be aided.

In 1951, the State rewarded citizens to run private schools, encouraged the masses in rural areas to run schools. So, many private schools were preserved; the enthusiasm of the masses for running schools was aroused.

Hereafter the number of private schools increased rapidly. In 1951, the number of students in private schools was 14.26 million, 33% of the total students in both public schools and private schools.

On 2 August, 1952, the Ministry of Education made a decision in the meeting on educational administrative. The decision stipulated that between 1951 and 1953, private schools should be taken over completely.

On 1 September, 1952, the Ministry of Education issued *Directives on Taking over Private Primary Schools and Secondary Schools*. The *Directives* stipulated that the Ministry should take over all private primary schools and secondary schools by the end of 1954. The guidelines for taking over private schools included five aspects: taking over the schools funded by the natives was preceded by taking over the schools funded by the foreigner; taking over the schools having poor achievements was preceded by taking over the schools having great achievements; taking over the schools having little expenses was preceded by taking over the schools having plenty of expenses first; taking over the primary schools was preceded by taking over the secondary schools.

To carry out the takeover of private schools smoothly, it was necessary to pay attention to the following aspects, such as, making investigation into private schools; assigning large amount of cadres who were good at political work in these schools; supporting the schools whose takeover was postponed; establishing a system of reporting and asking for direction.

In June 1952, the number of private primary schools was 8925; the number of teachers in private primary schools was 55,000. The enrollment of private primary schools was 1.6 million. The enrollment in private primary schools was 3% of the total number of students in all primary schools. The number of private secondary schools was 1412; the number of teachers in private secondary schools was 34,000. The enrollment in private primary schools was 0.53 million. The enrollment in private secondary schools was 26% of the total number of students in secondary schools.

On 26 November, 1953, the Administrative Council issued *Directives on Adjustments and Improvement of Primary Education*. The *Directives* stipulated that as the State was fulfilling the goals of industrialization, the population in urban areas was increasing rapidly, but the schools in urban areas were not increasing as fast as those in rural areas. So, efforts must be made to increase the number of schools in the urban areas. The localities should help masses to run the private schools, and the masses were permitted to continue to run the private schools so as to solve the problem.

In June 1955, the Ministry of Education issued *Directives on Supply of Teachers in Public Institutions, Army forces, Factories, Enterprises for Running of Schools*. The *Directives* stipulated that the educative administrative departments in provincial governments and governments of prefectures should be responsibilities for the supply of teachers. The principals and directors of kindergartens should be redistributed by the education administrative departments in provincial governments and governments of prefecture.

4.2.2   The Reform of the System of Provision of Education in Pubic and Private Universities and Colleges (1949–1956)

4.2.2.1   The Reform of the System of Educational Provision in Terms of Public Higher Education

A. The expansion of the People's Revolutionary Colleges

In the early years after the People's Republic of China came into being, in order to cope with society's urgent needs for personnel, the Chinese governments did make great efforts in expanding the People's Revolutionary Colleges, and continuously aimed at short-term political and Ideological education. Statistics showed that in 1950 there were 57 People's Revolutionary Colleges with the enrollment of 0.3 million students. Some years later, these colleges were transformed into regular higher education institution, and teachers became new personnel in these regular higher education institutions.

However, the overemphasis on the formalization of higher education thereafter seemed to be a deficiency that became more apparent later.

B. Restructuring of colleges and departments

In the early 1950s, higher education in China faced many challenges. The installation of colleges and departments was cumbersome. And the development between different areas was in balanced. Most of these colleges and universities were tightly clustered in the metropolises along the coastal areas. Very few personnel were adequately trained for the interior cities and rural areas.

In order to train all sorts of urgently needed personnel at the college level, a nation-wide reorganization of colleges and departments was undertaken in 1952 and 1953.

In 1950 the Minister of Education, Ma Xulun, pointed out that the politics and economy in New China was unitary, so education in New China needed to develop with good plans on the basis of political and economic development.

In May 1951, a meeting on education was held by the Administrative Council. Ma Xulun pointed out that the reorganization of HEIs should be conducted step by step. The main task in 1951 was the reorganization of engineering departments in HEIs in Huabei and Huadong Areas and the establishment of normal colleges in each great administrative region and some specialized higher education schools in each province.

In November 1951, the national conference on reorganization of colleges of engineering was held by the Ministry of education. The problems which colleges of engineering in China's HEIs faced were: irrational distribution of colleges, scattering of teachers and facilities, impractical instruction, and shortage of enrollment for the national construction. In the meeting, the scheme of reorganization was discussed. The principles for the reorganization were stipulated as follows: to transform old universities and colleges; to establish new special colleges; concentrate personnel, facilities and funds to form new colleges and departments; withdraw or adjust some poor universities and colleges. In the meeting, the scheme of reorganization for colleges of engineering was determined.

In Huadong great administrative region of East China, the work of reorganization was conducted early and effectively. After the reorganization of colleges and departments, the number of HEIs decreased from 75 in 1950 to 59 in 1951; the number of departments decreased from 548 in 1950 to 404 in 1951.

In May 1952, the Ministry of Education formulated national reorganization scheme in HEIs. The principle for the reorganization of colleges and departments was as follows: (1) reorganization should be step by step; (2) reorganization should center on cities with many HEIs; (3) reorganization should be conducted according to three type of HEIs, namely universities, colleges, specialized higher education schools; (4) colleges of engineering should be specialized on narrow fields; (5) agricultural colleges and normal colleges should be established in the Great Administrative Regions.

In 1952, the reorganization of colleges and department were conducted in the great administrative regions such as East China, Southeast China, South China, Central China Northeast of China and Northwest of China.

The scale of reorganization of colleges and department in 1952 was great. 75% universities and colleges participated in the reorganization.

By the end of 1953, there were 182 HEIs in China. Among them there were 14 comprehensive universities, 38 industrial universities and colleges, 31 normal universities and colleges, 29 agricultural and forest universities and colleges, 29 medical universities and colleges, 6 financial universities and colleges, 4 law universities and colleges, 6 language universities and colleges, 12 art universities and colleges, 4 physical universities and colleges.

4.2.2.2 The Reform of the System of Educational Provision in Terms of Private Higher Education

On 14 August, 1950, the Ministry of Education issued the Provisional Regulations on Management on Private Higher Education Institutions. The Regulations aimed at supporting and transforming private higher education institutions. The private HEIs should abide by the provisional regulations on HEIs. Private HEIs should be registered with the Ministry of Education. Presidents of private HEIs should be appointed by boards of trustees, but they should be submitted to the department of education in the great administrative regions and finally be approved by the Ministry of Education. The operation of instruction, administration and finance in HEIs should be reported to the Department of the Great Regions. The funds, assets, lands, buildings of private HEIs should be owned by private HEIs themselves. Funds could not be used for purposes other than educational goals. The removal and changes in the status of private HEIs should be notified to and approved by the Ministry of Education. By the end of 1952, all private HEIs were transformed to the public HEIs.

4.3 The System of Educational Provision at the Stage of Building Socialist Country with All Efforts (1957–1965)

4.3.1 The Organization and Policy Changes (1957–1965)

In 1957, Mao Zedong put forward the educational guideline, namely education must serve the proletarian politics and be combined with productive labor. From 1958 on, the Central Committee of the CCP stressed that education must be under the leadership of CCP.

In 1958, China began to implement the second development plan. In the 2nd plenary Session of the Eighth National Congress, the *Total Guidance* was promulgated, making all efforts to go ahead with the construction of the socialist country.

From 1958 to 1960 the "Education Revolution" was conducted. The main feature of this revolution was the rapid educational expansion. The "Great Leap Forward" in education was manifested in four aspects. Firstly, the production labor substituted for learning, disrupting the regular instruction order. Secondly, too dramatic devolution of power of management of education caused rapid educational expansion. Thirdly, mass movements were conducted in schools and educational laws were disobeyed. Fourthly, instructional reforms were conducted and the length of schooling was shortened.

4.3.2 The Reform of the System of Provision of Public Education and Private Education in Primary and Secondary Schools from 1957 to 1965

4.3.2.1 The Development of Public Education in Primary Schools and Secondary Schools

A. The reform of the system of schooling

On 19 September, 1958, the State Council issued *Directives on Educational Undertakings*. The Directives stipulated that the ways of running of schools should be diverse, namely education should be provided by state-run schools in conjunction with the factory-run schools, enterprise-run schools, schools run by agricultural cooperation units; general education should be given in conjunction with vocational and technical education; adult education in conjunction with children education; full-time education in conjunction with work-study education and part-time education; schooling in conjunction with self-study education; free education and fee-levied education.

The *Directives* stipulated that there were three kinds of schools, namely full-time schools, work-study schools and spare-time schools. Full-time schools should center on improvement of quality. They should help other schools to enhance the quality of education. These schools should have complete curricula, enhanced qualities of instruction and research. These schools should help other schools to make greater progress.

The work-study schools and spare-time schools should develop quickly so as to popularize education more quickly. Popularization of education would help the enhancement of technical levels in industrial production and agricultural production. These schools should be schools with complete curricula, facilities and teachers.

The *Directives* stipulated that education should serve the proletarian politics and be combined with productive labor. The schools were advocated to run factories and farms and the factories and agricultural cooperation units were advocated to run schools. The current schools should help factories and farms to establish new schools. In schools run by factories and farms, the combination of production and instruction should be stressed.

The *Directives* stipulated that within three to five years the goal of adult literacy, popularization of primary education, establishment of secondary schools in each commune, most preschool children's enrollment in the kindergartens should be fulfilled. The development of secondary education and higher education should be speeded up. In fifteen years, the goal of popularization of universities should be fulfilled.

On 24 May, 1959, the Central Committee of the CCP and the State Council issued *Regulations on Experiment of Reforms on the System of Schooling*. The *Regulations* stipulated that the Chinese Communist Party Commissions and educational administrative departments at various provincial governments should administrate the experiments of reforms on the system of schooling. If schools want to change the length of schooling, they should get the approved of the provincial governments and the Ministry of Education. Without the approval of governments the experiment of change of length of schooling should not be permitted.

B. Rapid development in primary and secondary education.

In the period of 1958–1960, educational undertakings in China developed extremely fast; many education reforms were carried out. This stage of reforms was called the Great Education Revolution.

In 1958, from January to August, the enrollment rate of school age children was 93.3%; 87% of the counties had achieved the goal of the popularization of primary education. 26,000 new secondary schools were set up.

From late 1959s to early 1960s, education developed quickly. There were 21,805 regular secondary schools and 6225 specialized schools.

In 1962 and 1963, primary schools and secondary schools were adjusted. The number of schools decreased.

C. Construction of key primary schools

In December 1962, the Ministry of Education issued *Directives on Running of Key Primary Schools*. The *Directives* stipulated that, among full time primary schools, some with good conditions should be run with great effort so as to enhance their educational quality and level of instruction as soon as possible. The government of provinces should choose primary schools with high-competence cadres and good teachers, good buildings, sufficient facilities. Each government of county should choose more than one key primary school. The areas with good educational conditions could have more key primary schools. Otherwise they could have less key primary schools. The number of key primary schools could not be too many. The requirements of key primary schools were the effective implementation of full time instruction programs and the improvement of educational quality. The measures taken included rational arrangement of size of schools, strengthening leaders' competence-building, increase in the number of good teachers, increase in necessary buildings, facilities, books. Under the guidance of the Party Commission, educational administrative departments should take overall responsibilities of these schools and manage them.

D. Construction of key secondary schools

The running of key schools attracted the attention of the Ministry of Education in the early 1960s.

On 21 December, 1962, the Ministry of Education issued *Circular on Running a Group of Full-time Primary Schools and Secondary Schools*. The *Circular* stipulated that among full-time Primary schools and secondary Schools, a group of full-time primary schools and secondary Schools with good basis should be run with great efforts so as to enhance educational their qualities and levels of instruction. The key primary schools should be administrated by governments of counties and communes.

In September 1963, there were 487 key secondary schools, which constituted 3.1% of the total number of secondary schools.

In 1963, three forums on running of full-time schools were convened by the Ministry of Education. The minister Yang Xiufeng presided over the forum in Shanghai. He pointed out that schools should not stress unitary requirement in instruction and should admit differences among students. It was not reasonable to require all students to get the highest scores in exams. In the meeting, the characteristics of running of schools were advocated. Each school should have its peculiarities; some schools may be good at instruction in natural sciences, some others in social science. The peculiarities meant the accumulation of experience and the school spirit.

E. Spare-time education

On 16 January, 1960, the Central Committee of the CCP and the State Council issued *Circular on establishment of Spare-Time Education Commission*. The *Circular* stipulated that Spare Time Education Commission under the State Council was established, and Lin Feng was the Director. The Ministry of Education and other ten ministries should cooperate with this commission to develop the spare-time education.

On 2 April, 1960, the Central Committee approved *Report on Literacy and Spare Time Education in Rural Areas and the Future Guidelines and Tasks*. The *Report* stipulated that by 1962, the rate of literacy among youth and adults should be 90%. Spare time primary education for adults aged below 40 should be popularized. Until 1965 spare time secondary education for adult aged below 40 should be popularized.

In order to fulfill the above tasks, three measures should be taken: they included assurance of learning time for masses, improvement in instruction and enhancement of education quantities, increasing quantities of teachers.

On 8 March, 1957, the Ministry of Education issued *Circular on Literacy Education*. The *Circular* stipulated that literacy education should be carried out according to plans. The plans should center on workers and peasants below the age of 40. Most spare time should be used for literacy education. The learning form should be diversified.

In 1964 and 1965, the work-study schools developed quickly. In August 1964, in the Journal of People's Education, an article titled 'Firmly Supporting Work-study Schools' was published. This article introduced some experiences on development of work-study education. Institutions in charge of work-study education were instituted

The development of work-study schools was quick. By the end of 1965, the enrollment of work-study primary schools in rural areas was 24 million. The number of work-study agricultural junior schools was 530,000 and their enrollment was 3.1 million.

F. The structures of secondary education

In 1958 the fourth conference on educational administration was held in Beijing. It was proposed at the meeting that agricultural secondary schools, industrial secondary schools should be run with great efforts.

In 1962 there were 6.46 million students in junior secondary schools; among them, 95% were in junior secondary schools and 5% in junior specialized secondary school. There were 1.92 million students in senior secondary schools; among them, 69% were in regular senior secondary schools and 31% in specialized secondary schools and technical schools.

In 1964, the Vice Chairman of the Central Committee of the CCP, Liu Shaoqi, pointed out that there were two labor systems and two educational systems. In the actual production process, a part of the labor system and a part of the educational system were present. The running of work-study schools in rural areas and in factories belonged to such a system.

In 1965 there were 11.70 million of students in junior secondary schools; among them, 69% were in junior secondary schools and 31% in junior specialized secondary school. There were 2.79 million students in senior secondary schools; among them, 47% were in regular senior secondary schools and 53% in specialized secondary schools and technical schools.

4.3.2.2   The Development of Private Schools

China was populous and the scale of education was very large. Primary education and secondary education could not be fully funded and administrated by the State. Various ways and forms of running of schools should be used so as to meet the requirement of enrollment and promotion of children. Except for schools run by the State, the running of schools by the masses should be encouraged. Citizens, factories, public institutions, social groups, universities and colleges and cooperation communes were encouraged to support and run schools on basis of need, willingness and possibilities. Individuals were encouraged to run schools.

In 1957, private schools mushroomed across whole country. According to statistics, in 18 provinces, in 1957, the enrollment in private secondary schools was 462,000, whereas in 1955, the enrollment in private schools was less than one 1000.

According to the statistics of 15 provinces, in 1957, the enrollment in private primary schools was 1,610,000, and in 1955, the enrollment in private schools was 882,000. In Henan province, there was only one private secondary school with the enrollment of 50 in 1956.

In 1958, the Vice Minister of the Ministry of Education, Dong Chuncai, said that development of public schools was not the only way of educational development. There were three ways. The first way was the State-run schools. The second way was the masses-run schools. The third way was part-work and part-study program.

On 21 April, 1962, the national conference on education was held in Beijing. The meeting maintained that private schools were permitted to be run and be administrated.

In 1962, the students in collective-run schools were 21.4% of the total students in all primary schools.

In 1963, the Central Committee of the CCP issued A *Directive*. It was put forward that the State-run schools should be the main part of primary schools and secondary schools. In rural areas collectives could run full-time or part-time primary schools, secondary schools, literacy classes, simple schools, and agricultural schools according to needs and possibilities of peasants. In urban areas the factories, enterprises, public institutions, social groups, and the masses could run various kinds of the primary schools, secondary schools, vocational schools.

In 1965, the students in private schools were 47.52 million, 49.9% of the total students in both public primary schools and private primary schools.

4.3.3   The Reform of the System of Provision of Public Education and Private Education in HEIs (1957–1965)

4.3.3.1   The Reform of the System of Educational Provision in Public HEIs

A.   The guidelines and policies for the reform and development of higher education

In this period, higher education development experienced both upward growth and downward slump. From 1959 to 1960, the number of HEIs increased from 229 to 1289; the entrants in HEIs increased from 100,500 to 323,000; the enrollment in HEIs increased from 440,000 to 960,000.

The rapid development, within one year, was an abnormal phenomenon. The development was only a pseudo development. Under these circumstances, many HEIs did not have the necessary material conditions and qualified teachers. Higher education development was beyond the support capacities of national economy.

In 1961, the national economy was going through a hard time. The Central Committee of the CCP put forward the policy of "regulation, consolidation, enrichment, improvement".

In January 1961, the first working meeting on adjustment of key higher education institutions was held in Beijing. The meeting stipulated the "Four Determination of HEIs", namely, the determination of scale, determination of target, determination of direction and determination of specialties. After the meeting, the key HEIs were adjusting their development scale, development direction, establishment of specialties.

After the meeting, the localities adjusted higher education institutions. In Beijing, the number of HEIs came down, from 90 in 1961 to 50 in 1962.

In July 1961, the first working meeting on adjustment of higher education institutions and specialized secondary schools was held in Beijing. Deng Xiaoping said that the level of education and science did not depend on the quantity but on the quality of education. Educational development should be slowed down. In the meeting, it was decided that the number of HEIs would be adjusted from 1251 in 1961 to 800 in 1962. The enrollment of HEIs should be cut by 22%.

The number of HEIs reduced from 1289 in 1960 to 407 in 1963. The entrants of HEIs decreased from 0.32 million in 1960 to 0.1 million in 1963.

B. The construction of key universities and colleges

In the late 1950s and early 1960s, great changes took place in the construction of key universities and colleges made.

On 22 March, 1959, the Central Committee of CCP issued *Decision on Designation of Some Key Universities and Colleges among HEIs*. The *Decision* stipulated that 16 HEIs, including Beijing University, were chosen as key universities and colleges. The Decisions stipulated that these key universities and colleges should make great effort to enhance educational quality.

In April 1960, the Ministry of Education issued the *Provisional Administrative Methods on National Key Universities and Colleges*. The *Methods* stipulated that key universities and colleges were guided and administrated by the Ministry of Education, the industrial Ministries under the State Council and provincial governments would take certain responsibility. The system of leadership was the system of sectoral guidance and provincial guidance.

In 1963, 4 universities, including the Zhejiang University, were designated as key universities.

By the end of 1965 there were 68 key universities and colleges.

The construction of key HEIs has been making progress in this period. These universities and colleges played an important part in the socialist construction.

C. The development of non-formal higher education

Spare time higher education was making steady progress. Spare time higher education included night universities and colleges, higher correspondence universities and colleges, broadcast and TV education.

On 21 February, 1957, the Ministry of Higher Education issued *Circular on Time of Learning and Educational Quality in Spare Time HEIs*. The *Circular* stipulated that the length of schooling in spare time HEIs was six years; instruction time per week was nine hours; the revision time per week was nine hours. In order to strengthen the administration of these HEIs, professional cadres should increase. The professional teachers should be recruited from normal colleges.

The system of half time in work and half time in higher learning was also making progress. In 1958, Liu Shaoqi repeatedly stressed two patterns of education (including higher education): (1) Full-time schools; (2) Part-time work-study schools.

In 1958, some provincial governments and ministries under the State Council established institutions for guidance of work-study schools.

In October 1958, a conference on Experiment on Work-study Schools in Higher Education Institutions of agriculture was convened in Beijing by the Ministry of Agriculture. In the conference it was put forward that the experiment of work-study form of education in agricultural higher education institutions should be conducted.

In 1964, Liu Shaoqi said that the system of national education had three forms, full-time education, spare time education, work-study education. Work-study education should cultivate new kinds of laborers with socialist consciousness, with cultural and scientific knowledge, with technologies and practical competence. Work-study education would be centered on the secondary and higher professional education.

In 1964, the Central Committee of the CCP issued *Written Instructions on the Document of Issues Concerning Development of Work-study System*. The *Instructions* pointed out that the number of work-study schools was not so many; but it signified the future development tendency.

Up to 1965, there were 434 HEIs, among them 177 had work-study programs. The total entrants of HEIs were 164,000; the entrants of work-study programs were 26,000. The total enrollment of HEIs was 320,000; the enrollment of work-study programs was 44,000.

D.   The specialties of higher education institutions

In 1957, there were 323 specialties in HEIs in China. Among them there were 183 specialties in engineering, 21 specialties in natural sciences, 18 specialties agriculture, 9 specialties in forestry, 7 specialties in medicine and pharmacy, 21 specialties in teacher training, 26 specialties in humanities, 12 specialties in finance and economics, 2 specialties in political science and law, 1 specialty in physical culture, 22 specialties in art.

In 1958, the increase in the number of specialties was as follows: 11 specialties in engineering, 19 specialties in natural sciences, 13 specialties in agriculture and forestry, 1 specialty in medicine and pharmacy, 4 specialties in teacher training, 3 specialties in art.

In March 1961, the State Council issued Report on Examination and Approval of Scale in HEIs and National Key Universities and Colleges and Establishment of Specialties. The *Report* put forward problems in establishment of specialties in HEIs. Some universities and colleges had many specialties, some of them were redundant. The specialties were narrow in scope. The average size of specialties was too small. Some specialties did not have sufficient teachers and facilities. To redress these problems it was necessary to take relevant measures such as determining the emphasis of development and guaranteeing key areas, widening the scope of specialties and readjusting narrow specialties, establishing the first class specialties, controlling the number of specialties and the size of specialties. The average size of specialties in each university or college should not be less than 50 students. Most HEIs should have 20–30 specialties.

In 1961, a conference on regulation of HEIs was convened in Beijing. Five principles for regulation of specialties were put forward. The establishment of specialties in key HEIs should stress cooperation. The establishment of specialties in HEIs should combine the requirement and possible conditions. The scope and goals of specialties should be specified. The structure of specialties should be rationalized.

In 1963, the general list of specialties in HEIs was revised; 432 specialties were revised. The adjustment of specialties was centered on the following four aspects: Firstly, the specialties were increased, for example, specialties in atomic science and technology, rocket technology, electronics. Secondly, the regulation of scope of specialties was conducted according to the principle of coexistence of narrow specialties and wide specialties and widening the scope of specialties.

In 1965, there were 601 specialties in HEIs. Among them, 315 specialties were in engineering, 55 specialties in natural sciences, 37 specialties in agriculture, 13 specialties in forestry, 11 specialties in medicine and pharmacy, 33 specialties in teacher training, 72 specialties in humanities, 21 specialties in finance and economics, 1 specialty in political science and law, 6 specialties in physical culture, 40 specialties in art.

4.3.3.2 The Reform and Development of Private Higher Education (1966–1976)

From 1966 to 1976 there was no private HEIS in China.

4.4 The System of Educational Provision at the Stage of the "Cultural Revolution" (1966–1976)

4.4.1 Reform of the System of Provision of Public and Private Education in Primary and Secondary Schools

At this period, many changes took place. (1) The length of schooling was shortened, from 1957 on, the length of primary education was five years, the length of junior secondary education was two years, and the length of senior secondary education was two years. (2) Learning Mao Zedong' Works became an obligatory course. (3) Regular secondary schools and vocational secondary schools stayed imbalanced. In 1965, the structure of secondary education was appropriate. By the end of 1976, the enrollment of regular secondary schools was 58.363 million. Among them, 14.836 million were in regular secondary senior schools, 43.53 million were in regular junior schools. The enrollment in secondary specialized schools, technical schools, agricultural schools, and vocational schools was only 1.16% of the enrollment of students in secondary senior schools. (4) The devolution of management of public primary schools to production units. From 1968 on, many schools in rural areas were changed to schools affiliated with the production units, many schools in urban areas were changed to schools affiliated with factories and affiliated with office of streets.

4.4.2   The Reform of the System of Provision of Higher Education

There were two main changes made in this period. One is about the suspension of enrollment of students in HEIs, and the other is about the adjustment of HEIs.

On 13 June, 1966, a decision was made by the Central Committee of the CCP to postpone the college enrollment. It was not until the end of 1969 that entrants of HEIs were recruited again. And in the same year, the Ministry of Higher Education decided to suspend postgraduate enrollment. For the next 12 years, enrollment of graduates was stopped across the country.

In 1971, the national conference on education was convened in Beijing and the *Scheme on Adjustment of HEIs* was issued. According to the Scheme, the number of HEIs would be reduced from 417 to 309. Among 106 HEIs, 43 HEIs were merged, 45 HEIs were revoked, 17 HEIs were changed into secondary specialized schools, and 3 HEIs were changed into factories. Many provinces, municipals and autonomous regions cut down the number of HEIs.

4.5   The System of Educational Provision at the Stage of Building Socialist Commodity Markets (1977–1991)

The diversification of the subjects of running of schools was an urgent task in the new period. China's system of running of schools was formed gradually after the founding of the People's Republic of China. The system was characterized by monotypic way of running of schools.

Monotypic ways of running schools had some disadvantages. Firstly, monotypic ways of running schools and monotypic ways of investment caused shortage of funds. China has the largest scale of education. But China is not a developed country. Public finance in China is limited. Public expenditure on education could not meet the requirement of education. Before 1977, the State ran most schools, and private schools were few. Schools depended on the limited public education expenditures. Public education could not develop very quickly.

Secondly, monotypic ways of running schools could not adjust to the various social requirements. As the reform was deepened gradually, most people began to have more free time. Many persons were not satisfied with formal education received in primary schools and secondary schools. They wanted to receive continuing education, vocational education and other kinds of education. As the socialized production developed, social divisions deepened. Many new kinds of professions increased rapidly. Under these circumstances personal requirements and social requirements of education increased. The monotypic way of running of schools did not meet the requirement of education.

Thirdly, Monotonous ways of running schools made the schools lack vigor; it was not beneficial to quality improvement. The monotonous ways of running of schools were the basic reasons for the lack of incentive for persons and organizations. Under the monotonous ways of state-run schools, educational mechanism did not fulfill their functions. The schools did not meet competition from other subjects of running of schools. The schools depended on the state's fund and management (Jin 2000).

4.5.1 Formulation of Policies on Mutual Sponsoring and Running of Schools by Both State and Private Agents

In 1982, *Constitution of the People's Republic of China* was revised. The Constitution stipulated that the State encourage the collective economic organization, state-run enterprises and public institutions, and other social forces conducting educational undertakings according to laws. The Constitution provided legal basis for educational reform and reform of the system of running of schools.

Decision on Reform of Educational System was issued in 1985, and it stipulated that localities should encourage and guide the state-run enterprises, social groups and individuals to run schools, on the volunteer basis; collectives and individuals were encouraged to endow for education. In order to develop vocational education, it was necessary to arouse the enthusiasms of enterprises, public institutions, industrial ministries and departments, and encourage collectives, individuals and other social forces to run schools. Units and departments running schools by themselves were advocated; also they were encouraged to work together to run schools or cooperate with education administrative departments to run schools.

Here, private agents meant the subjects besides the State; it included persons, other institutions, and groups.

4.5.2 Reform of the System of Educational Provision in Primary and Secondary Schools (1977–1991)

4.5.2.1 Reform and Development of Public Education in Primary and Secondary Schools

A. The reform of the structure of secondary education

On 8 October, 1980, the State Council approved *Outline on National Conference on Secondary Specialization Education submitted by the Ministry of Education*. The *Outline* pointed out that during the 17 years after the founding of People's Republic of China, secondary specialized schools had trained five million students; most graduates were key members in all fronts. But in the period of the "Cultural Revolution", secondary specialized education was suspended and one million students were not trained. The *Outline* pointed out that measures should be taken with regard to secondary specialized education. If the secondary specialized schools recruit the graduates of secondary junior schools, the school year would be four years. If secondary specialized schools recruit graduates of junior secondary schools, the length of schooling would be two years. All regions and departments should make complete plans and make adjustments. Running of some key secondary specialized schools was an important measure. Other measures include strengthening teachers' training, stabilizing instructional order and improving construction of textbooks, increasing the expenses and improving instruction conditions and strengthening leadership of schools.

From 1984 on, experiment and research on the reform of the system of schooling was carried out in many provinces and cities.

B. Adjustment of length of schooling in primary and secondary schools

On 3 December, 1980, the Central Committee of the CCP and the State Council issued *Decisions on popularization of primary education*. The *Decisions* stipulated that the system of schooling in primary schools and secondary schools should be changed into 12 years gradually. In the later period, primary schooling could be the five-year system in conjunction with six-year system. Primary schools could try the six-year system, and the primary schools in rural areas could keep the status quo. The Ministry of Education should put forward schemes on reform of the system of schooling and determine the basic system of schooling.

From 1980 on, in most cities the length of schooling in primary schools had changed into six years; the length of schooling in senior secondary schools changed into three years.

On 6 May, 1983, the Central Committee of the CCP and the State Council issued *Circular on Issues in Strengthening and Improvement of Schooling in Rural Areas*. The *Circular* stipulated that forms of running schools in rural areas should be diverse. The five-year system and six-year system could be used simultaneously.

C. The system of compulsory schooling

In 1985, the Decisions on Reform of Educational System was issued in 1985, it was pointed out that it was necessary to take the implementation of nine-year compulsory education as a matter concerning the enhancement of national competence and prosperity of the country. It was urged to mobilize the party, the whole society, and all citizens to implement compulsory education step by step in a planned way.

Compulsory education is national education that all children and youth should receive according to law. The State, the whole society, and all families should guarantee the educational rights of children. It was required by modern production and modern life; it was the sign of modern civilization. Implementation of compulsory education should be based on the localities' taking overall responsibility and managing at various levels.

On 12 April, 1986, the National Congress issued *Compulsory Education Law of the People's Republic of China*. The Compulsory Education Law stipulated that the

State should institute the system of nine-year compulsory education. Authorities of provinces, autonomous regions, and municipalities directly under the Central Government should decide on measures to promote compulsory education, in accordance with the degree of economic and cultural development in their own localities.

On 26 June, 1986, the State Education Commission, State Planning Commission, Ministry of Finance, and the Bureau of Personnel issued the *Opinions on Implementation of Law of Compulsory Education.*

D. Comprehensive education reforms in rural areas and urban areas

Since 1986, the State Education Commission had been choosing some localities in rural areas and urban areas to carry out comprehensive education reforms. In 1987, the State Education Commission decided to make experiments on economic development and education reform in Yangyuan Couty, Qinglong Man's Nationality Autonomous Region, Wan County, in Hebei Province. The first meeting on experiment was held in the same year. In 1988, the State Education Commission decided to choose 116 counties for experiments.

In 1989, the conference on comprehensive education reforms in rural areas was held by the State Education Commission. This experiment was considered as an effective way to promote the liaison between the rural economic development and rural education development. The experiment aimed at setting up liaison between agriculture, science and technology, education. The main tasks of the counties that took part in the experiment were to facilitate economic development, establish guidelines for serving education for economic development, reform educational structures in rural areas, reform curricula and instruction methods, facilitate teacher training. The counties taking part in the experiments engaged in education reform and used talents to promote economic development (Cao 2004).

By the end of 1991, 15 cities and 101 enterprises had taken part in experiments and made great progress in educational development as well as economic development. As a result the leaders of governments and enterprises paid more attention to education. The system of educational management in cities was reformed. The secondary education structures were optimized so as to adjust to the needs of economic development. Education commissions of districts were established in many cities, and the effectiveness of education was improved.

E. Key primary schools and secondary schools

In January 1978, the Ministry of Education issued *Provisional Scheme On the Running of Key Primary Schools and Secondary Schools.* The *Scheme* pointed out that running of key primary schools and secondary schools was very important to enhance the educational quality, summarize experiences of running of schools, and facilitate educational development. The provincial governments and ministries under the State Council should make and carry out plans for running of key primary schools and secondary schools. The *Scheme* made decisions on the purpose, tasks, planning, ways of recruitment, and guidance. As for ways of enrollment, key primary schools would recruit students according to the principle of enrollment in the nearest schools.

On 28 July, 1980, a national conference on key secondary schools was convened in Haerbing. On 14 October 1980, the State Council issued *Decisions*. The *Decisions* stipulated that key schools had two tasks. One task was to provide good entrants for higher education institutions. The other task was to train excellent labor forces for society. The difference between key schools and general schools is that key schools should train students with higher qualities.

On 21 January, 1982, the Ministry of Education issued *Circular on Problems Facing China in Current Primary Schools*. The *Circular* stipulated that governments and schools should pay attention to issues in dealing with the relationship between development of key schools and non-key schools. It was necessary to guarantee the development of key schools and give due consideration to non-key schools. Educational administrative departments should strengthen the guidance on non-key schools, especially the weak schools and schools with many problems. Key schools should create good examples and help non-key schools. Non-key schools should support running of key schools. They should learn from each other.

On 6 April, 1988, the State Education Commission issued *Circular on Reform of System of Enrollment in Junior Secondary Schools*. The *Circular* pointed out that the key junior schools should be revoked in the process of running of junior schools.

4.5.3   Reform of the System of Educational Provision in HEIs (1977–1991)

4.5.3.1   Reform of the System of Educational Provision in Public HEIs

A. Reform of the system of educational provision in terms of higher education in 1985

In 1985, the Central Committee of the CCP issued *Decisions on Reform of Educational System*. The *Decisions* stipulated that the system of higher education provision should be the system of provision by central governments, provincial governments and governments of central cities. This system of provision stressed localization of higher education as it advocated that central cities establish higher education institutions. The Decision also stipulated that HEIs that were set up by the Ministry of Education and other ministries under the State Council should firstly meet the needs of professionals in these departments, and HEIs set by local governments should meet the needs of professionals in the localities.

In 1985, there were 1065 regular higher education institutions. Among them, 36 were administered by the Ministry of Education, 305 were administered by the ministries under the State Council, and 713 were administered by the local governments.

C. Reform and development of non-formal higher education

Non-formal higher education was restored in 1978. On 21 November, 1978, the Ministry of Education approved the restoration of correspondence programs at Xiamen University.

On 23 February, 1979, the Ministry of Education and the Department of Central Broadcast Affairs established the Central Radio-TV University. Soon after this month, each provincial government established respective Radio-TV Universities. Radio-TV Universities were a kind of distance and open higher education institutions. The basic length of schooling for these kinds of universities was three years and the credit system was implemented.

On 5 September, 1980, the State Council approved *Notice on Development of Correspondence and Night University*. The State Council maintained that education needed great expansion in the 1980s. Higher education institutions not only needed full-time universities, but also needed correspondence and night universities, according to conditions and requirements. The Notice issued by the Ministry of Education stressed that it was necessary to make a tremendous effort to develop correspondence and night universities, to make this kind of education included in national education plans, to use various forms to run schools, to enhance educational quality, to solve problems in terms of personnel and expenditure, to solve problems in the use and allocation of graduates, to strengthen the leadership of this kind of HEIs.

On 13 January, 1981, the State Council Approved *Report on Experimental Examination System for Self-study Programs* submitted by the Ministry of Education. Pilot programs were to be initiated in Beijing, Shanghai, and Tianjin.

On 21 October, 1982, the State Council approved *Provisional Regulations on Problems in Strengthening Construction of College of Education*, submitted by the Ministry of Education. The *Provisional Regulation* stipulated that the task of the college of education was to train in-service teachers in secondary schools in many forms. One way was for teachers to take refresher courses. Another way was for teachers to engage in advanced courses at undergraduate level. In order to construct colleges of education, some measures should be taken; they included construction of teaching staff, increase expenditure, basic construction, instruction facilities, and strengthening of leadership in colleges of education.

On 18 May, 1983, the State Council approved *Notice on Setting up Colleges of Managerial Cadres* submitted by the Ministry of Education and other Ministries. The colleges of managerial cadres aimed at training cadres in all ranks. Students were graduates of senior secondary schools. This kind of colleges had three years of learning time. The curricula were based on the junior colleges.

D. Improvement of higher education and strengthening of specialized higher education.

For a long period of time, higher education in China was centered on the training of undergraduates. Development of specialized higher education fluctuated and was comparatively slow. This caused the imbalance in the strata of higher education.

So it was urgent to develop specialized higher education. After some years' hard work, specialized higher education developed rapidly. The ratios of entrants in undergraduate HEIs to entrants in specialized HEIs was 1:0.37 in 1982, 1:0.83 in 1986. The ratios of enrollments in undergraduate HEIs to entrants in specialized HEIs was 1:0.24 in 1982, 1:0.86 in 1986.

4.5.3.2   Reform and Development of Education in Terms of Private HEIs

Since 1978, private higher education developed gradually. In 1978 the first private higher education institution, Hunan Zhongshan Training School, was established. It showed that private higher education institution was rehabilitated after 25 years of suspension.

The development of private higher education development went through two phases from 1978 to 1991. The period from 1978 to 1986 was the stage of legalization of positions of private higher education. Social forces are encouraged to run educational institutions. By the end of 1986 there were 370 private higher education institutions.

The period from 1987 to 1991 was the stage of regulated development of private higher education. As development of private higher education speeded up; some problems and challenges became increasingly evident. These problems included poor conditions, and low educational quality in some private higher education institutions. So, in this period the State Educational Commission issued some regulations on the development of private higher education. The most important one was *Provisional Regulations on Social Forces' Engagement in Establishment of Educational Institutions*. In this period private higher education developed steadily. By the end of 1991 there were 450 private higher education institutions.

From 1978 to 1991 the development of private higher education was based on four forms. The first form was the establishment of regular higher education institutions. These institutions usually had relatively long history, good conditions and high educational quality. Only very few private higher educational institutions were included in this type.

The second form was the establishment of higher education institutions that had powers of issuance of record of education. These higher educational institutions were not many. In 1998 there were only a dozen private higher educational institutions had powers of issuance of record of education under the guidance of educational administrative departments. These private higher educational institutions could not issue record of education independently. They had only some powers and responsibilities of issuance of record of education. Students in this type of HEIs were enrolled according to the procedures of national college entrance examination and unitary recruitment.

The third form was the establishment of educational institutions that aimed at helping students to pass higher educational self-study programs which belonged to the scope of higher education. In these educational institutions students did not take part in the national college entrance examination and unitary enrollment in HEIs. Students who graduated from senior secondary schools had the right to enroll in this kind of educational institutions. The main tasks of these educational institutions were to conduct instruction according to the textbooks and instruction programs stipulated by the national higher education self-study regulations. After preparation for courses of examination, students took part in national examinations of courses. If these students passed all courses of examinations according to national self-study examination regulations, they could graduate and obtain a record of education.

The fourth was the establishment of educational institutions that aimed at providing vocational and technical training for students. These educational institutions had no long-run positioning of the level of education. In order to regulate the direction of development, they may adapt to social and economic needs actively.

The development of private higher education was a part of the development of higher education in China, and had some positive effects.

Firstly, the development of private higher education was useful in lessening the contradiction between the diversified needs of modernization and the limited scale of higher education, and was also helpful in lessening the pressure of employment on teenagers.

Secondly, the development of private higher education increased the selectivity and flexibilities of provision of higher education; more students had opportunities to receive education and select schools.

Thirdly, more resources from diversified channels were put into educational institutions, and the total funds were increased gradually, the deficiency of budgetary appropriation was eased to some extent; educational resource allocation was optimized.

4.6   The System of Educational Provision at the Stage of Building Socialist Market Economy (1992–2016)

4.6.1   Formulation of Policies for Running of Schools Mutually by the State and Private Agents (1992–2016)

In 1992, *the Eighth Five-year Plan for Educational Development* were issued by the State Education Commission. In this document the system of running schools was officially put forward. The document pointed out that, in order to meet the increasing demand for education, it was necessary to establish a system of running of schools mutually by taking the State as main subjects and social communities as auxiliary subjects. This system of running of schools was designed as follows. Preschools should be run mainly by social communities. Primary schools and secondary schools should be run mainly by the local governments. Higher educational institutions should be run by governments and private agents.

In 1993, *Program of China's Education Reform and Development* made concrete specification of the new system of running schools. It was necessary to reform the system of governments running schools. Government should be the main runners of schools and social communities should be auxiliary runners of schools.

In 1996, *the Tenth Five-year Plan for Education Development in the People's Republic of China* put forward several ways of running of schools by private agents. The *Plan* pointed out that, vocational education should preferably be provided by private schools. The current public schools could be transformed into a new type of public schools with the assistance of private funds and a new type of private schools with assistance from public funds. Till 2010 the system of running of schools by taking governments as main subjects and social communities as auxiliary subjects of running of schools was instituted and the schema of mutual development of public schools and private schools was formed.

In 1997, *Regulations on Running of Schools by Social Forces* were issued. The *Regulations* formulated social forces' positions, characteristics and functions in running of schools. The Regulations pointed out five principles. Educational institutions run by social institutions should abide by the laws, regulations, implement State's educational guidelines and policies, and assure educational quantities. Schools run by social forces should not be for profit. These schools should establish and perfect the system of property management and system of financial management.

In 1999, the Ministry of Education issued *Rejuvenation Action Plan for Education Facing the 21st Century*. It was pointed out in the plan that in the next 3–5 years, the system of running of schools by taking governments as main subjects of running of schools and private schools as auxiliary subjects would be instituted.

In 2001, in *the Tenth Five-year Plan for Educational Development in the People's Republic of China*, it was pointed out that reforms in the system of educational provision needed to be deepened so as to open wider avenues and attract more financial resources in facilitating expansion through various ways. Under macro-level regulation by the State, it is desirable to conduct pilot projects of higher education provision in the light of local socio-economic conditions through adoption of different mechanisms and modalities of educational delivery.

On 28 December, 2002, *Law of Promotion of Private Education* was issued. It aimed at normalizing private schools and facilitating the development of private schools.

On 25 February, 2004, the State Council issued *Implementation Regulations on Promoting Private Education*. More measures for facilitating private education were put forward.

On 29 July, 2010, the Central Committee of the Chinese Communist Party and the State Council issued *National Guidelines for Medium and Long-term Educational Reform and Development Program (2010–2020)*. The *National Guidelines* stipulated governments at various levels should regard the development of private education as the main responsibilities, and encouraged individuals and social bodies to invest in private education. The equal legal positions between private schools and public schools as well as the equal legal rights of teachers and students in private schools and public schools should be guaranteed. The policy of using public finance to support private education should be perfected. The management of private education according to laws and regulations should be strengthened.

On 18 June, 2014, the Ministry of Education issued *Implementation Opinions on Encouraging and Guiding the Private Funds into Private Education* The Implementation Opinions made clear the scope, ways, directions of bringing the private funds to educational fields and encourage private investment in education.

4.6.2   Reform of the System of Provision of Public and Private Education in Primary Schools and Secondary Schools (1992–2016)

4.6.2.1   Reform of the System of Provision of Public and Private Education in Primary and Secondary Schools

A. The development of compulsory education

In 1997, the State Education Commission issued *Main Opinions on Normalized Behaviors of Running of Schools in the Current Stage of Compulsory Education Development*. The *Opinions* stipulated that the development of compulsory education was chiefly the responsibility of governments. In the establishment of the socialist market economy, Governments at levels of provinces and prefectures should take the main responsibilities.

B. Involvement of enterprises in running of schools

In 1999, there were 20,000 primary schools and secondary schools run by enterprises. There were 9 million students and 0.9 million teachers in these schools. Schools run by enterprises were an important part of educational system in China. The enterprises run schools not only for children of administrators, workers and staff in these enterprises, but also for children outside of enterprises. But the reform of the system of modern enterprises poses many issues for enterprises.

Enterprises should be runners of schools continuously. The system of running schools by enterprises should be reformed so as to perfect educational functions of enterprises. Schools should not become burdens to the enterprises; these schools could be beneficial to the development of enterprises.

C. Development of private primary education and secondary education

In 1992, the 14th National Congress of the Central Committee of the CCP pointed out that it was necessary to support multiple-channel financing of education and private schools.

On 13 February, 1993, the Central Committee of the CCP and the State Council issued *Program of Educational Reform and Development*. The *Program* stipulated that it was necessary to reform the situation of state governments assuming the whole responsibility of running schools, and institute the system of the State-run schools as the main part in conjunction with the support of social forces. At present, the governments should take the main responsibility in establishing schools.

On 18 March, 1995, *Education Law of the People's Republic of China* was issued. The *Law* stipulated that the State should implement the system of nine-year compulsory education; the governments at various levels should take all measures to guarantee the enrollment of children. Organizations and individuals could not run schools and other institutions for profit.

In 1997, the State education commission issued *Provisional Regulations on Establishment and Administration of Schools by Social forces*. The *Regulations* stipulated that the so-called social forces included enterprises and other organizations that were legal entities, people's groups, and organizations in collective economy, academic groups, and independent runners of schools.

In 1997, the State Council issued *Regulations on Social Forces' Running of Schools*. The *Regulations* made specifications on the establishment of educational institutions, instruction and administration, funds and financial management, change of educational institutions, input and support, and legal responsibilities. The Regulations pointed out that the social forces should concentrate on conducting vocational education, adult education, and senior secondary education. The State should take strict control of establishment of higher educational institutions.

On 17 June, 1998, the Ministry of Education issued *Opinions on Reform on System of Running of Schools at the stage of Compulsory Education*. The *Opinions* declared that it was necessary to establish public schools supported by private funds and establish private schools supported by public funds.

By the end of 1998, there were 20,000 private kindergarten, 1800 private primary schools, and 1700 private senior secondary schools.

In 1999, *Decisions on Deepening Educational Reform and Pushing up Competence Education* was issued. The *Decisions* encouraged private educational development. It was necessary to encourage and support social forces to run schools in various ways so as to meet the needs of people and establish situations whereby governments took the main responsibility in running of schools, complemented by social forces running schools. Any ways of running of schools that were in accordance with laws could be explored. The social forces were encouraged to run senior secondary schools and other schools.

On 28 December, 2002, *Law on Facilitating Private Education in the People's Republic of China* was formulated by the National People's Congress. This law was the first law on private education. This law pointed out that private educational undertaking was a part of socialist educational undertakings; private education was of great public benefits.

On 1 March, 2003, the State Council issued *Regulations on Chinese and Foreign Cooperation in Running of Schools*. The *Regulations* decided that the State adopt guidelines for facilitating open policy, normalize running of schools, managing schools in accordance with laws, facilitating private education in terms of Chinese and foreign cooperation.

In 2006, *Compulsory Education Law of People's Republic of China* was revised. The governments' responsibilities for compulsory education were stipulated clearly. Governments at County level or above and other educational administrative departments should not change the nature of public schools.

4.6.3   Reform of System of Provision of Higher Education (1992–2016)

4.6.3.1   Reform of Public Higher Education Institutions

A. Guidelines of reform on higher education institutions

On 13 February, 1993, *Program of China's Educational Reform and Development* was issued by the Central Committee of the CCP and the State Council. The *Program* pointed out that the system of educational provision should be reformed. It further said that the situation of governments as only sponsors of schools should be changed, and the system of governments taking the main responsibility in the running of schools, complemented by social groups' involvement should be established.

B. Transfer of HEIs affiliated to ministries to HEIs under the jurisdiction of provincial governments

From 1992 on, the powers of provincial government in terms of control over HEIs has been increased. In 1994, 9 HEIs affiliated to 3 ministries were delegated to provincial governments, 2 HEIs affiliated to 6 ministries were delegated to provincial governments; 8 HEIs affiliated with 4 ministries were cooperating with provincial governments so as to make mutual construction of these HEIs; 9 HEIs affiliated with 5 ministries were prepared to cooperate with provincial governments so as to make mutual construction of these HEIs; 13 HEIs affiliated with 8 ministries were cooperating with enterprises so as to make mutual construction of these HEIs. Other 231 HEIs affiliated with 39 ministries were prepared to cooperate with local governments or enterprises. By way of delegation of power of management provincial government's function in managing public higher education institutions was strengthened.

4.6.3.2   Reform of Private Higher Education Institutions

In 1993, the State Education Commission issued the Provisional Regulations on the Establishment of Private Higher Education Institutions.

From early 1990s to 2003, many second-level private colleges were established in China. A public university or college may establish one or more colleges under its jurisdiction. They would be private colleges in which students are recruited based on scores for private undergraduate colleges; students in private HEIs pay higher tuitions and fees than students in public HEIs. Students with low scores in the national college entrance examination may be enrolled in these second-level private colleges.

Since 1999, many second-level private colleges have been established. From 1998 on, the entrants in HEIs increased rapidly. Each year, 600,000 were entering. Old public HEIs do not have sufficient buildings, dormitories, dining halls and libraries to attract these entrants. So, new HEIs should be established. Thus, public HEIs established many private HEIs under its jurisdiction.

The ways of establishing second-level private colleges were as follows: (1) Public HEIs establish second-level private colleges independently. (2) Public HEIs cooperate with enterprises so as to establish second-level private colleges. (3) Public HEIs, local government and enterprise establish second-level private colleges. (4) Public HEIs and foreign educational institutions establish second-level private colleges. (5) Public HEIs and local governments establish second-level private colleges. (6) The private HEIs merge into public HEIs.

The second-level private colleges had strengths and weaknesses. They had three strengths. Firstly, private funds could be used in higher educational development. Secondly, public HEIs made management of second-level private colleges and this was beneficial to guarantee instructional quality. Thirdly, a new way of reform of educational system was explored. There were also some weaknesses with this model of running of HEIs. Firstly, many second-level private colleges were not examined and approved by the Ministry of Education. Many of them were approved by provincial governments, and some of them were not approved by governments. Secondly, educational equity was damaged. The pure private HEIs could not stand fair competition with these second-level private colleges because they could obtain the strong support of public HEIs. Thirdly, some second-level private colleges did not have the necessary teachers, buildings, facilities and books for instruction.

Many provinces had established second-level private colleges. In 2003 there were more than 300 second-level private colleges and the enrollment amounted to 400,000. In Zehjiang Province, there were 22 second-level private colleges, and in Jiangsu Province, there were 36 second-level private colleges.

On 22 April 2003, the Ministry of Education issued Opinions on Management on Independent Colleges established by Public Regular HEIs. This *Opinions* stipulated that second-level private colleges would be renamed as independent colleges and they were restructured. The establishment of independent colleges would be useful in the fuller use of higher education resources with high quality and would help increase higher education resources.

The establishment of independent colleges should be according to three principles. Firstly, the establishment of independent colleges should have cooperators such as public institutions, enterprises or individuals.

Secondly, the establishment of independent colleges should use private mechanism.

Thirdly, the establishment of independent colleges should use new models such as independent legal entity, independent school area, independent enrollment, independent instruction and management, independent student certificate, independent financial accounting, independent higher education statistics.

On 15 August 2003, the Ministry of Education demanded all second-level colleges should be examined and approved by the Ministry of Education. In 2004 there were 249 independent colleges; the enrollment was 680,000. The restructuring of second-level colleges and the establishment of independent colleges is beneficial for all private HEIs to a fair ground.

4.6.4   Historical Experiences of the System of Educational Provision

There were five experiences which could be drawn from the historic development of the system of educational provision.

Firstly, reform of the system of educational provision should be adjusted to the needs of economic and social development, and adapted to the policy of reform and opening to the outside world.

Secondly, reform of the system of educational provision should be on consideration of the increasing requirements of the people.

Thirdly, reform of the system of educational provision should use all possible ways of running of schools and exploring good ways of running of schools. The reform of the system of running of schools should be based on the actual situations in China.

Fourthly, the reform of system of educational provision should arouse the enthusiasm of local government and social forces. The financing of education should be based on the State's appropriation as the main channel and many other channels of fund raising as the auxiliary channels.

Fifthly, the reform of the system of educational provision should both encourage social forces to participate in running of schools and make them run schools according to the laws and regulations.

4.7   Current Situation of the System of Provision of Education

4.7.1   Current Situation of the System of Educational Provision in Primary and Secondary Schools

Primary and secondary education consists of two parts, one part in public education, the other part is private education.

4.7.1.1   Current Situation of the System of Provision of Public Education in Primary and Secondary Schools

The current situation of the system of educational provision is characterized by following aspects.

As far as subjects in running of schools are concerned, the transformation from the system of State's taking the overall responsibility of educational provision to the new system of educational provision by enterprises, institutions, social group, individuals was fulfilled.

As far as the forms of running of schools are concerned, various ways of running of schools was guided by the State.

As far as the type of running of schools and the structures for the running of schools are concerned, governments are responsible for compulsory education, enterprises and social groups are responsible for vocational education. Governments and social groups are responsible for higher education. Enterprises are responsible for adult education.

As far as educational expenditures are concerned, the governmental budgetary appropriations are the main channels of financing of education and the other channels were sought in order to increase educational input.

The pre-primary education developed rapidly. In 2011, 2012, 2013 and 2014, the number of kindergartens in China were 0.1668, 0.1813, 0.1986, 0.2099 million, respectively.

The number of enrollment in kindergartens in 2011, 2012, 2013 and 2014 is 34.2445, 36.8576, 38.9469, 40.5071 million, respectively. The number is increasing gradually. The number of teachers in kindergartens in 2011, 2012, 2013 and 2014 is 1.496, 1.6775, 1.8851, 2.0803 million. The gross enrollment rate in kindergartens is in 2011, 2012, 2013 and 2014 is 62.3, 64.5, 67.5, 70.5%.

In 2011, 2012, 2013 and 2014 the net enrollment rate in primary schools is 99.79, 99.85, 99.49, 99.81% respectively.

In 2011, 2012, 2013 and 2014, the number of primary schools is 0.2412, 0.2286, 0.2135, 0.2014 million, and the enrollment in primary schools is 99.2637, 96.959, 93.6055, 94.51 million. The number of teachers in primary schools is 5.6049, 5.5855, 5.5846, 5.6339 million. The rate of teachers with qualified record of education in 2011, 2012, 2013 and 2014 is 98.62, 99.81, 99.83, 99.88%.

In 2011, 2012, 2013 and 2014, the gross enrollment rate in junior secondary schools is 100.01, 97, 104.1, 103.5% respectively. In 2011, 2012, 2013 and 2014, the promotion rate in junior secondary schools is 88.62, 88.4, 91.2, 95.1% respectively.

In 2011, 2012, 2013 and 2014, the number of junior secondary schools is 0.00541, 0.00532, 0.00528, 0.00526 million, respectively, and the enrollment in junior secondary schools is 50.668, 47.6306, 44.4012, 43.8463 million, respectively.

The number of teachers in junior secondary schools is 3.5345, 3.5044, 3.481, 3.4884 million. The rate of teachers with qualified record of education in 2011, 2012, 2013 and 2014 is 95.22, 99.12, 99.28 and 99.53%.

In 2011, 2012, 2013 and 2014, the gross enrollment rate in senior secondary schools is 84, 59.8, 86 and 86.5% respectively.

In 2011, 2012, 2013 and 2014, the number of all senior secondary schools is 27,638, 26,868, 26,200 and 25,700. In 2011, 2012, 2013 and 2014, the number of regular senior secondary schools is 13,688, 13,509, 13,400, 13,300, and the enrollment in all senior secondary schools is 46.8661, 24.6717, 24.3588, 24.0047 million.

The number of teachers in regular senior secondary schools in 2011, 2012, 2013 and 2014 is 3.49, 1.595, 1.629, and 1.6627 million. The rate of teachers with qualified record of education in 2011, 2012, 2013 and 2014 is 87.3, 96.44, 96.8 and 97.2%.

In 2011, 2012, 2013 and 2014, the gross enrollment rate in higher education institutions is 21, 30, 34.5, 37.5% respectively.

In 2011, 2012, 2013 and 2014, the number of all higher education institutions is 3167, 2790, 2788, and 2824. In 2011, 2012, 2013 and 2014, the number of regular higher education institutions is 2409, 2442, 2491, and 2529. In 2011, 2012, 2013 and 2014 the number of adult higher education institutions is 353, 348, 297, and 295.

In 2011, 2012, 2013 and 2014, the number of regular undergraduate higher education institutions is 1129, 1145, 1170, and 1202. In 2011, 2012, 2013 and 2014, the number of specialized vocational higher education institutions is 1280, 1279, 1321, and 1327.

In 2011, 2012, 2013 and 2014 in regular higher education institutions the enrollment is 6.815, 23.9132, 24.6807, and 25.477 million.

In 2011, 2012, 2013 and 2014, the enrollment of postgraduates who are pursuing doctoral degrees is 0.2713, 0.2838, 0.2983, 0.3127; the enrollment of postgraduates who are pursuing master degrees is 0.972, 1.436, 1.4957, 1.535 million.

4.7.1.2 Current Situations of the System of Provision of Private Education in Primary Education and Secondary Education

In 2014, there are 0.1552 million private educational institutions. In the private educational institutions the enrollment is 43.0191 million.

In 2014 there were 0.1393 million private kindergartens; the number of enrollment is 21.2538 million.

In 2014 the number of private primary schools is 5681; the number of enrollment is 6.7414 million.

In 2014 the number of private regular junior secondary schools is 4743; the number of enrollment is 4.87 million.

In 2014 the number of private vocational junior secondary schools is 67; the number of enrollment is 1.89 million.

In 2014 the number of private regular senior secondary schools is 2442; the number of enrollment is 2.3865 million respectively; the number of teachers is 314,622.

In 2014 the number of private vocational senior secondary schools is 2,343; the number of enrollment is 1.89 million.

In 2014 the number of private higher education institutions is 728; the number of enrollment is 5.8715 million respectively; the number of enrollment who major in undergraduate program is 3.7483 million. The number of enrollment who major in short cycle courses is 2.1228 million respectively.

4.8 Problems Facing China in the System of Educational Provision

4.8.1 Problems Facing China in the System of Educational Provision in Primary and Secondary Schools

4.8.1.1 Problems and Difficulties Facing China in the Development of Public Primary and Secondary Schools

A. Problems in the transformation from public schools to private schools

The reform of the system of educational provision faces some new problems in the process of the transformation of the nature of schools. The transformation of public schools into private schools in some places causes loss of national assets.

Recently, in public schools, experiments of public schools with assistance of private forces (*Gongban Minzhu*) and State-owned schools supported by private forces (*Guoyou Minban*) are conducted. Public schools may establish some new schools under general guidance and leadership of mother-like schools. The mother-like schools are usually famous schools and can attract much assistance from society. These schools are united into school groups. The school groups may have both a part of public schools and a part of private schools.

Experiments on the reform of the system of educational provision in the filed of basic education is a new thing. This kind of reform is beneficial to the flexible system of financing education, improving weak schools and introducing competition. The reform satisfies the choice of schools for the masses, facilitates diversification of models of running schools and facilitates formation of creatures in running of schools.

But this kind of reform is in the phase of experiment. Some problems need to be addressed. Firstly, some schools with good material conditions, teachers and quality were transformed into public schools with the assistance of private funds. These schools could charge very high tuitions and fees and make extremely selective enrollment. At present some public schools can attract more private finance by establishing new schools in other areas because the original schools are very good schools. Secondly, some private schools absorb one or more weak schools and construct school groups. They make weak schools a part of the private section within school groups. The absorbing of new schools opens a new avenue for obtaining more funds from parents of students and society at large. Thirdly, some good teachers in the original part of public school go to the later merged weak school. In this way the condition and quality of the weak school would be improved. After a period of structural adjustment, the private school could have sound reasons to charge high tuition fees from students. This kind of experiments changed the system of education provision greatly. These school groups charged tuition fees and collected funds from society in accordance with the regulations set by the governments.

These problems mentioned above disturb the regular order in basic education, stimulate behaviors in terms of choice of schools, spoil fair competition environment for public schools and private schools. These ways, to some extent, may induce corruption and may spoil the good name and the authority of governments. These behaviors are not in accordance with the essence and characteristics of compulsory education.

B. Increasing gap between good schools and poor schools

Weak schools need to be improved effectively. This is a difficult problem to be solved. Although the governments have formulated some policies and given financial and personnel support for these schools, they have not improved as much as people anticipated.

4.8.1.2 Problems and Difficulties in Development of Private Education

For development of private education, governments have not given enough support. Governments' support for private schools by way of appropriate policies was not enough (Fan 1999).

Governments have ambivalent policies regarding development of private education. On the one hand, governments advocate development of private education vigorously; they formulate laws and regulations to normalize education in private education institutions. On the other hand, they do not take into consideration seriously the problems in the development of private education. For instance, in the process of formulating the law of promotion of private education there are disputes regarding whether private schools can distribute the surplus and obtain sufficient returns in running of schools. Some managers maintain that private schools are competing for public education resources and they make constraints on private schools (Hao and Tan 1997, p. 310).

In the process of formulation of policies concerning private education, there exist discriminating policies. In fact, the development of private education supplements educational provision and meets the needs of the society. The policy goals of private education should supersede the constraints of the system of ownership and be in accordance with social development goals. To consider the difference in public education and private education seriously and make different policies is not a good policy choice. For instance, at present most private education policies focus on private education institutions but do not focus on the students. The ownership of property and the distribution of benefits attract the attention of lawmakers and public opinion. Viewed from the point of education, the students should be the focus of education policies. Students in private schools should be subsidized.

Law-making affairs relative to private schools have lagged behind the development of private education. Nowadays, private educational institutions cannot become for-profit organizations. The Education law does not recognize the possibility of for-profit education institutions. In some countries there are laws concerning for-profit education institutions. The for-profit education institutions develop very quickly in some areas. For the future development of private education, there are three models to choose from. The First model is based on the not-for-profit organization model. The second model is based on the for-profit organization model. The third is based on the combination of not-for-profit organization and for-profit organization model. According to the actual Chinese situation, the third model would be a rational choice. When the nonprofit organization and for-profit organization is differentiated, the rule for them is also different. The nonprofit education institutions can receive state's favorable taxation benefits, financial subsidies and other treatments, while the for-profit education institutions should be classified as a kind of enterprise; they should hand in the tax to the State. The change of policy concerning for-profit organization is beneficial to the future development of private education.

The tendency of seeking excessive profit was a threat for the sustainable development of private schools. Some private schools aimed at making profits. This way of doing things have negative effect of the running of the schools. Many investigations on private schools showed that there were only a few for-profit schools, but nearly every school is seeking surplus. They differ in the extent of seeking profit. A private school in Shenyang had 1000 students; the expense of construction and facilities amounted to 3 billion. The school was adopting all-around closure management. But as the tuition fees were too high, the entrants were decreasing, so in the fourth year the school was revoked.

The development of private education at some local levels, especially in some areas, through way of charging high tuitions and fees would cause inequalities. If these situations were not restricted, there would be the risk of widening of the social divisions. Even in some areas where public schools were the majority, private schools were provided to the students from rich families. This would bring problems of inequalities.

Some private schools did not establish good internal system of instruction management and system of financial management; they were running schools like running a family.

The policies of financing and policies of running schools should be different for compulsory education and non-compulsory education. At the stage of compulsory education, the government should be the main channel of providing funds and should make great efforts to improve the conditions of the buildings and facilities as well as the remuneration of teachers.

There are some problems in establishing schools which mixes characteristics of both public schools and private schools. At present most schools of dual nature are new born schools.

The instabilities of teachers have had negative effects on the development of private schools. In the past, many private schools did not have a stable personnel structure of teachers. In some private schools, by the end of the first year, a third of the teachers had moved out. Many teachers in private schools have not stayed for long periods in the same educational institution. The frequent mobility of teachers has caused much trouble for private schools. On the one hand, private schools cannot establish a stable contingent of teachers with long run goals. On the other hand, the instabilities of teachers have had negative effects on students' development.

4.8.2   Problems Facing China in the System of Educational Provision in Public and Private Higher Education Institutions

4.8.2.1   Problem Facing China in the System of Provision in Public Higher Education Institutions

A. The further development of vocational higher education

In a country such as China that is a developing country, the great expansion of vocational higher education is a good way of fulfilling the goal of massification of higher education or even universalization of post-compulsory education (Wu 1999).

Local universities and colleges, especially municipal universities and colleges and HEIS under the jurisdiction of governments of counties, have not developed as fast as anticipated. In China the most famous universities and colleges are national universities and colleges; they have made great contributions for national development. But economic development in China is very unbalanced. The relation between the State-run HEIs and local HEIs has not been treated seriously. The development of local higher education should be stressed more seriously. The establishment of municipal universities and colleges should be encouraged.

B. Problems facing China in adult higher education development

The development of adult HEIs faces some serious problems. Firstly, the internal efficiencies in adult HEIs are not very high. The average enrollment in adult higher education institutions is not so many as in regular HEIs and the average scale of adult higher education institution is relatively small. The purpose of adult higher education is to use the local resources to run schools. But the ministries under the State Council, educational administrative departments and social groups in localities can use limited resources. The allocation of resources is not balanced.

Sometimes in the same city there are many adult higher education institutions; the curricula of these institutions are the same. Many adult higher education institutions enroll too few students. Each adult higher education institution is making efforts to improve educational conditions and improve the quality of education, but they have too little resources. Secondly, the quality of instruction in adult higher education institutions is affected by teachers, instruction contents, facilities and instruction methods. Some teachers who have classes in adult higher education institutions are from other higher education institutions; teachers in senior secondary schools, retired teachers and part-time teachers in universities and colleges. Some teachers from other higher education institutions moved to adult higher education institutions because they did not have the qualifications for regular higher education institutions. Some adult higher education institutions do not have sufficient funds for instruction. Many adult higher education institutions have enough classrooms, but do not have auxiliary instruction facilities and facilities for experiments. The usual instruction methods are blackboards and lectures. The learning materials are mainly textbooks.

4.8.2.2   Problem Facing China in the System of Educational Provision in Private Higher Education Institutions

A.   Weakness in management of private higher education

There are two kinds of management of private higher education, namely the external management of private higher education and the internal management of private higher education. External management is micro-management; it concerns questions about how to manage private higher education institutions, how to deal with public higher education and private higher education management, how to establish fair competition environments. With regard to the macro-management of private higher education, the main problem is the lack of the State's unitary and authoritative management institutions. Private higher education institutions are managed by adult education bureaus under educational administrative departments at various levels. Actually private higher education is not only concerned with adult education.

B.   Weakness in teacher staff' construction

In many private HEIs, some teachers are part-time workers. Even in those successful private HEIs, the proportion of full-time teachers is not as high as many persons anticipate. This is restricted by shortage of funds. Most private HEIs do not have public subsidies. They should use their own funds to fulfill definite tasks. But on consideration of the long development needs, private HEIs should increase full-time teachers.

4.9 Strategies and Measures for Reform of the System of Educational Provision

4.9.1 Strategies and Measures for Reform of the System of Educational Provision in Primary and Secondary Schools

4.9.1.1 Strategies and Measures for Public Schools

A. Normalization of transformation of the nature of schools

The normalization of running schools is important for the healthy development of basic education. The experiment on the reform of the system of educational provision should follow three principles. It should be beneficial to the consolidation and improvement of basic education; it should be beneficial to the implementation of competence education; it should be beneficial to construction of weak schools.

The transformation of the nature of schools should be under the scrutiny of governments. In most cases, public schools can not be changed into private schools without legal procedures. Public schools with a division of private school should be forbidden.

As far as basic education is concerned, the following measures should be taken. Firstly, compulsory education is public goods; compulsory education activities should not be for-profit activities. Secondly, fees-collection should be in accordance with regulations issued by the State and local governments. Fees above the criteria of national and local standards and charging of specified fees should not be permitted. The salaries in private section of schools should not be too high so as to avoid the big difference between teachers' salary in public school and in private schools. The national assets in schools that make experiments of transformation of nature of schools should be preserved. The financial management and audit of funds in the schools that take part in experiments should be strengthened. The transformation of the nature of schools and carrying out experiments should be approved by governments. The experiments should be centered on the weak schools. The school that takes the experiment should be independent legal entity with independent grounds, buildings, accounting system, and independence in running of schools.

B. Strengthening the construction of weak schools

Now that compulsory education has been universalized, the task of governments and educational administrative departments at all levels is to run every school efficiently. While maintaining high standards in key schools, great efforts should be made to improve other schools. Key primary schools and secondary schools, though small in number, are precious educational resources. So they need to be supported so as to bring their exemplary role into full play. At the same time great efforts to strengthen weaker schools should be made. Human resources and material and financial support should be given to weak schools. The key factors are principals and teachers. So governments and educational administrative departments should help principals and teachers to improve their own qualifications through training. At the same time, outstanding principals and teachers from good schools should be transferred to weaker schools. Exchange of principals and teachers between schools, school co-management or mergers of schools, famous schools helping weak ones, are some of the methods to turn things around in weak schools.

4.9.1.2   Strategies and Measures for Private Schools

A.   More support from governments and educational administrative department

Governments should take the responsibility for private schools. In order to change the attitude of governments, it is necessary to implement educational policies according to educational laws and other laws pertaining to private education. The reform of the system of educational provision is an important task for local economic development; it is a systematic engineering. Governments should do the following things. They should make unitary policies and formulate relevant policies and establish good environment for the reform of educational provision. Meanwhile the concerned educational administrative departments should take unitary actions and coordinate effectively.

In order to set up correct guidelines for private education development, governments should use the same yardsticks for the development of private education and public education. Private schools need to achieve minimum criteria of quality. Education quality is very important for private education institutions. Educational policy goal should direct toward benefits of students other than educational institutions. The students in private schools should have the same national citizen's treatment as those in public schools.

B.   Strengthening lawmaking concerning private education

To redress problems of lag in law-making in private education, it is necessary to formulate different kinds of rules for different kinds of private education institutions. The best way to facilitate private education development is to make differentiation of nonprofit education institutions and for-profit educational institutions as well as make concerned laws and regulations.

C.   Enhancement of educational quality in private schools

The quality of education is of utmost importance, not only for public schools but also for private schools. Educational quality is not only required by the State, but also needed by parents and students. Private schools should not aim at seeking the surplus. Under the principle of cost accounting, private schools should spend for ordinary items and charge due tuition fees. The surplus should be used to increase the facilities and enrollment.

4.9.2 Strategies and Measures for Reform in the System of Educational Provision in Higher Education

4.9.2.1 Strategies and Measures for Reform in the System of Educational Provision in Public Higher Education Institutions

A. Expansion of vocational higher education

Development of vocational higher education should be based on development of specialized higher education. At present some specialized higher education institutions can be transformed into vocational higher education colleges. Viewing from the requirement of skilled manpower and professionals, China needs a great deal of skilled manpower that has received short-cycle higher education. There are three reasons for the expansion of short-cycle higher education. Firstly, many town-owned enterprises and collective-owned enterprises need skilled manpower; these enterprises need manpower with strong manual labor competence. Secondly, China is at the stage of building a primary socialist country; the development of vocational higher education is suitable to national situation. Thirdly, the need for higher education cannot be met by development of undergraduate higher education alone. In order to develop vocational higher education rapidly, governments should advocate diversification of higher education system, HEIs should establish more suitable disciplines, take more effective instruction methods and more open policy of enrollment in the field of vocational higher education. Students should change their academic-orientation concept of higher education and establish practice-orientation concept of higher education and become willing to accept vocational education and respective jobs. Higher education institutions should make good strategic positioning and features in running of schools. Employers should change their criteria of choosing graduates from HEIs. In order to develop vocational higher education rapidly, it is necessary to reform the administrative system of vocational higher education. The powers of establishment of vocational higher education institutions should be delegated to provincial governments. Localities have more autonomous power of running schools. The relation between regular undergraduate higher education and vocational higher education should be adjusted so students' transition at different levels and types of higher education institutions is possible.

Local higher education is characterized by the establishment in localities and serving local development. In order to develop local HEIs, especially municipality-run HEIs, four measures should be taken. Firstly, different regions should aim at making higher education development goals and models with local features. For instance, in the economically developed areas or in the coastal areas, local higher education development should center on training high-level comprehensive professionals, professionals in foreign trade, applied professionals. Secondly, secondary-level municipalities should establish municipal universities actively. The central municipalities have the possibilities of establishing HEIs for local social and economic development. The establishment of these kinds of HEIs can facilitate economic development. Thirdly, local HEIs are advised to cooperate with each other. The local HEIs should center on development of vocational higher education. Fourthly, some policies for the development of local HEIs should be implemented. The autonomic powers of running schools in local HEIs should be increased. The laws and regulations of local higher education institutions especially at the local levels should be perfected.

B. Facilitating adult higher education development

Adult higher education institutions usually are small in size. So, in the near future, the restructuring of adult higher education institutions should be conducted. Some adult higher education institutions should be merged into public higher education institutions. Some adult higher education institutions can be transformed into educational institutions by using distance education models. Some adult higher education institutions can cooperate with educational institutions in other regions so as to increase the size and lower the operation cost.

At present, the quality of adult higher education is controlled by means of entrance examination and approval of degrees. But these methods of controlling quality center on the student resources and the final outcome of learning in HEIs. The process control of instruction is lacking. So, the improvement of process control of instruction should be attended to. Training of teachers and guidance on instruction skills should be conducted regularly in adult HEIs. The learning materials should be relevant to students' professional development needs and work requirement.

4.9.2.2 Strategies and Measures for Reform in the System of Educational Provision in Private Higher Education Institutions

A. Strengthening management of private higher education.

Authoritative private education administrative departments should be established. The bureau of management of private education under the Ministry of Education and the divisions of private education management under the educational administrative departments under the provincial governments should be established. These administrative institutions can make complete management of private education. They can coordinate with other administrative departments. They can enhance the efficiency of management in private education.

The discriminating viewpoint of private education is partly caused by poor management of private education. So, it is necessary to strengthen the management of private higher education institutions. The system of ownership of private schools should be specified clearly; the organizational structure should be optimized; the system of management should be established and perfected, and teacher management and financial management should be strengthened (Wan 2002, p. 154).

B. Improvement of teachers' qualities

To address the problem of shortage of full time teachers, it is necessary for private HEIs to make long term planning of teachers and implement planning of teachers step by step. Private HEIs should make a good positioning. Based on this positioning, private HEIs should train and construct their professional teachers.

References

Cao, S. (2004). *An economic analysis of educational system and educational organization.* Beijing: Beijing Normal University.

Fan, J. (1999). *A theoretical research on higher education development and practice in China.* Shanghai: Fudan University Press.

Hao, K., & Tan, S. (Eds.). (1997). *Chinese education facing the 21th century.* Guiyang: Guizhou People's Education Press.

He, D. (Ed.). (1998). *Important documents in the People's Republic of China (1949–1975).* Haikou: Hainan Press.

Jin, Y. (Ed.). (2000). *A history of Chinese socialist education.* Shanghai: East China Normal University Press.

Mao, L., & Sheng, G. (Eds.). (1989). *A history of education in China.* Jinang: Shangdong Education Publishing House.

Wan, J. (2002). *A macro-analysis of higher education.* Beijing: Higher Education Press.

Wu, D. (1999). *A study on education reform in China.* Beijing: The Central Party's College Press.

Chapter 5
Strengthening Educational Autonomy: Educational Enrollment System in China

5.1 Introduction to the System of Enrollment

5.1.1 The Concept of the System of Enrollment

The system of enrollment deals with the processes and requirements of the enrollment of students in educational institutions. The system of enrollment is an important part of the educational system. The system of *enrollment* is concerned with the criteria of enrollment of students in various schools and the management and methods of enrollment of students. The system of enrollment is linked to the rights and obligations of citizens to receive education; it is also related to the issue of equality of educational opportunity.

5.1.2 Classification of the System of Enrollment

The system of enrollment can be classified in different ways. According to the school's autonomous power of enrollment, the system of enrollment can be classified as independent recruitment of students by individual schools or common recruitment by groups of schools. HEIs, for example, can recruit students by using their own criteria based on either scholastic record in secondary schools or general performance in secondary schools. HEIs can also recruit students by common unified efforts.

According to whether enrollment of students is based on the examination results or otherwise, the system of enrollment can be classified as exam-based enrollment and non-exam-based enrollment. In the former system, students are required to take part in an examination, and the results of the examination are the basic criteria for selecting students. In the later system, students are not asked to participate in any examination and the criteria of enrollment are based on the schools' need.

© Springer Nature Singapore Pte Ltd. and Higher Education Press 2018
M. Yang and H. Ni, *Educational Governance in China*,
https://doi.org/10.1007/978-981-13-0842-0_5

According to whether governments have the final decision making power of enrollment of students or not, the system of enrollment can be classified as unitary management system and devolved management system. If the enrollment of students is finally approved by the educational administrative departments, then this system of enrollment is called unitary management system. Otherwise schools have some or even much powers of selecting the suitable students; such an enrollment system is called devolved management system.

5.1.3 Functions of the System of Enrollment

The system of enrollment pertains to human rights, especially the educational rights of citizens. Educational rights are a very important part of human rights. In many countries the Constitutions stipulate the rights of citizens to receive education as a basic civic right that cannot be revoked for any reason. The system of enrollment affects the operation of schools. Different schools have different localities, community conditions, natural environments, buildings and facilities with special features, cultural atmosphere as well as traditions and ambitions. Enrollment of students is the starting point in the educational process; it is also the connecting point between educational institutions and the society.

Students are very important resources for schools. Good student resources determine the educational quality in schools, to some extent. In some cases they may be more important than teachers in making a school famous. Schools often compete for good students. So the design of enrollment system is an important influencing factor in school development as well as educational development.

5.2 System of Enrollment at the Stage of Completing Socialist Restructuring (1949–1956)

5.2.1 The System of Enrollment of Students in Primary and Secondary Schools (1949–1956)

Before the founding of the People's Republic of China the enrollment of students in primary schools and secondary schools was under the jurisdiction of school authorities.

On 6 January, 1950, the First National Conference on Education was held in Beijing. In the meeting the scheme of establishing fast secondary schools was formulated. This kind of schools recruited managers and workers; the length of schooling was three to four years.

The regular secondary schools had two tasks. One task was for students to enter higher-level schools; the other task was for students to participate in national construction activities. On 19 March, 1951, the Minister of the Ministry of Education, Ma Xulun, said that the nature and tasks of regular secondary schools was to give general education, and to lay the foundation for entering higher-level schools or for joining national construction.

On 10 August, 1951, the Administrative Council issued *Decisions on Reform of the System of Schooling*. The *Decisions* stipulated that primary schools and secondary schools should provide complete basic education for children. Schools implementing primary education for youth and adults who missed opportunities of enrollment in schools included fast primary schools for workers and peasants, spare-time primary schools and winter schools. Graduates in primary schools should pass the entrance examination and enter the secondary schools. Graduates in fast primary schools should pass the entrance examination and enter fast secondary schools. Graduates in spare-time primary schools should pass the entrance examination and enter spare-time secondary schools. Graduates in junior secondary schools should pass the entrance examination and enter senior secondary schools. Graduates in senior secondary schools, fast secondary schools and spare-time secondary schools should pass the entrance examination and enter HEIs.

On 18 March, 1952, the Ministry of Education issued *Provisional Regulations on Secondary Schools*. The *Regulations* stipulated that the entering age for junior secondary schools was 12 years and for senior secondary schools it was 15 years. Graduates from primary schools that apply for junior secondary schools and graduates from secondary schools that apply for senior secondary schools who take examination and are accepted, should be enrolled regardless of sex, race and religious belief.

In 1952, the Ministry of Education issued *Directive on Unitary Enrollment in Senior Secondary Schools, Technical Schools and Normal Schools*. The *Directives* stipulated that Senior Secondary Schools, Technical Schools and Normal Schools implement the system of unitary enrollment. In order to assure that plans of enrollment are fulfilled, the great administrative regions should make plans by taking provinces as the basic units.

The Ministry of Education issued *Directives on Enrollment in National Secondary Schools in 1953*. The *Directives* pointed out that in 1952 the regions did not take strict control over the number of entrants so that the education quantity increased rapidly while the education quality decreased. So, in 1953 each region should take strict control of the number of entrants stipulated by the central government. The students who graduated from junior secondary schools and primary schools were so many that each region should choose good students to enroll in higher-level schools so as to assure quality of entrants. Except for the degree of culture and physical conditions, students from families of workers and peasants should be given priority. Each province should set up an enrollment commission. The minister of education department should be the director of this commission.

In 1955, the Ministry of Education issued *Regulations on Enrollment in Secondary Schools*. The *Regulations* stipulated that enrollment in secondary school should be administrated by provincial governments and that unitary enrollment should be implemented in the provinces. Students who graduated from primary schools should submit diplomas and behavior assessment materials when they make application for junior secondary schools or junior secondary normal schools. Students who graduated from junior secondary schools should submit physical examination certificate within one year when they make application for senior secondary schools or senior secondary normal schools.

The date of examination for junior secondary schools, senior secondary schools, and senior normal schools should be from 21 July to 25 July. Each region should persuade students to take part in examination in their own localities and enroll in local schools.

The subjects of examination were Chinese and mathematics for junior secondary schools and junior normal secondary schools. In senior secondary schools and senior normal secondary schools, the subjects of examination were Chinese, mathematics, and general knowledge of politics.

When schools enroll new entrants they should choose on merit and on the basis of scores in examination, physical health, performance in ordinary time. In order to encourage students to pay attention to ordinary learning and to inspire them to be good at physical health and learning, secondary schools and normal schools could carry on with the system of recommending good students for enrollment to higher-level schools. Schools could recommend students with good learning result, moral conduct and physical health for enrollment to higher-level schools.

5.2.2   The System of Enrollment in HEIs (1949–1956)

5.2.2.1   National College Entrance Examination and Enrollment in the Transitional Period

In this period there were two systems of college entrance examination and enrollment: one, independent examination and enrollment by HEIs; two, the common examination and enrollment across the whole country.

5.2.2.2   The System of Examination and Recruitment by Individual University or College

In 1949, there were 207 HEIs; some of them were private HEIs (*Editorial Board of China's Education Yearbook* 1984). The system of examinations and recruitments by individual university or college was implemented. Each university or college determined the time of examinations, number of enrollment, requirement of recruitment, and ways of recruitment. The examinees could choose to take examination in one university or college or in more HEIs.

At the beginning of the founding of the People's Republic of China, China's Government adopted the principle of "Preserving the Status Quo and Restructuring Gradually". So, higher education institutions still used the old system and recruited students on their own.

The recruitment of students directly by higher education institutions themselves had some disadvantages. Some famous HEIs recruited enough students with one time of enrollment examination. But the weak HEIs could not recruit enough students even after many times of examinations and enrollment. As many good students took many times of examinations and got approval for admission from several HEIs, they would forgo the admission offers from some HEIs; as a result, the final rate of enrollments in some HEIs was very low. In some HEIs the rate of enrollment was lower than 20%. Some students could not be recruited by the targeted higher education institutions which had more than enough students; these students had no time to take examination, and so they lost the chance to go to HEIs finally.

The system of examination and recruitment by university or college on its own had obvious shortcomings. This system was not adapting to the needs of higher education development and national construction. In order to cultivate professionals and professionals for national construction, the old system of recruitment by university or colleges on their own needed change.

5.2.2.3 The System of Common Enrollment in the Great Administrative Regions

In 1950, the Ministry of Education advocated the system of common enrollment by a group of HEIs. In this year, 73 HEIs, more than one-third of universities and colleges, were adopting this way of enrollment, and most HEIs recruited enough students in one timen of examination and enrollment.

On 26 May, 1950, the central government issued *Regulations on Recruitment of Students in HEIs*. The *Regulations* advocated a part of or even all of HEIs in the great administrative regions to adopt common enrollment examination and enrollment.

The qualifications for the examinees included willingness to serve people and being healthy. Students who graduated and had diplomas from any public or private senior secondary schools, senior normal schools, secondary technical schools, senior vocational schools could make application for taking part in the examinations.

The subjects of examinations were Chinese, foreign language, general knowledge of politics, mathematics, geography, physics, chemistry. Examinees could make application for exemption from foreign language test.

The test questions were to be based on the textbooks in secondary schools. The test questions should be provided by experts who were invited by the great administrative regions.

The date of examination in this period was from 21 July to 10 August. The final date to deliver notice of approval of enrollment was to be earlier than 25 August.

On 14 August, 1950, the Administrative Council issued *Provisional Regulations on Higher Education Institutions*. The *Regulation* stipulated that anyone who was 17 years old or above, healthy, graduated from senior higher schools, passed in the examinations, could be admitted in HEIs regardless of sex, race, religious belief.

On 1 October, 1951, the State Council issued *Decisions on Reform of System of Schooling*. The *Decisions* stipulated that universities, specialized colleges, specialized schools should recruit graduates from senior secondary schools or schools at the same levels.

In 1951, the system of common enrollment was implemented in the great administrative regions. In July and August 1951, the system of common enrollment in the great administrative regions achieved the anticipated results.

5.2.2.4 Establishment of the System of National Entrance Examination and Enrollment

In 1952, China established a system whereby higher education institutions enrolled the best students through the system of national unified examination and enrollment.

The Ministry of Education issued *Regulations on Enrollment in HEIs during the Summer Vacation of 1952*. The *Regulations* stipulated that all HEIs should take part in national entrance examination and enrollment, except for some HEIs which could make application to and receive approval by the Ministry of Education. The number of enrollment was to be submitted to and approved by the department of education under the great administrative regions according to national enrollment plans. The manner of enrollment was determined by the Ministry of Education.

On 30 April, 1952, the Ministry of Education issued *Directives on Enrollment Plans of HEIs and its Implementation*. The *Directives* pointed out that in the case of universities, independent colleges, specialized higher education institutions that recruited students from senior secondary schools, the number of enrollment should be included in the national plans. The number of enrollment should be approved by the great administrative regions and finally ratified by the Ministry of Education. The number of enrollment in 1952 was 50,000. In the process of recruitment, the number of students in great administrative regions should be adjusted. The number of enrollments in schools and specialties of national defense, industry, medicine, normal schools should be guaranteed.

In 1952, the National College Enrollment Committee was established. The respective commission of enrollment in each great administrative region was also established. The branch of commission of enrollment in each province was also established.

The new system of national examination and enrollment unified the formation of test papers, conditions for registration for examination, subjects for examination, criteria for political censorship, and criteria for physical exanimation across the whole country. The enrollment guidelines, enrollment policies, methods of enrollment were formulated by the Central Government and the executive branches. From 1952 to 1956 the system of national entrance examination and enrollment was carried out step by step in a planned way.

In 1952, the system of common examination and enrollment by a group of HEIs was revoked entirely.

In 1956, the State Council issued *Directives on Fulfillment of Enrollment Plans in HEIs in 1956*. The *Directives* stipulated that in 1956 students who graduated from senior secondary schools did not meet the requirement of enrollment in HEIs. So, except for mobilizing all students who graduated from senior secondary schools to take part in examinations, cadres in administrative institutions, teachers in primary schools, students who graduated from secondary normal schools, soldiers who retired from active military service, workers in factories, youth who stopped learning in schools and were at home, students who graduated from secondary specialized schools, were to be mobilized to take part in the examinations.

In this process, the qualifications of examinations for students were made lower than those of the previous year. This may have negative effects on instructional quality and education quality.

5.2.2.5 The Subjects of Examination

In 1952, the system of national examination and enrollment was established. The recruitment of enough students in each higher education institution was assured.

The subjects for the unified entrance examinations in 1953 are listed below. For general students, the respective subjects of examination were general knowledge of politics, Chinese, foreign language (Russian or English), Chinese history, foreign history, Chinese geography, foreign geography, mathematics, physics, chemistry, biology. Students who wanted to enroll in disciplines such as physical training, music, and art needed to take examination on the relevant subjects.

In 1954, the Ministry of Education and the Ministry of Higher education stipulated that the subjects of examination should include two kinds. For specialties in liberal arts, engineering, hygiene, agriculture, forestry, the subjects of examination were Chinese, political course, math, chemistry, biology, a foreign language. For specialties in liberal arts, politics, law, finance, physical training, art, the subjects of examination were Chinese, Political course, history, geography, a foreign language.

In 1955 the subjects of examination included three kinds. For specialties in liberal arts, engineering, the subjects of examination were Chinese, general knowledge of Politics, math, physics, chemistry, and a foreign language. For specialties in medicines and agriculture, forestry, biology, psychology, physical training, the subjects of examinations were Chinese, general knowledge of politics, basics of Darwinism, chemistry, and physics. For specialties in politics, law, finance, physical training, and art, the subjects of examination were Chinese, general knowledge of politics, history, geography.

5.2.2.6 The Organization of Enrollment of Students

From 1952 on, the National Enrollment Commission was set up. The tasks of this Commission were to make out unitary test questions and organize test subjects, stipulate unified ways and rules for enrollment. The commission of enrollment in each province had to be set up. This kind of commission had to take responsibility for taking the examination on application of students, taking the political examination of students, taking the health examination of students and giving marks for tests.

5.3 The System of Enrollment at the Stage of Completion of Building Socialism (1957–1965)

5.3.1 The System of Enrollment of Students in Primary and Secondary Schools (1957–1965)

In 1962, the Ministry of Education issued *Circular on Running of Full-Time Primary Schools and Secondary Schools with Emphasis on These Schools*. The *Circular* pointed out that it was necessary to run these full time primary schools and secondary schools. They are the backbone of primary and secondary schools. These schools could expand their scope of choice of students. They could recruit good new students from wider regions on the basis of students' moral development, intellectual development, and physical development. The scope of enrollment in primary schools could not be limited by definite districts.

5.3.2 The System of Enrollment of Students in Higher Education Institutions (1957–1965)

5.3.2.1 The Enrollment Reform in 1957

Under the state planned economic system, governments implemented the system of unitary planned enrollment. Central government decided the national enrollment amount and structure; this enrollment plan was divided into regions and HEIs, and sent to HEIs.

On 29 March, 1957, the Ministry of Education, the Central Committee of the Chinese Communist League and the Ministry of Higher Education issued *Notice on Political Education Concerning Entering Higher Schools for Students Who Want to Enter HEIs*. The *Notice* pointed out that in 1957 the enrollment plan was 0.1 million; the number in 1957 was lower compared with that of 1956. Students should make prepare well for the examination and take part in the examinations. HEIs should give a complete introduction of the specialties in HEIs and guide students to make wise choices of target HEIs. HEIs should have different propaganda contents in the different process of enrollment.

On 24 July, 1957, the Ministry of Higher Education and the Ministry of education issued *Regulations on Enrollment in HEIs*. The *Regulations* stipulated that students who graduated from specialized secondary schools should take part in labor and should not make application for examination and enrollment in HEIs.

5.3.2.2   System of United Enrollment Conducted by Universities or Colleges in 1958

On 1 July, 1958, the Ministry of Education issued *Regulations on enrollment of entrants in HEIs*. The *Regulations* stipulated that in order to make enrollment in HEIs adapt to the needs of localities and HEIs, and to arouse the enthusiasm of localities and HEIs, the system of enrollment by individual university or college or united enrollment would be implemented. Students who graduated from fast secondary schools and had long period of work would be considered as qualified after examination, could be recommended to enroll in HEIs.

In 1958, the Working Commissions of Enrollment in the Great Administrative Regions were revoked. Instead of them, there were the Provincial Enrollment Commissions in charge of enrollment of students.

In 1958, the subjects for examination were of three kinds, but all students had to take part in the examination on foreign language.

The guidelines for recruitment were: enroll the best students after considering academic performance and physical conditions on the basis of the assurance of the political qualities.

5.3.2.3   Resumption of the System of National Entrance Examination and Enrollment

In 1959, the system of national entrance examination and enrollment was restored. On 5 June 1959, the Ministry of Education issued *Regulations on Enrollment in HEIs in 1959*. The *Regulations* stipulated that the system of enrollment in HEIs should be implemented by unitary guidance and decentralized management. Educational administrative departments under the Governments of Provinces should establish unitary institutions to administrate enrollment affairs such as conditions of examination, subjects of examination, date of examination, principles of enrollment.

On 28 May, 1960, the Ministry of Education issued Regulations on Enrollment in HEIs. The *Regulations* stipulated that key HEIs and HEIs under the jurisdiction of ministries should be implementing the system of national unitary enrollment. The enrollment in other HEIs should be determined by provincial governments.

In 1962, the criteria of recruitment were reformed. The Ministry of Education stipulated that HEIs should examine political and physical conditions of examinees, based on scores in examination and target HEIs for students, based on the principle of recruiting by criteria of the scores.

5.4   The System of Enrollment at the Stage of the "Cultural Revolution" (1966–1976)

5.4.1   The System of Enrollment of Students in Primary and Secondary Schools (1966–1976)

5.4.1.1   The System of Enrollment of Students in Primary Schools

On 12 July, 1966, the Ministry of Education issued *Circular on Enrollment, Examination, Vacation, Graduation in Primary Schools and Secondary Schools*. The *Circular* stipulated that in the autumn of that year, recruitment of students in primary schools could be continued. If some localities could not recruit students in time because they had to take part in revolutionary movements, the enrollment could be postponed. In areas that primary education had been universalized, pupils could enter primary schools directly without taking part in the examination.

5.4.1.2   The System of Enrollment for Students in Secondary Schools

The reform of the system of enrollment centered on the following aspects: Firstly, the method of examination and recruitment was suspended. The enrollment of students in senior secondary schools was based on recommendation in conjunction with the selection. The children from families of workers, peasants and soldiers should be given priority in enrollment to senior schools.

5.4.2   The System of Enrollment of Students in HEIs (1966–1976)

On 27 June, 1966, the Central Committee of the CCP and the State Council issued *Circular on Postponement of Enrollment of Students in HEIs for Half Year*. Enrollment of students in HEIs was postponed by half a year. The Students in senior secondary schools could participate in social activities further. Students could also go to the rural areas to work or go to factories to work.

But actually in 1967 the enrollment of students in HEIs was suspended further.

The enrollment method was through recommendation of the masses, leader's approval, and HEIs' examination.

5.5   The System of Enrollment at the Stage of Building Socialist Commodity Economy (1977–1991)

5.5.1   The System of Enrollment of Students in Primary and Secondary Schools (1977–1991)

5.5.1.1   Resumption of the System of Enrollment Established Before 1965

In 1983 the Ministry of Education issued *Opinions on Improvement of Education Quality in Regular Secondary Schools*. The *Opinion*s stipulated that it was necessary to establish and perfect the system of entering the next grade and staying in the original grades and system of Graduation. Localities should improve educational quality on the basis of actual situations in local schools.

5.5.1.2   Revoking of the System of Unitary Examination for Promotion to Junior Secondary Schools in Primary Schools

In 1984, the Ministry of Education issued *Opinions on Instruction Program in Primary schools in Full Time Schools*. The *Opinions* stipulated that in cities where secondary education had been popularized, students' promotion from primary schools to secondary schools should not be based on unitary examination. Students should enter higher-level school according to the principle of entering the nearest schools. For key secondary schools, they could determine target district for recruitment of students and allocate quota of enrollment to relevant primary schools. Primary schools made recommendation of good students and secondary schools choose on merit.

In Changcun Municipality, the educational administrative department carried out the reform of system of enrollment in junior secondary schools. The unitary examination for students' promotion from primary schools to junior secondary schools was revoked. Students who graduated from primary schools had to take part in graduation examination. If they passed the examination they could enter senior secondary schools naturally.

In 1987, the educational administrative department in Shanghai began to conduct general graduation examination in senior secondary schools. In 1989, Shanghai and Zhejiang implemented graduation examination in senior secondary school. It was proved that graduation examination in senior secondary school was useful for universities and colleges to choose good students.

In 1990, the State Education Commission issued *Notice on Graduation Examination in Senior Secondary School*. From 1991 on, this kind of examination conducted across whole country.

5.5.2   The System of Enrollment of Students in Higher Education Institutions (1977–1991)

5.5.2.1   Resumption of National College Entrance Examination in 1977

In August 1977, Deng Xiaoping convened some forums on development of education and science. In the forums many persons asked for the rehabilitation of national entrance examination system. Deng Xiaoping said that our country would like to catch up with the advanced countries. Deng Xiaoping said that China should begin this arduous task from the development of education and science. When the participants asked for the resumption of national entrance examination, Deng Xiaoping consented that even we had to postpone half year we would rehabilitate the national entrance examination in this year.

On 5 October, 1977, the Political Bureau of the Central Committee of the CCP discussed problems of rehabilitation of national college entrance examination.

On 21 October, 1977, the Xinhua News Agency, the People's Daily, the Central People's Broadcast Radio publicized the news on resumption of national college entrance examination. The masses, especially the youth, were excited.

On 12 December, 1977, the State Council approved *Opinions on Enrollment Work in Higher Education Institutions and Specialized Secondary Schools in 1977* submitted by the Ministry of Education. The *Opinions* stipulated that from 1977, the method of recommendation by the masses would be revoked. The national college entrance examination system, which was suspended for eleven years, was restored.

In 1977, 5.7 million examinees took part in the national college entrance examination. Among these, 0.22 million were enrolled in higher education institutions.

5.5.2.2   Qualifications for Application for National Entrance Examination

In 1979, the *Opinions on Enrollment in HEI* stipulated that examinees should advocate Chinese Communist Party, love socialist country, study hard, love labor, abide by disciplines, and be younger than 25 years and unmarried. Students who graduated from specialized secondary schools could make application for examination after two years of work.

On 4 May, 1985, the State Education Commission issued *Regulations on Enrollment in HEIs*. The *Regulations* stipulated that students who graduated from specialized secondary schools could make application for national college entrance examination after recommendation by specialized secondary schools. But the number of students recommended by schools should be less than 1% of the total graduates in specialized secondary schools; in 1986 it was raised to 2%.

5.5.2.3   Physical Health Examination and Political Censorship

On 9 June, 1978, the Ministry of Education and the Ministry of Hygiene issued *Criteria of Physical Health Examination and Implementation Rules*. The Document stipulated that the criteria of physical health examination in 1958 would be used as usual.

On 3 April, 1984, the Ministry of Education and the Ministry of Hygiene demanded good hospitals with good conditions administrated by the government of counties or above the level of counties should take responsibilities of physical health examination.

5.5.2.4   Subjects of National College Entrance Examination

In October 1977, the State Council approved *Opinions on Enrollment in HEIs in 1977*. The *Opinions* stipulated that the subjects of examination included two kinds: one kind was for students who majored in liberal arts; their subjects included politics, Chinese, mathematics, physics and chemistry. The other kind was for students who majored in humanities; their subjects of examination included politics, Chinese, mathematics, history and geography. The students who majored in foreign languages would have to take part in the examination of foreign languages.

In 1978, the subjects of examinations for students who majored in liberal art were politics, Chinese, mathematics, physics, chemistry, foreign language. The subjects of examinations for students who majored in humanities were politics, Chinese, history, geography, foreign language. The subjects of examinations in foreign languages could be any one from English, Russia Japanese, French, Germane and Spanish.

From 1983, biology was added to the subjects of examination for students who majored in liberal arts.

5.5.2.5   Organization and Guidance of Enrollment in HEIs

In 1977, the Ministry of Education issued *Opinions on Enrollment Work in HEIs*. The *Opinions* stipulated that governments of provinces, governments of prefectures, and governments of counties should establish respective HEIs Enrollment Commissions.

On 21 April, 1987, the State Education Commission issued *Provisional Regulations on Enrollment in HEIs*. The *Regulations* stipulated that the State Education Commission should take responsibilities for enrollments in regular HEIs. HEIs Enrollment Commission at the level of governments of provinces, prefectures, and counties should take responsibilities for enrollments under the guidance of the SEC.

5.5.2.6   Reform of Methods of Formulation of Enrollment Plans in HEIs

The reform of the yearly enrollment plan was an important task. As far as the Higher Education Institutions were concerned, there were two kinds of yearly enrollment plan: one was business plan. It was decided by educational administrative departments on the basis of the following conditions: (1) requirement for labor forces and professional workers; (2) possibilities of national financing of education; (3) actual conditions of higher education institutions.

The other was the plan of the source of students. It was decided by administrative agencies at different levels. It was based on such condition as future requirement for graduates, the principle of making choice on merit. The educational administrative agencies combined the source of students and the target working place of graduates and determined the number of enrollment of universities and colleges. The "target plan" assured the balance of the requirements of economic development for labor forces and quantities of the enrollment, the balance of specialties and the balance of each level in higher education institutions.

In the mid 1980s, the enrollment plan was changed from the single directive plan to coexistence of national target plan and regulative plan. The national plan referred to central and local education administrative departments target plan. The regulation plan referred to the plan proposed by the higher education institutions; this plan was based on own capacities of training and society's needs. The regulation plan included joint enrollment in higher education institutions and other institutions.

5.5.2.7   Establishment of HEIs' Accountabilities in Enrollment

The transformation from the system of "HEIs taking in students but governments actually recruiting the students" to the system of "HEIs taking responsibilities for recruitment and the enrollment office supervising" was very important for the reform of system of enrollment.

From 1984 to 1985, the system of unitary enrollment was carried out. The rights and responsibilities centered on enrollment offices under provincial governments. The system of enrollment was called "the HEIs like to take in the students but the enrollment office finally recruit definite students". Even the enrollment methods had been changed; HEIs did not have enough rights to recruit students.

5.5.2.8   Reforms on Recruitment Methods from 1984 on

From 1977 to 1986, the system of enrollment was changed from the old system into a system whereby enrollment of students was conducted by enrollment office at provincial levels. Under the unitary guidance of the enrollment office under the provincial governments, the HEIs recruited the students according to the score line. The list of recruited students should be approved by the enrollment office under the provincial governments. The enrollment method was 'recruitment according to the score spans'. HEIs were classified as three types, namely the key HEIs, the undergraduate HEIs, the specialized higher education institutions. The score criteria of each type of HEIs were different. When the recruitment began, the candidates were classified into several divisions with different score spans on basis of the total score of these students. The recruitment was carried out according to the score spans.

From 1984 on, the recruitment method was changed from "enrolling according to the span of the scores" system to "basing on the candidate's target HEIs and specialties based on their aspirations and wishes and sending the candidate's record proportionally in the process of recruitment" system.

5.5.2.9   Enrollment Through Recommendation by the Excellent Senior Secondary Schools

In 1984, some colleges were trying to recruit some good students directly from senior secondary schools. These students were called students recommended for studying in colleges. These students did not take part in the national college entrance examination. The criteria of recommendation were good performance in moral development, intellectual development and physical development. Senior secondary schools determined the list of commendation. The colleges interviewed these students and decided if they would like to recruit them. According to the new system, when a higher education institution would like to recruit a fixed number of students, more files of students than the predetermined enrollment quato was sent to HEIs. Under the new system higher education institutions had more scope to choose students.

5.5.2.10   Enrollment of "Contract Training Students"

Contract training of students meant enterprises and public institutions provided expenses for training of students in higher education institutions and students should work in these units after graduation.

On 21 July, 1978, the State Council issue *Circular on Problems of "Contract Training Students"*. The *Circular* stipulated that before 1977 there were some "contract training students" in higher education institutions. After the reform of the system of enrollment in 1977, the enrollment of "contract training students" was suspended. But in 1977 some higher education institutions still enrolled "contract training students". Most "contract training students" had poor cultural basis, did not study hard, had a special life, and were separated from the masses. The State Council stipulated that enrollment of students in higher education institutions was included in the national plan. The "contract training students" enrolled since 1977 were sent back to the original units. For the "contract training students" enrolled before 1977, they would be permitted to finish study in higher education institutions but they could not get diplomas. They could get a certificate of finishing the courses.

In 1983, the national meeting on enrollment was convened in Beijing. At this meeting it was decided that the national enrollment system needed steady reform. The main measures that were taken included making good enrollment plans, enrolling more students from the countryside, introducing enrollment of contract training students.

In 1983, the number of enrollment of contract training students was 3200, and in 1984, the number was 22,000. We could see the rate of increase was very high.

On 24 June 1984, the Ministry of Education, the State Planning Commission, and the Ministry of Finance issued *Provisional Measures on Accepting Contract Training Students by Colleges and Universities*. The *Measures* stipulated that measures on accepting contract training students by colleges and universities under the premise of finishing national plans were favorable for realizing the potentialities of the universities and colleges, useful for increasing the educational expenditure, useful in connecting universities and the users of graduates, and beneficial for the reform of higher education.

On 11 January, 1986, the State Education Commission issued Provisional Regulations on Management of Work for Accepting Contract Training Students by Regular Universities and Colleges. The Regulations stipulated that regular higher education institutions enrolled"contract training undergraduates".

5.5.2.11 Enrollment of Paying Their Ways Students

On 27 May 1985, the Central Committee issue *Decisions on the Reform of Educational System*. The *Decision*s stipulated that the planning system of enrollment should be reformed. Three ways of enrollment were to be adopted hereafter.

The first kind of was enrollment according to national plan. In this kind of enrollment, students did not need to pay for training costs. They should have enough or usually very high scores for enrollment in higher education institutions.

The second kind was enrollment of "contract training students". The units paid an amount of fee to the HEIs for students and students would work for these units after graduation.

The third kind was "paying their way'" students for receiving higher education. These students would pay training fees themselves.

The *Decisions* stipulated that all students should take and pass the national college entrance examination.

From 1985 on, the paying-their-ways students increased rapidly.

In 1986, the State Education Commission issued *Regulations on Enrollment in Regular HEIs*. The *Regulations* stipulated that enrollment plans included state plans, "contract training plans, and paying their ways" students's plans. The scores for enrollment of paying-tuitions students should not be lower than the minimum control score line.

5.5.2.12   Directive Enrollment in Special Industries and Regions

In rural areas and areas with difficult living and working conditions, for a long time, few students were recruited; students who graduated from HEIs could not be sent there and workers who worked there could not stay for a long time. From 1980 on, the system of directive enrollment was implemented

On 21 February, 1983, the Ministry of education decided that the job-oriented enrollment and employment in HEIs should be implemented on consideration of the students' source of regions in enrollment and target place in assignment. From 1983 on, agricultural universities and colleges, forest universities and colleges, medical universities and colleges, normal universities and colleges that were affiliated with the ministries under the State Council should implement the system of job-oriented enrollment.

In 1985, the Ministry of Education issued *Regulations on Enrollment in Regular HEIs*. The *Regulations* stipulated that in order to send graduates to work in rural areas and regions with difficult living and working conditions, universities and colleges with specialties in agriculture, forest, coal collecting, electricity, geography, petroleum, metrology, construction materials and army, should implement the system of job-oriented enrollment and assignment. The graduates should be assigned to farms, ranches, forestry, mining areas, bases, oilfields, field geological exploring units, electronic stations. The HEIs that implement the system of directive enrollment could lower 20 scores to enroll entrants. If enrollment plans could not be fulfilled, HEIs could recruit entrants from other areas.

On 24 November, 1988, the State Education Commission issued *Provisional Regulations on Directive enrollment and Assignment*. The *Regulations* stipulated students who are recruited by job-oriented enrollment and assignment should be exempted from tuitions and fees. They could obtain scholarship on the basis of scholastic achievement and personal performance.

5.6   The System of Enrollment at the Stage of Building Socialist Market Economy (1992–2016)

5.6.1   The System of Enrollment of Students in Primary and Secondary Schools (1992–2016)

On 27 April, 1999, the Ministry of Education issued Circular on Guiding Opinions on Reform of Graduation Examination and Enrollment Examination in Junior Secondary Schools. The Circular pointed out the graduation examination and promotion examination should be reformed.

In junior secondary schools, graduation examinations are important examinations at stage of basic education. Reform of examination is important for conducting the competence education. Graduation examination and promotion examination can be merged into one examination. In this case, the new kind of examinations should embody characteristics of compulsory education in junior secondary education when the selection function of examinations was fulfilled. Graduation examination and enrollment examination can be separated. In this case, for graduation examination test questions should be provided by schools and examinations organized by schools. For enrollment examination subjects of examination, organization of examination, conducting of examination, should be determined by educational administrative departments at provincial levels.

On 3 January, 2000, the Ministry of Education issued *the Circular on Lessening Students' Excessive Learning Load*. The Circular stipulated that in areas where the nine-year compulsory education had been popularized, the system of promoting students who graduated from primary schools to junior secondary schools without graduation examination should be instituted. Junior secondary schools should not conduct any written examinations for the purpose of selection of students.

On 14 March, 2000, the Ministry of Education issued *Circular on Guiding Opinions on Reform on Graduation Examination and Enrollment Examination in Junior Secondary Schools*. The *Circular* stipulated that graduation examination and enrollment examination in junior secondary schools should be administrated by educational administrative departments. The subjects of examinations and organization of examinations should be administrated by the educational administrative departments.

On 16 August, 2002, the Ministry of Education issued *Circular on Guiding Opinions on Facilitating Basic Education by Classification and Evaluation*. The *Circular* stipulated that unitary examination in junior secondary schools should be conducted in the whole prefecture.

On 14 January, 2014, the Ministry of Education issued *Implementation Opinions on Improvement of Junior Secondary Schools' Enrollment for Graduates in Primary Schools*, The Opinions stipulated that every junior secondary school should be designated one or several primary schools, it may be one primary school versus one junior secondary school, or several primary schools versus one junior secondary school. In the former situation, all graduates from a primary school should be enrolled into the junior secondary school, in the latter situation, if graduates of primary school is less than the enrollment of junior secondary school, then all graduates would be enrolled in this junior secondary school, if graduates of primary school is more than the enrollment of junior secondary school, then students' preference should be considered, and the method of using computer to distribute the quato randomly should be adopted.

On 27 May, 2015, the Office of General Affairs under the Ministry of Education issued *Notice on the Enrollment of Students in Senior Secondary Schools*. The *Notice* stipulated that the enrollment of regular senior secondary schools should be approximately the same as the enrollment of secondary vocational schools, the enrollment platform for regular senior secondary schools and secondary vocational schools should be built. The equal opportunity and procedural equality for enrollment in regular senior secondary schools and secondary vocational schools should be guaranteed.

5.6.2 The System of Enrollment of Students in HEIs (1992–2016)

Prior to 1994, the government policy stipulated that students who enrolled in regular universities or colleges as state-funded students would receive education at government's expenses, and these graduates were assigned jobs in line with the unified State plan for job assignment. In this way, governments covered most educational costs.

Since the mid 1980s, colleges and universities adopted a "double-track" system in enrollment of students. In this system, the State paid only for those students who scored more than the passing mark in national college entrance examination and enrolled as state-funded students, while those who failed to score the minimum points but enrolled as the "above-quota" had to pay their ways through college.

On 26 December 1992, the State Education Commission issued *Circular on Strengthening Management of Enrollment Plans for Regular HEIs*. The *Circular* stipulated that there were some problems in the system of enrollments. The macro-management of enrollment was not as good as people anticipated. Some HEIs disobey rules in enrollment, collecting fees. Some HEIs enrolled too many students. Some unqualified HEIs began to enroll students. To solve these problems, the State Education Commission stipulated that governments should strengthen macro-management and control the total enrollment. Enrollment of student was administrated by the central government and provincial governments. HEIs that enrolled too many students should increase the financial input or lessen enrollment in the following year. HEIs should not run schools in other places without the approval of the educational administrative departments.

According to *Program of China's Educational and Development,* the enrollment of students as the "above quota" part in university and college enrollment was abolished along with the double-track system that categorized students as either government-funded or self-funded type. In other words, the double-track is now changed into a single-track, where students were neither totally government-funded nor totally self-funded but all of students paid a part of educational costs in HIEIs. The reform was endorsed by the State Council and carried out on a trial basis among the first batch of the 50 universities. When parents' opinions were canvassed in Shanghai International Studies University and some other universities which were involved, the overwhelming majority of parents supported the reform of the system of enrollment, which was really unexpected. After the experience in two universities was summarized and reform plan improved, further experiments were carried out in the second batch of 240 universities. By the time of the third batch of 234 universities were involved in the experiments, the reform had been carried out smoothly in virtually all the universities except those in such fields as agriculture, geology and mining, and teacher training. It took more than six years to basically complete the reform and introduce the single-track system of enrollment for students in universities and colleges, toward the end of the previous century.

When reform of higher education was being implemented, adjustments have been made of the system of entrance examination and recruitment. For example, explorations have been made about reducing the number of subjects to be examined upon: in examinations, students 'ability' and overall quality as well as their knowledge are tested; and examinations were held twice a year rather than once a year, as was the case in the past.

On 18 April, 1994, the Office of General Affairs under the State Education Council issued *Opinions on Reform on System of Enrollment and Assignment in Regular HEIs*. The *Opinions* stipulated that the system of enrollment was reformed so that graduates were not assigned jobs by the State at the time of graduation. The fee-charging system was instituted. The criteria of fees were rationalized. The system of scholarship and loan was instituted.

The rapid development of vocational higher education was brought about in late 1990s. In 1999, the Central Committee of the CCP and the State Council issued *Decisions on Deepening Educational Reforms and Carrying out Competence Education*. The *Decisions* stipulated that provincial governments with good conditions in educational reforms were advocated to carry out reform on national examination reforms and enlarge enrollment autonomy in HEIs.

On 16 April, 2014, the Ministry of Education issued *Notice on Increase the Number of Enrollment in Key Universities Targeted for Students living and Studying in Rural Areas*. This Notice aimed at equality of opportunity of higher education. The *Notice* stipulated that the State instituted a special enrollment program in Key Universities with the number of enrollment of 50,000, so as for key universities to attract more students from rural areas. The *Notice* also stipulated that the universities and colleges affiliated to the Ministry of Education should make arrangement of 2% of the total number of enrollment for recruitment of students in rural areas.

On 3 September, 2015, the State Council issued *Implementation Opinions on Deepening the System of Examination and Enrollment*. The *Implementation Opinions* decided on basic principles of reform of the system of examination and enrollment and new system of examination and enrollment with China characteristics should be instituted in 2020. As far as the reform of planning of enrollment, the rate of enrollment in west regions and populous provinces should be increased, the enrollment of students in rural areas in key universities should be increased, students' enrollment in neighbouring schools without graduate examination should be guaranteed. As far as the mechanism of enrollment and examination the autonomous enrollment by universities and colleges should be perfected, the criterion, conditions and procedures of enrollment should be made public or more transparent, the methods of enrollment should be improved.

5.6.3 Historical Experiences of Reform of the System of Enrollment

In the past sixty years, the reform of the system of enrollment facilitated the reform and development of education, provided new entrants for higher-level schools at various levels. A great deal of experience has been accumulated.

Firstly, it was necessary to establish the system of enrollment characterized by Chinese culture and in accordance with national situations. Although we need to learn useful advanced experiences in reform of system of enrollment from foreign countries, we could not imitate foreign models, and we could not establish systems of enrollment completely based on the requirement of market economy.

Secondly, we needed to reform and perfect the system of enrollment on the basis of requirements of social and economic development and on the basis of requirements of the youth for education and the requirements of the rank and file. Only through meeting the requirements of the society could the reform of the system of enrollment be deepened.

Thirdly, the reform of the system of enrollment should help push up competence education. In order to fulfill this goal, it is necessary to regulate educational structures, to expand the scale of senior secondary education and higher education, to increase the channel of cultivation of talents, and to decrease the pressure of promotion to higher-level schools. In the near future, it is necessary to expand higher vocation education and secondary vocation education, to construct an educational system with good horizontal and vertical mobility. By this way, the educational system could provide students more opportunities of learning and development.

Fourthly, the college entrance examination should be in accordance with the principle of choice of entrants from students who graduated from senior secondary schools and choice of students on merit. The practice in the past show that high criteria of choice of entrants among good students who graduated from senior secondary schools are the basis of guaranteeing the quality of entrants. choice of entrants on merit.

5.7   Current Situation of the System of Enrollment

The characteristics of the system of enrollment in the past sixty years can be summarized as follows.

Firstly, the influence of national unitary examination and enrollment is decreasing so as to adjust to requirements of the development of market economy and construct a new system of enrollment on the basis of autonomous powers of HEIs. Students should find jobs by themselves by adjusting to needs of markets.

Secondly, the reform of the system of enrollment in HEIs was deepened. The reform of the subjects of examination, contents of examination, methods of examination are carried out, test on students' competence and comprehensive abilities are stressed. New ways and new systems of enrollment, examination and evaluation in accordance with the characteristics of regions and schools are introduced.

5.7.1   Current Situation of the System of Enrollment in Primary and Secondary Schools

5.7.1.1   The System of Enrollment of Students in Primary School

Primary education is compulsory education. *The Compulsory Education Law of the People's Republic of China* stipulated that all children who have reached the age of six should enroll in school and receive compulsory education for the prescribed number of years.

Local governments at various levels should establish primary schools and junior secondary schools at such locations that children and adolescents can attend schools near their home.

So every child at the age of 6–11 should enter primary school and finish primary education. The enrollment in primary schools is based on the age of children. If the child is over 7 full years old, he or she should enroll in primary schools.

5.7.1.2   The System of Enrollment of Students in Junior Secondary Schools and Senior Secondary Schools

A.   The System of enrollment of students in junior secondary schools

Most regions abandon the entrance examination for junior secondary schools. But after graduation from junior secondary schools, the entrance examinations for students to enter senior secondary schools were conducted in most junior secondary schools. The main examination subjects are Chinese, mathematics and foreign languages.

The entrance examination in Tianjin has some features. The graduation examination and examination for promotions to senior secondary schools was separated. The examination for promotion to senior secondary schools was administrated by the enrollment and examination institutions. The subjects of examination for promotion to senior secondary schools were Chinese, mathematics, English. The test questions in politics were all open questions. The test of oral English was conducted and consisted of 30% of the total score of English.

B.   The System of enrollment for students in senior secondary schools

The enrollment of entrants in senior secondary schools is based on the scores and target of schools that are chosen by students. The entrance examination is a vital examination for students who graduate from senior secondary schools.

The enrollment in regular schools should follow the principle of comprehensive evaluation, and select students on merit.

The experiment on distribution of quota in excellent senior secondary schools and recommending good students from junior secondary schools to senior secondary schools should abide by the strict procedures and use open choice methods.

The system of publicity, the system of confidence, and the system of supervision are carried out in enrollment in senior secondary schools. The reform scheme of enrollment in senior secondary schools, including the content, methods, procedure of comprehensive evaluation concerning graduates from junior secondary schools, should be publicized. The costs of examination, various schemes of enrollment in senior secondary schools should be publicized.

5.7.2 Current Situation of the System of Enrollment for Students in HEIs

At present there are two ways of becoming entrants in HEIs. One way is for students to take part in national college entrance examination and to be recruited by HEIs. The other way is for students to be recommended to be enrolled in HEIs without taking part national college entrance examination. But more than 99% of entrants of HEIs take part in national college entrance examination. There are two entrance examinations and they are held in February and June.

The subjects of this kind of examination is using of "3+3" model. The first "3" stands for the three subjects of Chinese, mathematics and foreign language, these three subjects are the same examination subjects for all examinees. The latter "3" has many forms for examinees in different provinces. It may be three subjects choosing from politics, history, geography, physics, chemistry and biology in Shanghai, and it may be three subjects choosing from politics, history, geography, physics, chemistry biology and information and general technologies in Zhejiang. And in other provinces the latter "3" subjects may have other combinations.

After this kind of examination is conducted, the test questions will be examined and scores given. Ten days later students can know their examination scores. Then they will make application for HEIs. The HEIs are classified into four types. The first type is the key undergraduate HEIs and general undergraduate HEIs. The second type is short-cycle colleges. Applicants should make application for HEIs on the basis of their scores and personal preferences.

The recruitment process is conducted according to unitary plans. The steps begin from enrollment of students in the first type HEIs; the enrollment of students in the short-cycle colleges is conducted in the last period.

The recruitment is conducted by using recruitment network. HEIs may receive electronic records of applicants sent by the provincial enrollment office by using special network in CERNET. Then they put forward suggestions on recruitment and these lists of recruitment will be examined and approved by the provincial enrollment office. At this time recruitment of students is over.

The independent recruitment was conducted in some HEIs recently. In 2001 Nanjing University, Northeast University and Nanjing Aviation and Aerospace University made experiment on independent recruitment. In 2002 the participating universities increased to six. In 2003 the Ministry of Education decided that 22 key national universities take part in this kind experiment. The number of recruitment is less than 5% of the total number of recruitment in individual university. The Ministry of Education put forward three principles. Firstly, the university should publicize the objects of recruitment, methods of recruitment and number of recruitment. Secondly, graduates from senior secondary schools should make application and be examined and approved by schools and expert groups. Thirdly, the list of recruited students should be publicized.

5.8   Problems Facing China in the System of Enrollment

5.8.1   Problems Facing China in the System of Enrollment in Primary and Secondary Schools

5.8.1.1   Problem in Basic Education Concerning the Transformation from Examination-Oriented Education to Competence Education

At present, the system of enrollment is examination oriented to some extent. Examination oriented education included four features.

The choice of instruction content is based on requirements of entrance oriented education. Examination-oriented education may only cares about examination results and ratio of enrollment, so social economic construction and actual development has not been cared about seriously. Students are not trained to take part in social and economic construction immediately.

Examination-oriented education only cares about a few students who can enroll in higher-level schools. Students who can enroll in HEIs are a third of the students graduating from senior secondary schools at present.

Examination-oriented education increases students' learning loads. The enrollment competition is fierce. This kind of competition causes teachers to increase learning load.

5.8.1.2   Problems Facing China in the System of Enrollment in Primary Schools

Primary education is a kind of compulsory education. So in areas where compulsory primary education has been popularized, all students who are over six full years of age are eligible to enter primary schools automatically. But in areas where compulsory primary education has not been popularized, some students may face problems in enrollment in primary schools. One problem is economic difficult the students and their family face. The free compulsory education has not been fulfilled entirely in China. Students may incur some direct and indirect costs for schooling.

In the case of fees charged for dwelling in schools or some special fees for learning, some students may face difficulties. They may not be able to enter school.

The second problem facing China in the system of enrollment in primary schools is the difficulty faced by students from families of migrating laborers. Nowadays, many peasants in rural areas go to cities or other places to work. They may take their children with them or leave their children in their hometowns under the care of their relatives. If their children go with them to cities or other places they need to let their children receive education. But governments in the place where these parents work do not have enough public schools to accept their children. A more serious problem is that there are no special educational expenditures for educating these children. Governments have great financial pressure for educating these children. So in most cases, public schools would charge fees for enrollment of these children while children from local areas need not pay. It is unfair for the migrating laborers' children, but governments and schools cannot operate without sufficient financial support. Because of fees some migrating laborers' children may not enter primary schools eventually.

The choice of good primary schools is a disturbing problem in the stage of primary schools.

5.8.1.3 Problems Facing China in the System of Enrollment in Junior Secondary Schools

The reform of entrance examination in junior secondary schools is vital for the educational reform and instructional reform at the stage of primary education and junior secondary education and it would be beneficial to the implementation of competence education.

Students' choice of good junior schools is a serious problem. At present, among junior secondary schools, there are good schools and poor schools. Usually students should be enrolled in neighboring public schools. The way of enrollment is determined by educational administrative departments. If a student would choose a good public schools that is situated out of the school district where he or she dwells, he or she need to pay a fee for choosing a good school. The number of entrants in public schools for migrating laborers' children is very limited because a large portion of entrants is reserved for students dwelling near the schools, so the competition of choice of good schools is fierce. And this choice of good school causes unfair competition between schools, because these schools can get much money from the choice of schools. This choice of good school causes unfair competition between students because some students may choose a good school by using money. The parents who do not have enough money or are reluctant to spend such a sum lose the opportunity to choose a good school.

5.8.1.4 Problems Facing China in the System of Enrollment in Senior Secondary Schools

At present, compulsory education is nearly popularized in China. With the great expansion of higher education, the gross rate of higher education is higher than 37.5% in China in 2014. But development of senior secondary education is slow in comparison with the rapid development of higher education.

A more rapid development of senior secondary education is necessary. Only by this way can the educational structure be optimized. There are some non-harmonious factors in the reform of the structure of compulsory education and senior secondary education, and the structure of senior secondary education and higher education. The relatively slow development on the side of senior secondary education can make competition in entering HEIs more fierce.

The main problem is the single criterion of enrollment. The senior secondary schools use score line to recruit students. This way of recruitment restricts the development of schools with features. Many schools pursue the same target of enrollment ratio.

5.8.2 Problems Facing China in the System of Enrollment in Higher Education Institutions

Taking the scores in national college entrance examination as the single criterion in assessing basic education is not wise. Goal of secondary education is double. Secondary schools should provide qualified entrants to HEIs, but they should also train qualified labor forces for society. Using the results of examination in assessment of performance of schools is not a complete and equitable way. At present nearly one third of the students who graduated from senior secondary schools could be enrolled into HEIs to study further. In some senior schools the percentage in very low. In some senior secondary schools only a few students have the opportunities to be enrolled in HEIs.

Now the registration for national college entrance examination has been conducted by the community. National college entrance examination is a social examination. Persons who take part in national college entrance examination are from all ranks and files. Many affairs concerning college entrance examination are determined by situations in senior secondary schools. This kind of situations provides a pretext for the pursuit of enrollment in senior secondary schools. As the registration for national college entrance examination was done by senior secondary schools, the calculation of ratio of enrollment is easy.

The enrollment of students on the basis of recommendation by HEIs is very few. Less than 3% entrants in HEIs were enrolled in this way. So the system of recommendation has made little influences on the running of senior secondary schools.

5.9 Strategies and Measures for Further Reform of the System of Enrollment

5.9.1 Strategies and Measures for Further Reform of the System of Enrollment in Primary and Secondary Education

5.9.1.1 Strategies and Measures for Implementation of Competence Education

To redress the problems of the use of the single criterion in enrollment, it is necessary to establish more diversified criteria of assessment of students. Except for the use of scores in school entrance examination, students' ordinary performance in junior secondary schools should be stressed. The receipt in junior secondary schools should be listed as reference criteria of promotion to senior secondary schools.

5.9.1.2 Strategies and Measures for Solving Problems in the System of Enrollment in Primary Schools

Firstly, free compulsory education across the whole country should be implemented effectively. The central government has made decisions about achieving free and universal compulsory education. So the central government and local governments should provide enough public educational expenditure for free and universal compulsory education. Students at the stage of compulsory education should not pay tuition fees and other miscellaneous fees. Only after economic difficulties are overcome, students can enroll in primary schools without any fear of difficulties in paying for educational costs.

Secondly, governments should eliminate all discriminative policies concerning enrollment of transient population's children in primary schools. The main policy choice is establishment of enough public primary schools so as to recruit all migrant children. Meanwhile some special schools for migrant children can also be established, and these schools should be public ones and should meet the basic requirements of running schools.

5.9.1.3 Strategies and Measures for Solving Problems of the System of Enrollment in Junior Secondary Schools

The current graduation examination and entrance examination are centering on written cultural knowledge. It cannot be used to check the level of students' moral, intellectual, physical, aesthetic, labor skill development. As this kind of evaluation cannot tell much about the situation of students' development, the strategies and measures for improvement of instructional quality and educational quality are not easily put forward by researchers and practitioners.

It is necessary to conduct scientific evaluation on educational quality. The establishment and perfection of this kind of evaluation system can be beneficial to actual monitoring of education quality, solving practical problems, determining the requirements of enrollment. The use of this evaluation system will give a sound basis for the reform of enrollment.

The choice of good schools is a serious problem facing China in its system of enrollment in secondary schools. By the end of the third year in secondary schools, students would take part in a final examination. The final score in this examination is important to enroll in a good school. So the choice of good junior secondary schools is fascinating for students. The main measure for tackling the problems of choice of good senior schools is to make a balanced development of junior secondary schools.

5.9.1.4 Strategies and Measures for Solving the Problems of the System of Enrollment in Senior Secondary Schools

The development of senior secondary education is the bottleneck of educational development in China. So speeding up senior secondary education development should be an important task for the Chinese governments. The educational development strategies should be adjusted so as to make senior secondary education the priority of basic education. The development of senior secondary schools is the main task of the governments of counties. The central government and provincial governments should support government of counties to develop senior secondary schools. They should transfer more funds to governments of counties. The structure of senior secondary schools should be optimized. More students should enroll in vocational secondary schools. Otherwise the pressure of enrollment in regular senior secondary schools would be too much.

5.9.2 Strategies and Measures for Further Reforms of the System of Enrollment in Higher Education

The fame of senior secondary schools should not be determined by the ratio of enrollment of students in HEIs. The school's fame should be determined by the professionals the schools provided and the social contribution the schools make.

In order to increase the number of enrollment of students on the basis of recommendation by HEIs, it is necessary to reform the system of recommendation. The State Council should formulate regulations on the system of recommendation for selection of entrants for HEIs. The concerned regulation should stipulate the goal, function, organization, way of management, and procedures for the enrollment of students on the basis of recommendation by HEIs. The schools that can recommend students who are eligible to enter HEIs are limited to schools with good fame in society. The recommended students should meet some basic requirements.

Reference

Editorial Board of China's Education Yearbook (ed.) (1984). *China's Education Yearbook.* Beijing: Chinese Great Encyclopedia Publishing House.

Chapter 6
Moving Towards Market Orientation: The System of Employment in China

6.1 Introduction to the System of Employment

6.1.1 The Concept of the System of Employment

The system of employment aims to answer questions like who have the power of assigning jobs for students as well as who has the powers of acceptance of jobs.

The system of employment concerns the exit of educational process. Graduates from schools are educational products. The quality of educational output determines the future development of schools.

The system of employment is the total policies and regulations pertaining to the entry of the graduates from schools at various levels into the labor market and graduates' choice of jobs. The system of employment concerns the entry of graduates from various schools into the society by choosing various kinds of jobs.

6.1.2 Classification of the System of Employment

The system of employment can be classified in different ways as follows:

According to whether governments or markets decide the process of personnel-job matching, system of employment can be classified as government-dominated employment and f market-dominated system of employment.

Within the government-dominated system of employment, graduates from schools at various levels are assigned jobs by unitary governments' employment plans. Governments not only take the overall responsibilities of dispatch of students, but also take overall responsibilities for full employment of graduates. Schools do not have the rights of assignment of graduates from schools. Graduates themselves do not have the rights to choose schools freely.

© Springer Nature Singapore Pte Ltd. and Higher Education Press 2018
M. Yang and H. Ni, *Educational Governance in China*,
https://doi.org/10.1007/978-981-13-0842-0_6

In the market-dominated system of employment, graduates from schools are seen as a part of human resource allocation; the basic manner of human resource allocation is the market. The demand side and supply side of labor market determine the relation of employment by using two-sided free choice in labor markets. The demand and supply of labor determines the level of wages, the level of wages and its difference determine the final result of demand and supply of labor forces and the mobility of labor forces. The governments provide guidance and service by provision of training and education as well as by provision of information through vocational intermediary institutions and the media. The governments also carry out the supervision of labor markets according to laws and regulations. The governments indirectly monitor the labor force's supply and demand by income policies and welfare policies so as to make rational and effective allocation of labor forces.

6.1.3   Functions of the System of Employment

The reform of the system of employment plays an important part in the optimization of educational resource allocation and labor resource allocation. It also affects the system of training of students and management in schools.

6.2   The System of Employment During the Completion of Socialist Restructuring (1949–1956)

6.2.1   The System of Employment for Students in Primary and Secondary Schools (1949–1956)

At the beginning of the founding of the People's Republic of China, students who graduated from primary schools and secondary schools had two choices. On choice was to enter higher-level schools. The other choice was to go back to their hometown to be a worker or a peasant. The State did not assign a job for them. They had to find a job after graduation.

In 1953, *Directive on Enrollment in National Secondary Schools* pointed out that in this year many students who graduated from primary schools could not be enrolled in junior secondary schools. They had to take part in labor. Only a part could be enrolled in junior secondary schools.

On 3 December 1953, the People's Daily published an editorial, '*Organizing Graduates to Participate in Agricultural Work*'. The *Article* pointed out that the development of agricultural production was the only right way for peasants to get rich. It was an important task to organize graduates from primary schools to participate agricultural work. Many graduates from primary schools would like to enter higher schools to study. This reflects the people's desire for higher-level material life and spiritual life. The State was making great efforts to meet the requirements. But as the limited development level of economy and the limited financial support, the requirement could not be met in a short time. The graduates from primary and secondary schools would engage in agricultural work actively after the teachers' patient persuasion.

On 27 January, 1954, the vice-minister of the Ministry of Education, Qian Junrui, said that we should approach the problems of graduates' employment with a positive attitude. The graduates from primary schools were not many. Primary schools should recruit more students.

On 22 April, 1954, the Central Committee of Chinese Communist League issued *Directives on Organizing Graduates Who Could Not Enter Higher Schools to Participate in Labor Production*. The *Directives* pointed out that the attitude of letting children to study more and acquire much knowledge was an ordinary attitude for they had no opportunity to study in the past. But the State's purpose to run schools was to build active constructors for society. The schools had two tasks, one was to provide entrants for higher schools and the other was to provide labor force for production. Only a small portion of the graduates could enter the higher schools; most graduates would participate in labor production. Millions of new workers with knowledge and political consciousness taking part in socialist industrialization were an important task for socialist construction. To make graduates participate in labor production actively, three measures were taken. Firstly, the educational administrative department should strengthen labor education for students. Secondly, the Communist League should make active propaganda and help to form correct social opinions. Thirdly, excellent graduates who produce brilliant achievements in labor production should be given wide publicity.

On 6 April, 1954, the Ministry of Education and the Ministry of Higher education issued *Directives on Ideological Education Concerning Entering Higher-level schools for Students Graduating from Senior Secondary Schools*. The Directives pointed out that in the past some students could not be relived to study after enrolling in higher education institutions and some quit study in HEIs. Because of this, the national enrollment plans could not be fulfilled. The reason for this phenomenon was that they did not have clear knowledge about the disciplines and specialties in higher education institutions. Idcological education for graduates was fragmentary; so the outcome was not as good as people anticipated. The Directives suggested that three measures should be taken. Firstly, the main content of ideological education would focus on the establishment of correct thoughts about the relationship between entering higher-level schools and conducting socialist construction. Secondly, the State could fulfill the enrollment plans completely. Thirdly, the respective departments should make full propaganda of booklets on enrollment.

6.2.2 The System of Employment for Students in HEIs (1949–1956)

6.2.2.1 The System of Governmental Appointment and Regional Adjustment

Before the founding of the People's Republic of China, graduates from HEIs found jobs by themselves. Since late 1949, the State established the system of assignment of graduates through planning, and stopped the situation of "graduation means unemployment" before 1949.

On 22 June, 1950, the Administrative Council issued *Notice*. The *Notice* pointed out that in 1950 graduates in HEIs were 17,539. The assignment of graduates would guarantee the needs of national key construction. Each Great Administrative Region (GRA) made different assignment plans.

The Northeast GRA Regions had only 530 graduates. So, 4900–6200 graduates from Eastern China GRA, Southern China GRA, and Southwest GRA would be assigned to Northeast GRA to support key construction within this region.

In the Northern China GRA, 2600–3300 graduates were assigned within the region, 500–800 graduates were assigned to departments of central government; 2500–3000 graduates were assigned to the Northeast GRA.

In South Central China GRA, 1400–2000 graduates were assigned to the Northeast GRA; 2500 graduates were assigned within this region.

In Southeast GRA, 1000–1200 graduates were assigned to the Northeast GRA, the rest were assigned within this region.

In Northwest GRA, all graduates were assigned within this region.

In Northern China GRA, 1200 graduates were assigned to the Northeast GRA; the rest were assigned to five provinces.

The *Notice* also stipulated that graduates in public and private HEIs should be assigned through planning. The Notice pointed out that assignment of graduates should be based on the qualities of graduates. Governments and HEIs should persuade graduates to obey assignment plans. If they would like to find work by themselves, they were assured of the freedom. Graduates had one year's probation period.

From 1952 on, the system of State's unitary assignment was established and perfected.

6.2.2.2 The Establishment of National Unitary Assignment System

The problem of matching graduates with jobs was a challenging issue. Since the first reorganization of higher education in 1949 the State was responsible for assigning jobs for graduates in accord with State's planning. At the beginning this highly centralized system did not work very well. Because authorities in HEIs knew not much about the requirements of the job market, the State's authorities responsible for graduates' employment was not easy to coordinate their needs with the actual situation of universities and colleges. Each some graduates were assigned jobs that mismatched their specialties while hundreds of thousands of jobs were begging for want of applicants.

On 30 June 1951, the Administrative Council issued *Directives on Unitary Assignment of Graduates in HEIs*. The *Directives* stipulated that job assignment plan in this year was focusing on adjustment of assignment process between the regions; job assignment should be adapted to the needs of national construction and managers should care about the regions with too few graduates. Political work and mobilization work should be done effectively; 90% of graduates should follow job assignment plans made by the State. Localities and departments should overcome selfish departmentalism.

On 1 October, 1951, the State Council issued *Decision on Reform of School System*. It was decided that from then on, jobs assignment for graduates in universities and colleges were managed by governments.

On 3 January, 1952, the Ministry of Education issued *Directives on Students in Liberal Arts and Engineering Colleges in the Third Years to be Graduated Ahead of One Year*. The *Directives* pointed out that as the restructuring of universities and colleges took place, a lot of students should be graduated in 1954. But the State needed a great deal of personnel to construct the socialist country. So it was decided that students in engineering colleges were graduated one year ahead of time.

On 18 June, 1952, the Administrative Council issued *Directives on Adjustment of Assignment of Graduates of HEIs*. The *Directives* pointed out the problems facing China in the job assignments for graduates in HEIs. These problems included: (1) some institutions took position of departmentalism and cared too much about their needs so that some graduates changed their specialties; what they learned could not be used in posts; (2) some institutions stressed organizations' job assignment procedures and neglected graduates' personal needs and thoughts; (3) some institutions did not care about the difficulties of graduates. To solve these problems, it was necessary to overcome selfish departmentalism; the mismatch between what students learned and what students used should be lessened.

On 19 July, 1952, the Administrative Council issued *Directives on Assignment of Graduates in HEIs in 1952*. The *Directives* pointed out that the system of unitary job assignment for graduates in HEIs by the governments was established in the past two years. This system was adjusting to the needs of our country and the actual situations.

On 1 August, 1953, the Administrative Council issued *Directives on Assignment of Jobs for Graduates in HEIs in 1952*. The job assignment methods were changed. The Administrative Council determined the general scheme for job assignment for students. Then the Ministry of Personnel considered thee needs and situation of the concerned departments and formulated a job assignment scheme for each higher education institution on the basis of the general scheme. Higher education institutions were responsible for the implementation of the job assignment plans by deploying graduates to their respective jobs and posts.

In 1954, the Ministry of Personnel was revoked, so the Ministry of Higher Education took responsibilities for the assignment of jobs for graduates in HEIs.

In 1956, the State Planning Commission took the responsibility for the formulation of the job assignment plans for graduates. The Ministry of Education was in charge of providing information of distribution of graduates in disciplines and specialties and responsible for deployment and dispatch of graduates.

6.3   The System of Employment at the Stage of Completion of Building Socialism (1957–1965)

6.3.1   The System of Employment of Students in Primary and Secondary Schools

On 1 January, 1957, the Ministry of Education issued *Circular on Political Education and Ideological Education in Secondary Education*. The *Circular* pointed out that labor education for students who graduated from secondary schools should be strengthened.

On 5 June, 1957, the Ministry of Education issued *Circular on the Issues about Education of Students Who Graduated from Primary Schools and Secondary Schools*. Four measures were proposed for improvement of job assignment.

Firstly, the social propaganda and social investigation of students' job assignment should be conducted.

Secondly, a short period of ideological education for students should be conducted.

Thirdly, educational administrative departments should make research on job assignment for students who graduated from schools in this year.

Fourthly, students who had special difficulties should be taken care of on a priority basis.

6.3.2   The System of Employment of Students in HEIs (1949–1965)

6.3.2.1   The System of Sharing Graduates Between Central Government and Localities

From 1959 to 1965, the process of job assignment for graduates in HEIs was reformed. The job assignment method used by the central government had two parts: the central governments taking some of the graduates for their use; and leaving the others to be assigned to local areas.

On 2 June, 1959, the Central Committee of the CCP approved *Report on Provisional Regulations of Assignment of Graduates in HEIs*, submitted by the

State Planning Commission. The *Report* stipulated that graduates from HEIs, which were administrated by the Ministry of Education and other ministries under the State Council should be assigned jobs by the central government. Graduates from HEIs which were administrated by the governments at province level should be assigned jobs using the method of delivering some graduates to the ministries under the State Council and others to the respective provinces for local use.

From 1959 to 1961, the job assignment of for graduates in HEIs was administrated by the Bureau of Personnel under the State Council, and the formulation of job assignment plans was administrated by the National Economic Commission.

On 27 April, 1962, the Central Committee of the CCP approved *Opinions on Improvement of Assignment of Jobs for Graduates in HEIs*. This *Opinions* was submitted to the Bureau of Secretary of Central Committee by Zhou Enlai. The Opinions pointed out that the current manner of job assignment for graduates in HEIs was divided into three kinds, namely, the central unitary assignment, direct assignment by ministries under the State Council, and direct assignment by provincial governments.

For central unitary assignment, the National Planning Commission formulated the job assignment plan; the Ministry of Internal Affairs formulated the job adjustment plan while HEIs took responsibility for dispatching graduates toothier respective posts.

The Ministry of Education took responsibility for the training of students but it was not taking part in the work of assignment. This would cause a mismatch between training of graduates and the use of graduates. To solve the problem, the *Opinions* suggested that: (1) the assignment of jobs for graduates in HEIs should have intimate connection with training of students; (2) The Ministry of Education should not only take the responsibility for training, but also take the responsibility for the assignment of jobs for graduates.

In order to improve job assignment for graduates in HEIs, three steps were to be taken. Firstly, the Ministry of Education assembled and provided information concerning graduates all over the country; the National Economic Commission got information about the need for graduates. Secondly, based on information provided by the Ministry of Education and based on consideration of the need for graduates, the National Economic Commission made out the assignment plan, and sought suggestions from different departments and provinces. Thirdly, the State Planning Commission in conjunction with the General Office of the State Council made the adjustment plan, and the State Planning Commission formulated the final job assignment plan and submitted it to the Central Committee of the CCP and the State Council for approval. Fourthly, the Ministry of Education took the responsibility for job assignment of jobs for graduates in HEIs.

6.3.2.2   Reform of Assignment of Jobs for Graduates Through Assignment Commissions for HEIs

On 20 August, 1962, the Central Committee approved *Report on Assignment Plan for Graduates in HEIs*, submitted by the National Assignment Commission for

Graduates in HEIs. The *Report* stipulated that the job assignment for graduates according to proportionate sharing of the total graduates was revoked. The method of national unitary assignment was reformed. The structures of specialties were adjusted so as to make those less unpopular specialties change into required specialties.

On 30 August, 1963, the Ministry of Education, the Ministry of Internal Affairs, and the State Economic Planning Commission issued *Provisional Regulations on the Deployment of Graduates*. The *Regulations* stipulated that the Ministry of Education should consult with other ministries under the State Council to formulate the job assignment plans for different HEIs, regions, and departments on the basis of national assignment plan approved by the Central Committee of CCP and the State Council.

6.3.2.3   The System of Direct Assignment by Ministries Under the State Council and Direct Assignment by Provincial Governments

On 14 June, 1965, the Central Committee issued *Directives on the Assignment of Jobs for Graduates Who Would Like to Work in Grassroots Organizations*. The *Directives* stipulated that the assignment of some jobs in grassroots organizations for graduates was an important means to combine intellectuals with workers and peasants and an important measure to strengthen the construction of grassroots organizations. After the assignment of these graduates to grassroots organizations, the most important issue was how to administrate and educate them well. Before assignment of jobs to the graduates, the training of graduates within a period of time was necessary. After these graduates were assigned to the grassroots organizations, governments should specify definite persons responsible for the administration and education of these graduates.

6.3.2.4   Treatment of Graduates Who Did not Obey Assignment Plans

In the 1950s, most graduates in HEIs obeyed the job assignment plans made by governments. But in the 1960s, a lot of graduates did not obey the job assignment plans. In 1962 there were 2000 graduates who did not obey the assignment plans. In 1963, 2% of the graduates in HEIs did not obey the job assignment plans. So on 10 May 1963, the Central Committee of the CCP and State Council issued *Report on Assignment Plans for Graduates in HEIs*. The *Report* made it clear that graduates who did not obey the assignment plans were to be persuaded to accept them. If graduates in HEIs did not accept the job assignment plans, they would be deprived of job assignment chance. Educational administrative department told other units not to recruit these graduates. If they would obey the assignment plans within three months, they would be assigned jobs on the basis of job assignment plans as usual.

6.3.2.5   The Probation System (1957–1966)

On 25 October, 1957, the State Council issued *Regulations on Temporary Remunerations for Graduates in HEIs*. The *Regulations* stipulated that in order to strengthen the training of graduates and make rational use of graduates, all graduates should have at least one year's probation. In this period graduates could not be given formal remunerations as usual, but they could be given temporary remunerations.

On 17 August, 1963, the State Council issued *Circular on Graduates in HEIs Who Took Part in Fieldwork*. In order to implement the Chinese Communist Party's Guidelines, the system of one year's probation was changed into a system one year's work plus one year's period of probation. Graduates from specialties of engineering and agriculture in HEIs were chosen to take part in such experiments.

6.3.2.6   The Assignment of Graduates in HEIs to Privately-Owned Units

In early 1960s, the collective economy developed rapidly. In order to meet the collective units' requirements of professionals, some graduates in HEIs were assigned jobs in collective units.

On 1 July, 1964, the Central Committee and State Council issued *Report on Issues of Assignment of Graduates from HEIs*. The *Report* stipulated that some graduates in agricultural specialties in HEIs would be assigned jobs in collective-ownership units. They kept the status of managers and took part in labor in collective—ownership units and got remunerations as others did. But if their remunerations were lower than the definite criteria for graduates in HEIs, the State would give them subsidies. Graduates from specialties in medicine, education and engineering should follow this way.

In 1966, the system of assignment of jobs for graduates in HEIs to collective units was revoked.

6.4   The System of Employment at the Stage of the "Cultural Revolution" (1966–1976)

6.4.1   The System of Employment for Students in Primary and Secondary Schools (1966–1976)

On 21 May, 1966, the Central Committee of the CCP approved *Report on Conference of Work-study Education in Urban Areas*, submitted by the Ministry of Education. The *Report* pointed out that work-study education was beneficial to training a new type of labor force that had cultural knowledge and practical skills.

Students should be told that after graduation they could have jobs or enter higher-level schools; they could work as workers and peasants, or technicians.

On 14 October, 1972, Premier Zhou Enlai pointed out that after students graduated from senior secondary schools they did not need to work for two years and then were enrolled in HEIs. They were eligible to be enrolled in HEIs. Most graduates should go to work immediately; they should improve their competences in production practice. After several years' work they could be enrolled in HEIs to study further.

6.4.2   The System of Employment for Students in HEIs (1966–1976)

On 15 June, 1968, the Central Committee of CCP, the State Council, the Central Military Commission of the CCP, the Central Leadership Group of the "Cultural Revolution" issued *Circular on Assignment of Some Graduates to Farms Administrated by the People's Liberation Army*. The *Circular* stipulated that some graduates should be assigned jobs in the farms administrated by the People's Liberation Army. The ministries under the State Council made out concrete plans. The provincial governments should put forward plans for assignment of jobs for graduates in HEIs; graduates were sent to farms administrated by the People's Liberation Army.

6.5   The System of Employment at the Stage of Building Socialist Commodity Economy (1977–1991)

6.5.1   The System of Employment for Students in Primary and Secondary Schools (1977–1991)

In April 1978, the National Conference on Education was held in Beijing; Deng Xiaoping pointed out that each department should implement the policy of all-around examination and recruitment according to merits.

In August 1980, the Central Committee issued *Decision on Open Multiple Channel for Resolution of Problems of Employment*. The *Decision* pointed out that in the past in new vocational schools the method of unitary assignment was not used. Students could find jobs by recommendation from labor departments and they are examined by employers. Students could also find jobs by themselves. Hereafter employers were encouraged to use students who had received vocational training.

In October 1980, the Ministry of Education and State Labor Bureau submitted *Report on Reform of Structure of Secondary Education to the State Council* and it was approved. The *Report* stipulated that students who graduated from secondary schools were not assigned jobs by the State. Students who graduated from secondary schools could be recommended by labor departments, examined by employers, and selected on merit. Students could find jobs freely. In communes and production brigades, students who graduated from schools had priority in employment.

6.5.2   The System of Employment for Students in HEIs (1977–1991)

6.5.2.1   Establishment of Job-Directive Enrollment and System of Employment

A. Reform of the system of job assignment for graduates in HEIs

The system of unitary job assignment failed to solve the problem of posting sufficient trained manpower away from coastal cities, or in major sectors of the economy such as agriculture. The number of graduates from agricultural colleges was minute, and half of these graduates soon sought employment in other sectors.

Employment is an economic issue. So for a long time in China when we talked about jobs for graduates from HEIs, we used a special term, namely, job assignment for graduates in HEIs.

In 1983, the government delegated some administrative powers of job assignment for graduates from colleges and universities. These powers include making suggestions of job assignment for graduates, deciding job assignment list, making adjustment of job assignment plan.

In 1983, the Ministry of Education decided that Tsinghua University, Shanghai Communication University, Xian Communication University, Shangdong Oceanology University make experiments on reform of job assignment by "interviews between suppliers of jobs and demanders of jobs".

In 1985, Tsinghua University and Shanghai Jiaotong University carried out experiments on "letting employers have rights to choose graduates". The University sent out their letters to employers for information on supply of jobs available one year ahead of graduation. This kind of information was conveyed to graduates, who filled in job application forms accordingly. Those on the short lists for jobs were interviewed by units, and introduced to talk about job conditions, salaries, housing and so on. The final decision was made by the employers and the successful applicants, with no intervention of the State. This method proved very successful and quickly spread to other prestigious universities and colleges.

In 1986, some colleges and universities conducted comprehensive tests for students and made selective job assignments. Colleges and universities permitted 3% good students to choose jobs on basis of top priority.

From 1983 on, the system of job assignment was changing, national direct control was lessening and indirect control on job assignment was increasing.

On 24 November, 1988, the State Education Commission issued *Provisional Regulations on Job-directive enrollment and Assignment of Jobs by Regular Universities and Colleges*. The *Regulations* stipulated that in order to assure a definite number of graduates working in regions and industries under difficult circumstances, the State implement the system of job-oriented enrollment and system of employment. The regions included all Western regions in China as well as the units under difficult circumstances. The special industries included agriculture, forestry, geology, energy, construction materials, and meteorology.

6.6 The System of Employment at the Stage of Building Socialist Market Economy (1992–2016)

6.6.1 The System of Employment for Students in Primary and Secondary Schools (1992–2016)

By the end of the 1990s, the nine-year compulsory education was universalized rapidly. The scale of education of all levels and types was increasing. People's need for education was expanding. In each year, there were 21 million students who graduated from junior secondary schools; among them, 8 million students entered senior secondary school, 7 million entered vocational secondary schools; the remaining 6 million entered labor markets, worked in villages or in urban areas. These students were mainly from rural areas and from remote and poor areas. They may be the most disadvantaged groups in the process of employment.

Since 1992, the governments have formulated some important policies on reform of the system of job assignment in secondary education.

On 6 March, 1992, the Ministry of Labor issued *Circular on Implementing Decisions on Vocational and Technical Education Development*. The *Circular* pointed out that vocational training includes pre-employment training and on-the-job training. For students who had graduated from vocational and technical schools, the system of graduation certificates and technical level qualification for posts should be established. When enterprises employed workers, they should give priority to students who had these two certificates.

On 9 February, 1993, the Mechanical and Electrical Ministry and the Ministry of Labor issued the *Circular on Those Using New Workers in Mechanical and Electrical Jobs*. The *Circular* stated that they should use students who graduated from vocational and technical secondary schools. The *Circular* pointed out that the vocational and technical secondary schools should make good plans.

On 2 May, 1995, the Ministry of Labor issued Circular on Appraisal of Vocational Skills for Graduates from Technical Secondary Schools, Vocational Schools and Vocational Training Centers. The scope of appraisal of skills included many kinds of knowledge and skills. Examination for knowledge was conducted by using written tests. Examination for skills was conducted by students' participating production work and projects.

6.6.2   The System of Employment of Students in HEIs (1992–2016)

On 13 February, 1993, *Program of Educational Reform and Development* formulated a future action strategy for reform of the system of employment. It stipulated that the unitary job assignment system for graduates from HEIs should be reformed. In the near future, some graduates should be assigned jobs by the State; most graduates should find jobs independently. For the "contract-training students", their employment should be arranged by contracts. For fees-paying students, their employment should be decided by themselves independently.

On 18 April, 1994, the Office of General Affairs under the State Education Commission issued *Opinions on Reform of the System of Enrollment and Assignment in Regular HEIs*. The *Opinions* stipulated that the system of job assignment for graduates in HEIs should be reformed. A system of scholarship and loan that coordinated with the fee-collecting system was instituted. The differences between the State plan and the regulative plan was manifested in the fee-collecting system and the system of scholarship and loans. As for personnel in national key construction, defense construction, cultural and educational construction, basic disciplines, remote areas, industries, HEIs should establish scholarships to enroll students so as to meet the needs of these areas and industries on the top priority of national development.

On 28 December, 2007, the Office of General Affairs under the Ministry of Education issued *Notice on Instruction Requirement for Courses of Vocational Development and Vocational Guidance in HEIs*. The *Notice* stipulated that from 2007 on the course of vocational development and vocational guidance should be included in the instruction program as a common required course.

On 8 October, 2012, the Office of General Affairs under the Ministry of Education issued *Basic Requirement on Instruction of Entrepreneurship Education in regular HEIs*. The *Basic Requirement* put forward the instructional goals, instructional principles, instructional contents, instructional methods, and instructional ways of entrepreneurship education.

On 20 May, 2016, the Office of General Affairs under the Ministry of Education issued *Notice on Improvement of Graduate's Employment and Entrepreneurship*. The *Notice* stipulated that it was necessary for HEIs to combine the employment with entrepreneurship and to exert the multiplier effect brought by entrepreneurship. HEIs should set and perfect the employment services.

On 2015, the Office of General Affairs under the State Council issued *Implementation Opinions on Deepening of Reform on Employment and Entrepreneurship*. The *Opinions* stipulated that four measures should be taken, such as perfecting the standards of higher education quality, innovating the training mechanisms, improving employment and entrepreneurship related courses, and reforming the instruction and examination methods.

6.7   Current Situation of the System of Employment

6.7.1   Current Situation of the System of Employment for Graduates in Primary and Secondary Schools

In China, compulsory education has been universalized in most regions. In 2014, the net rate of enrollment in primary schools was 99.81%, the gross rate of enrollment in junior secondary schools was 103.5%. 95.1% of the students who graduated from junior secondary schools can enter senior secondary schools in 2014. So nearly all students who graduate from primary schools do not need to find jobs; they are required to study in junior secondary schools. Students who have graduated from junior secondary schools are free to choose to enter senior secondary schools or to find jobs. But most of them are entering senior secondary schools to study further. Students who have graduated from junior secondary schools and would like to find jobs may rely on their own competence. Governments do not make formal arrangement on job assignment for them.

The enrollment of entrants in senior secondary schools depends on the scores in the graduation examination in the last year of junior secondary schools.

Schools at the stage of secondary education could be classified as regular secondary education and vocational secondary education. Students who are receiving regular secondary education are willing to enter higher education institutions. Students who are receiving vocational secondary education are willing to work after they have graduated from these schools, only a small part of graduates could be enrolled in higher vocational colleges.

Most of students who have graduated from vocational secondary schools should find jobs soon after graduation. So for these students finding jobs is a very important issue. Recently the guidance on employment in vocational secondary schools is centering on three aspects.

Firstly, these schools are orienting to employment, running of schools by facing society and markets, adapting to social needs, and market needs, establishing specialties concerning modern industries and new industries.

Secondly, these schools are deepening instruction and educational reform, renovating educational models, improving instruction methods, and laying emphasis on competence building.

Thirdly, these schools strengthen guidance on employment, entrepreneurial education and employment service. In many regions, employment information service network in vocational secondary schools have been established. Schools make efforts to provide better information service.

In 2015, the number of graduates in vocational secondary schools was 515.47 million, and 496.42 million found jobs instantaneously. The employment rate was 93.3%. For all graduates, 52.04% finds jobs in governments, enterprises and public institutions, 16.7% belonged to the kind of self-employment, 11.67% found jobs in other ways. For all graduates, 10.87% were working in the first industry, 32.93% were working in the second industry, and 56.20% were working in the third industry. For all graduates, 89.26% have made labor contracts formally, 10.74% were waiting for the opportunities to make contracts.

In 2014, the graduates in vocational secondary schools was 577.70 million, 558.54 million found jobs instantaneously, the employment rate was 96.68%.

The rate of employment of graduates in vocational secondary school was higher now than it was in the 1990s. In 2002, 2003, 2004, 2005, 2006, the rate of employment was 94.6, 92.3, 94.3, 95.35 and 95.60% respectively. In 2006 there were 3.64 million graduates in vocational secondary schools; 3.48 million have been employed instantaneously. Among these students, 2.55 million went to enterprises, 0.36 million were engaged in individual labors, 0.57 million entered higher level schools to study further. Among these students 0.25 million were working in the primary industry, 1.34 million were working in the secondary industry, 1.88 million were working in the tertiary industry. Among these students 2.192 were working in localities, 1.27 million were working in other places, 0.0018 milliohm were working abroad.

6.7.2   Current Situation of the System of Employment for Graduates in HEIs

At present the system of employment in HEIs is a market-oriented system. A perfect market-oriented system of employment should have the following necessary conditions. The socialist market economic system is relatively perfect. The labor market and professional market reform has been deepened. The reform of the system of labor management and personnel management has achieved results. The equitable competition environment in society has been established, and the guidance system for employment of graduates has been set up. The service system for graduates' employment has been established.

In this market-oriented system of employment, there are four important factors. The first factor is governments' guidance and monitoring. Governments make rational higher education planning and strategies to guide the balance of supply and demand of higher education. Governments also make supervision and monitoring on labor markets and professional markets. Governments should guarantee the meeting of special needs in some industries and professions. Every year the Ministry of Education publishes a circular on improvement of the employment of students who have graduated from HEIs. This document has been a guideline for one year's employment affairs.

The second factor is the employment market for students who have graduated from HEIs. From 1995 on, the name of employment market for graduates has been accepted by the masses. Graduates and employers meet each other to match the job with personnel.

In the employment market, graduates make application for jobs, and employers provide information suitable for jobs. Graduates may make an outline of his or her career. Usually employers receive these applications from graduates. After examination and selections they ask the candidates to meet again. In many cases the selection process may have more than one round. Finally employers may decide to select suitable employees from among the candidates.

The third factor is the HEIs. HEIs are responsible for the training of students; they also should care about the rate of employment.

At present the State makes decision that the rate of employment by the deadline of May or June should be assessed and publicized. The rate of employment should be a factor influencing the number of entrants in HEIs in the next year.

Under these circumstances, HEIs are making great efforts to make sure that the rate of employment does not decrease.

HEIs may do some important work for graduates. Usually a department of employment is established and is responsible for employment affairs in HEIs. The main task of this department includes five aspects. Firstly, they will make propaganda and conduct graduation education for graduates and mobilize students to take part in various activities of employment. Secondly, they will make arrangements for employment-oriented market activities such as communicating with employers and determining the process and procedures of employment market activities. Usually the on- the-spot meetings concerning employment are held in universities and colleges or in other places. Thirdly, they may conduct vocational, professional and employment guidance though curricula, lessons, lectures, meetings, advertisements. Fourthly, they will coordinate among many stakeholders concerning employment. Fifthly, they will supervise and monitor employment process and make examination and assessment of the result of employment of the graduates.

The fourth factor is students. They are the main actors in the system of employment. Since 1997, the system of paying tuition and fees has been introduced in higher education system. Students are cost conscious. Nowadays students find jobs by themselves after graduation. Students are keen to find a nice university or college, a fascinating department and specialty. After entering HEIs they may choose curricula more seriously. Many students learn foreign languages and computer technology eagerly, for they know these are useful tools for students' purpose of finding good jobs. Many students decide to learn more than one main specialty so as to be professionals with multiple talents. These practices are stressed by students. Students are eager to know how society is operating. In the final stage of finding jobs, students may have many choices. Some of them choose to study abroad after graduation. Some of them decide to be postgraduates, so they prepare to take postgraduate entrance examinations. Some of them choose to be clerks in government office, so they take part in the public servant examination. Many students choose to engage in a job as soon as possible.

Report on Employment of Graduates in HEIs in 2015 was published by MyCos Institute. The *Report* indicated that the graduates' employment rate after half year later than the time of graduation was 90.9, 91.4, 92.1% in 2012, 2013, 2014. For undergraduate-level HEIs, the graduates' employment rate after half year later than the time of graduation was 91.5%%, 91.8%,92.6% in 2012, 2013, 2014; for vocational higher educational institutions, the graduates' employment rate after half year later than the time of graduation was 90.4, 90.9, 91.5% in 2012, 2013, 2014. The graduates' self-initiated employment rate after half year later than the time of graduation was 2.0, 2.3, 2.9% in 2012, 2013, and 2014. Half of graduates of the self-initiated employment stop the self-initiated employment after three years; it showed that it is difficult for graduates' innovation and entrepreneurship to be continued. The graduates' full-time employment rate after half year later than the time of graduation was 81.3, 80.6, 79.2% in 2012, 2013, and 2014.

In 2014, 91.5% of HEIs published their employment reports officially. The employment rate for graduates in undergraduate-level HEIs was 91.5%, and the employment rate for graduates in the top 100 HEIs was 95.5%. The employment rate for graduates in HEIs in more developed regions was higher than those in less developed regions.

6.8 Problems Facing China in the System of Employment

6.8.1 Problems Facing China in the System of Employment in HEIs

There are four main actors in the reform of system of employment; they are governments, markets, employers, graduates. Each of them should play their respective roles in the reform of the system of employment in HEIs.

6.8.2 Lack of Strong Guidance by Governments

Recently governments are deepening the reform of the system of employment, and are cultivating graduates' employment markets actively. With the efforts of the governments, China has established a system of employment whereby graduates make autonomic choice of vocations. But some problem concerning governments' role exist in terms of the system of employment. Firstly, the idea that "governments have done nothing" means "governments have done well" is a misunderstanding of market mechanism. The effective market mechanism can not go without government's functioning. In the process of the reform of the system of employment, market failure and governmental failure exist. Both of these failure need to be prevented. So these two mechanisms are all necessary. Recently the government's role in the reform of the system of employment has been weakened.

6.8.2.1 Employers' Roles in Reform of the System of Employment

Some issues concerning employers exist. Firstly, some managers of enterprises may be manifesting nearsightedness. Usually the terms of appointment of managers in some state-owned enterprises are four to five years. As new employees can play full role after several years, the managers in enterprises may hesitate to use new employees. Secondly, in great cities, some enterprises or other units may raise the requirements of employment to unlimited levels so as to intimidate many suitable candidates. Thirdly, some employers are short of consciousness of competitions, and they may choose employees through nepotistic practices.

6.8.2.2   Graduates' Unrealistic Attitudes Toward Employment

There are some problems with regard to the graduates. Some graduates are only interested in choice of great cities, and jobs with high salaries. They neglect other job opportunities.

6.8.2.3   Discrepancy Between Demand and Supply

The imbalance between demand and supply of graduates in some regions and fields are very evident.

Generally speaking, in recent times, the total requirement for graduates has slowed down. According to investigation conducted in 2002, 58.5% of graduates had signed contracts with employers before leaving HEIs. The rest, who had not signed such contracts needed to seek other opportunity later. The employment pressure comes due to several factors: the new increase in urban and rural labor forces, the unemployment in enterprises, the lowering of requirements for labor forces in traditional industries.

Statistics show that the lower a group's educational levels, the higher the rate of unemployment for the group. There is a decreasing rate of employment on the basis of the level of schools. The rate of employment in specialized higher schools is 70% for the best specialized higher schools and 29% for the poorest specialized schools.

The rate of employment among male graduates is higher than that among female graduates. The rate of employment among graduates from rural areas is higher than that among graduates from urban areas.

6.8.2.4   Weakness in Guidance on Employment

The guidance on employment in HEIs has not been adjusting to the needs of complete bilateral choice among employers and employees. Reform of the system of employment brings about both hope and difficulties for graduates. Some graduates may have expectations of bright future and free choice and be too optimistic about finding jobs; but when they cannot find jobs temporarily, they become pessimistic. The aimless search for jobs causes wastage of human resources.

Educational employment is an impending challenge. As the supply of qualified graduates' increases and the demand for educated graduates' decreases in a harsh time, some graduates will have no chances of finding suitable jobs. Although the number of graduates from HEIs is only a low percentage of the total labor force, some graduates find it hard to get jobs.

6.9   Strategies and Measures for Further Reforms of the System of Employment

6.9.1   Strategies and Measures for Further Reforms of the System of Employment For Graduates in Higher Education Institutions

6.9.1.1   Strengthening Functions of Government Management

In order to strengthen the functions of government management, three measures are necessary.

Firstly, governments should strengthen macro-management and guidance of reform of the system of employment. Governments should make economic regulations on human resource allocation in special regions and professions. For graduates who would like to work in remote areas and areas with difficult working and living conditions, better remuneration and subsidies should be given by governments or favorable policies should be made for localities. These graduates can be exempted from tuitions and fees in HEIs.

Secondly, governments should recognize the importance of ideological education. In the past, ideological education played an important part in the assignment of graduates. In new situations, the ways and methods of ideological education should be innovated. And it should not be discarded.

Thirdly, governments should make guidance on HEIs. The establishment of specialties in HEIs may be intimately oriented toward market needs. So the "cold" specialties may be in danger. Some basic disciplines may vanish. Some "hot" disciplines may not reflect the true social needs; they may be a temporary fashion. So governments should make guidance and management of the information and provision of subsidies for the so-called "cold" specialties which are important for national development.

6.9.1.2   Active Participation by Enterprises

In order to solve problems in enterprises, on the one hand, the modern enterprise system should be established so as to make the long term development of enterprises the main task of managers. On the other hand, employers should not set very high criteria of employment too high because students who have graduated from HEIs are still scarce human resources. How to use these precious resources to get maximum benefit is the challenge for the governments and enterprises.

6.9.1.3 Strengthening Ideological Education for Graduates

In order to solve problems faced by graduates, ideological education is necessary. The graduates' social responsibilities should be increased.

6.9.1.4 Increase in the Requirements for Graduates

In order to tackle the decrease in requirements for graduates, the main task is to maintain a fast economic growth rate. One percent of economic growth rate in national economy means millions of new jobs. The economic construction should be adjusted so as to make balanced developments of labor-intensive industries, capital-intensive industries and knowledge-intensive industries. Scientific and technological advance should play a much more important part in the economic growth. The allocation of labor resource should be regulated so as to contain more job opportunities.

Specialized higher education should be reformed. Vocational and technical education should be the main features in these schools. Students' practical competence and innovative competence in these schools should be cultivated more effectively.

Measures should be taken to change the disadvantaged position of female graduates and graduates from rural areas. Employment should be based on merit. Contest-based system in employments should be strengthened.

6.9.1.5 More Effective Guidance on Employment

In order for graduates to adjust to labor markets and find jobs with rational ways, it is necessary to make correct guidance on employment (Cai 1997).

Firstly, HEIs should take guidance on employment as a basic discipline and make efforts to research on this discipline. The course of guidance on employment should be open and include in institution program. Selective courses about employment should be opened. This kind of courses aim at helping students to establish correct viewpoint of life, viewpoint of moral development and helping students to know correct ways and methods of choosing jobs.

Secondly, HEIs should use modern information technology to conduct guidance on employment. Movies, videos, special websites can be used to conduct vivid guidance on employment.

Thirdly, face to face guidance also should be conducted. When students are in the stage of actual choice of jobs, psychological counseling, career counseling, guidance on techniques and methods should be given to students.

In order to facilitate counseling service in employment guidance, the following measures should be taken. The system of employment counseling and information services should be established and perfected. This system should make HEIs to collect, store and find information about graduates who are needed by employers.

This system should also make employers provide information about requirements for labor forces and professionals. The national or regional internets should be the basis of such a system. All graduates across all over the whole country should be included in this system. Modern information means should be used, and the complete information data bank should be established. The accuracy and punctuality of information provision should be guaranteed. HEIs should strengthen the connection with employers and make systematic research on employment markets.

Reference

Cai. (1997). The *reform of the system of higher education and analysis of its comprehensive benefits*. Beijing: People's Education Press.

Chapter 7
Expanding the Channels: Education Financing System in China

7.1 Introduction to the System of Financing of Education

7.1.1 The Concept of the System of Financing of Education

The system of financing of education is a part of the educational system. It deals with issues such as how to get funds for education, how to distribute educational investment between various levels and types of education and schools, how to use educational investment efficiently. The system of financing denotes the policies, laws, regulations, mechanisms that pertain to obtaining and using of educational investment so as to facilitate educational development. Research on the system of financing of education is useful for making scientific arrangement of educational investment, obtaining and allocating educational investment effectively, making better use of educational investment (Min 2002).

Financing of education is a part of the national financing process and outcome. The term of China's education input encompasses all funds for running schools in the national education system. It includes allocations from the state budget, i.e. budgetary appropriations at different administrative levels, urban and rural education surcharge, expenditure by enterprises for setting up their own primary and secondary schools, and tax breaks for business run by schools. It also includes financing outside the state budget, such as monies for schools set up by individuals or community organizations, donations to educational institutions, tuition and miscellaneous fees paid by students.

Financing of education reflects some economic relations such as the relations between educational departments and other departments, relations between governments and schools, relations between national education investment and individual investment.

© Springer Nature Singapore Pte Ltd. and Higher Education Press 2018
M. Yang and H. Ni, *Educational Governance in China*,
https://doi.org/10.1007/978-981-13-0842-0_7

7.1.2   Classification of the System of Financing of Education

The sponsors of educational institutions are the bearers of educational investment, but they are not necessarily the only bearers of investment. Educational investment can be classified in different ways.

According to the financing basis, the system of financing education can be classified as the system of input-oriented financing, system of throughput-oriented financing and the system of output-oriented financing. When financial means are made available to cover distinct costs such as costs of faculties and staff, material operating costs, and costs of investment, this system of financing of education can be called input-oriented financing of education. When governments provide funds for throughputs in the educational process, the activities performed by an institution are paid for, the system of financing is said to be throughput-oriented financing. When the financing of education is based on achievements of the institution, the system of financing of education it is said to be output-oriented financing.

Wan Shanmei, the author of *Study on Educational Input and Output*, classified the system of financing of education into three kinds, namely the system of educational budgetary management, the system of budgetary appropriation and the system of tuitions and fees (Wan 1996).

National budget includes the state's budget and local budgets. The system of educational budgetary management refers to the basic system concerning the distribution relationship between central government and local governments and the relationship within various local governments.

The System of budgetary appropriation refers to ways and methods of educational budgetary appropriation. Basic ways of budgetary appropriations include incremental budgeting, formula budgeting, performance budgeting.

The System of tuitions and fees refers to ways and methods of students' paying for education.

According to sources of educational investment, there are three systems of financing education. The first system is the State dominance system of financing of education. In this case, the State-run schools receive all their financing from the government which also subsidizes students' living expenses. Typically, public funds are channeled to schools directly from ministries or departments of finance. However, some governments may establish intermediate financing organizations that lie between governments and schools. There are many reasons, historical, institutional and political, that may account for the central role of governments in financing of education.

The second is the cost-recovery system. Educational institutions may be seen as service institutions that can be relied on to serve the wider interests of society and the economy, and alternatively they can be regarded as commercial enterprises that provide services for the benefit of individuals.

The third system is the system of diversification of educational financing. The possibilities of extensive cost-recovery may be constrained in many developing countries. The system of diversification of financing means that not only the government appropriation and cost-recovery means that not only the governmental appropriation and cost–recovery means are the source of educational finance, but also educational institutions can raise funds on their won; they can engage in selling instruction service, and receive donations from society at large.

7.1.3 Functions of the System of Financing of Education

Financing of education is the first driving force and the continuous driving force of educational development. Without the necessary educational funds, education activities cannot be embarked on. Financing of education is the fundamental guarantee for making education a strategic priority.

7.1.4 Factors Influencing the System of Financing of Education

What kind of system of financing of education a State should adopt in a definite given period depends on the economic system, finance system and system of educational management. As the economic system, the finance system and the educational management system change, the system of financing of education will change inevitably.

The historical development of financing of education in China can be classified into five stages.

7.2 The System of Financing of Education at the Completion of Socialist Restructuring (1949–1956)

7.2.1 The Reform of the System of Financing of Education (1949–1956)

7.2.1.1 Establishment of Central Unitary Finance Administrated at Different Levels

One cannot understand the operation mechanism of financing of education without knowing how the system of finance functions in a country. No doubt, the system of financing of education is closely connected with the system of finance.

At the beginning of the founding of the People's Republic of China, the system of finance was not unitary across the whole country. The institutions which obtained revenue and the institutions which used the expenditures did not have an effective coordination concerning the management of finance. So in 1949, the system of central finance was set up in PRC.

7.2.1.2 Transition from the System of Unitary Financial Management System to Multi-level Financial System

In 1950, PRC decided to establish a highly centralized and unitary financial management system. In other words, funds were in the hands of the central government and under the control of the central government. The central government had the powers of management of finance. The central government followed a policy of uniform management of revenue and expenditure. Local governments got funds from central governments and spent money in accordance with the rules and regulations issued by the central government. This system was in operation in the period 1950–1952.

In the period of 1952–1953, the central government established another system of finance. This system of finance is characterized by a separation of financial revenues and financial expenditures, and devolved financial powers to lower-level administration. This system was called the system of three-level financial management.

In 1953, the Administrative Council stipulated that universities and colleges under the jurisdiction of the central government would get funds from the central government, and the funds must be listed in the budget of the central government (He 1998a, b). The funds in universities and colleges under the jurisdiction of the great administrative regions must be listed in the budget of the great administrative regions.

In 1953, the Administrative Council stipulated that various educational administrative departments must strictly implement the system of three-level financial management.

In the period of 1950–1953, China set up a system of three-level financial management, namely management at level of the central government, the governments of the great administrative regions, and the provincial governments.

In November 1952, the Central Committee of the CCP decided that the People's Commission was changed into Administrative Commission. The administrative Commission should represent the central government to guide and supervise local governments under the guidance of the Central Committee of the CCP. Here the governments of the great administrative regions were an administrative level whose functions were to be in charge of several provinces. The whole country was divided into six great administrative regions.

In 1952, the financial system at the level of the counties was established. By the end of 1952, there were 2149 counties in China. The People's Commission at the level of county is a kind of local government. This year, the financial system at the central government, provincial government and county government was set up.

7.2.1.3   The System of Unitary Management of Finance of Revenues and Expenditures from 1950 on

On 24 March 1950, the Administrative Council issued *Decisions on Unitary Management of Revenues and Expenditures*. The *Decisions* stipulated that, in order to overcome the imbalance in the national revenues and expenditures and the split between revenues and expenditures, it was necessary to establish a system of unitary management of financial revenues and expenditures.

The *Decisions* stipulated that expenditures for primary schools and normal schools could be raised from the local additional tax on agriculture paid by peasants. This kind of local additional tax was raised in conjunction with the State tax on agriculture. The rate of additional tax on agriculture paid by peasants should not exceed 15% of the same type of additional tax levied by the State.

Expenditures for primary schools in urban areas and expenditures for educational administrative department in suburbs could be provided by levying surtax. The methods, rules and rates concerning this kind of surtax should be examined and approved by the government of the great administrative regions. The current situation of expenditure and revenue would be put on records of Ministry of Finance. Only after being approved by the central government could the surtax be levied by the provincial governments.

Schools at various levels administrated by the Central Government should be supported through the budget of the Central Government and be administrated by the Ministry of Finance.

The county-run schools or schools that were administrated by the governments of prefectures, governments of provinces, and the Governments of the great administrative regions should be supported by the budget of the great administrative regions governments and the budget of government of provinces.

7.2.1.4   Reform of the System of Budget for Education in 1951

On 15 November, 1951, the Administrative Council issued *Circular on the Methods of Formulation of Budgetary Expenditures and Expenditures for Training of Cadres*. The *Circular* stipulated that expenditures in schools of all types and levels and all organizations for training of cadres that are run by governments at various levels, except for expenditures in schools run by the social groups, should be listed in the total budget of governments through budgetary expenditures or expenditures for training of managers.

The expenditures in schools at various levels that are sponsored by the ministries under the Administrative Council but administrated directly by Ministry of Education should be formulated as budget of the Ministry of Education. For schools sponsored by the ministries under the Administrative Council, the ministries should formulate the whole plan at the beginning of year. The plans and the expenditures in the year with detailed explanation of expenditure scheme should be examined and approved by the ministry.

The expenditures of training organizations should be administrated according to the above methods.

The expenditures for schools and training organizations that are administrated by the governments of the great administrative regions and governments of provinces should be administrated according to the above methods.

After examination and approval of educational expenditures, the ministries should avoid change of plans of expenditures.

It could be seen from the above Circular that the Ministry of Education had powers of establishment of educational institutions and expenditures in these educational institutions. This kind of system of budget had its strength in normalization of management of educational revenues and expenditures.

7.2.1.5 Budgeting Process of Educational Expenditures in the Early 1950s

On 20 March, 1953, the Ministry of Education, the Ministry of Higher Education, and the Ministry of Finance issued *United Circular on Budget of Educational Expenditures*. The *Circular* pointed out that the principles for educational budgeting was "making regulation and consolidation, facilitating development of key areas, making assurance of educational qualities, pushing forward educational undertakings steadily". As concerned with educational budgeting, the general expenditures such as the people's grants for students, expenditures for instruction and administration, expenditures of general facilities should be calculated according to the national budgeting criteria. The remunerations of teachers, staff and workers were calculated according to the criteria of salaries. The expenditures for architectures should be calculated according to the situations of climates in localities, price of products and services in the Great Administrative Regions. The expenditures of constructions and instruction facilities for key schools should be calculated on consideration of the key areas. Schools in same areas and with the same characteristics should be calculated according to the same criteria. Governments should make adjustment on educational budgeting by suiting measures to different local conditions.

The expenditures in primary schools were based on the controlled quotas for primary schools that were distributed to each region by the Ministry of Finance.

Teachers' remunerations in schools of various types and levels were based on the quantities of salaries calculated according to the adjusted criteria of 1952, plus 2.6% increase in the total amount of salaries in the previous year.

The *Circular* stipulated the scope of expenditures. The operating expenses of preschool education included the operating expenses of kindergartens that were administrated by educational administrative departments. The operating expenses of primary schools included operating expenses of public primary schools. The operating expenses of secondary schools included the operating expenses of public secondary schools. The operating expenses of secondary specialized education did not include the operating expenses of secondary technical schools and secondary hygiene schools. The operating expenses of higher education included the operating expenses of regular higher education institutions. The operating expenses of higher normal universities and colleges included the operating expenses of higher normal universities and colleges as well as the operating expenses of some teachers' training in these HEIs.

7.2.1.6   Administration of Educational Budgeting

From 1952 to 1953, the revoking of the great administrative regions was a great challenge for the reform of management of education. The education administrative departments made great efforts to set up new management institutions and formulate methods of management, strengthen the examination of financial budgeting and implementation of capital construction plans, and to improve the efficiency of the use of funds. The administrative responsibilities were delegated to the provincial governments. So the administrative system in terms of financing of education should be changed.

In 1954, in order to adapt to the needs of the reform of financial management system, the Ministry of Finance in conjunction with other ministries worked out and revised the fixed number of persons and quota for key public institutions. The system of fixed number of persons and quota aimed at making the financing of operation expenses for public institutions more rational.

On 30 July, 1954, the Culture and Education Commission under the Administrative Council issued *Directives on Strengthening the Management of Financial Affairs and Capital Construction.*

As the great administrative regions were revoked, the tasks of provincial governments in the management of educational financing were becoming increasingly heavier.

The *Directives* stipulated that cultural and educational administrative departments of provincial governments should establish and perfect the management institutions concerning the management of educational finance and capital construction. The bureau of education under provincial governments should establish an accounting department and capital construction department. If the tasks of capital constructions were too heavy, the department of capital construction would be set up.

The culture and education department under the provincial governments should strengthen the work of fixed personnel and fixed quota and budgeting management in terms of management of finance. At present the most important task was to establish and perfect units budgeting and accounting system. This system was useful to increase the vigor of the concerned departments, decrease the chaos of financial management, and increase the intimate connection between financial management and institution development.

The cultural and educational departments should pay attention to the economic management of construction capital and assure the qualities of projects in terms of capital management.

On 14 September, 1954, the Ministry of Education and the Ministry of Finance issued *Circular on Procedures of Solving Problems of Educational Expenditures*. The *Circular* stipulated that ministries under the Administrative Council, except for the national enterprises affiliated with the central government, should not receive applications of expenditures from subordinate administrative departments and allocate funds to subordinate administrative departments. The people's governments should transfer funds within the same kinds of expenditures.

In 1954, the State Council issued *Directives on Formation of Budget Draft*. The *Directives* stipulated that national budget was divided into central budget and local budgets; different levels of governments had different budgets.

7.2.1.7 Reform of Fixing the Number of Persons and Setting Quota of Facilities in Terms of Education Appropriation

In the early 1950s, public institutions in the fields of education, culture and hygiene faced certain problems like excessive size of staff, too many personnel, too high rate of administrators, too high criteria for building and facilities, too low of utilization of facilities, wastage of funds. So it was important to fix the number of persons and set quotas of facilities.

In 1955, the Ministry of Finance, in cooperation with the Ministry of Higher Education, the Ministry of Culture, and the Ministry of Hygiene issued *Joint Announcement on Improvement of Working out a Scheme for Fixing the Number of Persons and Setting Quotas for Facilities*. The *Joint Announcement* stipulated certain criteria of fixing number of staff, criteria for amount of buildings and facilities, criteria for expenses for administration and business, criteria for necessary quantity of equipment and material.

The system of fixing the number of persons and setting quota of facilities was to assure rational allocation of personnel and facilities and eliminate wastage of funds.

In the past, the number of staff was determined according to students-teacher ratios, the criteria of funds was an estimation, the fixing of quota of areas of building was also an estimation, and there was no quota of facilities

The system of fixing the number of persons and setting quotas for facilities was aimed at assuring the requirements of educational development. It was the true scale for measuring the needs for development of public institutions. Without the system, it was difficult for governments to allocate limited funds correctly and proportionally to public institutions. If we fixed the number of persons and quota for public institutions, public institutions would have the necessary material conditions, and people could improve the efficacy in using personnel, materials and funds.

The *Circular* also pointed out that there were three kinds of expenses. As concerned with personnel, fixing the number of persons should be determined by work load of staff in a unit. In a secondary school, the number of teachers was determined by total instruction hours with regard to instruction programs and the instruction hours that each teacher had. The number of administrators and workers was determined according to number of classes. The class size should be optimized according to regulations of education so as to allocate the teachers, staff and workers effectively.

As concerned with recurrent expenses, the items of concrete expenses were so many that the criterion of each item could be determined by the real quantities of consumption of facilities and materials and the prices of facilities and materials. The fixing of quota of facilities and materials should firstly be based on the consumption of facilities and materials, then on the monetary or the financial criteria of these facilities.

Concerning assets, the expenses of assets included the expenses for purchasing of high-price facilities and the expenses for basic construction. The criteria of assets should be determined according to the requirements of materials. The requirement of facilities should be determined according to the scale of the institutions and the actual use of these facilities.

In 1956, the Ministry of Education and the Ministry of Higher Education issued *Joint Directives on Quota for Expenses of Instruction, Administration, Facilities of Instruction, General Facilities*. The Joint Directives stipulated concrete quota for facility. The budget quota was the criteria for the Ministry of Finance to determine the budget of each university or college under the jurisdiction of various ministries.

In summary, in the 1950s, the framework of the system of financing of education in China was formed. Educational institutions receive state appropriation according to the unitary state budgetary plan. Unused funds had to be returned to governments at the end of year. Thus, the tightly controlled budgetary system provided no incentives for efficiency gains, and hampered the incentives of institutions and governments.

7.2.2 Financing of Primary Education and Secondary Education (1949–1956)

7.2.2.1 Financing of Private Education

From 1952 on, the development of private schools was encouraged by governments. On 15 November, 1952, the Ministry of Education issued *Directives on Rectification and Development of Private Primary Schools*. The *Directives* stipulated that public primary schools were developed rapidly. But as budgetary appropriation of government was limited, development of public schools did not meet the needs of citizens. So many persons in rural areas collect funds to set up schools by themselves. Governments advocated the development of education through governmental support and the running of schools by the masses. But in the process of running schools by the masses, there were some problems.

Firstly, the rich villages and big villages established primary schools; usually these schools were public schools. The expenses of running the schools were taken from governments. But in the poor and small villages there were not a school in the past; the masses could set up schools by themselves, but the expenses were to be born by themselves. The masses often criticized this phenomenon.

Secondly, in the process of running of primary schools, the masses lacked planning and guidance. Although schools were established, some schools could not run well or even were suspended for shortage of funds and qualified teachers.

Thirdly, in some counties, some former public primary schools were transformed into private schools, and these schools could not be preserved; the masses bore great loss.

In order to solve these problems, governments should establish public schools with good plans and encourage the masses to develop the private schools if they had definite conditions. With regard to the development of private schools, the establishment of private schools should be based on volunteer actions of the masses; the masses were mobilized for financing these schools on the basis of equity and rationality. The running of private schools should be centered on the rich and big villages. The establishment of private schools should be conducted through planning. The establishment of public schools should center on the factories and poor villages. Those private schools that had difficulties in operation funds could be transformed into public schools and receive public funds. For those private schools that were short of expenses, they could receive subsidies from governments.

On 26 November, 1953, the Ministry of Education issued *Directives on Consolidation and Improvement of Primary Education*. The *Directives* stipulated that from 1954 on, localities should put educational expenditures into the budgeting of governments at various levels according to administrative relations. The expenses of construction of buildings and renovation of facilities should be born by budgeting expenditures of governments in counties or cities. The expenses of construction of buildings and renovation of facilities for public schools in rural areas should be born by governments of counties.

7.2.2.2 Charging Fees in Primary Schools and Secondary Schools

On 19 1955, the Ministry of Education and the Ministry of Finance issued *Circular on Management of Fees in Primary Schools and Secondary Schools* (He 1998a, b). The *Circular* pointed out that the State spent a lot of funds in education, and that the amount was increasing. But primary education and secondary education could not meet the requirements of the masses. To fulfill the aspirations of the masses, charging of fees in primary schools and secondary schools was an effective measure for solving problems faced by development of education and meeting requirements of the masses.

The *Circular* stipulated that the criteria of fees should be rectified. At present the criteria across schools and regions were not consistent. The Ministry of Education and the Ministry of Finance therefore put forward new criteria on the basis of local economic and cultural conditions and balanced development of neighboring localities. The fees in rural areas were lower than that in urban areas. The fees in primary schools were lower than those in secondary schools. The fees in junior primary schools were lower than those in senior primary schools.

The *Circular* stipulated that reduction of or exemption from fees should be considered. Students who had difficulties in paying fees could make an application for reduced fees or for exemption from fees, partially or wholly. The proportion of reduction of fees could not be over 20 percent of the total of fees in a school, the number of students that had privileges of reduction of or exemption from the fees could not be over 30 percent of the total number of students in a school.

The revenues from fees should be hand into the educational administrative department under the governments of counties, except for a part of the fees used for water supply for students and expenses for cleaning the houses. The main part of fees administrated by governments of counties should be used as fees for instruction and administration as well as fees for renovation of building and for supplementing facilities.

7.2.3 Financing of Higher Education in This Period

The Ministry of Education took responsibility for the supply of financial sources for those universities and colleges under its direct control. Other Ministries under the State Council financed universities and colleges under their jurisdiction. For those higher education institutions sponsored by local authorities, the financing of education was under the responsibility of governments at provincial or lower levels. Funds were channeled through the Ministry of Finance or Bureau of Finance to various ministries and local governments.

In 1949 and 1950, public HEIs administrated by the central government received public expenditure regularly.

On 5 May, 1950, the Administrative Council issued *Provisional Regulations on Management of HEIs Affiliated with the Great Administrative Regions.* The *Regulations* stipulated that the budget draft and final budget of HEIs affiliated with the great administrative regions should be submitted to and approved by the educational administrative departments in the great administrative regions.

On 23 September, 1954, the Ministry of Higher Education decided that the buildings and facilities of HEIs are owned by the State and administrated by the Ministry of Higher Education.

7.3 The System of Financing of Education at the Stage of Completion of Socialist Restructuring (1957–1965)

7.3.1 Reform of the System of Financing of Education (1957–1965)

7.3.1.1 Devolution of Management in Terms of System of Financing of Education

In the late 1950s, China made great efforts in economic and educational development. Great changes had taken place in the system of administration in China.

On 4 August, 1958, the Central Committee of the CCP and the State of Council issued *Regulations on Delegation of Powers of Management of Educational Undertakings*. The *Regulations* pointed out that in order to conduct activities in provincial governments, to strengthen cooperation between different regions, and to facilitate the running of schools by the whole Chinese Communist Party and all Society, the system of administration by mainly relying on industrial ministries should be reformed. Local governments' guidance on educational undertakings should be strengthened on the basis of the principle of combination of central governments holding the main powers with localities sharing powers.

The devolution of powers in educational administration forced localities to take great responsibilities in the establishment and development of schools at various levels.

In 1958, many provincial governments laid emphasis on allocation and use of educational expenditures, some provincial governments made specific examinations on allocation and use of educational expenditures. But in some regions there were some problems concerning allocation and use of expenditures. One government of prefecture reduced 26% of the budget for educational expenditures that was designated by government of province. One government of county reduced 5% of the amount of budget for educational expenditure designated by the government of prefecture. In the process of use of educational expenditures in some areas, the people's grants were reduced, expenditure for adult literacy was reduced, and teachers' salaries were reduced. As reduction in educational expenditure was universal, these problems could not be solved by increasing national budgets. Educational expansion and enhancement of educational quality could not be assured without commensurate financing of education.

7.3.1.2 Strengthening Financial Management in Schools

On 24 November, 1959, the State Council ratified *Suggestions for Further Strengthening Management of Educational Expenditure* put forward by the Ministry of Education and the Ministry of Finance. The *Suggestions* maintained that the Ministry of Finance or the Bureau of Finance under provincial governments should consult with the administrative agencies at the same level and be ratified by local governments.

So the Ministry of Education and the Ministry of Finance stipulated that hereafter financial administrative departments and educational administrative department should make intimate connection, strengthen cooperation and manage educational expenditures effectively. Departments of finance at various levels of governments should negotiate with departments of education and submit budget draft to governments at the same level for approval. Governments should classify educational expenditure as separate items. Governments at provincial levels decide the outline of educational expenditures on the basis of indicators issued by the central government. Provincial governments should formulate the criteria of educational expenditures according to national unitary criteria of education expenditure.

In the past educational expenditures which were formerly a part of the budget of education expenditure in government of counties were now delegated to the education expenditure in the government of commune; this situation should be changed; they should be listed in the budget of educational expenditure of the government of counties.

On 12 January, 1962, the Ministry of Education and the Ministry of Finance issued *Supplemented Opinions about Strengthening the Management of Educational expenditures*. The *Opinions* stipulated that the budgeting indicators for educational budgeting should be arranged on the basis of management of schools through hardworking and thrift, educational plans set by governments, and the requirement of the enhancement of educational qualities.

Education expenditure indicators should be used by educational administrative departments according to the principle of thrift. Provincial governments could allocate a part of surtax of agriculture in order to support the renovation of public schools and subsidize private schools. The fees collected in primary schools and secondary schools should be managed as special funds. Educational administrative departments should use funds in educational undertakings. The management of revenues and expenditures should have plans, be based on policies, have records, forbid wastage and corruption.

7.3.2 Financing of Primary Education and Secondary Education (1957–1965)

On 11 May, 1957, the Ministry of Education and the Ministry of Finance issued *the Opinions on Fees in Primary Schools and Secondary Schools* (He 1998a, b). The *Opinions* pointed out three problems faced in fees collection.

Some students complained that the criteria of fees was too high and were increasing. Some schools punish students by forbidding them to go to school because they did not pay fees. Some schools used fees to compensate for teachers' salaries and expenses for instruction and administration.

The charging of fees increased the burdens for teachers and influenced the relation between schools and families, between teachers and students.

The *Circular* stipulated that the criteria of fees should be rational. Students' right of learning should be guaranteed. Teachers' salaries should not be lessened because teachers did not collect fees. The task of collection of fees should not be born by teachers wholly.

On 21 March, 1960, the Ministry of Finance and the Ministry of Education issued *Regulations on Subsidies for Commune-run Schools*. The *Regulations* stipulated that People's Commune-run schools should rely on one's own efforts. The sources of educational expenditures could be diversified. People's Communes could use a part of public accumulations of funds to develop primary and secondary education. People's Communes could increase educational expenditures by collecting fees or using workforce of peasants for construction of schools. People's Communes could get a part of the lands allocated by People's Communes. The revenues from students' production labor could use as expenditures of schools.

7.3.3   *Financing of Higher Education (1957–1965)*

In 1957, the Ministry of Finance and the Ministry of Higher Education issued Provisional Regulations for Concerned Department Financial Management and Responsibility of Higher Education Expenses. The Regulations pointed that the Ministry of Higher Education put forward budgetary appropriation for each item line in universities and colleges on the basis of financial indicators for higher education expenses that were determined by the Ministry of Finance. The Ministry of Finance determined the financial indicators and made it known to concerned provinces, autonomous regions and municipalities.

7.4   The System of Financing of Education at the Stage of the "Cultural Revolution" (1966–1976)

7.4.1   *Reform of the System of Financing of Education (1966–1976)*

From 1966 to 1976, generally speaking, the society lessened investment. The underlying reason was that education was generally seen as a form of social consumption and its economic benefits were not easily recognized. Ironically, while the study of economics of education began to blossom in the Western countries during the 1960s, and the human capital revolution was seen as a revolution on economic thoughts.

7.4.1.1   The System of Finance (1968–1975)

In 1968, the system of centralized and unitary finance with the separation of expenditure and revenues was instituted. All revenues were provided to the central government by localities and then the central government distributed these expenditures to localities so as to meet the financial requirements in localities.

From 1971 to 1973, the system of finance was called the system of fixing total revenues and expenditures in localities. The central governments determined the total revenues and expenditures of each locality according to national economic plans. If in a locality the revenues surpassed expenditures, the locality should provide the surplus to the central government according to a fixed portion of the total revenues and expenditures. If in the locality the revenues were less than expenditures, the locality should be provided with a sum of money by the central government according to fixed portion of the total revenues and expenditures.

In 1974 and 1975, where localities obtained planned revenues, a part of the revenue was reserved by the locality, and a part of the revenue was handed into the central government.

7.4.2 Financing of Primary Education and Secondary Education (1966–1976)

On 15 October, 1966, the Ministry of Education and the Ministry of Finance issued *Opinions on Charging of Fees during the Great Cultural Revolution*. The *Opinions* stipulated that graduates who postponed graduation time should not pay fees any more.

On 10 March, 1967, the Ministry of Education and the Ministry of Finance issued *Circular on Fees in Primary Schools and Secondary Schools*. The *Circular* stipulated that the schools that were opened could collect fees as usual. The reduction of and exemption from fees should be taken seriously.

In 1973, a national forum on financing of education and hygiene was convened in Beijing. In the forum some opinions were put forward. Educational administrative departments should strengthen planned management of educational undertakings and educational expenditures through cooperation and negotiation. Educational administrative departments and financial administrative departments should put forward allocation scheme under negotiation by concerned departments; the scheme should be separated from the total budget, and made known to subordinates. Administrative departments should make examination and supervision on educational expenditures that are made known to subordinates.

7.4.3 Financing of Higher Education (1966–1976)

During the "Cultural Revolution", a limited sum of higher education expenditures was from the central government and provincial governments.

From 1970 on, some HEIs recruited workers and peasants as students. These students who were from factories could obtain remuneration from factories.

7.5 The System of Financing Education at the Stage of Building Socialist Commodity Markets (1977–1991)

In 1977, the Chinese economists and educators have begun to lobby for a guaranteed increase in educational expenditure in a way which reflects a strong faith in the tenets of human capital theory.

The shortcomings of the old system of financing of education were very evident. Firstly, educational expenditures were arranged on the basis of ministries' distribution and regional distribution; there were no ratios determined by laws.

Secondly, the increase or decrease of educational expenditures was not known to educational administrative departments ahead of time, so they could not make comprehensive arrangements for educational expenditures effectively.

Thirdly, the distribution of education expenditures had been imbalanced at various levels; the distribution was affected by artificial factors.

Fourthly, the sources of educational expenditure were relatively too few, so the system of financing of education should be reformed systematically.

7.5.1 Reform of the System of Financing of Education (1977–1991)

7.5.1.1 Favorable Conditions for Reform of the System of E System of Financing of Education

From 1978 on, the reform of economic system in rural areas made the change of the system of educational financing feasible. On the basis of improving living conditions, peasants wanted to consider their children's education more seriously. They wanted to invest in the education of their children actively.

In urban areas, State-owned enterprises have been reformed to increase the autonomy of enterprises. State-owned enterprises had more financial autonomy. Increase in revenues in these enterprises provided new ways of increasing the finance in education.

The national income distribution scheme changed greatly. In the total national income, the share of citizens and enterprises' income increased and the share of government's income decreased. The income of citizens in urban areas and rural areas increased rapidly. Statistics showed that in 1978 among the national gross domestic product, the share of the State's income, the collective's income, and the individual's income was 32.1, 17.9, and 50%, respectively. But in 1991, the of these three sources was 12.9, 22.4, and 64.7% respectively. Great increase in collective's income and individual's income made diversified investment possible.

7.5.1.2 Reform of the System of Finance in China (1977–1991)

In 1980, the State Council issued *Provisional Regulations on Reform of the System of Finance*. The new system was called the system of making division of revenues and expenditures and sharing of total revenues and expenditures by governments at various levels. The Regulations stipulated that from 1980 on, except for Beijing, Tianjin, and Shanghai, the other 14 provinces implemented the new system of finance. In terms of revenues, three factors should be mentioned. Firstly, the total revenues in central government and local governments were determined. Secondly, the ratio of sharing total revenues between the central government and local governments was determined. Expenditure was also divided into expenditures of the central government and expenditures of local governments.

Other 11 provinces implemented the original systems.

From 1985 on, the new system of the "making divisions of kinds of taxes, determining total revenues and expenditures, sharing revenues and expenditures at various levels" was implemented. Revenues were divided into fixed revenues in central governments, fixed revenues in local governments, sharing revenues between the central government and local governments.

7.5.1.3   The System of Taking Overall Responsibilities of Budget Within HEIs

In order to improve the system of financial management in higher education institutions, to enhance the efficiency of the use of funds, it was necessary to reform the system of internal financial management.

On 23 November, 1979, the Ministry of Finance issued *Circular on Promulgation of Provisional Methods of Taking Overall Responsibilities of Budget.* The *Circular* stipulated that any unit that adopted the system of total amount management in budgeting management, would transform from the old system of "approval of budgeting by the State and taking surplus back to department of finance" into the new system of "taking responsibilities of budget and reserving surplus by themselves". I

On 28 April, 1980, the Ministry of Education issued Announcement about the Promulgation of 'provisional method of taking responsibilities of budget in higher education institutions affiliated with the Ministry of Education'.

This *Announcement* noted that the new method was "taking responsibilities for the budget by higher education institutions and reserving surplus and put it into use at the end of the year."

According to the method, the surplus should be used for the improvement of instruction and research conditions and institutional development.

The budget was determined year after year. If financial situation, educational plans and criteria of expenditures changed, educational budget would be changed.

Each university and college should establish and perfect the economic accountability and the system of financial management, increase revenues and economize expenses.

Each university and college should determine the teachers' work load, formulate personnel's accountabilities and establish reward system.

On 11 June, 1980, the Ministry of Education, the National General Labor Bureau, and the Ministry of Finance jointly issued *Provisional Methods of Setting up Higher Education Institutions' Fund and System of Reward.* The *Provisional Methods* stipulated that higher education Institutions' fund came from HEIs 'affiliated factories' net profits, returns from transfer of research achievements, returns from the use of facilities by other institutions.

7.5.1.4　Diversification of Educational Expenditures

A.　Measures of increase in appropriations

In 1985, *Decision on the Reform of Educational System* pointed out that it was necessary to increase investment in education. Hereafter the increase in the central government's and local governments' educational appropriations should be higher than the increase in regular financial revenues. The increase in average cost of per student in schools should be guaranteed.

Party Commissions and governments at various levels should consider education as the strategic key, taking educational development as main tasks. Governments at higher levels should take these tasks as criteria of assessment of lower-level governments' performances.

B.　Charging of Surtax for education operation expenses

In early 1980s, conditions in schools in rural areas were poor; educational funds were deficient, teachers' remunerations were low. These phenomena affected the educational development in rural areas seriously.

On 13 December, 1984, the State Council issued *Circular on Raising Funds in Rural Areas* (State Education Commission 1992).The Circular stipulated that multi-channels of raising funds for schools in rural areas should be established. Except for the State's budgetary appropriations, governments of towns could collect additional tax on educational operation expenses. And social forces and individuals would be encouraged to run schools by using their funds. These funds should be used for special purposes.

Governments of towns collected additional tax. Agriculture units and enterprises in towns should hand in additional tax. The rate of additional tax could be based on revenues. The rates and methods of collecting additional tax should be determined by governments of towns on the basis of economic situations, bearing capacity of the masses, and the requirement of educational development. The scheme of additional tax should be approved by governments of towns.

Governments of towns should establish the management commission of education operation expenses. Commissions took responsibilities for managing expenditures of schools in the whole town.

C.　Charging fees from students

On 27 May, 1985, the Central Committee and the State Council issued *Decisions on Reform of Educational System*. The *Decisions* stipulated that charging of fees was an important way to increase educational funds. Except for enrollment through national plans whereby students were trained through state's appropriations, HEIs could recruit "contract training students". The production units give funds to HEIs according to contract. Students go to production units to work after graduation according to contract.

HEIs could recruit some students who paid fees to HEIs, for they could enter HEIs with relatively low scores in the national entrance examination. These students could find jobs by themselves after graduation.

After 1985, the Ministry of Education advocated a "Multi-Channel" strategy for raising educational funds from all possible sources. Local educational authorities were encouraged to raise funds through education surtax, profits from school-run enterprises, fees coming from students and different donations.

7.5.2 Financing of Primary Education and Secondary Education (1977–1991)

7.5.2.1 Implementation of the System of Compulsory Education and Reform of the System of Finance

On 12 April, 1986, the Fourth Session of the Sixth National People's Congress revised the Compulsory Education Law of the People's Republic of China.

This revised *Law* stipulated that the State should not charge tuitions for students receiving compulsory education. The State should establish a system of grants-in-aid to support the school attendance of poor students. The State Council and the local people's government at various levels should be responsible for raising funds for the operating expenses and capital construction investment needed for the implementation of compulsory education, and the funds were to be fully guaranteed. State appropriations for compulsory education should increase at a faster rate than regular state revenues, and the average expenditure on education per student should also increase steadily. In accordance with the provision of the State Council, the local people's governments at various levels should levy surtax for education, which should be used mainly for compulsory education. The State should subsidize those areas that are unable to introduce compulsory education because of financial difficulties. The State should encourage individuals and all segments of society to make donations to help educational development. The State should assist areas inhabited by ethnic minority groups to implement compulsory education by providing them with teachers and funds.

On 26 June, 1986, the State Council issued *Circular on the Implementation of Compulsory Education Law*. The *Circular* stipulated that local governments should provide a part of the income from extra revenues in localities to support compulsory education. The revenues in governments of counties should be used mainly for compulsory education. The central government provided funds for supporting the poor areas, subsidies for construction of border areas, subsidies for minority areas. The local governments which receive these kinds of funds or subsidies should use a part of these funds or subsidies to support compulsory education in these areas. The construction of building and increase in facilities should be included in the construction planning in urban areas and be coordinated with the development of compulsory education. The construction, renovation and expansion of State-run primary schools, secondary schools, and normal schools should be included in the capital construction planning of administrative departments that are in charge of these schools. The construction of primary schools and secondary schools that are run by communities should be supported by the communities.

7.5.3 Financing of Higher Education (1977–1991)

7.5.3.1 Budgetary Appropriation for HEIs

In October 1986, the State Education Commission and the Ministry of Finance issued *Methods of Reform on Financial Management in Higher Education Institutions*. The *Methods* stipulated that the yearly operational expenses in higher education institutions were calculated by the "comprehensive quota plus specific subsidy". Here comprehensive quota was the expenditure per student. According to different disciplines and graduate level or undergraduate level that the students majored in, on basis of possibilities of national financial capacities, the respective ministry would decide the "comprehensive quota plus specific subsidy" for each higher education institutions.

7.5.3.2 Reform of System of Enrollment and Change of
Financing of HEIs

On 27 May 1985, the Central Committee of the Chinese Communist Party issued *Decisions on Reform of Educational System*. The *Decision* stipulated that the system of enrollment of students in HEIs and the system of employment in HEIs would be changed. Students should be divided into two basic enrollment categories. One category belongs to directive or state-assigned plan, while the other category is the more flexible guided plan. Students enrolled under the directive plan will generally be exempted from paying tuition, and their other learning expenses will be incurred by the State. They must also accept state-assigned jobs in the area for which they were trained. Other students, under the guided plan, would be free to apply for more popular specialties that were prone to train for better-paying and more prestigious careers, and they would find employment on their own after graduation. This institutional arrangement could allow students from poorer families to attend college and guarantee enrollments in specialties that were unpopular. Usually, those fields included teacher training, agriculture, water conservancy, geology, petroleum engineering, and mining.

7.5.3.3   HEIs' Funds

On 11 June, 1980, the Ministry of Education, the State Bureau of Labor, the Ministry of Finance issued *Provisional Methods of establishment of HEIs' funds and System of Reward.*

The *Methods* stipulated that there were five sources of HEIs' funds: (1) the net profits from factories and farms affiliated with HEIs; (2) the net revenues from transfer of research product or the share of profit between HEIs and enterprises and the revenues of sale of research products after fulfilling the research product; (3) the net revenues from laboratories for use of laboratories and computers by other units or individuals, and the sale of product of laboratories; (4) the net revenues from delegated work by other institutions and individuals; (5) the net revenues from the use of facilities in HEIs.

The accounting of revenues should be conducted. There were clear divisions between the budget revenues and expenditures and non-budgetary revenues and expenditures. Budgetary revenues and expenditures should not be transferred into non-budgetary revenues and expenditures.

In order to obtain revenues, HEIs should formulate rational prices and HEIs' funds should be used in instruction, research, development of HEIs, the increase in welfares of teachers and rewards of teachers. They could be used in the improvement of instruction conditions and research conditions. They could also be used in renovation of facilities, experiment on new products, technological reform, supplement the circulating funds, establishment of new productive buildings. Funds of HEIs could be used in increasing the collective welfare of teachers, and the cultural and life facilities. Funds of HEIs could be used to reward teachers.

7.5.3.4   People's Grant in HEIs

On 17 December, 1977, the Ministry of Education and the Ministry of Finance Issued Methods of Setting up the People's Grant System for Students in Regular Higher Education Institutions, Secondary Specialized Schools and Technical Schools.

The *Methods* stipulated that the people's grants were classified as three kinds and nine subsidy levels. Students who majored in sports, navigation, dancing, drama, acrobatics would have extra subsidy for consumption of foods. Grants would be determined through self-application, discussion in the class, examination by the dean, and ratification by the school or college.

7.5.3.5   The System of Paying Unitary Fees in HEIs

On 22 August 1989, the State Education Commission, the State Bureau of Price, and the Ministry of Finance issued *Regulations on Tuitions and Fees for Accommodation in HEIs*. The *Regulations* stipulated that the criterion of fees would be 100 RMB Yuan per year in general areas. The criteria were based on the level of economic development, income of the masses, and competence of bearing fees. From 1989 on, entrants should pay fees for accommodation if they got accommodation in HEIs. The criteria of this kind of fees would be 20 RMB Yuan per year. The criteria of fees should be determined by the department of education, department of price, department of finance. Students who enrolled in normal universities and colleges could be exempted from fees.

To sum up, by the end of the 1980s, a system of financing of education was characterized as the budgetary appropriations of the government as the main source, to be supplemented by the funds raised through multiple channels.

7.6   The System of Financing of Education at the Stage of Building Socialist Market Economy (1992–2016)

In 1992, Deng Xiaoping made a supervision trip to the southern part of China, which boosted the reform process. Deng Xiaoping pointed out that science and technology were the first productive forces; sciences and technology was the key for national development; and education was the foundation for four modernizations.

In October 1992, Jiang Zemin said at the 14th Plenary Session of the Central Committee of the CCP that Education must be placed as the top priority in national development.

7.6.1   Reform of the System of Financing of Education (1992–2016)

7.6.1.1   Laws Concerning Educational Expenditures

On 31 October, 1993, the Fourth Plenary Session of the Eighth National People's Congress issued Teachers' Law of the People's Republic of China. The Law stipulated teachers' remuneration.

On 18 March, 1995, the National Congress issued *Education Law of the People's Republic of China*. In the eighth chapter of the *Education Law*, the input to education and guarantee of conditions were stipulated in detail.

On 15 May, 1996, *Vocational Education Law of the People's Republic of China* was issued. The input to vocational education was stipulated.

On 29 August, 1998, *Higher Education Law of the People's Republic of China* was issued. The input to higher education was stipulated.

In 2002, Law of Promotion of Private education of the People's Republic of China was issued. The input to private education was stipulated.

On 29 June, 2006, *Compulsory Education Law of the People's Republic of China* was revised. The new mechanism of educational expenditure in compulsory education was stipulated.

On 27 December, 2015, the Eighteenth Plenary Session of the 12th National People's Congress revised *Education Law of the People's Republic of China* and *Higher Education Law of the People's Republic of China and.* New regulations of financing of education were implemented.

7.6.1.2   Establishment of the System of Governments Taking Leading Role in Financing Education and Raising Funds Through a Variety of Other Channels

In 1993, *Program of China's Educational Reform and Development* pointed out that at present education expenditures were deficient and could not meet requirements of the open reform policies and requirements of professionals in the process of modernization. Increase in educational investment was a fundamental measure for the establishment of the strategic position of education. Governments at various levels, society, individuals should increase education funds with great efforts. The governments were taking a leading role in financing education.

In 1995, *Education Law of the People's Republic of China* stipulated that the State should institute a system of financing of education in which fiscal allocations constituted the main source, to be supplemented by funds raised through a variety of avenues in an effort to gradually increase input of financial resources directed to education so as to ensure that state-run educational institutions have stable source of revenues.

In 1996, *the Ninth Five-year Plan for Educational Undertaking and the Development planning in 2010* stipulated that it was necessary to establish and prefect the system of taking governmental appropriations as the main channel in conjunction with the auxiliary channels in surtax on education, tuition fees at the stage of non-compulsory education, development of factory-run schools, social donations, educational endowments.

On 14 October, 2003, the Third Plenary Session of the 16th Congress of Central Committee of the CCP issued *Decision on Perfection of Socialist Market Economy. The Decision* stipulated that the State should perfect and normalize the system of governments taking leading role in financing of education and raising educational expenditures through various channels, and the common development of public schools and private schools would be guaranteed.

On 29 June 2011, the State Council issued *Opinions on Further Increasing Budgetary Appropriation for Educational Development.* The *Opinions* stipulated that the ratio of national public educational expenditures to GNP should be increased to 4% in 2012. In order to achieve this goal, three measures should be taken, namely increasing the percent of public educational expenditures to public expenditures, unify education surtax from all kinds of enterprise (foreign and domestic-funded) and setting a certain percent of benefits of government's land sale into education.

7.6.1.3 Amount and Ratios of Financing of Education by the State

In order to solve the problems of arbitrariness of distribution of educational expenditure and the unstableness of increase in educational expenditures, the State made specifications of the amount and ratios of educational expenditures.

In 1993, *Program on China's Educational Reform and Development* put forward some important measures for increasing in educational expenditures. State's public education expenditures included budgetary appropriations at various administrative levels, urban and rural educational surcharges, and expenditure by enterprises for setting up their own primary schools and secondary schools, and tax breaks for business run by schools. The ratio of state's public education expenditure to GNP in China should be increased. The administrative departments of planning, finance, tax management should take measures to fulfill these goals. The proportion of education expenditures to the public expenditures should be increased and should be no less than 15% on average. The ratio of education expenditures to public expenditures should be determined by provincial governments.

On 13 January, 1999, the State Council issued *Circular on Education Rejuvenation Action Program Facing the 21st Century*. The *Circular* stipulated that from 1998 on, the central government should increase its total revenues for education by 1% over the previous year. In 2000, the central government should increase its total revenues for education by 3% over the previous year. The original public expenditure on education should not be changed. Provincial governments should increase total revenues for education by 1–2% over the previous year. From 1998 on, the part of revenues that surpassed the planned revenues should be used in education partially according to the ratio of educational expenditures to public expenditures.

On 13 June, 1999, the Central Committee of the CCP issued *Decisions on Deepening Education Reform and Pushing up Competence Education*. The *Decisions* stipulated that from 1998 on, the ratio of educational expenditures to total revenues of the central government should increase 1% compared with the rate in the previous year.

The ratio of national public educational expenditures to GDP increased to 4% in 2012, and the 4% goal stipulated in the *National Guidelines for Medium and Long-term Educational Reform and Development Program (2010–2020).* has been finally achieved.

In 2013, the ratio of national public Educational expenditures to GDP was 4.16%, and in 2014, the ratio was 4.15%.

7.6.1.4 Formulation of One Year's Requirement Plans for National Educational Expenditures

From 1994 on, under guidance of the Ministry of Finance, the State began to establish one year's requirement plans for national educational expenditures. One year's requirement plans for national educational expenditures was formulated by educational administrative departments at various levels, and submitted to the departments of finance at the same levels, and were approved by the People's Congress. This was an important reform in terms of management of educational system. This reform was beneficial to making balance of supply and demand of education expenditures at various places.

7.6.1.5 Surtax on Education in Rural Areas and Urban Areas

In 1993, *Program of China's Educational Reform and Development* stipulated that methods of levying surtax or additional tax on education should be perfected. Any units and individual that hand in tax on product, tax on added value, tax on business should be levied 2–3% of surtax on education in urban areas. In rural areas the ratio of surtax on education should be determined by provincial governments. Surtax on education should be used on education. Local governments could levy other surtax on education according to the requirement of localities, economic situations of the masses and the potentialities of the masses.

On 13 January, 1999, the State Council issued *Circular on Education Rejuvenation Action Plans.* The *Circular* stipulated that the management of levying surtax on education in rural areas and urban areas should be strengthened so as to get enough funds and these funds should be used in education after consulting with local industrial and commercial administrative departments.

On 29 July 2011, the State Council issued *Opinions on Further Increasing Budgetary Appropriation for Educational Development.* The *Opinions* stipulated all enterprises at home and abroad, as well as individuals of self-employment should be levying surtax, and the surtax is calculating on the actual amount of taxes for enterprises and individuals, and the rate is 3%.

7.6.1.6 Separation of Education Expenditures from Other Kinds of Expenditures and Independent Management of Education Expenditures

The national budget includes state budget and local budgets. State budget includes educational budget. The system of educational budgeting refers to examination, approval, formulation, distribution, management, supervision of educational budget.

In order to make sure that public education expenditures increased steadily, it was necessary to establish a rational system of educational budget. Although a system of educational budgeting was established in the past, it needed further reform.

In 1995, *Education Law of the People's Republic of China* stipulated that education expenditures coming from governments at various levels should be separated as items in the budget according to the principle of unity of power of task and power of funds.

In order to establish the system of separation of educational budget from other budgets and independent management of education budgets, three steps should be taken.

Firstly, operation expenses and capital construction expenses should be merged into one kind of educational expenditures.

Secondly, educational budget should be formulated by the education administrative departments, financial administrative departments, planning administrative departments. Educational administrative departments should put forward the draft of education budgets.

Thirdly, educational budgets was examined and approved by the governments and the people's congress. Financial administrative departments should allocate funds to educational administrative departments. Educational administrative departments should exercise the powers of allocation, powers of management, and monitoring.

At present, the new system has not been instituted. In the national budget draft and final budget report total education expenditures was specified. But the budget rank about educational expenditures did not change. Educational administrative departments did not have relevant powers of formulation of educational budget.

7.6.1.7 Establishment of the System of Monitoring of National Educational Expenditures

The respective system of monitoring of educational expenditures was required to know whether governments made enough input into education according to the laws and policies. 1n 1995, the State Education Commission and the State Statistical Bureau formally established the system of monitoring educational expenditures. Monitoring centered on implementation of policies in Program and Law of Education of PRC. The system of monitoring educational expenditures stressed that if education expenditures of government did not meet the requirements of laws and policies, measures should be taken by concerned departments. In order to let the society know and supervise educational input by governments, from 1995 on, the results of operation of the system of national monitoring of educational expenditures was publicized. It showed that the system of monitoring of educational expenditures was an effective measure for supervision on governments' performance in implementing laws and policies of educational expenditures and it facilitates the governments' establishment of strategic positions of educational development.

7.6.1.8 Normalization of Management on Charging Fees in Schools at Various Levels

Under wide survey and research on collection of fees in schools of all types and levels, the State Education Commission issued Provisional Regulations on

Collection of Fees in Primary Schools and Junior Secondary Schools, Provisional Regulations on Collection of Fees in Regular Senior High Schools, Provisional Regulations on Collection of Fees in Secondary Vocational Schools, Provisional Regulations on Collection of Fees in Higher Education Institutions. These four regulations were important polices to normalize collection of fees in schools.

On 12 January, 1993, the State Council approved and issued a proposal submitted by the State Education Commission, namely, *Speeding Up Reform and Actively Developing Regular Higher Education.* It was proposed that in the 1990s, the development of higher education would be aiming at raising the quality, quantity, structure and benefits of higher education all together. It was stressed that the system of unitary financing of higher education should be reformed, reform of system of financing of higher education should be explored, which should correspond to socialist market system, bringing the initiative of society into full play, and exploring new ways for higher education development.

In 2016, the Ministry of Education, The Commission of National Reform and Development, the Ministry of Finance and the Bureau of National News, Publishing and Broadcasting issued Opinions on the Normalization of Fees-charging and Check on Irrational Fees-charging. The Opinions stipulated that teachers were not permitted to have lessons for students after they leaving schools and charging fees for such activities, schools were not permitted to charge fees for enrolling students that were not qualified for enrollment in these schools on basis of the registration regulations. Criterion of tuitions and fees in HEIs should be based on the cost-monitoring, hearing and publishing.

7.6.2   Financing of Primary Education and Secondary Education (1992–2016)

7.6.2.1   Strategies and Polices of Input in Compulsory Education (1992–2000)

In 1993, Program on China's Educational Reform and Development stipulated that the surtax on education should be used for compulsory education. The criteria of fees and methods of collecting fees should be determined by provincial governments on the basis of the masses' potentialities. Management of fees should be strengthened. Students who were from poor families could be exempted from fees.

On 3 July, 1994, the State Council issued *Opinions on Implementation of the Program of Educational Reform and Development in China.* The *Opinions* stipulated that the State Council should formulate and promulgate Regulations on Educational Expenditure in Compulsory Education and governments at various levels should take effective measures to guarantee and increase compulsory education input. Teachers' remuneration in public schools in rural areas at the stage of compulsory education should be paid by the funds of governments of counties. In some very developed rural areas, teachers' remuneration could be paid by governments of towns. The community-supported teachers' remuneration should be paid partially by governments of counties and partially by the surtax on education collected by government of counties. The criteria of public expenses per student in schools at the stage of compulsory education should be determined by provincial governments. Government should make budgetary appropriation. The establishment, renovation, and expansion of schools at the stage of compulsory schools should be included in the capital construction plans in local governments. The central governments, governments of provinces, governments of prefectures, governments of counties should establish special funds for and increase expenditures to the remote regions and poor regions that used to conduct compulsory education. These special funds from the central government for compulsory education in remote regions and poor regions should be increased from this year's 0.2 billion RMB Yuan to 1 billion RMB Yuan in two years. Governments of counties and above should make arrangements for distribution of these expenditures and supervise the use of these expenditures.

7.6.2.2 Establishment of County-Based Management System and the Reform of Financing of Compulsory Education (2001–2007)

On 29 May, 2001, the State Council issued *Decision on Reform and Development of Basic Education*. The *Decision* stipulated that the change of system of management of basic education. The system of local governments' taking overall responsibilities, and managing at various levels was changed into the system of governments of counties taking main responsibilities. The central government and provincial governments should increase input on compulsory education in poor regions and minority regions though transfer of expenditures. Governments of provinces and governments of counties should strengthen the overall planning of education, make effective coordination, and guarantee the development of compulsory education in rural areas when making transfer of educational expenditures. Governments of counties should take main responsibilities in compulsory education especially in rural areas; they should make the overall planning of education, make regulation of geographical distribution of schools, establish schools and manage schools. Governments of counties should pay teachers' remuneration unitarily and timely.

From 2001 on, the Ministry of Education and the Ministry of Finance took the measure of providing textbooks to students from poor families in rural areas without paying for them. In March 2005, Wen Jiabao, the Premier of the State Council declared in Government Report that the tuitions and fees would be waived for students in primary schools and junior secondary schools in 529 poor counties, and students in primary schools and junior secondary schools in rural areas of West Regions were waived in 2006, students in primary schools and junior secondary schools in rural areas of Middle Regions were waived in 2006, students in primary schools and junior secondary schools in rural areas of East Regions were waived in 2006.

7.6.2.3   Establishment of County-Based Management System and the Reform of Financing of Compulsory Education (2008–2016)

In 2008, the State Council issued *Notice on the Waiving of Tuitions and Fees for Students in Urban Schools of Compulsory Education*. The *Notice* stipulated that from the autumn of 2008, tuitions and fees for students in all public schools in urban areas should be waived. Government provides students from poor families with free textbooks and some living expenses. In 2008, 28.21 million students received the policy bonus, 190–350 yuan was waived for each student in different urban areas.

From 2008 on, all students in public primary schools and secondary schools receive compulsory education needless of paying for it. Students should pay for textbooks, but students from poor families need not pay for it because of governments' support. Students should pay for lunch in schools, but students from poor families don't have to pay for that.

On 1 January, 2013, the Ministry of Education issued *Financial Regulations in Primary Education and Secondary Schools*. the Financial *Regulations* stipulated the management in schools. In comparison with the original system, the implementation of the new *regulations* should be beneficial to a more open and efficient financial management system.

7.6.3   Financing of Higher Education (1992–2016)

7.6.3.1   Great Expansion of Higher Education and Measures for Financing of Higher Education

In the period of 1999–2009 great expansion of higher education, the scheme of higher education input in China changed a lot. The old scheme of only relying on governments to support higher education institutions has changed; cost sharing, creation of revenues by HEIs, revenues from other non governmental resource, became important channels of financing of higher education.

The central government took 70 billion from the long national debts of national construction and used these funds for capital construction of HEIs.

From 1998 on, the central government increased its input of higher education; 1% of its yearly additional funds were put into higher education. Under the guidance of the central government, many provincial governments increased their input into the education.

7.6.3.2 The Changes of Main Channel and Supplementary Channels of Financing of Higher Education

On 27 December, 2015, the Eighteenth Plenary Session of the 12th National People's Congress revised *Higher Education Law of the People's Republic of China and*. The revised *Higher Education Law* changed the statement of system of financing of higher education, the 60th article of the original *Law* is "the State institutes a system wherein government appropriation constitute the bulk of the funds for higher education, to be supplemented by funds raised through various of avenus, so as to ensure that the development of higher education is suited to the level of economic and social development. The 60th article of the revised *Law* is "The State should institutes a mechanism of the runners of HEIs contributing the main part of finance, supplemented by students' rational cost-sharing and funds raised through various avenus. The reason for emphasis of runners' role in investment is that the governments are not the main investors for private HEIs.

In 2015, the Ministry of Education made an announcement that the former documents about the "211 Project" and "985 Project" were abolished. On 24 October, 2015, the State Council issued *Total Program of Pushing up the Building of World-class Universities and Disciplines (so called "double world-class")*. The total goal of higher educational development can be divided into three stages. At the first stage, some universities and disciplines become world-class universities and disciplines (from now to 2020). At the second stage, more universities and disciplines become world-class universities and disciplines (2020–2030). At the third stage, both the quantity and power of China's world-class universities and disciplines lead the world (2030 to 2050) and basically make China a county with strong higher education. In order to achieve these goals, the central government and local governments should give budgetary appropriation for building of world-class universities and disciplines.

7.6.3.3 The Financial Management in HEIs

On 2013, the Ministry of Finance and Ministry of Education issued revised Accounting System in HEIs. The revised system aimed at improving the ordinary accounting in HEIs and enhancing the efficiency of financial management.

In 2013, the Ministry of Finance and Ministry of Education issued *Notice on long-term Financing Mechanism for HEIs under the Jurisdiction of Ministry*. The Notice stipulated that Each HEI under the jurisdiction of ministry should establish this long-term financial mechanism, and in this year the budgetary appropriation for these HEIs would be 2.9 billion RMB yuan.

7.7 Current Situation of the System of Financing of Education

7.7.1 Law and Policies for the System of Financing of Education and Basic Sources of Revenues

7.7.1.1 Law and Policies on Educational Input

Up to now there is no separate educational input law, but there are some stipulations on financing of education within the concerned educational laws. *Education Law of the People's Republic of China* makes stipulations on input to education and guarantee of conditions. *Compulsory Education Law, Higher Education Law, and Vocational Education Law of the People's Republic of China* also make some stipulations on educational input in these fields.

7.7.1.2 Basic Funding Sources of Education

A. State and local budgetary appropriation

The system of financing of education in China is a system in which fiscal allocations constitute the main source, to be supplemented by funds raised through a variety of avenues.

The proportion of educational expenditure in the total fiscal expenditure of governments at various levels was gradually rising with national economic development.

The amount and ratios of educational expenditures are stipulated by the *Education Law* and regulations issued by the National People's Congress and the State Council. The increase of educational expenditure allocated by the governments at various levels should be at a higher rate than the growth of normal financial revenues so that the average educational expenditure per student increases gradually and a steady increase in teachers' salaries and in average public expenditure per student is guaranteed.

B. Surtax on education

Before 2005 surtax on education was levied by local governments to support compulsory education. The State Council and governments at or above county level set up a special education fund used mainly for the implementation of compulsory education in remote areas and poverty-stricken areas and in areas inhabited by ethnic minorities. Taxation authorities collected in full the educational surtax. These funds was managed by educational administrative departments and used mainly for the implementation of compulsory education. In 2011, in order to increase educational public expenditure, the State Council stipulated that this kind of educational surtax should be levied again.

C. Tuitions and fees

In schools at thee stage of compulsory education tuitions and miscellaneous fees are not permitted from September of 2008 onwards. The true free compulsory education has been implemented completely. Normally students should pay for textbooks and lunch at schools.

In senior secondary schools and senior vocational schools, tuitions and fees are collected by schools. The criteria of tuition and fees are determined by educational administrative departments, departments of price and departments of finance.

From 1997 on, students in universities and colleges should pay tuition and fees to HEIs. The amount of tuition and fees is different in different regions and HEIs. Usually local governments will determine the criteria of tuition and fees.

D. Revenues from industries affiliated with schools at various levels

The State adopts preferential measures to encourage and support schools in carrying out work-study programs, community services and in setting up schools affiliated with factories, provided that they do not interfere with the normal activities of education and instruction.

7.7.1.3 Structure of Financing of Education in China

The total educational expenditure in 2011, 2012, 2013, and 2014 is respectively 2386.929, 2769.597, 3036.472, 3280.646 billion RMB yuan in China.

The national public educational expenditure in 2011, 2012, 2013, and 2014 is respectively 1858.67, 2223.623, 2448.822, 2642.058 billion RMB yuan in China.

The governmental budgetary appropriation in 2011, 2012, 2013, and 2014 is respectively 1680.456, 2013.417, 2140.567, 2257.601 billion RMB yuan in China.

The ratio of national public educational expenditure to GNP in 2011, 2012, 2013, and 2014 is 3.93, 4.28, 4.16, 4.15%, respectively.

Per student's public expenditure on education in regular primary schools in 2011, 2012, 2013, and 2014 is 4996.04, 6128.99, 6901.77, 7681.02 RMB Yuan, respectively.

Per student's public expenditure on education in primary schools in rural areas in 2011, 2012, 2013, and 2014 is 4764.65, 6017.58, 6854.96, 7403.91 RMB Yuan, respectively.

Per student's public expenditure on education in regular junior secondary schools in 2011, 2012, 2013, and 2014 is 6541.86, 8137, 9258.37, 10,359.33 RMB Yuan, respectively.

Per student's public expenditure on education in regular junior secondary schools in rural areas in 2011, 2012, 2013, and 2014 is 6207.10, 7906.61,7906.61, 9711.82 RMB Yuan, respectively.

Per student's public expenditure on education in regular senior secondary schools in 2011, 2012, 2013, and 2014 is 5999.60, 9477.75, 8448.14, 9024.96 RMB Yuan, respectively.

Per student's public expenditure on education in vocational secondary schools in 2011, 2012, 2013, and 2014 is 6148.28, 7563.95, 8784.64, 9128.83 RMB Yuan, respectively.

Per student's public non-personnel expenditure on education in regular higher education institutions in in 2011, 2012, 2013, and 2014 is 13,877.53, 16,367.21, 15,591.72, 16,102.72 RMB Yuan, respectively.

Per student's public non-personnel expenditure on education in regular primary schools in 2011, 2012, 2013, and 2014 is 1366.41, 1829.14, 2068.47, 2241.83 RMB Yuan, respectively.

Per student's public non-personnel expenditure on education in primary schools in rural areas in 2011, 2012, 2013, and 2014 is 1282.91, 1743.41, 1973.53, 2102.09 RMB Yuan, respectively.

Per student's public non-personnel expenditure on education in regular junior secondary schools in 2011, 2012, 2013, and 2014 is 2044.93, 2691.76, 2968.37, 3120.81 RMB Yuan, respectively.

Per student's public non-personnel expenditure on education in regular junior secondary schools in rural areas in 2011, 2012, 2013, and 2014 is 1956.66, 2602.13, 2983.75, 2915.31 RMB Yuan, respectively.

Per student's public non-personnel expenditure on education in regular senior secondary schools in 2011, 2012, 2013, and 2014 is 1687.54, 2593.15, 2742.01, 2699.59 RMB Yuan, respectively.

Per student's public non-personnel expenditure on education in vocational secondary schools in 2011, 2012, 2013, and 2014 is 2212.85, 2977.45, 3578, 3578.25 RMB Yuan, respectively.

Per student's public non-personnel expenditure on education in regular higher education institutions in 2011, 2012, 2013, and 2014 is 7459.51, 9040.02, 7899.07, 7637.97 RMB Yuan, respectively.

7.7.2 Financing of Primary Education and Secondary Education

7.7.2.1 Financing of Compulsory Education

In public primary and secondary schools, educational funds are provided mainly by governments. Governments of counties are responsible for providing educational expenditures for schools under their jurisdiction. Teachers' salaries are provided to each teacher' special salary account by governments of counties in each month. The funds come from budgetary appropriation in government of counties. The criteria of teachers' salaries are determined by the system of salaries. As far as operation expenditures is concerned, for each student who is enrolled in school, the government of county will provide a sum of money being equal to the definite criteria of public expenditures per student.

7.7.2.2   Financing of Senior Secondary Education

Senior secondary education is not compulsory education. Senior secondary education is a kind of selective education. Students who have graduated from junior secondary schools can either choose to go to senior secondary schools or leave schools to work. All senior secondary schools charge tuition and fees from students.

Regular senior schools are funded by governments. In public regular senior secondary schools, teachers receive salaries from local governments' budgetary appropriations. In these schools for every student who is enrolled in school, a sum from public expenditure would be given to the schools for operation of schools.

In senior vocational schools, students should pay for education. If these schools are sponsored by educational administrative departments, governments should make budgetary appropriation for these schools. If these schools are sponsored by other departments, the departments should arrange support for them.

7.7.3   Financing of Higher Education

7.7.3.1   Tuitions and Fees in HEIs

In 1993, *Program on China's Educational Reform and Development* stipulated that the criteria of tuitions and fees for students in schools at the stage of non-compulsory education should be increased. The criteria should be determined by provincial governments. Management of collection of fees should be strengthened. The collection of fees should be in accordance with the laws and policies.

On 13 June, 1999, the State Council issue *Decision on Deepening Education Reform and Pushing up Competence Education*. The *Decision* stipulated that at the stage of non-compulsory education the ratio of tuitions and fees to the training cost should be increased. The cost sharing mechanism in accordance with the socialist market economy should be instituted. Educational loan, system of subsidy and scholarship should be established and perfected.

7.7.3.2   The Funding of Higher Education in "211 Project" and the "985 Project" and the Evaluation of Disciplines

In 1993, *Program on China's Educational Reform and Development* proposed that, in order to meet the challenges of new technological revolution in the world, 100 key HEIs and 100 key disciplines should be run well by concentrating the State's efforts and locality's efforts. In the beginning of the 21st century, some university and some disciplines and specialties should be among the top institutions in educational quality and scientific research competence.

In 1995 the State Council approved *Total Construction Plan for "211 Project"*. Thus the "211 Project" was launched. The so-called "211 project" aims at setting up 100 key HEIs and 100 key disciplines in the beginning of 21st century.

In 1996, the State Council, the State Education Commission, the State Planning Commission, and the Ministry of Finance instituted a coordinating group for "211 Project".

During the period of 1996-2000, 99 HEIs were approved for inclusion in the "211 Project"; 602 Key disciplines were approved to be included in the "211 Project". A sum of 10.9 billion RMB Yuan was spent for the "211 Project".

The "211 Project" has achieved the original goal. Firstly, the improvement of conditions of running schools, the enhancement of educational quality was assured. Secondly, a large number of key disciplines have been the main bases of national knowledge innovation and technological innovation. Thirdly, management mechanism in higher education institutions has been instituted.

In 2016, the disciplines evaluation covering all universities has been conducted; the issue of connecting evaluation result to the financing of universities and disciplines have been a debated issue. According to international experience, formula-based performance funding is beneficial to leading to an objective evaluation and funding results.

7.8 Some Problems Facing China in the System of Financing of Education

7.8.1 Problems Facing China in the Macro-management in Financing of Education

7.8.1.1 Lack of Specific Law of Educational Input

From 1986 on, there are laws concerning compulsory education, teachers, education, higher education, vocation education, private education. In these laws, there are some articles talking about educational revenues and expenditures. But these articles only talk about educational revenues and expenditures in a simple way; many articles talk about the basic principles but they do not talk about the procedures and methods of financing of education in details. For instance, the *Education Law* does not make detailed statements about subjects of financing, channels of financing of education, the education cost accounting, ways of delivering education expenditures. As there is not a specific law concerning educational input, the rights and responsibilities of governments, schools at various levels, enterprises, families, and social groups are not formulated clearly.

7.8.1.2 Need for Establishing a System of Independent Budgeting in Educational Revenues and Expenditures

From the early 1990s on, independent educational budgeting was put forward by some scholars. And the central government supported the idea. In 1995, *Education Law of the People's Republic of China* stipulated that educational revenues and expenditures of governments at various levels should be listed as independent items in financial budgeting in accordance with the principle of the combination of powers for fulfilling tasks and powers for financing these tasks.

At present, only the central government and provincial governments list the total education expenditures in the budgeting report submitted to the People's Congress for examination and approval. The delegates at various levels do not know the details of education budgeting and they cannot make effective examination of education expenditures. So the government listing the total education expenditures as an item for examination is an initial step for assuring the necessary education expenditures. The governments of prefectures and counties did not list as educational expenditures as independent items.

The obstacle is the lack of education input law that formulates procedures and methods of a system of independent educational budgeting.

7.8.1.3 Lack of Normalized Transfer of Educational Expenditures Between Governments

One of the main tasks of the governments in China is to provide relatively equal public service to all citizens. Education, especially compulsory education, is an important part of public services. As the economic development and financial competence across regions is not balanced, the public services across regions are also not balanced. So the transfer of expenditures and the different ways of provision of public services are necessary for governments.

There are two ways of transfer of expenditures between governments, namely, unconditional transfer and conditional transfer. The former is the direct grant. The later is the specific subsidy. At present, China takes unconditional transfer as the main way of transfer, supplemented by the conditional transfer. The unconditional transfer of educational expenditures is conducted through procedure of application, examination and approval. This way of transfer is on the basis of personal judgments and is not as objective as most persons anticipate. The amount of transfer of educational expenditures is not enough. The way of transfer is not as normalized as most peoples anticipate. So the system of transfer of educational expenditures needs to be reformed.

7.8.1.4 Lack of Criteria of Financing of Education in Monitoring and Evaluating of Educational Expenditure

As far as we know, there are no systematic criteria of cost-sharing and system of accounting in schools at various levels. The lack of cost norms make financing of education and distribution of funds among various schools a difficult task. The administrators responsible for the financing of education cannot know exactly how much funds the units need for fulfilling definite tasks without objective criteria of operation cost. As there are no definite norms in scale of schools and size of staff in units, education cost cannot be calculated on a solid basis.

7.8.2 Problems Facing China in Financing Primary Education and Secondary Education

7.8.2.1 Deficiency of Educational Expenditure in Rural Areas

The deficiency of educational expenditure in rural areas is serious. The shortage of educational expenditure causes three results.

Firstly, in some cases teachers' remuneration in rural primary and secondary schools cannot be paid on time. The delay of payment of remuneration to teachers is a problem that has not been solved for a long time. Except for the great and middle municipalities and developed provinces, the problem exists in a few rural areas.

Secondly, the basic conditions for running of schools at primary and secondary levels in rural areas have not been guaranteed completely. In rural areas there are dangerous buildings.

Thirdly, some primary schools and secondary schools in rural areas have been getting into debt. Since the 1990s, many primary schools and secondary schools obtained money from other persons and institutions in order to fulfill the task of the popularization of nine-year compulsory education. The money was used to construct of buildings and increase facilities for schools.

7.8.2.2 Indiscriminate Collection of Fees in Primary and Secondary Schools

The schools at the stage of compulsory education cannot charge fees from students. The tuitions and fees in public primary schools and junior secondary schools are waived completely. But some primary schools and junior secondary schools can charge fees from students coming from other school districts. In some developed regions the fees can be more than 20 thousand RMB Yuan. Miscellaneous fees charged by schools for provision of services such as buying learning materials and provision of lunch for students need to be monitored more strictly.

7.8.2.3 Marked Overinvestment in Higher Education at the Cost of Basic Education Development

At present, the distribution of education expenditure among primary education, secondary education, and tertiary education is biased toward tertiary education. In 1993 the education operation expenses per student among primary education, secondary education and tertiary education was 1:2.23:25. The ratio of educational operation expenses per student in HEIs was very high compared with other schools.

7.8.3 Problems Facing China in Financing Higher Education

7.8.3.1 After the Great Expansion of HEIs, Some HEIs Face Problems of Shortage of Educational Operation Expenditures

In some cases some HEIs have classes with over 100 students in a class. The dormitories are deficient and students have to rent rooms in areas far from universities and colleges. The dinning rooms are also deficient. Students do not have favorable learning conditions in some HEIs.

7.8.3.2 High Level of Tuitions and Fees

The increase in tuition and fees has been very high. In 2001 the central government stipulated that the tuition and fees in HEIs should not be further increased. So the expansion of higher education cannot be supported by increase in tuitions and fees. How governments and the society can maintain the rapid development of higher education becomes a new challenge.

7.8.3.3 Lack of Mechanism and System of Determining Rational Tuitions and Fees

From the late 1990s, the tuition and fees have become an important part of the revenues in HEIs. In 1999 the average tuitions and fees per student for all HEIs was 23.4% of the recurrent expenditure per student. In 2007 the average tuitions and fees per student for all HEIs is as 24.8% of the recurrent expenditure per student. The criteria of tuitions and fees are determined by provincial governments. Most students and their parents think that the criteria of tuitions and fees are too high; the increase of tuitions and fees is very salient. Some students feel that tuitions and fees are beyond their capacities. How to determine the quantity of tuitions and fees becomes an important issue.

Higher education is quasi-public goods. The criteria of tuitions and fees should be determined on consideration of higher education cost, income of most citizens, rate of return of higher education, supply and demand of higher education, and higher education policies.

At present there is no system of cost accounting in HEIs; higher education administrative departments and HEIs cannot provide accurate information on higher education cost, especially higher education cost in terms of recurrent expenditures. So the information of recurrent expenditures per student in HEIs cannot be obtained timely. The ratio of tuitions and fees to higher education cost cannot be determined on solid basis. The administrators determine criteria of tuitions and fees by personal judgments. This way is not a rational way to determine criteria of tuitions and fees, ignoring consideration of most factors affecting the tuitions and fees.

7.9   Strategies and Measures for Reform of the System of Financing of Education

7.9.1   Strategies and Measures for Reform of Macro-management of Financing of Education

The formulation and implementation of Law of Education Input is a very important measure for guaranteeing the steady increase in education expenditures and facilitating the reform and development of education. The Law of Education Input aims at solving problems facing the legal responsibilities of governments, society, individuals in educational input. The Law of Education Input should specify the responsibilities of governments at various levels, the system of financing of education, the ratio of public education expenditures to GNP, the system of independent education budgeting, the ratio of budgetary appropriations in education to the total budget for various governments, the responsibilities of individuals and social groups in financing of education, the supervision, examination and punishment of behaviors that are not in accordance with laws and regulations.

The system of independent education budgeting can guarantee the strategic position of education in national development. Some persons worry about the effect of independent education budgeting. If other departments also want to make independent budgeting, the State budgeting would be difficult to formulated. This anxiety is comprehensible but not necessary. Education departments take a much more important position in national economy and its strategic position cannot be superseded by other departments. Some persons are suspicious of the fact that other departments may not like to invest in education further, if the system of independent education budgeting is formulated. This worry is also not necessary because educational departments should take the main responsibilities in financing of education, supplemented by other departments' education input.

In order to establish the independent education budgeting system, five steps should be taken. Firstly, the respective laws and regulations should be formulated and implemented. Secondly, governments at various levels should list education budgeting as special items in total budgeting and separate educational budgeting from other budgeting. Thirdly, formulation of education budgeting should be the main responsibilities of departments of education and departments of finance. Fourthly, departments of education should make educational planning and formulation of education budgeting according to education planning. Fifthly, the People's Congress should pass regulations about the system of independent educational budgeting so as to assure the system of education budgeting can be implemented smoothly.

Governments should increase the amount of transfer of educational expenditures rapidly so as to address problems of imbalanced development of education across regions. The transfer of educational expenditures should be concentrated on compulsory education development in rural areas and poor areas so as to assure all children receive relatively equal education service, especially compulsory education service across all regions.

In order to reform the ways of transfer of educational expenditures, important measures should be taken.

Firstly, in determining the amount of transfer, ways of examination and approval should be substituted by the ways of factor analysis. The factor analysis includes various steps. The first step is rational classification of powers of fulfilling tasks and powers of financing of these tasks between governments at various levels. The second step is to determine standardized competence of obtaining revenues and standardized requirement of expenditures on the basis of the objective factors affecting revenues and expenditures. The third step is to determine the amount of transference of educational expenditures.

Secondly, powers scheme and benefit scheme across governments should be changed so as to make transference of educational expenditures feasible.

In order to evaluate the effectiveness of education, it is urgent to establish some evaluation indicators concerning effectiveness. In order to make financing of education more open, more equitable and fairer, it is urgent to use criteria-reference financing. So it is necessary to establish a system of management and evaluation in terms of financing of education in China. By using such a system, education revenues and expenditures can be distributed among regions and schools more objectively and rationally.

7.9.2   Strategies and Measures for Reform of the System of Financing Primary and Secondary Education

According to the guaranteeing mechanism of educational expenditure in compulsory education, governments of counties should take responsibilities for paying remuneration for teachers. But actually some governments of counties are short of competence for support basic operation cost in public institutions. So the central government and governments of provinces should make transfer of educational expenditure to compulsory education.

Governments at various levels should increase special funds for capital construction in poor areas. The governments of counties should make good plans for use of capital construction.

The geographical regulation of schools should be done systematically and completely. In the 1980s and 1990s, many villages established primary schools and junior secondary schools in localities. These schools were in good condition in the early 1980s. As time lapsed, the implementation of one-child policy and the transfer of rural work force to urban areas caused a rapid decrease in the number of children eligible for entrance into primary schools. So the rural primary schools set up by villages should be regulated as soon as possible. The government of counties should make a ten-year education plan or twenty-year education plan. In these educational plans, the geographical regulation should be considered seriously.

The debt of primary schools and secondary schools should be tackled prudently. In some areas, the debtors come to ask the schools to pay the debts and disturb regular educational order in schools. These phenomena should be prevented. The schools should make arrangement for paying their debts. If some schools cannot pay their debts after making sincere efforts, the government should give support for paying these debts by lawful procedures.

7.9.3   Strategies and Measures for Reform of the System of Financing of Higher Education in China

The pace of education expansion should be slowed down gradually. After many years of expansion of higher education, the scale of higher education in China is very large. Compared with the level of economic development, the pace of higher education development is not slow. Nowadays the main task of higher education institutions is to enhance quality (Li 2002).

The structures of higher education should be changed so that vocational higher education can be developed more rapidly.

There are three models for the development of higher education across the world.

One is the European model, in which the HEIs are mainly public HEIs; the governments provide the main part of educational expenditure; tuitions in HEIs are low, or higher education is free for students.

The second model is the East Asia model in which governments run very few public HEIs; the tuitions in public HEIs are low; most HEIs are private; tuitions in private HEIs are high.

The third model is the United States' model, in which public HEIs and private HEIs are of the same importance in the development of education. Levy called this model as parallel model.

China should learn from the East Asia model so as to develop higher education more rapidly. If China uses the European model, then governments should increase tuitions and fees in public HEIs, and the function of assurance of educational equity will not be guaranteed; governments should take responsibilities for financing public HEIs and responsibilities of assignment of graduates in public HEIs.

The central government and provincial governments should establish the system of cost accounting on higher education cost. Based on this system the training cost of students can be calculated on time. The researchers should give estimation of the rate of return in higher education so as to help determine tuitions and fees rationally. Administrators should establish a model to forecast supply and requirements of higher education. The policy factor and supply-demand factors cannot be estimated with accuracy. But we cannot use the model of forecasting tuitions and fees only by considering limited factors such as policy factors. The most important element in the model is the attitudes and competences of consumers in higher education.

Three steps should be taken. Firstly, governments, HEIs, intermediary organizations should provide information on factors affecting tuitions and fees as fully as possible. They should provide several schemes on determination of criteria of tuitions and fees. The hearing of tuitions and fees participated by respective administrative departments of governments including department of education, department of finance, department of planning, department of price as well as HEIs, students, parents, social groups should be held several times. Finally, governments should make decisions on criteria of tuitions and fees after making complete consideration on all respective opinions (Hao 1996).

References

Hao, K. (1996). *Market economy and education reform*. Guilin: Guangxi Education Press.
He, D. (Ed.). (1998a). *Important documents in the People's Republic of China (1949–1975)*. Haikou: Hainan Press.
He, D. (Ed.). (1998b). *Important documents in the People's Republic of China (1976–1990)*. Haikou: Hainan Press.
Li, F. (2002). *Research on efficiency in higher education institutions*. Beijing: Beijing Normal University Press.
Min, W. (2002). *A study on operation mechanism of higher education*. Beijing: People's Education Press.
The State Education Commission. (1992). *Important documents since the third plenary session of the 11th National Congress of the Central Committee of the CCP*. Beijing: Educational Science Press.
Wan. (1996). *Educational input and output*. Shijiangzhuang: Hebei Education Press.

Chapter 8
Balancing Between Social Equality and Meritocracy: The System of Examination in China

8.1 Introduction to the System of Examination

8.1.1 The Concept of the System of Examination

Examinations are both a subject of research and a subject of practice. Research about examinations attempt to solve a range of dichotomies: a big range of marks in one subject (such as mathematics) and a small range of marks in another subject; the measurement of actual attainment against the need to provide a form of rank order for grading; the ease of measurement using short questions against the difficulty of using longer essay-type questions.

Much of research on examinations has investigated styles of question, marker variations, multiple marking, and statistical procedures for utilizing the data available.

8.1.2 Classification of the System of Examinations

The system of examinations can be classified in various ways. One kind of classification is the system of internal and external examinations. In an educational system, examinations are normally conducted within the schools, especially in classes or out of schools. Internal examinations are tests or inquires conducted by persons who are usually teachers and managers in schools. External examinations are tests and inquires conducted by outsiders, that is to say, people who are not directly connected with the schools concerned. The underlying reason for instituting external examinations is an egalitarian one, stemming, as it does, from a desire to remove all traces of favoritism or patronage in the process of the examination.

© Springer Nature Singapore Pte Ltd. and Higher Education Press 2018
M. Yang and H. Ni, *Educational Governance in China*,
https://doi.org/10.1007/978-981-13-0842-0_8

8.1.3 Functions of the System of Examinations

The system of examination, then, plays an important part in modern society. Viewing from the outside, examinations have the functions of testing the knowledge of persons in view of certifying their competence in the subject or field of study. In modern society, the professions develop their own entrance tests. Young people intending to become doctors, apothecaries, engineers, or other specialists, take these tests to prove their competence and capabilities. For the public who seek their services, it is always a comforting thing to know, that these people have successfully gone through the professional examinations and have proved they have certain minimum reliable standards.

In schools, the examinations have the functions of making assessment of the level of students' learning so as to make plans of instruction and learning rationally.

Viewing from sociological perspectives, the system of examination has two functions. Firstly, system of examination was used to assess the extent to which an individual has benefited from the education he or she has received. What does he or she know? Has he or she learned what he or she was supposed to learn and were taught? The function of measurement of attainment or achievement has always received explicit recognition. The system of examinations designed to this end may be taken place frequently throughout the process of education. The second function of system of education is selection of individuals. This process implies that the examinees are being selected for something, either for further education or for some task or role in society. It implies that not all young people are expected to reach the same levels of achievement and that societal roles are differentiated and specialized. That is to say, even if a society is egalitarian and based on the concept of equal rights, its functioning depends on the fact that not all individuals are expected to perform the same duties and to accept identical responsibilities.

The historical development of the system of examination in China can be classified into five stages.

8.2 The System of Examination at the Stage of Completing Socialist Restructuring (1949–1956)

8.2.1 The System of Examination in Primary and Secondary Schools from 1949 to 1956

8.2.1.1 Instruction Program in Primary Schools and Secondary Schools and the Scope of Examinations

On 1 August, 1950, the Ministry of Education issued *Directives on Provisional Instruction Program and School Calendar in Secondary Schools* (He 1998a, b). The *Directives* stipulated the instruction subjects, the hours of instruction per week for these subjects, the total hours of instruction in three years, the average hours per subject in secondary schools.

The subjects for examination were based on the instruction program. Usually Chinese, mathematics, politics, natural science, biology, physics, chemistry, history, geography and foreign language would be tested in mid-term or at the end of term.

8.2.1.2 Dual Tasks of Regular Secondary Schools and the Relation Between Instruction and Examination

Instruction and examination was intimately connected to each other. Instruction was the main task in schools, and examination was taken an important means to pursue a good instruction. Without instruction, examination had no purpose; without examination, instruction would not be conducted effectively.

On 31 March, 1951, Ma Xulun, the Minister of Education, made a speech in the concluding ceremony of the national conference on secondary education. Ma Xulun pointed out that schools should conduct instruction effectively. Instruction was the basic work in schools. Also, the system of examination should be helpful to the instruction.

On 6 August, 1951, the Administrative Council issued Decisions on Improvement of Students' Health in Schools at Various Levels (Editorial Board of China's Education Yearbook). The Decisions pointed out that the poor health of students in schools at various levels was causing serious concern. The poor health of students was caused by the heavy load of lessons, too many activities conducted by social groups and poor administration of food and dormitories. The Decisions stipulated that schools should cut down duplication and unnecessary curricula and teaching contents and improve the methods of instruction. Teachers should let students practice more in the class, and reduce their after-school activities. The examination questions should not be too difficult or too complicated for students to answer.

8.2.1.3 The Establishment of System of Examination in Primary Schools and Secondary Schools

The systematization of examinations began in 1952 when two regulations on schools were issued. On 18 March, 1952, the Ministry of Education issued *Provisional Regulations on Secondary Schools* and *Provisional Regulations on Primary Schools*. The *Regulations* made important decisions on the system of examinations. The *Regulations* stipulated that tutors of students should be accountable for the performance of the students. Teachers must master contents in textbooks, use correct instruction methods, conduct instruction step by step on the basis of the instruction program, criteria of curricula, psychological laws of students' development.

The examinations on academic learning were classified as ordinary examinations, examinations in the process of lessons, examinations at mid-term, examination at the end of term.

For the score of each subject, the ordinary test and mid-term test should consist of 60% of the total score, and the examination at the end of the term should consist of 40% of the total score. The score for one year's learning result should be calculated as the average scores in two terms.

The method of showing the score was the percentage system. The score of 60 was the criterion for passing examination. The five-level system could be used by schools under approval of educational administrative departments.

The score for physical training was based on performance in the class of training and the physical conditions of student at the end of term.

The scores for ordinary behavior or conduct were based on the daily examination of students' behaviors. The teachers should write down remarks on students' conduct and give levels or grades for students' conduct. The levels are usually classified as 'extremely good', 'quite good', 'good', 'medium', and 'poor'.

The students who pass the examinations in all subjects could enter a higher grade. When students fail in one or more subjects, the school should organize extra learning for them during the vacation, and at the beginning of the next term, take the examination again.

On 1 July, 1955, the Ministry of Education issued *Directives on Lessening Excessive Learning Loads for Students in Primary and Secondary Schools* (He 1998a, b). The *Directives* stipulated that ordinary examinations should be strengthened. Answering question in classes should be increased; ordinary observation should be stressed. The written work and examination should be easy to tackle. The kind and times of examination should be lessened. Only examination in the end of year and examination for graduation should be permitted. The unitary examination should not be conducted. In some regions the tests and examination were conducted too often; this should be curbed. Test questions should be based on the textbooks and *National Unitary Instruction Programs*.

8.2.2 The System of Examination in HEIs (1949–1956)

8.2.2.1 Transition from Old System of Examination to New System of Examination

On 14 August, 1950, the Administrative Council issued *Provisional Regulations on Higher Education Institutions* (Editorial Board of China's Education Yearbook 1984, p. 776). The *Regulations* stipulated that the HEIs should formulate curricula for all departments. The examinations in universities and colleges included college and university entrance exanimations, examinations in normal time, mid-term examinations and examinations at the end of terms.

Students in universities and colleges should submit topics of papers and designs to the dean of department; the dean should give approval of the topics. Under the guidance of supervisor, the students should finish their papers and designs.

Students in universities and colleges should finish the necessary courses and pass examinations. The universities and colleges submitted the list of students who pass examinations and the Ministry of Education examined and approved the diploma of graduation for graduates.

8.2.2.2   The Subjects of Examination in the Early 1950s

On 26 May, 1950, the Ministry of Education issued *Regulations on Enrollments.* The *Regulations* stipulated that subjects of examinations were Chinese, foreign language, general knowledge of politics, mathematics, Chinese history and foreign history; Chinese geography and foreign geography, physics, chemistry.

In 1953, the subjects of examination were Chinese, foreign language, general knowledge of politics, mathematics, Chinese history and foreign history, Chinese geography and foreign geography, physics, chemistry. Students who wanted to be enrolled in specialties of music, art, drama, physical training should take extra examinations in these subjects.

In 1955, the subjects of examination included three types for students who were enrolled in different specialties. For students who were enrolled in engineering, liberal arts, agriculture and forestry, the subjects of examination were Chinese, general knowledge of politics, mathematics, physics, chemistry. For students who were enrolled in medicine and biology, the subjects of examination were Chinese, general knowledge of politics, basis of Darwinism, physics, chemistry. For students who were enrolled in humanity, laws, finance, economy, physical training and arts specialties; the subjects of examination included Chinese, general knowledge of politics, history, and geography.

8.2.2.3   The Systematization of Examinations in Higher
Education Institutions

On 9 July, 1954, the Ministry of Higher Education issued *Regulations on Examinations and Checks on Curricula in HEIs.* The *Regulations* stipulated that examinations and checks on curricula were not only the criteria of examination of students' learning results, but also the main methods of mastery of knowledge. The main methods of examination were oral tests. Even if some courses needed written tests, the oral tests were necessary.

On 15 December, 1955, the Ministry of Higher Education issued *Circular on Regulations on Examinations on Curricula in HEIs* (He 1998a, b). The *Circular* stipulated that examinations and checks on curricula was the unique criterion for assessing the learning achievement of students. The schedule of examinations were determined by the deans of departments and presented to the presidents of

Universities for approval. The schedule should be publicized one month prior to the time of examination. The schedule should take into consideration the full contents and difficulties of examinations so as to leave two to four days for students' revision.

Ways of assessment of learning achievement included formal examinations and check on courses. The methods of exams should be based on the program of instruction.

The ranks of examinations were classified as excellent, very good, passed, failed. The ranks of checking a course could be classified as pass and failure.

The examinations were conducted by teachers who had lessons. The checks were conducted by teachers who were in charge of practices, experiments, class discussions. The checks of theoretical courses were conducted by teachers who taught the lessons.

The checks on courses should be finished before the formal exams were conducted. If students had special reasons, the checks could be postponed. If a student failed in checks of courses, in designs or papers, he or she could not be permitted to take part in the final exams.

In order to check how students understand what they learned and how they use the knowledge, the examinations should be in the form of oral tests.

Test questions should be determined according to the instruction program. In the process of oral test, test questions should be distributed evenly in test bulletins. Test questions should be approved by the directors of instruction research group.

The scores of examinations and checks should be written in the students' record. The examiners should present scores and test papers to departments and the instruction research groups.

8.2.2.4 The Establishment of National Examination in 1956 and the Revoking of National Examination in 1957

On 14 May, 1956, the Ministry of Higher Education issued *Circular on National Examinations in HEIs* (He 1998a, b). The *Circular* stipulated that those HEIs that had graduates should establish national examination commissions. The scheme of examinations and the reports on examination should be submitted to the Ministry of Higher Education in time. The *Circular* stipulated that the purpose of national examinations were to examine whether the academic performance of graduates was in accordance with the requirements set by instruction program so as to assure educational quality. Graduates who passed the examination would be given the title of professionals. There were three ways of examinations: they were the tests of courses, making statements about papers and answering questions, or the combination of the above two ways. The national examinations were conducted once a year.

On 14 March, 1957, the Ministry of Higher Education issued *Circular on the Suspension of National Examinations in HEIs*. The *Circular* pointed that although national examinations had achieved a lot, but as too many graduates took part in examinations, there were not enough examiners, and so much time was spent on examinations. So the examinations met with difficulties. If the examination were continued, the format would be serious. So the Ministry on Education decided to revoke this kind of examinations in 1957.

8.2.2.5   The Objective Assessment of Scores in Examinations

On 20 August, 1956, the Ministry of Higher Education issued *Opinions on Assessment of Instruction on Political Theories in HEIs* (He 1998a, b). The *Opinions* pointed that in some HEIs administrators and teachers maintained that the scores in examinations could not reflect the real achievements of students in learning. Some students did not behave properly, but through keeping notes and recitation they could get good scores. Some students behaved better and studied harder, but they could not get good scores. Some administrators and teachers proposed that teachers could give scores based on students' ordinary behavior. The *Opinions* objected to this proposal. It was not proper for teachers to give scores by referring to students' behavior and learning attitudes. The basic goal of learning was to understand and use basic theories. The problems students faced in political thoughts and behavior should be solved through the political education.

8.3   The System of Exanimation at the Completion of Building Socialism (1957–1965)

8.3.1   The System of Examination in Primary Schools and Secondary Schools (1957–1965)

8.3.1.1   Establishment of Regular Instruction and Examination Order

On 30 January, 1957, the Ministry of Education issued *Circular on Graduation Examination in Secondary Schools*. The *Circular* pointed out that there were some problems in the reform of examinations in schools. Some schools did not abide by the instruction programs, cut contents of textbooks randomly, speeded up the process of instruction, finished the lessons ahead of time and conducted examinations in junior secondary schools and senior secondary schools. This kind of behaviors made students nervous, influence regular instruction, affected mastery of knowledge. The *Circular* stipulated that content of examination included all textbooks in the three years in junior secondary schools and senior secondary schools. The length of instruction in the third year of all senior secondary schools should not be less than 32 weeks. The length of instruction in the third year of all junior secondary schools should not be less than 34 weeks. Students should have enough time to prepare for examination.

8.3.2   The System of Examination in HEIs (1957–1965)

8.3.2.1   The Reform of National Entrance Examination

On 8 August, 1961, the Ministry of Education issued Circular on Scores on Foreign Language Test Should Be Listed as Formal Test Scores in the National College Entrance Examinations. The Circular stipulated that before 1961, test scores in foreign language were not taken as formal test scores in the enrollment of students in HEIs. The Circular pointed that senior secondary schools had been teaching courses of foreign languages for a long time. In order to increase the quality of higher education and stress foreign language instruction, test scores in foreign language in national college entrance examination were taken as formal test scores in the enrollment of students from 1962 on.

8.3.2.2   Reform of Examination on Students' Achievement

From 1959 to 1962, some HEIs faced problems such as irregular instruction order, incomplete examination system and poor mastery of knowledge among students. So it was urgent to strengthen instruction and examination in HEIs.

On 20 November, 1962, the Ministry of Education issued *Circular on Regulations on Examinations on Students' Achievements in HEIs Affiliated with the Ministry of Education*. The *Circular* stipulated that the scope of examination on students' achievement was to examine and assess students' academic achievement as well as political consciousness, moral qualities and labor performance.

The method of assessment of academic achievement was examinations and checks. The purpose of examinations and checks was to help students to review and consolidate knowledge systematically, examine the level of students' understanding and knowledge and students' competence of use of knowledge.

The courses that were listed in instruction program in the first time should be examined in every term. The number of courses for examination and checks should be determined by instruction program. In lower grades, the courses for examination should be no less than three. In higher grades, the number of courses of examination could be more than three.

The assessment on students' achievements should use the levels of 'excellent', 'good', 'fair', 'failed'. Some courses could use the percentage system.

The assessment of courses by way of checks could use the levels of qualified level and unqualified level.

The examinations of courses usually were conducted by teachers who taught the lessons themselves. Other experienced teachers could participate in the assessment. The scores for courses by way of checks were given by teachers who took responsibilities of these courses.

The ways of examination should be oral tests, written tests or both of them on the basis of the characteristics of courses, size of class and number of teachers.

8.4   The System of Examination at the Time of the Great Cultural Revolution (1966–1976)

8.4.1   The System of Examination in Primary and Secondary Schools (1966–1976)

8.4.1.1   Lessening Students' Learning Loads and Times of Examination in the Early Period of 1966

On 17 January, 1966, the Central Committee of the CCP approved *Report on Lessening Learning Loads and Guaranteeing Students' Health submitted by the Ministry of Education* (He 1998a, b). The *Report* pointed out that schools should control the amount of activities for students, lessen learning and homework loads for students, strengthen political work, make proper arrangement of labor, carry out proper activities of physical training, amusement and scientific activities, care about students' life conditions. The methods of examination should be reformed.

8.4.1.2   Suspension of Examination in Primary Schools and Secondary Schools

On 16 May, 1966, the Great Cultural Revolution started; students were urged to take part in this movement. Schools were taken as the important base for training proletarian revolutionaries.

On 12 July, 1966, the Ministry of Education issued *Circular on Enrollment, Examination, Vacation, and Graduation* (He 1998a, b). The *Circular* stipulated that students at various levels in primary and secondary schools should not take part in examinations in the end of term if they had not taken part in examinations. The scores for students could be determined by democratic assessment within the schools.

8.4.2   The System of Examination in HEIs (1966–1976)

8.4.2.1   Revoking of Examination for Enrollment to HEIs

On 24 July, 1966, the Central Committee of the CCP and the State Council issue *Circular on Reform on Enrollment in HEIs*. The *Circular* stipulated that from this year on, the national entrance examinations was revoked. The enrollment of students would be conducted on recommendations and selection.

The revoking of enrollment examinations for entrants in HEIs had a great negative effect on higher education.

8.5   The System of Examination at the Stage of Building Socialist Commodity Markets (1977–1991)

8.5.1   The System of Examination in Primary Schools and Secondary Schools (1977–1991)

8.5.1.1   Correction of One-Sided Pursuit of Enrollment Rates and the Constraint of Examinations in Secondary Schools

In 1983, the Ministry of Education issued *Opinions on Further Improvement of Educational Qualities in Regular Secondary Schools*. The *Opinions* stipulated that it was necessary to establish and prefect the system of promotion. The courses in instruction programs should be offered. After finishing a course, the course should be examined or checked. The scores should be recorded; the graduation examination should focus on courses in the whole year.

On 31 December, 1983, the Ministry of Education issued Ten Opinions on Full Implementation of Party's Educational Guideline and Correction of One-sided Pursuit of Rates of Promotion in Regular Secondary Schools (State Education Commission 1991). The Opinions stipulated that regular secondary schools should stress students' understanding of learning content, and not conduct examination frequently. In each term, examinations in the mid-term and at the end of the term were conducted, and the number of courses for examination were not too many. Some courses should be examined only at the end of the term. The examination for graduates should be limited on the last year's courses which the students were studying. Except for the examination for enrollment and graduation, no unitary examinations were conducted without the approval of provincial governments. Test questions should not replace the scope of instruction programs and textbooks.

8.5.1.2   Lessening of Students' Heavy Learning Load of Courses and Homework in Primary Schools

In 1984, the Ministry of Education issued *Opinions on the Arrangement of Instruction Program in Full-time Six-year Primary Schools*. The *Opinions* stipulated that localities and schools with good conditions should not conduct the midterm examinations in many subjects; the examinations at the end of the term could be limited to Chinese and mathematics. The system of graduation examinations should be reformed. In rural areas, graduation examinations should be guided by educational administrative departments; central primary schools should make out test papers for schools according to instruction programs. The use of methods of examinations should consider situations of schools. The methods of examinations in primary schools should be decided by educational administrative departments. In the near future, the schools could determine the test questions themselves.

On 11 May, 1988, the State Education Commission issued *Certain Regulations on Reducing Work Load for Primary School Pupils*. The *Regulations* stipulated that educational administrative departments and schools should not organize examinations beyond requirements of instruction. The times of examination should be limited. The examination in subjects of Chinese and Mathematics should be conducted twice, in mid-term and at the end of the term or one time, at the end of the term. The examinations of other disciplines should be conducted in the process of instruction. The content of graduation examination for graduation was limited to the year's curricula. Except for graduation examination, educational administrative departments should not organize any unitary examinations. In places where secondary schools were popularized, enrollment of graduates from primary schools should be based on the principle of enrollment in the nearest schools. Departments and units should not determine the indicators of scores of examination and rate of promotion of students for instructional classes and teachers. The rankings of schools, classes, and teachers were not permitted; evaluation of teachers should not be the criteria of assessment for teachers. Schools should not publicize students' scores and make rankings of students.

8.5.1.3 Revoking of Graduation Examination of in Primary Schools

The reform of examinations had important guiding role in educational development. The reform of the system of examination was an important task of instruction reform in primary schools and secondary schools.

In 1984, the Ministry of Education advocated the revoking of graduation examinations in places where the junior secondary education was popularized. From 1985 to 1988, the State Education Commission issued four documents stressing the reform of examinations. By the end of 1991, 70% of the cities revoked graduation examinations.

8.5.1.4 General Examinations for Graduates in Senior Secondary Schools

In 1985, the State Education Commission decided that educational administrative departments in Shanghai make experiment on the establishment of general graduation examination in senior secondary schools as well as the reform on national college entrance examination. In Shanghai nine courses were listed as courses of examination. From the first term to the fifth term, after one course was finished, an examination was conducted. The general graduation examination in senior secondary schools was a kind of examination that assesses whether students had achieved the level of being qualified for graduation.

The experiment in Shanghai showed that all secondary schools could form characteristics in terms of general graduation examination in senior secondary schools. The students could learn much more in some subjects listed in the subjects of national entrance examination. The general examination of graduates in senior secondary schools should be easier than the national entrance examination.

From 1983 on, tl administrative department of Zhejiang Province made an experiment on general examination of graduates in senior secondary schools. In 1988, the general examination of graduates in senior secondary schools was conducted in all secondary schools in Zhejiang Province.

In 1990, the State Education Commission convened a conference on general examination of graduates in senior secondary schools. In the meeting, it was decided that general examination of graduates in senior secondary schools will be conducted across the whole country.

8.5.2 The System of Examination in Higher Education (1977–1991)

8.5.2.1 The Rehabilitation of National Entrance Examination

On 8 August, 1977, Deng Xiaoping said in the symposium on science and education that the enrollment of students in HEIs should be rehabilitated. The entrants of HEIs should be recruited from graduates in senior secondary schools. Recruitment of entrants on the basis of recommendation should be forbidden.

On 12 October, 1977, The State Council issued *Opinions on System of Enrollment in Higher Education Institutions*. The *Opinions* stipulated that the national examination entrance examination would be rehabilitated in 1977, and this kind of examination would be held in 1977.

Since 1978, the unified examination for college enrollment has included the following subjects: (1) For students who want to major in humanities and social sciences, political science, Chinese, mathematics, history, geography, and foreign language were the subjects. (2) For students who want to major in science and technology, agriculture, medical science, Chinese, mathematics, physics, chemistry, and foreign language were the subjects of examination.

8.5.2.2 Standardization of Examination in Terms of National Entrance Examination

The so-called standardization of examination aimed at reforming the traditional methods and contents of examinations and created new ways of standardization of examinations by using theories of modern education measurement, theories of educational statistics and computers.

In 1985, the department of higher education in Guangdong province, the Enrollment Office of Guangdong Province, Guangzhou Foreign Language Colleges, Zhongshan University, Guangzhou Normal College took part in the reform of standardization of examinations.

In 1989, the State Education Commission issued the Implementation Plans for Standardization Scheme on National Unitary Examination in Regular Higher Education Institutions. The standardization scheme was implemented hereafter.

8.5.2.3 Self-study and Examination Program in Higher Education

On 3 March, 1988, the State Council issued *Provisional Regulations on Self-Study Examinations in terms of Higher Education Fields*. The *Regulations* stipulated that and examination program in higher education were a kind of national examinations. It was a form of higher education using the way of self-study. The self-study and examination programs in higher education were beneficial to cultivation of professionals with good character and talents, beneficial to improvement of citizen's moral, cultural and scientific competence.

The specialties should be established according to needs of economic and social development, scientific forecast of requirement of manpower and professionals, and conditions of conducting of examinations.

The national guidance commission for self-study and examination program in higher education took responsibilities of supervision on self-study and exams program in higher education. The members of this commission included some leaders of departments under the State Council, some leaders from Army and social groups, and presidents of HEIs.

The commissions at provincial levels should take responsibilities under the guidance of national commission.

HEIs which take responsibilities of supervision of examinations should be HEIs with strong power of teachers.

New specialties for self-study and examination program in higher education should be expounded and approved by national commission. The new specialties should have conditions such as complete work institutions, necessary professionals and expenditures.

The learning period for obtaining the degree of specialized higher education was three to four years; the learning period for undergraduate study was four to five years.

According to the examination plans, students conducted examination of each course at one time. If students passed examination, the would obtain the certificate of being qualified for this course. The credit would be accounted. If students failed in the examination, he or she could participate in the next examination.

Examinees could choose specialties on their own. The examinees on-the-job were advocated to choose specialties according to actual needs.

Examinees could obtain diplomas if they were in accord with the following conditions: finishing examinations in all courses and pass in all examinations; finish graduate papers and pass moral examination.

8.6   The System of Examination at the Stage of Building Socialist Market Economy (1992–2016)

8.6.1   Reform of the System of Examination in Primary Schools and Secondary Schools (1992–2016)

8.6.1.1   Reform of Graduation Examination in Junior Secondary Schools

The graduation examination in junior secondary schools was an important examination in the phase of compulsory education.

In 1999, the Ministry of Education asked the Beijing Normal University and East China Normal University to conduct a research on test questions and management of examinations in junior secondary schools. The research report on evaluation of examination of graduates and enrollment in junior secondary schools was issued.

The specialists thought that test paper in 2000 was competence education oriented; localities made great efforts to reform the system of graduation examination in junior secondary schools. Test paper stressed the relations between social actualities and students' life, stressed examination of competence in analysis of problems and solving of problems.

8.6.1.2   Use of System of Grades and Writing of Remarks for Students

In 1999, the primary schools and secondary schools in the County of Dehua in Fujian Province made reform on the system of examination. Three measures were taken by these schools. One measure was to revoke the percentage system in assessment of students. Instead, the old system of grade plus remarks on students was established. The old scores reports were changed into evaluation manuals for competence development. In the evaluation manuals students' performance in schools were written down.

8.6.1.3   Reform of Examination in Senior Secondary Schools

On 3 September, 2014, the State Council issued *Implementation Opinions on the Reform of System of Examination and Enrollment*. The *Implementation Opinions* stipulated that examination of students' academic level in senior secondary schools should be perfected. This kind of examination covered all subjects taught in senior secondary schools. The provincial governments should issue the *Opinions on Perfecting the Examination of Students' Academic Level in Senior Secondary Schools* and organizing and implemented this kind of examination.

8.6.2   Reform of the System of Examination in HEIs (1992–2016)

8.6.2.1   The "3+X" Model of Subjects of Examination(1992–2014)

In 1991, on basis of implementation of general graduation examinations in senior secondary schools, the Ministry of Education decided that Hunan Province, Yunnan Province, Hainan Province should make experiments on the reform of the establishment of subjects of national college entrance examination. One year later, the scheme in these three provinces were objected by persons in most other provinces because they were too characterized by the big changes.

In 1992, the Ministry of Education decided that from 1993 on, the "3+2" model of subjects of examinations was implemented. "3" meant that three subjects of examination namely Chinese, mathematics, and foreign languages. "2" meant that for students who are prone to learn social science, politics, history were subjects to be examined further, and for students who are prone to learn natural science, physics, chemistry were subjects to be examined further.

In 1993, the State Council issued *Opinions on Deepening the Reform and Development of Regular Higher Education.* The *Opinion*s stipulated that on the basis of general graduation, examination in senior secondary schools, the subjects of examination should be less.

In 1993, the "3+2" model of subjects of examinations was objected to by teachers in the fields of geography and biology. Some educators also thought that divisions of two courses batch between social sciences and natural sciences were not adapted to the needs of scientific development.

In 1999, the Ministry of Education decided that "3+X" model of subjects of examination scheme was implemented in Guangdong Province. Here '3' stands for Chinese, mathematics, foreign language. These subjects were examined by every examinee. 'X' stands for selective subjects; it was open system, and it was of various combinations.

'X' could include politics, history, geography, physics, chemistry, biology; 'X' could also include comprehensive examination that consisted of these six subjects.

In 2002, most provinces implemented the "3+X" model of subjects of examination scheme.

8.6.2.2   The "3+3" Model of Subjects of College Entrance Examination (from 2015 on)

On 3 September, 2014, the State Council issued *Implementation Opinions on the Reform of System of Examination and Enrollment.* The Implementation Opinions stipulated that the reform aimed at the provision of education satisfied by all citizens. The reform initiated in 2014, pushed forward completely in 2017, and aimed to establish a new system of examination and enrollment in 2020. The reform of national entrance examination focused on three aspects. Firstly, the subjects of national entrance examination should be the "3+3" model, the former "3" meant the subjects of Chinese, mathematics, foreign language as the subjects on unitary examination subjects, the score of each subject was 150 points; the latter "3" subjects meant the three subjects of academic-level examination in senior secondary schools, the three subjects could be chosen from politics, history, geography, physics, chemistry, biology etc. of students' own will, Foreign language examination chances should be provided twice a year.

In 2014, government of Shanghai Municipality and government of Zhejiang Province issued the *Trial Program of Comprehensive Reform of College Entrance Examination*. In Shanghai, the three subjects of examination of academic learning level in senior secondary schools could be chosen from politics, history, geography, physics, chemistry, biology, and the score for each subject was 70 points, while in Zhejaing Province, the three subjects of examination of academic level in senior secondary schools could be chosen from politics, history, geography, physics, chemistry, biology and technology (Information and general technology), and the score for each subject was 100 points. The examination of academic learning level in senior secondary schools would be conducted by each senior secondary school. The examination would be conducted after the instruction task of course has been finished.

8.7 Current Situation in the System of Examination

8.7.1 Current Situation in System of Examination in Primary Education and Secondary Education

8.7.1.1 The System of Examination in Primary Schools

A. Internal examinations in primary schools and junior secondary schools

The graduates in primary schools are usually assigned to junior secondary schools on the basis of choice of a neighborhood school.

In primary schools, the mid-term examinations were revoked entirely. The examinations at the end of term were permitted.

But the subjects of examinations were limited. From 1997 on, educational administrative departments in Jiangsu Province stipulated that Chinese and mathematics were permitted to be examined at the end of the term. From 2002, educational administrative departments stipulated that the subjects of examinations at the end of the term were Chinese, mathematics, and foreign language; other subjects could not be listed as subjects of examination.

From 2017 on, the academic learning level examination would be conducted in each junior secondary school, the subjects of examination would be Chinese, mathematics and foreign language, the examination contents would be oriented to the competence of analysis of problems and solving problems. The ways of showing academic learning could be scores or grades.

B. Reform on students' reports

Before 1997, student could get reports on scholastic achievements when the term was over. The reports may list students' score in each subject. Also, remarks on students were written on the reports by teachers. The score for each examined subject was given in the report.

From 1997 on, in primary schools in Jiangsu province the form of report was changed. The original score in the report was substituted by rank. The ranks included the five-level, such as, excellent, very good, good, satisfactory, and ordinary. Also, remark on students characterized by personal description and evaluation was given by teachers. The form of "rank plus remarks" was adopted widely by nearly all primary schools.

From 1997 on, subjects of examinations in primary schools, the score may not be permitted to be shown in test papers. In primary schools, the entrance examination for entering junior secondary schools was revoked entirely. The assessment of students' scholastic achievements should use the form of "rank plus remarks".

C. The internal examinations in junior secondary schools

The graduates in junior secondary schools needed to score well to be qualified to attend the key senior secondary schools. These senior secondary schools were usually provided with better teachers, better equipments, and better students. Many families would relocate their home in order to have access to good schools, or they may turn to private tutors for supplementary teaching.

In junior secondary schools examinations was permitted to be conducted. The examination at the end of the term was very important for students and teachers. Although ranking was not permitted, the publication of scores had a visible influence on the concerned students and teachers.

8.7.1.2 Current Situation in the System of Examination in Senior Secondary Education

A. Internal Examinations in senior secondary schools

Senior secondary education is non-compulsory education. The senior secondary schools have more autonomous powers in designing and implementing the system of examination.

In senior secondary schools, students take examination at mid-term and at the end of the term. Before 2006, the system of percentage was used in senior secondary schools. But from 2006, the reform of curricula in senior secondary schools was conducted. The credit system has been introduced in senior secondary schools. The credit system is similar to the credit system in HEIs. The courses are divided into required courses and selective courses. Students can arrange their own learning plans.

The examinations are managed by schools. The teachers provide examination papers, read and mark examination papers.

B. The graduation examinations in senior secondary schools

The graduation examinations in senior secondary schools are useful for the implementation of the policies of competence education.

Usually nine subjects were examined. But now the subjects of examinations decreased.

In the graduation examinations the check on students' experiment competence and practice competence was emphasized.

From 2015 on, in senior secondary schools, students should take part in academic learning level examination in each subject. Only after they pass all these examination could they be permitted to get the diploma. In some provinces, the academic learning level examination would be conducted two times for each subjects which were chosen as the three subjects included in the national college entrance examination subjects, and students could choose the score of the better examination result as the score for national entrance examination.

8.7.2 Current Situation in the System of Examination in Higher Education Institutions

8.7.2.1 College Entrance Examination

Great changes have been taken place in the organization and implementation of college entrance examination recently. The change could be summarized as three stages.

In the period of 2002–2014, the "3+X" model was used in the provinces, municipalities and autonomous regions. The subjects of examination follow the model of "3+X". From 2002, this basic model is followed by all provinces; here '3' stands for Chinese, mathematics, and foreign language. The score of each subject is 150. 'X' stands for one or two subjects. The total score of 'X' is 300. 'X' has several models.

The first model is the comprehensive subject that consists of several humanities; they are politics, history, and geography.

The second model is the comprehensive subject that consists of several liberal arts; they are physics, chemistry, and biology.

The third model in the comprehensive subject consists of several humanities and liberal arts; they are politics, history, geography physics, chemistry, biology.

The fourth model is consists of any one subject from politics, history, geography, physics, chemistry, and biology.

The fifth model is consists of a subject from politics, history, geography, physics, chemistry, biology and comprehensive subjects. Here the comprehensive subject is the independent combination of several subjects.

The content of examination is focused on the content specified in the instruction programs of senior secondary schools. From 1981, there are national unitary instruction programs for subjects in senior secondary schools. The Ministry of Education does not publish the revision program for examinees, but the Ministry of Education publishes a simple program of revision for students in the national college entrance examination.

The reform of contents of examination is focused on three aspects: firstly, the transformation from knowledge-centered examination to competence-centered examination.

Secondly, examination on students' potentialities of learning in HEIs and examination on basic cultural competence and innovation competence is emphasized. The comprehensive competence in learning is stressed by using new types of examination questions.

Thirdly, the content of examinations is focused on the use of knowledge, and the cultivation of competence.

The test paper for college entrance examination subjects was made out by the national examination center and used by many provinces. But in some provinces the test paper for college entrance examination was made by themselves independently. After finishing tests the examination papers were read and marked.

At present the frequency of college entrance examination has increased to twice a year, one in March, the other in June. The change of frequency is beneficial to the instruction and education in senior secondary schools. Examinees can choose one or both of these examinations.

In the period of 2015–2012, the college entrance examination was at the stage of transition. In 2015, the reform programs of college entrance examination in Shanghai municipality and Zhejiang Provinces were published. From 2015 on, the new "3+3" model of college entrance examination was introduced in Shanghai municipality and Zhejiang Provinces. In senior secondary schools the academic learning level examination was introduced. The instruction planning in schools also changed rapidly. In 2016, more provincial governments issued the programs of reform of college entrance examination. The "3+3" model of college entrance examination was introduced in many provinces. The three examination subjects of academic learning level would be conducted in respective senior secondary schools.

Since 2021, the "3+3" model of college entrance examination would have been introduced in every province.

8.7.2.2 The Internal Examinations in HEIs

At present HEIs establish and perfect the system of internal examinations. Usually after entrants enter HEIs, they are assigned to definite colleges, departments and specialties. But in some cases, HEIs can conduct special tests for selecting good students to advanced colleges.

Usually the time for instruction of a course is a term. Some courses have two or more terms of instruction time. There are no midterm examinations in the instruction in courses. But in most cases, the examinations or checks at the end of the term is necessary.

Check on courses refers to summative assessment on learning outcome. Teachers keep a record of students' performance in the process of instruction. Students' homework, practice or experiment reports, speeches made in classes are checked by teachers. The courses suitable for checks include practice courses, experiment courses, and technical courses.

For some courses teachers can make application for adoption of form of check in a course. For most courses the written examinations are necessary. Teachers provide examination papers, read and mark these examination papers.

In universities and colleges there are no graduation examinations. The credit system is followed across the whole country. If a student gets a score of 60, he has the necessary credits for the course. The credit point is four for score span of 90–100, three for score span of 80–89, two for score span of 70–79, one for scores span of 60–69. A student should obtain a definite amount of credits so as to graduate from university.

8.8 Problems Facing China in the System of Examination

8.8.1 Problem Facing China in the System of Examination of Primary and Secondary Schools

8.8.1.1 Problem Facing China in the System of Examination in Primary Schools

In some primary schools all examinations were revoked entirely.

The graduation examination has made great influence on instruction in junior secondary schools. Many junior schools care about the ratios of enrollment in key senior secondary schools among their students graduated in a specific year. Sometimes they would make comparisons of the ratios of enrollment between different junior schools. Those have high ratios would be respected by educational administrative departments, parents, students. They may get more funds from governments. The parents may be eager to send their children to these schools.

The courses listed as the subjects of graduation examination can be stressed in the instruction. Test questions and the criteria of examinations can be studied thoroughly by the teachers. Much time is spent on the subjects of examination in the process of instruction.

8.8.1.2 Problems Facing China in the System of Examination in Secondary Education

A. Problems facing China in the internal examination in junior secondary education

There are some limitations with the cultural examinations. The internal examination was normally based on paper-and-pencil test. It focuses on knowledge embodied in books. But much useful knowledge in daily life and production could not be reflected completely in written examination. Parents and students lay emphasis on learning of knowledge from books and practice on test questions from books. Most students do not care about extra-curricular knowledge and neglect moral, intellectual, physical development. Using a single criterion to assess performance of schools and students has negative effects.

B. Problems facing China in graduation examinations in senior secondary schools

The graduation examinations in senior secondary schools have some problems.

Firstly, there are some function limits concerning the graduation examinations in senior secondary schools. There are two functions concerning graduation examinations in senior secondary schools. One is to assess educational quality in senior secondary schools. The other is to assess qualified persons to be enrolled to HEIs.

Secondly, there exists a problem concerning ambiguity of criteria. The establishment of criteria is based on instruction programs. The instruction programs are outlines of instruction contents and requirements of instruction. Actually there are no systematic researches on the objectives of instruction and assessment.

Thirdly, public confidence on graduation examinations in senior secondary schools is not very high as many peoples anticipate. As graduation examinations in senior secondary schools are perfecting, the design and implementation of examination are short of sound theoretical guidance and strict supervision. The information of graduation examinations in senior secondary schools is not used fully by the concerned departments and it is not used fully.

Fourthly, the powers and responsibilities of graduation examination in senior secondary schools are not clear enough.

Fifthly, when students in senior secondary schools should choose three academic learning subjects from six or seven subjects such as politics, history, geography, physics, chemistry, biology and information technology s stipulated by the national college examination regulations, the schools prefer student's choice of more popular subject mixture to student's choice of less popular subject mixture, this is not beneficial to students' free choice of course, and hinder students' all-around development.

8.8.2   Problems Facing China in the System of Examination in Higher Education

The reform of college entrance examination is a social engineering; it pertains to benefits for millions of families. At present, the law of examination in China is not formulated. Although there is a regulation about the enrollment in HEIs, it is issued by the Ministry of Education; it does not have strong constraining power for many stakeholders concerning entrance examination. The college entrance examination and other examinations are having great influence on the masses. So it is urgent to formulate and issue a law of examination.

The relation between graduation examinations and college entrance examination is not harmonious. The graduation examinations are a kind of certificate examinations; it is based on the goals of secondary schools. Its functions are to make sure that the students graduating from secondary schools are qualified. The results of graduation examinations in senior secondary schools can be the main criteria for assessing the educational quality in senior secondary schools. The entrance examination is a kind of selective examination. It aims at choosing qualified entrants for HEIs. But now, most senior secondary schools use the result of college entrance examination to assess instruction quality and educational quality in senior secondary schools. In this situation, senior secondary schools can lead all students to pursue good performance in college entrance examination in senior secondary schools. Some students take the high scores in college entrance examination as the foremost task and neglect the other aspects of personal development.

In the past, HEIs increased some powers in determining subjects. At present the "3+X" model is used by every province.

8.9   Strategies and Measures for Reform of the System of Examination

8.9.1   Strategies and Measures for Reform of the System of Examination in Primary and Secondary Education

8.9.1.1   Strategies and Measures for Reform of the System of Internal Examination in Primary Schools

Primary school education and junior secondary education is compulsory education. For schools at the stage of compulsory education, the criteria of evaluation should be focusing on whether they have fulfilled the task of compulsory education, whether students have achieved the goal of compulsory education, whether they have conducted the courses according to instruction program. These tasks and goals have been stipulated by the State. The model of evaluation on the basis of these tasks and goals is called goal attainment model or criteria-reference model.

There is another evaluation model called selective model. In the selective model, the ratios of enrollment and the criteria of scores are used to assess performance of schools. If a school has high ratio of enrollment in higher-level schools, especially key schools, this school is thought of as a good school. If a student has obtained high scores in a course and a type of examination, the student can be thought of as intelligent student; the higher the ratios of enrollment, the better the schools; the higher the scores, the better the student.

In primary schools and junior secondary schools the selective model is not beneficial to the implementation of competence education. The evaluation model in primary schools and junior secondary schools should be transformed from selective model to criteria-reference model.

The ratio of enrollment should be analyzed dialectically. The ratio of enrollment is ratio of students who graduated from lower-level school to students who are promoted to higher-level school. The ratio of enrollment is a basic indicator for educational management. Educational administrative departments can use ratios of enrollment to regulate educational activities and evaluate schools. The ratio of enrollment can affect lower-level schools and higher-level schools.

The abstract talk about ratio of enrollment is meaningless. Peoples' attitudes on the ratio of enrollment should be complex. Schools and the students, teachers in lower-level schools think that the higher the ratios of enrollment, the better the schools. But in the higher-level schools the teachers may think that strict selection in enrollment is the prerequisite for enhancement of educational quality. The 100% ratio of enrollment means that all students can enroll in higher-level schools irrespective of their performance in learning.

The ratio of enrollment is not complete and accurate criteria for assessment of schools. The ratio of enrollment is based on scores of examinations. At present ratio cannot reflect students' comprehensive performances. Some aspects in moral development, intellectual development, and physical development cannot be assessed by written examinations. So the ratio of enrollment cannot be the best indicators of the educational quality in these cases. The criterion of assessing whether a student is good or excellent in lower-level schools cannot be the same as the criterion of selecting an entrant in higher-level school.

The selective model is used as the unique criterion of assessment of students. As the methods of measurement have been introduced in educational fields, the objective and rational measurements and evaluation are pursued by many persons. The scores may be indicators of reflecting outcomes of education. They are quantitative indicators that are used to make comparisons feasible. But the scores have its own limitations. Character, competence, affective development cannot be assessed with accurate quantitative methods. Sometimes, the more accurate the measurement, the more non-scientific the evaluation will be.

In primary schools there are examinations at the end of term. These examinations aim at formative evaluation of students' performance. These examinations cannot be used for selective purpose.

In junior secondary schools there are some examinations in mid-term and at the end of the term. But these examinations should be used for instruction purposes.

The graduation examinations in junior secondary schools are used for issuing of certificates for students who meet the requirements of compulsory education. They should not be used for selective purposes.

The entrance examinations in junior secondary schools are used as the means to select qualified students to enter senior secondary schools.

8.9.1.2   Strategies and Measures for Reform of the System of Examination in Senior Secondary Education

Seven measures should be taken concerning graduation examinations in senior secondary schools.

Firstly, the position of the graduation examination in senior secondary schools should be reconsidered. What kinds of position graduation examination in senior secondary schools should have, and what functions should graduation examination in senior secondary schools should fulfill, are fundamental questions. In the future reform of educational system, graduation examination in senior secondary schools may have four functions.

The first function is to assess the educational quality of senior secondary education.

The second function is the diagnostic function. Graduation examination in senior secondary schools should appraise instruction plans, instruction contents, instruction methods and the feasibility of educational policies, regulations, and measures in senior secondary education.

The third function is monitoring. Graduation examination in senior secondary schools is an excellent way for monitoring the educational standards in various schools and regions.

The fourth function is the function of guidance. Graduation examination in senior secondary schools could be beneficial to the healthy development of senior secondary education and implementation of the Party's education guidelines and polices.

Secondly, in order to address the problem of ambiguity of criteria in graduation examination in senior secondary schools, some measures should be taken. Great efforts should be made to establish the criterion system for all subjects of examination, and to evaluate the educational quality. Multiple assessment criteria should be established. The criteria of assessment of cognition development should be perfected. The criteria of assessment of affective development should be established and perfected. Professional aptitudes, competence aptitudes, sense of taking responsibilities, ambition, and cooperative spirit should be included in the assessment of affective domain. Criteria of assessment of motor skills should be established and perfected. Students' skills in computer, calligraphy, music, dancing, drawing, chess, and technological invention should be assessed.

Thirdly, in order to increase public confidence in graduation examination in senior secondary schools, it is necessary to take following measures.

The system of operation rule and social service system of graduation examination in senior secondary schools should be established.

Data on graduation examination in senior secondary schools should be collected and refined so as to provide more information and services for society. Meanwhile the research on graduation examination in senior secondary schools should be conducted more effectively. The administrators of graduation examination in senior secondary schools should increase the consciousness of research and make more research on reform and perfection of graduation examination in senior secondary schools. Research expenditures for study on graduation examination in senior secondary schools should be increased.

It is necessary to optimize the management of graduation examination in senior secondary schools. Powers and responsibilities concerning graduation examination in senior secondary schools should be specified clearly. The competence of administrators, staff and workers responsible for graduation examination in senior secondary schools should be enhanced. The training and education of administrators should be strengthened. Modern technologies should be used more widely and effectively in graduation examination in senior secondary schools.

In order to improve students' free choice of subject mixture, it is necessary for schools to increase number of teachers and diversify teachers' capacity to have more kind of courses pertaining to the six or seven academic learning subjects.

8.9.2 Strategies and Measures for Reform of the System of Examination in Higher Education

The reform of college entrance examination should abide by three basic principles. Firstly, it should be beneficial for HEIs to select students with high quality and high competence. In the near future, the system of college entrance examination should be reformed so as to cultivate professionals with better quality and competences in HEIs.

Secondly, it should be beneficial to the implementation of competence education in secondary education and solving problems connected with examination-oriented education. Efforts should be made to correct the shortcomings of examination-oriented education and push up competence education. National entrance examination should be beneficial to laying emphasis on enhancement of competence so as to make students grow and develop in a lively environment.

Thirdly, it should be beneficial to increase the autonomy of HEIs. Some HEIs should have powers to introduce special subjects of examination so as to adapt to their requirements. Some students also should have power to choose from subjects.

Chinese, mathematics, and foreign language are the mandatory subjects of examination. But other subjects should be chosen by HEIs. HEIs of different levels and types should have different combinations of subjects. Students also can choose HEIs and subjects of examinations according to their ambition and advantages.

8.9.2.1   Reform of College Entrance Examination

The system of college entrance examination should be reformed step by step, in a planned way. Governments should transform their functions, and speed up the process of lawmaking concerning examination. Governments should strengthen macro-management of examination affairs. Each enrollment office should be a legal entity. The enrollment office should take more responsibilities regarding the management of service for students and schools at various levels (Zhu 2001).

8.9.2.2   Relationship Between Graduation Examination and College Entrance Examination

To address the problems of graduation examination and entrance examination, it is necessary to explore comprehensive evaluation models in senior secondary schools. These two examinations differ in natures and functions. The graduation examination is a kind of criterion-reference examination; it aims at checking whether students in senior secondary schools meet the requirements of instruction programs. And the college entrance examination is a selective examination for selecting qualified students for HEIs.

The graduation examination should be perfected. In the near future, the graduation examination and entrance examination should be complementary in functions. The nine subjects in senior secondary schools should be examined more thoroughly. So the subjects in college entrance examination should be decreased. The new training models of selecting good students and pushing up the competence education should be explored.

As far as the college entrance examination is concerned, the "3+X" model is a good model under the current situation. The methods of combination of subjects should be perfected. The best way is increasing the powers of HEIs' determination of the combination of subjects of examinations so that the subjects of examination can be more adapted to the requirements of HEIs. The complete independent examination and recruitment by individual university and college cannot be fulfilled overnight. The increase in autonomy of HEIs in determining the subjects of examination is a step in the right direction for fulfilling this task.

References

Editorial Board of China's Education Yearbook (ed.) (1984). *China's Education Yearbook.* Beijing: Chinese Great Encyclopedia Publishing House.

He, D. (Ed.). (1998a). *Important documents in the People's Republic of China (1949–1975).* Haikou: Hainan Press.

He, D. (Ed.). (1998b). *Important documents in the People's Republic of China (1976–1990).* Haikou: Hainan Press.

The State Education Commission. (1991). *Collections of educational laws and regulations in China.* Beijing: People's Education Press.

Zhu, G. (2001). *Challenge and innovation: Restructuring Chinese higher education in era of new economy.* Nanjing: Nanjing Normal University.

Chapter 9
Aiming at School Improvement: Educational Evaluation System in Primary and Secondary Schools

9.1 Introduction to the System of Educational Evaluation

9.1.1 The Concept of the System of Educational Evaluation

The system of educational evaluation is an important part of the educational system.

The system of educational evaluation aims at answering the question of who have powers of assessment of persons and affairs, as well as how they make such assessment.

Evaluation means determination of the value or worth of something. In a broad sense, evaluation is a process of making value judgment on education and making improvement of education by systematic collection of information and making scientific analysis on the basis of definite educational goals and criteria.

The procedures of educational evaluation can be stated as follows. Firstly, the objects of evaluation should be determined. Secondly, the educational goals and criteria should be formulated. Thirdly, it is necessary to collect accurate and complete information on educational states after analysis of information. Fourthly, value judgment is given. Finally, the evaluation result should be used for putting forward suggestion for improvement of education.

9.1.2 Classification of the System of Educational Evaluation

There are different ways of classifying the system of educational evaluation. The most common way is to differentiate the prescriptive system of evaluation from the descriptive system of evaluation. This kind of classification aims to answer questions on whether evaluation is to describe what evaluators do or to prescribe what they should do. Generally speaking, evaluators are concerned with determining the value of the current status of things or state of affairs.

© Springer Nature Singapore Pte Ltd. and Higher Education Press 2018
M. Yang and H. Ni, *Educational Governance in China*,
https://doi.org/10.1007/978-981-13-0842-0_9

In the first way, it is called the prescriptive system of evaluation. The most common prescriptive type is a set of rules, prescriptions, prohibitions, and guiding framework that specify what a good or proper evaluation is and how evaluation should be carried out. In the second way it is called the descriptive system of evaluation. It is the use of a set of statements and generalizations which describe, predict, or explain evaluation activities. Such a type of evaluation is designed to offer empirical information.

Understanding of different evaluation types may provide insights and offer a framework for conducting evaluations. Prescriptive types may help to provide consistent frameworks and strategies for performing evaluations, and descriptive models present arrangement of validated possibilities for conducting evaluation.

9.1.3 Functions of the System of Educational Evaluation

There are two basic functions of the system of educational evaluation. Firstly, the system of educational evaluation aims to strengthen governments' management of schools. Education is a kind of normalized business. The standards of education are key factors for operation of schools and the fulfillment of the tasks of educational development.

Secondly, the system of educational evaluation aims to make better educational resource allocation. Although not every kind of educational resource allocation uses educational evaluation results as basis of financing education, it does use evaluation activities to direct resource allocation.

9.2 The System of Educational Evaluation in Primary Schools and Secondary Schools (1949–1956)

9.2.1 The System of Evaluation of Primary Schools and Secondary Schools (1949–1956)

Since the founding of the People's Republic of China, great progress has been made in primary and secondary education development. Managers and teachers in schools have been trained, facilities have been enriched, and managerial institutions have been established in schools.

On 18 March, 1952, the Ministry of Education issued *Provisional Regulations on Primary Schools*. The *Regulations* stipulated that primary schools aimed at providing all-round basic education for children and to make them love the motherland and the people and become active members. Governments of municipalities and counties should choose one, or more good schools in suitable locations as key schools on the basis of the geographical distribution of administrative regions and schools. These key schools should organize other primary schools to conduct professional research and political learning, and communicate their experience with each other.

On 18 March, 1952, the Ministry of Education issued *Provisional Regulations on Secondary Schools*. The *Regulations* stipulated that secondary schools aimed at providing youth with education in Mao Zedong's Thoughts and cultural knowledge. The secondary schools should conduct all-around education in terms of intellectual education, moral education, physical education, aesthetic education, and comprehensive technical education.

9.2.2   The System of Evaluation of Teachers (1949–1956)

On 26 November, 1953, the Administrative Council issued *Directives on Regulations and Improvement of Primary Education*. The *Directives* stipulated that the main task of principals and teachers was instruction. They should not take part in too many social activities and non-instruction activities. The teachers' work could not be regulated without keeping the relevant regulations. Teachers should improve instructional methods and enhance instruction quality. The Directive stipulated that primary schools should formulate tables of curricula and schedules of instruction, and institute systems of attendance of examination, organizing vacation, and assessment of achievement. But the *Directives* did not make detailed specifications on the system of evaluation of teachers.

9.2.3   The System of Evaluation of Students (1949–1956)

On 26 November, 1953, the Administrative Council issued *Directives on Regulations and Improvement of Primary Education*. The *Directives* stipulated that the five-grade system of scoring should be used in examination of scholastic achievement of students. Within the five-grade system of scoring, grade three was regarded as satisfactory. The system of percentage could be used before the new system was introduced in primary schools. The assessment on scholastic achievement should be determined by several ways, such as ordinary examination, one-year's examination, graduation examination.

On 26 November, 1953, the Administrative Council issued *Directives on Regulations and Improvement of Secondary Education*. The *Directives* stipulated that the achievement of students in secondary schools include scholastic achievement, conduct, and achievements of physical training. The scholastic achievement can be examined by ordinary examination, examination at the middle stage of learning and examination at the end of the term. The conduct of students was assessed by the directors in classes. The physical training scores should be assessed by the test in course of physical training. The students with very good scholastic achievements should be appraised and rewarded by secondary schools.

The students who passed examination in all subjects should be permitted to enter higher level grades. Students who failed in some examinations should take lessons after school and take examination again. If they still failed in two subjects, they would stay another year in the same grade. Students who took all lessons and passed the examinations could graduate from primary schools.

9.3   The System of Educational Evaluation in Primary and Secondary Schools (1957–1965)

9.3.1   The System of Educational Evaluation in Schools (1957–1965)

In March 1963, the Central Committee of the CCP issued *Provisional Regulations on Full-time Primary Schools*. The *Regulations* stipulated that the task of primary schools was to train potential labor force for socialist construction and provide qualified students for higher-level schools. Primary schools should conduct instruction on the basis of unitary instruction program, syllabus and textbooks.

In March 1963, the Central Committee issued the Provisional Regulations on Full-time Secondary Schools. The Regulations stipulated that the task of secondary schools is to train potential labor force for socialist construction and to provide qualified students for higher-level schools.

9.3.2   The System of Evaluation of Teachers (1957–1965)

In March 1963, the Central Committee issued *Provisional Regulations on Full-time Primary Schools*. The *Regulations* stipulated that the educational administrative departments and educational labor unions should convene regular meetings to appraise and reward teachers, sum up experiences and listen to their personal opinions and suggestions. Good teachers should be appraised and rewarded by the education administrative departments.

In March 1963, the Central Committee issued *Provisional Regulations on Full-time Secondary Schools*. The *Regulations* stipulated that the education administrative departments should pay attention to teachers' idea of serving educational undertakings over a long period; that governments should encourage and reward excellent teachers, especially teachers that had been working hard for a long time and were excellent in work. The assessment of teachers' salaries and regulation of salaries should be done well. The system of subsidies for the number of years in instruction was instituted. Some good teachers could be promoted to higher levels of salaries in a short time.

9.3.3 The System of Evaluation of Students (1957–1965)

In 1955, the Ministry of Education issued *Directives on Lessening Students' Learning Load in Primary Schools and Secondary Schools*. The *Directives* pointed out that importance should be given to ordinary examinations; the practice of raising questions and answering them in the classroom should be promoted; the ordinary observation on students in the class and written tests should be improved.

In March 1963, the Central Committee issued *Provisional Regulations on Full-time Primary Schools*. The *Regulations* stipulated that check on courses and examinations aim at knowing the actual situation of students' learning, encouraging students to review the lessons and consolidate knowledge, facilitating research on and improvement in instruction. There should be one or two mid-term examination in Chinese and mathematics and only one examination at the end of the term in Chinese and mathematics.

9.4 The System of Educational Evaluation in Primary Secondary Schools (1966–1976)

During the "Cultural Revolution", great changers took place in the system of evaluation of schools.

The criteria of evaluation of schools focused on the implementation of educational policies.

The evaluation of students focused on students' political consciousness.

9.5 The System Educational of Evaluation in Primary and Secondary Schools (1977–1991)

9.5.1 The System of Evaluation of Primary and Secondary Schools (1977–1991)

9.5.1.1 Establishment of Key Schools and Its Exemplary Effects

In order to train advances specialties, one of the first priorities was to reconstitute the system of key schools, in the autumn of 1978, many key schools were established.

9.5.2 The System of Evaluation of Teachers (1977–1991)

In 1978, *Provisional Regulations on Primary Education and Provisional Regulations on Secondary Education* pointed out that the system of appraisal of teachers should be instituted. But no detailed rule of appraisal of teachers was formulated in 1978.

9.5.2.1 Choice and Appraisal of Top-Class Teachers

On 17 December, 1978, the Ministry of Education and the State Planning Commission issued *Provisional Regulations on Choosing and Appraising Top-class Teachers* (Editorial Board of China's Education Yearbook 1984). The aim of choosing and appraising of top-class teachers was to enhance teachers' social and political positions and reward teachers for their great contributions. Teachers who were apprised included teachers in kindergartens, primary schools, secondary schools. The top-class teachers should advocate the CCP, solism and devote themselves to the educational undertaking. The top-class teachers should love students, work hard and have high prestige among teachers and in the education field. The choice and appraisal of top-class teachers should be strict. Among ten thousand teachers, five teachers can be chosen and appraised as top-class teachers. The top-class teachers can be provided with certificates; some of them can be elected as delegates to the People's Congress and be consultants after retirement. The remuneration of top-class teachers should be enhanced greatly. In 1978, subsidies for the top-class teachers in primary schools were 20 RMB Yuan per month, subsidies for the top-class teachers in secondary schools was 30 RMB Yuan per month.

In 1985, *Decision on Educational Reform and Development* pointed out that the establishment of teachers force with enough number, stable personnel, and high quality is the key for implementation of compulsory education and enhancement of educational qualities. Special measures for improvement in teachers' social positions and remunerations should be undertaken. The current teachers should be trained and examined seriously. The development of normal education and on-the-job training of teachers should be the strategic measures for educational development.

9.5.2.2 The System of Certificate in Examination of Teachers

In 1986, the State Education Commission decided to institute the system of certificate in examination of teachers. In September 1986, *Provisional Regulations on the System of Certificate of Examination of Teachers in Primary Schools and Secondary Schools* was issued (State Education Commission 1991). The system of certificate for teachers in primary schools and secondary schools is an important measure. It aims at constructing a qualified teacher force. The teachers who did not have the necessary academic records of schooling should obtain certificates.

9.5.2.3 Professional Titles for Teachers

In 1986, the State Education Commission issued the Regulations on Professional Titles for Teachers in Primary Schools (State Education Commission 1991, p. 626). The Regulations stipulated that schools should conduct examination on the teachers' political and ideological performance, cultural and professional knowledge, and competence in instruction and education, achievements, fulfillment of personal functions. The records of examination should be instituted so as to provide a basis for the teacher's promotion and appointment.

9.5.3 The System of Evaluation of Students (1977–1991)

From 1977 on, Students' academic learning was evaluated systematically in schools. Under the pressure of enhancement of educational quality, in primary schools and secondary schools tests were frequently conducted. In addition to mid-term tests and end-of-the-term tests, tests in all units of textbooks were also conducted regularly. Students who were good at moral development, cultural development and physical development were examined and selected each year in schools.

9.6 The System of Educational Evaluation in Primary and Secondary Schools (1992–2016)

9.6.1 The System of Evaluation of Primary and Secondary Schools (1992–2016)

In 1993, *Program on China's Educational Reform and Development* was issued by the Central Committee of the CCP and the State Council. The *Program* pointed out that it was necessary to improve and standardize the conditions of schools. Primary schools and secondary schools should facilitate students' all-round development. The system and model of running schools at senior secondary level should be diversified. It was necessary to establish the criteria of education and evaluation indicator systems at various levels. Educational administrative departments should make examination and assessment on educational quality in schools as the regular tasks. The examination and guidance on school work and educational quality should be strengthened. For vocational education, various ways of assessment of educational quality should be made by leaders, experts and employers.

On 13 June, 1999, the Central Committee of the CCP and the State Council issued *Decisions on Deepening Educational Reform and Pushing up Competence Education*. The *Decisions* pointed out that in terms of evaluation of schools' performance, human resources forecast and guidance on graduates' employment, social organizations and social intermediary organizations should play an important role. The mechanism of evaluation of schools, teachers and students on the basis of competence education should be established. Governments at various levels should not direct indicators on rate of enrollment, should not take rate of enrollment as the unique criteria of evaluation of school's performance. Social groups, parents and students were encouraged to take part in evaluation of school performance.

On 7 March, 2014, the Ministry of Education issued *Opinions on Comprehensive Evaluation Reform of Educational Quality of Primary and Secondary Schools.* The *Opinions* maintained that the tendency of evaluation of schools according to ratio of enrollment should be transformed. The *Opinions* constructed a new system of evaluation of schools' quality; the five indicators include students' moral development, scholastic achievement, physical and mental development, interest and strengths, learning loads.

9.6.2 The System of Evaluation of Teachers (1992–2016)

On 31 October, 1993, T*eachers Law of the People's Republic of China* was promulgated (State Education Commission 1991). *Teachers Law* stipulated that schools or other institutions of education should conduct assessment of teachers' political awareness, professional qualifications, attitude toward work and their performances. Educational administrative departments should guide and supervise the assessment of teachers. The assessment of teachers should be conducted in an objective, fair and accurate manner. In the process of assessment, opinions from teachers themselves, their colleagues and students should be taken into full consideration. The assessment results should be the basis for appointment and increase in remuneration as well as rewards and punishments.

On 6 September, 2012, the Ministry of Education, the Commission of National Reform and Development issued *Opinions on Deepening Teacher Education Reform.* The Opinions stipulated that the standards of teacher education should be set up and teacher quality should be evaluated systematically.

On 20 August, 2012, the State Council issued *Opinions on Strengthening the Teachers Team's Construction.* The Opinions stipulated that the system of teacher evaluation should be improved. The assessment criterion of teachers should be focused on teacher's moral character, capacity, achievement and contribution. Teachers' performance should be assessed by schools, students, colleagues and social bodies. The ratio of enrollment and students' scores should not be used as the basic criterion to evaluate teachers. The assessment of teachers should be based on teachers' post and work characteristics.

In 2013, the Ministry of Education made reform of teachers' qualification exams. In 2013, the new kind of exams were piloted in ten provinces, and 0.37 million of teachers took part in this exam, the passing rate was 25.8%.

9.6.3 The System of Evaluation of Students (1992–2016)

Since the middle of the 1990s, Chinese governments actively formulated and implemented the policy of competence education.

In terms of evaluation of students, new ways of evaluation were used. Firstly, the complete indicator as the core part of evaluation system was used. Evaluation indicators included not only indicators concerning students' intelligence development, but also concerning students' non-intelligent factors, psychological competence and technological competence. The basic criterion of each dimension was stipulated. Many schools put forward the slogan "all-round development for a solid basis, formation of features for cultivation of talents".

Secondly, the complete process of evaluation of students was stressed. Evaluation of learning process was emphasized. Formative evaluation became a necessary part of instruction process.

Thirdly, various ways of evaluation were used in schools. Students' self-evaluation, mutual evaluation by students, teachers' evaluation on students, and social evaluation on students were all used in schools.

From 1997 on, the system of percentage was reformed; the system of level was implemented. The system of credit was explored. Scores were not regarded as the most powerful criteria on evaluation of students.

On 22 December, 2014, the Ministry of Education issued *Opinions on Strengthening and Improving the Evaluation of Students' Comprehensive Competencies in Senior Secondary Schools*. The Opinions stipulated that the main evaluation indicators for students in senior secondary schools should be focused on five aspects, namely the moral development, scholastic achievement, physical and mental health, artistic competence, performance of taking part in social practice. The evaluation procedures should be based on the objective description of students' activities.

In 2013, the National Educational Examination Center established PISA 2015 National Center, this new center made independent PISA 2015 research. Twenty thousand 15-year old students took part in tests of reading literacy, mathematics literacy, scientific literacy, finance and monetary literacy. The data were collected and analyzed, the report was published.

9.7 Current Situations of the System of Evaluation

9.7.1 Current Situation of the System of Evaluation in Primary Schools and Secondary Schools

Schools' self-evaluation is regular evaluation on school activities on the basis of the evaluation criteria accepted by schools. Schools' self-evaluation is centered on the implementation of schools' strategies and concrete goals.

Schools' self-evaluation is the basis of school evaluation. Schools' self-evaluation is beneficial to strengthen self-construction of schools, enhancement of educational quality.

Self-evaluation is different from evaluation by other agents. It is evaluated by school itself on the basis of definite criteria and evaluation principles.

There are three steps in schools' self evaluation.

The first step is making preparation. Schools should establish self-evaluation guidance group, formulate developmental indicators system and organize specific self-evaluation groups.

The second step is implementation of evaluation. Schools should make diagnostic evaluation, make self-evaluation and make summative self-evaluation.

The third step is to make a summary. Schools should write down the report of self-evaluation on the basis of the summative report of various specific self-evaluation groups. The evaluation guidance group should hold meeting on summary of evaluation.

Schools are also evaluated by other institutions. Governments and social groups may make evaluation of schools. Among various evaluation methods, unitary criteria are used to make evaluation of schools. Such evaluations are directed toward standardization of running schools. The evaluation outcomes have great influence on schools.

In 1995 the State Educational Commission issued *Circular on Examination and Approval of 1000 Exemplary Senior Secondary Schools*. From 1995 on, this evaluation activity has been conducted regularly. The criteria of evaluation were formulated by the Ministry of Education. There were six steps for this kind of evaluation. Firstly, senior secondary schools wrote down self-evaluation report and application form to government of county. Secondly, government of county examined whether these schools had the qualification for application. Thirdly, after examination of qualification of application, the county government wrote a report and sent it to the provincial government. Fourthly, the division of the education administrative department at the provincial level held an examination, then an expert group visited the schools. Fifthly, the expert group wrote a report and sent it to the educational administrative department under the provincial governments. Sixthly, the school is approved as an exemplary senior secondary school.

Governments also make evaluation of schools' development levels. This kind of evaluation covers all schools of the same level and type. The governments of counties formulate criteria of evaluation of schools' development. The criteria of evaluation are indicator systems which consist of three levels of indicators.

9.7.2 Current Situation of the System of Evaluation of Teachers

Evaluation of teachers is an important part of system of basic education evaluation. Evaluation of teachers has been a hotly debated issue in the process of the reform of basic education. All education reforms have to be implemented by teachers finally.

Competences, educational ideals, educational behaviors of teachers have direct influence on the effectiveness of educational reform.

9.7.2.1 The System of Choice of Advanced Teachers

The system of choice of advanced teachers means that advanced teachers are chosen by all teachers on the basis of general criteria of moral behavior, competence, working load, performance at the end of the term or at the end of year. This system of choice of advanced teachers is used by primary schools and secondary schools in rural areas and remote areas.

Recently some schools made some reforms on the system of the choice of advanced teachers. The aim is to let more teachers be chosen as advanced teachers. The types of advanced teachers are increased. Advanced teachers include skilled instructors, advanced researchers, good directors, as best friends of students, best teachers in instruction as well as other types being appraised. As the types of advanced teachers increase, most teachers have opportunity to win rewards.

9.7.2.2 The System of Levels of Teachers

The system of levels of teachers is not to choose some advanced teachers, but to make assessment on all teachers, and all teachers are classified as teachers of different levels of capabilities. There are three kinds of levels. One level includes excellent teachers and good teachers. The second level includes excellent teachers, good teachers, and general teachers. The third level includes excellent teachers, good teachers, general teachers, and unsatisfactory teachers.

The system of levels of teachers is used in primary schools and secondary schools in rural areas and urban areas. Compared with the system of choice of advanced teachers, the system of levels of teachers has greater influence on teachers. In fact, most teachers are included in the objects of evaluation.

There are two shortcomings with the system of levels of teachers. Firstly, the criteria of assessment are as ambiguous as the system of choice of advanced teachers. The guiding role for teachers is not definite. Secondly, the system of levels of teachers may cause great pressures on teachers; the relationship between teachers and administrators and between different teachers may be intense. The conflict between teachers may be great.

9.7.2.3 Developmental Evaluation of Teachers

Developmental evaluation is a way of evaluation whereby teachers make evaluation by themselves and aim at facilitating professional development. Developmental evaluation is centered on affairs. Its goal is not to make comparison between teachers or. Its goal is directed toward whether teachers do right things and how they do these things so as to find out the scientific and effective educational methods. The criterion is not determined ahead of time; it is open and can be revised in the process. In the developmental evaluation of teachers, teachers are subjects in evaluation process.

Developmental evaluation has put forward some new challenges for teachers. Firstly, developmental evaluation is centering on teachers' development, centering on finding out problems and solving the problems; this requires that participants should have some theoretical levels and practical work levels. Otherwise the evaluation can be a kind of formalism. Secondly, developmental evaluation should deal with the relation between certification and management. Schools are a kind of social organization. Teachers are social workers. Teachers should be assessed and managed. Without assessment many problems can arise. At present some teachers do not achieve the requirements stipulated by the State. So the assessment and evaluation of teachers should be promoted.

9.7.3   Current Situation of the System of Evaluation of Students

At present there are five models of evaluation of students. They are as follows:

9.7.3.1   The Hundred-Mark System

The hundred-mark system is a grading system for registering students' marks, with 100 as the highest score, and 60 points as the passing score. Students' grades are reported to parents. The hundred-mark system is a way of assessing students' scholastic achievement. In the late 1990s and in this decade, the hundred-mark system has changed its form. One variable form is the combination of hundred–mark and remarks on conduct. The other variable way is a combination of hundred-mark with ranking in the class.

9.7.3.2   Remark on Conduct

In recent times, the use of remark on conduct has been reformed. Four ways have been used. The first way is writing a comprehensive remark on conduct. The second way is writing remark on moral learning; the third way is writing remarks on homework. The fourth way is writing instant remarks on students.

The principles of writing remark on conduct are summarized by teachers. These principles include respecting students' esteem and adapting to their age and psychological characteristics, fulfilling the functions of all-round education, making concrete, emotional, normalized remarks on students.

The procedures for writing remarks on conduct are perfected. The first step is to make self-evaluation by students. The second step is to make a review in small groups. The third step is to obtain the opinion of students in the whole class. The fourth step is to make a comprehensive remark by the director of the class.

9.7.3.3   Comprehensive Evaluation

As the transformation from examination-oriented education to competence education is carried forward, comprehensive evaluation model is adopted at the stage of basic education. Some schools use models of combination of three factors. These factors include levels, features and remarks.

The system of determination of student's level substitutes for the system of hundred-mark. The way of examination has been reformed. Concerned with the examination result, two levels or four levels are used. Two levels include pass or not pass. Four levels include excellent, good, satisfactory and unsatisfactory.

Features are centered on students' personalities.

Remarks are centered on students' conducts.

At present there are four characteristics concerning the model of comprehensive evaluation.

Firstly, evaluation indicators are complete. The new model is based on the goal of competence education and instruction program.

Secondly, evaluation result is classified as different levels. Various systems of levels have been used in primary schools and secondary schools.

Thirdly, evaluation indicators are pointed to students' development. The evaluation model is a developmental model.

Fourthly, evaluation system has various dimensions. The content of evaluation has various forms such as students' moral, intellectual, physical, aesthetic development. The ways of evaluation are diverse; they include checks, surveys, questionnaires, practice, selection, competition. The way of showing results include scores, levels, and remarks.

9.7.3.4   The Credit System

From 2006 on, the new curriculum reform in senior secondary schools has been implemented in China. The credit system is introduced in senior secondary schools. There are two kinds of credit systems. One is the school-year credit system. The course is given some credits, students are asked to obtain the required credits in each school year. When a student obtains minimum credits within three years, they can graduate from senior secondary schools. The second kind is the credit system on the basis of stage. There is no definite number of credits that students should obtain in one school year. Students can graduate if they obtain a definite total credits.

9.8 Problems Facing China in the System of Evaluation in Primary and Secondary Schools

9.8.1 Problems Facing China in the Evaluation of Schools

9.8.1.1 Lack of Various Evaluation Subjects and Tendency of Administration-Orientation

The present model of evaluation of schools is dominated by educational administrative departments. There are no active participants from society, community and parents. Subjects who make evaluation are monotypic. As a result of single subject of evaluation, the objectivity of evaluation of schools is not guaranteed.

Many persons suggest that subjects in making evaluation of schools should be diverse. Recently some intermediary organizations have been instituted. But the number of intermediary organizations is very small, so the functions of this kind of organizations have not been fulfilled effective.

9.8.1.2 Shortage of Development-Orientation in Evaluation of Schools

Up to now, evaluation of schools has been focusing on what schools have achieved in the past, and has been neglecting the future development in schools. The present model of evaluation of schools is a kind of summative evaluation; the formative evaluation and the diagnostic evaluation of schools are not considered seriously by education administrative departments. The formative evaluation of schools is centering on the enhancement of educational quality in the educational process. Educational activities should be oriented to future development.

At present, in some regions there are experiments on introducing formative evaluation of schools. In Shanghai many schools have introduced a new system of evaluation on the basis of fundamental indicators and developmental indicators.

9.8.1.3 Lack of Rationality in Evaluation Indicators

In the quantitative evaluation of schools and norm-reference evaluation of schools, the criteria in terms of hardware are of foremost importance for evaluation results. The criteria in terms of software are not as important as criteria in terms of hardware.

IN some cases the determination of indicators is full of accidents because the design of indicator system is based on researchers' personal efforts without complete pilot tests. Some indicators that do not relate to the core task of schools are included in the system of evaluation indicators.

There are too many evaluation indicators that aim to cover all aspects of schools. Too many evaluation indicators mean that the core indicators are not salient and are changed into trivial indicators.

9.8.1.4 Too Many Evaluation Indicators in Terms of Prohibited Behaviors

There are too many indicators in terms of prohibited behaviors and necessary conditions, so there are few indicators concerning innovation and development in schools. Competence education is the key element of schooling. In some cases many criteria of evaluation center on prohibited behaviors in schools. For instance, homework is prohibited, lessons conducted outside of schools are prohibited, and purchasing learning materials outside of schools is prohibited. These measures are beneficial to restriction of class hours in schools for students and decrease in students' learning loads, but it is a kind of temporary measure for school development. The parents will make compensation for reduction in school time by asking teachers have lessons for their children at home.

9.8.2 Problems Facing China in Evaluation of Teachers

9.8.2.1 The Positioning of Evaluation of Teachers

The positioning of evaluation of teachers refers to what kind of roles should evaluation of teachers play in schools' reform and development. The main issues that concern evaluation of teachers include why we need to make evaluation on teachers, and what changes will evaluation of teachers bring about for schools' development. Only after we have a rational positioning of evaluation of teachers, can we consider the issues of design of indicators and criteria effectively. If the total goal of evaluation is not clear, the design of indicators can be separated from the whole goal in schools.

There are two ways of irrational positioning of evaluation of teachers. Firstly, some persons regard evaluation of teachers as a simple thing. They maintained evaluation of teachers does not have internal and intimate connection with instruction and education reform, and regular management in schools. Actually this viewpoint does not recognize the importance of evaluation of teachers. Under this circumstance, evaluation of teachers is only conducted at the end of school-year and can be as simple as possible.

Secondly, evaluation is taken as if it is the same as management, or evaluation may substitute for management. In some schools some managers think that evaluation of teachers aims at making complete, objective and equitable appraisal of teachers, so they would like to use the system of determination of teachers' level or system of evaluation indicators used by managers. For schools it is necessary to make examination and appraisal of teachers, but if the aim is to make final certification of teachers and make ranking of teachers, it is not suitable.

Two points need to be considered. Firstly, it is difficult to make an accurate ranking of teachers on the basis of comprehensive criteria. Each teacher has his/her own characteristics. For the same work such as instruction, management of classes, teachers can be assessed, but it is difficult to make an accurate evaluation. If teachers have different tasks, it is more difficult to make assessment. Some teachers have much work load, while some teachers have higher level of proficiencies in work; hence how to make comparison between them? Some teachers are good at management of classes, while some teachers are good at instruction; hence how to make a comparison between them?

Secondly, if the aim of evaluation of teachers is to make ranking of teachers, the pressure on teachers could be increased. Such evaluation is centering on differentiation of teachers and normalization of teachers' behaviors; it is not centering on solving problems facing schools in instruction and education. Teachers cannot be guided and encouraged effectively.

9.8.2.2   Irrationality of Criterion of Evaluation of Teachers

The criteria of evaluation of teachers are hotly debated issues in the process of reform of evaluation of teachers. Many schools take appraisal and management as the basic goal of evaluation of teachers. They bring up the slogan, "objective, equitable, complete evaluation". Teachers care about the rationality of the criteria of evaluation. If the criteria are not rational, the evaluation would be misleading.

The irrationality of criteria of evaluation is manifested in three aspects. Firstly, there are some problems with the basic value criteria that the evaluation of teachers is drawn from. There are different opinions on the relationship between knowledge and competence, knowledge and learning habits, knowledge and personality, conduct and achievement. In the process of evaluation of teachers, some schools pay attention to teachers' language, gesture, climate in classroom, but do not pay attention to teachers' educational thoughts, students' learning states, teacher-students relationship. This kid of evaluation is misleading.

Secondly, there are tendencies of mechanization in the use of the criteria of evaluation of teachers. Some schools lay emphasis on unitary criteria but disregard differences in teachers' actual situations. Some schools lay emphasis on the horizontal comparison but disregard the vertical comparison. Some schools disregard the total quality and effectiveness.

9.8.2.3   Teachers' Passive Positions Under Great Pressure
from Schools and Society

Many schools use evaluation of teachers as a means to constrain teaches and urge them to work hard. They use the system of determination of teacher's level and system of evaluation indicator. Such way of evaluation put teachers in positions of being examined and assessed. Some teachers come under great pressure; some of them lose mental balance.

Statistics show that there are serious psychological problems among teachers. The incidence of psychological illness among teachers is higher than among ordinary groups. The psychological problems arise from many factors. The evaluation of teachers also has an influence on the teachers' mental states. Some schools take evaluation of teachers as a means of management and constraint.

A part of the teachers feel that much pressure or threat arises from the evaluation of teachers. They think it is difficult to improve work actively. The pressure can be transferred. If teachers have much pressure, it will show in the educational process; they can transfer the pressure and nervous feeling onto the students consciously or unconsciously. The imbalanced mind causes distorted behaviors and finally influences educational result.

There are tendencies of over elaborated and quantified evaluation of teachers. Some schools have made too elaborated systems of evaluation of teachers. The over elaborated system of evaluation of teachers increases the workload of managers and teachers in schools. When evaluation of teachers is conducted, the principals and teachers feel very tired because they need to make various evaluations and make statistics.

9.8.3 Problems Facing China in the System of Evaluation of Students

9.8.3.1 Limitation in Examination and Appraisal of Students Being "Good at Moral, Intellectual and Physical Development" Has Its Limitations

In the past, the examination and appraisal of students being 'good at moral, intellectual and physical development' has played many important roles in facilitating students' development. But as competence education is carried out gradually, the traditional way of determining students being good at has some moral, intellectual and physical development is of limitations. Firstly, the three aspects do not cover the basic competence of modern citizens. At present independence, initiative, creativity, practice competence, competence in information collection and processing, the competence in communication, competence in aesthetic examination, consciousness of openness, should be basic requirement for students. These aspects are not considered in the former criterion of examination and appraisal of students being 'good at moral, intellectual and physical development'. Secondly, the examination and appraisal of students being 'good at three moral, intellectual and physical development' is a process in which only a few students are selected as good students while other students are not chosen as good students, so most students have been despised to some extent.

9.8.3.2 New Evaluation Model Need to Be Perfected

The system of remark on conduct needs to be improved. One shortcoming in the system of remark on conduct is formalism. If the remarks on the conduct of students are the same, or do not change over a period time, the students are likely to ignore them. Another shortcoming is the unfair appraisal of students. How to master the scale of appraisal is a difficult task for students. Students should be encouraged to know their strengths and weaknesses objectively.

There also exist some problems with the comprehensive evaluation of students. Firstly, by using the system of levels, students and parents feel confused with the actual performance of students themselves. Students could ask the question, what "good" means? The elimination of scores in primary schools brings about the cooling effects on scores among students. But it also causes the problem of ambiguity. Teachers often obtain scores in examination papers and then transform the scores into various levels, but they do not have precise criteria to make this transformation. So they may use their personal judgment.

Now the evaluation of moral development is based on the system of levels. The levels are given according to teachers' observation and the students' ordinary performance. The level is given by way of quantitative analysis. Some students show the discrepancy between what they say and what they do. It is connected with the way of evaluation. The evaluation of competence is important for implementation of competence education.

9.9 Strategies and Measures for Reform of the System of Educational Evaluation

9.9.1 Strategies and Measures for Reform of the System of Educational Evaluation in Schools

9.9.1.1 Transformation from Unique Subject to Multiple Subjects in Evaluation of Schools

In order to make sure that the effectiveness of evaluation of schools is achieved, it is necessary to invite authoritative institutions and professional institutions to take part in the evaluation of schools. The relevant laws and regulations should be formulated and implemented. Educational administrative departments and schools should take responsibilities in evaluation of schools. Schools should be encouraged to invite social accreditation institutions to make accreditation on schools. Intermediary organizations should be instituted and perfected so as to play a more important part in evaluation of schools.

9.9.1.2   In Pursuit of the Process of Evaluation and Developmental Evaluation

The fundamental goal of evaluation of school is to facilitate school development. In the process of evaluation of schools, the assessors should find various problems in the examined schools and put forward suggestions and counter measures. The evaluation of schools not only focuses on what these schools have achieved and what these schools are doing now, but also what kind of goals these school are making effort to achieve.

9.9.1.3   Rationalization of Evaluation Indicators

The evaluation indicators concerning evaluation of schools should be determined by the need of evaluation. The weight of evaluation indicators should be determined by Delphi Methods. The system of valuation should have feasibility in practice.

9.9.1.4   Increase in Positive Evaluation Indicators

There are two ways of evaluation of schools. One way is using negative evaluation indicators so that many behaviors in schools are not permitted. The other way is using positive evaluation indicators so that many actions are advocated. The latter way is encouraged to be used widely.

9.9.2   Strategies and Measures for Reform of the System of Evaluation of Teachers

9.9.2.1   Making Rational Positioning of Evaluation of Teachers

In order to reform the evaluation of teachers more effectively, it is necessary to make accurate positioning of evaluation of teachers. Only by using a suitable model of evaluation of teachers can evaluation of teachers be coordinated with the work in schools and bring about good effect.

Three measures should be taken for making good positioning of evaluation of teachers. Firstly, the evaluation of teachers is not an independent work; it is a sensitive school work; it brings about multiple effects and functions. Evaluation of teachers should be taken as an important part of school work and has a strategic position. Evaluation of teachers may bring about various effects on teachers. In some cases the effects on teachers may not be brought about by the objective and scientific criteria of evaluation. Under different positioning of the evaluation, the evaluation process and results is will be different even if the evaluation criteria are the same.

For different teachers' work, evaluation of teachers should play different roles. Some teachers' work may have definite norms such as minimum working load, abiding by regulations and rules, definite quantities of homework, objective criteria of scholastic achievement. For these works, evaluation of teachers should play important roles of appraisal and management because these works are easy to make appraisal. But for some work that are very complicated, evaluation of teachers should play limited roles in terms of research, diagnosis, guidance, and development.

9.9.2.2   Principals' and Teachers' Correct Educational Ideals and Rational Evaluation Criteria

The principals and teachers should have correct education ideals. Firstly, principals and teachers should have correct viewpoints of professionals. Professional development should center on three aspects. The first aspect is teachers' physical development. The second aspect is teachers' socio-cultural development. The third aspect is teachers' external behaviors and results.

There are two basic aspects in the evaluation of teachers. One aspect is the basic requirements of teachers, and the second aspect is requirements for teachers' educational behavior. Correct viewpoints of instruction, viewpoints of total educational quality and viewpoints of educational effectiveness are needed for evaluation of teachers.

In order to formulate rational criteria of evaluation of teachers, it is necessary to take three measures. Advanced education ideals should be used to guide the formulation of criteria. For those behaviors that need to be normalized, the criteria of evaluation should be concrete, operative. For complicated behaviors, the criteria of evaluation should leave teachers to probe and no definite criteria should be formulated. Various ways of evaluation of teachers should be used. Evaluation of teachers can be divided into several parts.

In order to make teachers play an active role, it is necessary to take three measures. The self-evaluation of teachers should be the main form of evaluation. The managers in schools should not impose their subjective hypotheses on teachers; otherwise the evaluation of teachers will not be supported by teachers and will not bring about good results. Developmental evaluation combines external evaluation with internal evaluation and takes self-evaluation as the main form of evaluation. External assessors can make suggestions for teachers, but only teachers themselves can be conscious of their own strengths and weakness, promote strengths and overcome shortcomings, enhance levels of instruction and education.

In order to assure the greatest development effects for teachers, evaluation of teachers should be connected with the teachers' personal development plans. Teacher development plans should have concrete and specific requirements so as to guide teachers on enhancement of levels of instruction and education.

9.9.3   Strategies and Measures for Reform of the System of Evaluation of Students

The hundred-mark system should be reformed. The hundred-mark system has been used for many years, and it still has some reasonable factors. So it is useful to make some adjustment on this system. In senior secondary schools it can be used as the basic model. The hundred-mark system is used in college entrance examination. So for the smooth transition from senior secondary schools to higher education institutions need to retain the hundred-mark system in senior secondary schools.

Students being 'good at moral, intellectual and physical development' should be reformed. The criteria of being good at moral, intellectual and physical development should be perfected. Some schools have reformed the ways of choice of students that are good at moral, intellectual and physical development.

Remark on conduct is a new form of making reform in evaluation of students. It is in accordance with competence education. In the future two measures should be taken. Firstly, teachers should show their active feelings for students in making remarks on the conduct. Secondly, remark on conduct is only one form of evaluation.

References

Editorial Board of China's Education Yearbook (Ed.) (1984). China's Education Yearbook. Beijing: Chinese Great Encyclopedia Publishing House.

The State Education Commission. (1991). Collections of educational laws and regulations in China. Beijing: People's Education Press.

Chapter 10
Ensuring Higher Education Performance: Quality Assurance System of Higher Education in China

10.1 Introduction to the System of Quality Assurance of Higher Education

10.1.1 The Concept of System of Quality Assurance of Higher Education

Quality assurance of higher education refers to a set of approaches and procedures regarding the measurement, monitoring, guaranteeing, maintenance or enhancement of the quality of higher education institutions or providers and their programs of education, and the processes of evaluation by which are measured the achievements of education, and program standards, as established by institutions, professional organizations, government and other standard-setting bodies, are measured.

The main tool of quality assurance is the evaluation of higher education which is defined as a process in which the value of activities of higher education is judged through data systematically gathered, in order to achieve the cardinal goal of strengthening the link between higher education and society and accelerating the overall quality progress. In essence, evaluation of higher education is to evaluate such themes as the quality of management, quality of education, quality of discipline and students' achievements.

10.1.2 Classification of the System of Quality Assurance of Higher Education

The system of quality assurance of higher education consists of the institutions of quality assurance of higher education and the activities these institutions carry out. There are four classifications of the system of quality assurance of higher education.

© Springer Nature Singapore Pte Ltd. and Higher Education Press 2018
M. Yang and H. Ni, *Educational Governance in China*,
https://doi.org/10.1007/978-981-13-0842-0_10

Viewing from structure and functions, we can classify the system of quality assurance of higher education into four parts, and they are: quality assurance in training of manpower, quality assurance in scientific research, quality assurance in social service, quality assurance in international exchanges. Among these four parts, the system of quality assurance in training of manpower is the core. Higher education institutions should make efforts to activate teachers and students' enthusiasm and bring about good results. Quality assurance in scientific research refers to more and better scientific achievements brought about by researchers. Higher education institutions have been the axial institutions, and they need to provide sufficient social services. International exchange has become the important mission of higher education institutions.

An evaluation model consists of four factors. They are: context, input, process, and output. According to Stufflebeam, higher education evaluation is to judge whether higher education goals have been achieved or not and to make suggestions for decision making in higher education field. Based on this model, the system of quality assurance may consist of four factors: context evaluation, input evaluation, process evaluation and output evaluation.

The system of quality assurance of higher education is a process of dynamic monitoring of higher education process and outcome. So this system can be divided into four aspects. They are assurance of goal attainment, assurance of sufficient input, assurance of rational process, and assurance of effective monitoring. The assurance of goal attainment is the premise of assurance of quality of higher education. The assurance of sufficient input is the responsibility of governments and other sponsors. The assurance of rational process pertains to instruction and education. The assurance of effective monitoring is the responsibility of governments and society at large.

The formation and change of quality of higher education is both affected by factors within higher education system and by factors such as political, economic and cultural development. In order to enhance the quality of higher education, both internal assurance and external assurance are needed. So the system of assurance of quality of higher education can be classified as internal assurance system and external assurance system.

10.1.3   Functions of the System of Quality of Assurance of Higher Education

Quality assurance has been one of the major concerns in the Chinese higher education debate in the last two decades. In adapting to the emerging structure of the socialist market economy for the time being, China's higher education is committed to develop an autonomous system under the government's general guidance. The quality assurance of higher education is now playing an increasingly important role in assessing educational performance, the efficiency of running higher education institutions and teaching efficiency within government guidelines. So it is necessary to summarize the Chinese experience in quality assurance practice and strengthen the study of the quality assurance theory to bring China's higher education evaluation up to a new level.

There are three developmental stages of quality assurance of higher education in China as given below.

10.2   The System of Assurance of Higher Education (1949–1956)

China has had a long history of evaluation of higher education, but the history of evaluation in the modern sense is comparatively brief. It was only after 1949 that evaluation of higher education in the modern sense was able to develop.

After the founding of the People's Republic of China, higher education was reformed step by step. Firstly, Chinese Communist Party strengthened the leadership on HEIs. The basic length of schooling was determined and curriculum in HEIs was reformed. So the quality of higher education was enhanced gradually.

On 1 June, 1950, the first national conference on higher education was convened in Beijing. Higher educational guidelines were put forward. Higher education aimed at cultivating high level professionals who had high cultural level, mastered modern scientific and technological knowledge and skills, and served the people.

In October 1954, the Administrative Council issued *Decisions on the Revision of Relationship in HEIs*. The *Decisions* stipulated that the unitary instruction plans, instruction programs and textbooks should be used in HEIs across country.

On 20 June, 1956, Yang Xiu Feng, the Minister of Education, pointed out that thereafter reform and development of higher education should center on enhancement of the quality of higher education. Students' competence in independent thinking and independent work should be cultivated with great efforts.

10.3   The System of Assurance of Higher Education (1957–1965)

In 1957, the higher education reform was conducted. The principle of training of teacher staff that was both red and professional was emphasized. The principle of combination of theories with practice was strengthened so as to train students' independent work competence. The combination of research and instruction was taken care of.

In 1958, the basic curricula were lessened, theoretical instruction was weakened, instruction in classroom was neglected, too much production labor was conducted, and teachers' and students' time in learning and instruction was cut.

From 1961 on, the regulations on higher education were carried out. In September 1961 *Provisional Regulations on HEIs Affiliated with the Ministry of Education* was issued. The quality of higher education was enhanced gradually.

10.4   The System of Assurance of Higher Education (1966–1976)

During the "Cultural Revolution", the quality of higher education was lowered to a certain extent.

10.5   The System of Assurance of Higher Education from 1977 to 1991

In this period there were two small stages, from 1977 to 1984 and from 1985 to 1991.

10.5.1   Preparatory Stage (1977–1984)

There were three reasons for the quick development in modern quality assurance of higher education in China during this period of time.

Firstly, we needed to evaluate the reform of bringing order to higher education shortly after the so-called the "Cultural Revolution". During the period of 1966–1976, Chinese universities and colleges suspended enrollment for ten years, and this caused great shortage of trained personnel in 1980s and 1990s. Meanwhile key universities and colleges were eliminated so as to make higher education opportunity more equal. The content of curricula of universities and colleges on the average were probably reduced.

From 1977 on, China began to implement the policy of reform and openness to outside world. HEIs were now expected to provide students with a sound understanding of basic theory that could be broadly applied to the development of solutions dependent upon high technology. They were also required to provide research and development that were essential to the four modernizations.

As far as higher education was concerned, four important measures were taken shortly after 1977. The national college entrance examination was restored in 1977, and more than 100,000 students entered universities and colleges each year. More than 30 key universities and colleges were renamed in 1978; they were recognized as best HEIs (Higher Education Institutions) and set models of quality education for other HEIs. In 1980 the States Council issued *Regulations on Degrees Accreditation in the People's Republic of China*, bachelor's, master's and doctorate's degree system were reinstated in universities and colleges (He 1998a, b). New curricula in universities and colleges were also reformed, standards of curricula were made out, a lot of new textbooks were rewritten. Learning modern advanced science and technology from western countries was stressed.

Secondly, new disciplines, especially evaluation theories, were introduced to China from the West. Taylor's theory of curriculum and teaching as well as Bloom' theory of taxonomy of educational objectives and Cronbach's theory of evaluation were introduced and put into use in schools and colleges.

Thirdly, the government's line to seek the truth and to emancipate the mind helped to pave the way towards the quality assurance of higher education in China. In the past, education was the main tool of class struggle and ideological control. Since 1978, the function of production concerning education has been recognized. The human capital theory was introduced into China. The essence of education was re-evaluated. As the national development strategies centered on the economic development, higher education system must provide a great quantity of qualified personnel for economic and cultural development.

Major studies on evaluation of higher education were undertaken in some regions and departments. For example, in 1982, the Ministry of Hygiene carried out an evaluation of teaching quality in its subordinate colleges of medicine by means of a unified examination. Also, in order to meet the demand for theoretical study, some foreign academic achievements were successively introduced to China. But on the whole, the higher education evaluation at this time was still dispersed rather than coherent.

10.5.2   All-Round Development Stage (1985–1991)

The promulgation of *Decision on Reform of Educational System* in May, 1985, marked a fruitful era for China's quality assurance of higher education (Editorial Board of Chinese Educational Yearbook 1985). In this document, higher education institutions are depicted as being responsible for two main tasks. One was the training of advanced personnel, essentially the same role as was described in the fifties; the other was developing science, technology and culture, a new and more open-ended agenda that called for new research initiatives and direct involvement in economic and social reform. The problems of the past were seen as resulting from "excessive government control", which was to be eliminated in favor of "extending the decision-making power of the universities and colleges under the guidance of unified educational policies and plans of states." (Editorial Board of Chinese Educational Yearbook 1985). The promised new autonomy was to take concrete form in a number of ways according to the provisions of this document. Enrollments were now no longer to be entirely restricted to state allocated quotas set in accordance with national planning; universities were allowed to enroll additional students whose expenses were paid through contracts with enterprises as well as private students. Possibly the most significant new freedom promised to universities was concerning their curricula. Universities were assured power to "redefine the goals of different specializations, draw up teaching plans and syllabi and compile and select teaching materials". Major activities of quality assurance in this period included:

The first national session on the evaluation of higher education held in Jingpohu of Heilongjiang province in June 1985. Follow-up sessions were held in Hefei of Anhui province, Beijing and Tianjin to continue studies on the nature of evaluation of higher education, especially its purposes, principles, processes and criteria.

Multi-level higher education evaluations were brought into full play in which at least eight Ministries or Commissions, six Education Committees at provincial and municipal levels and 500 regular higher education institutions were involved. The Ministry of Coal Industry and Shanghai Municipality worked together to make evaluation of universities and colleges in Shanghai.

External exchanges concerning evaluation of higher education were stressed. Two Sino-American symposia on education evaluation were held and supervision groups were sent to the USA and Canada as a part of collaboration projects with these countries.

A number of theoretical advances were made and academic periodicals were published during this time; for instance, *Reports on Evaluation of Higher Education* which was first issued in 1988.

By the end of the seventh Five-Year Plan, a capable cohort of higher education evaluation researchers had been formed in which higher education administrators, experts on higher education, and faculty on campus were the backbone.

10.6   The System of Assurance of Higher Education (1992–2016)

Since the 1990s, great changes have taken place in higher education in China. Firstly, the transitions from socialist planning economy to socialist market economy promoted the breakthrough of reforms of management in higher education. The impetus for this kind of development came from Deng Xiaoping's talk during his tour in South China in 1992. The goal of building up a socialist market economy system set at the fourteenth National Congress which broke with the convention of the planned economy system provided a good environment for educational evaluation in China. From 1992 on, Chinese universities and colleges were restructured. The restructuring of universities and colleges lays a solid basis for quality assurance of higher education.

Secondly, the advocating and implementing of competence-oriented higher education changes the objective and curricula of higher education institutions. The competence-oriented higher education is characterized by the following five aspects: (1) every student is well cared for; (2) student's all-round development is stressed; (3) innovative capabilities and practical abilities are cultivated: (4) student's personality is well respected; (5) student's lifelong learning and lifelong development is cared for.

Thirdly, the transition from elite higher education to mass higher education needed to construct a new quality assurance system. Since 1998, China has been increasing the enrollment of higher education rapidly; the students in HEIs increased from 7.53 million in 1998 to 9.53 million in 1999, 11.84 million in 2000, and 13 million in 2001. In 2003 the entry rate of tertiary education amounted to about 15%. According to Martin Turow's theory of higher education development, China has been making the transition from elite higher education to mass higher education recently. On the one hand, the rapid expansion of higher education increases the opportunity of higher education for graduates in secondary schools and makes the higher education more equal and more democratic. On the other hand, the rapid expansion of higher education also makes the supply of higher education resources a major concern; quite a few HEIs are short of staff, facilities, dormitories, dining halls, classrooms, books. Many people are worried about the lowering of quality in HEIs. The impetus to build up new quality assurance system is urgent.

Fourthly, in 2001 China become a member of WTO. China made a partial promise for higher education; foreign organizations and institutions can supply higher education service in China. The internationalization of higher education brings opportunities as well as difficulties to Chinese higher education institutions. The quality assurance of overseas students is also a major concern.

The main activities of quality assurance in this period included:

(1) The Bureau of Higher Education in Shanghai made an evaluation of four new HEIs; it is recognized by the State Education Commission. Other provinces and cities also made the similar evaluation.
(2) The State Education Commission delegated the Institute of Degree and Graduate Education to assess 34 graduate schools of universities and colleges.
(3) The fifth National Session on evaluation of higher education which was held in Changchun in Jilin province in January 1994 at which the Higher Education Evaluation Society was founded; it was the first of its kind in China.
(4) A symposium on evaluation of higher education in counties around the Pacific Rim was held. National evaluation of higher education lectures and a Sino-American Evaluation Seminar on higher education were also sponsored in the same year, which were of benefit to Chinese scholars.
(5) In 1994, an Appraisal Committee on Universities and Colleges evaluated the newly booming non-state run universities and colleges, six of which were approved.
(6) In July 1995, the State Education Commission organized a group of 140 experts and scholars from various universities and colleges all over China to appraise as many as 2700 monographs, papers, reference books and research reports published during the past decade. More than 500 items were given the grading of "Academic Excellence."
(7) New progress was also made in theoretical study. More than one thousand papers on the evaluation of higher education were published.

(8) In 1995, the National Education Commission (SEC) published "*Methods and Procedures of Evaluation of Undergraduate Instruction in Regular Higher Education Institutions*" (He 1998a, b). In 1997, it provided some evaluation scheme, in 1998 it made some suggestions on evaluation schema, in 1999 it made out the guideline for expert's examination. Since 1995 many universities and colleges were evaluated by SEC.

(9) Since the 1990s, more than ten non-governmental assessment agencies of higher education have been set up; they have been conducting many evaluation activities.

(10) University ranking activities are attracting more and more people's attention.

(11) In 1998, Higher Education Law stipulated that development levels and educational quality in higher education should be supervised by educational administrative departments and be assessed by other organizations. Evaluation of quality in higher education obtained a legal position. Evaluation of higher education became an important tool and means of management of higher education in accordance with laws.

(12) In 2001, the ministry of Education issued Some Opinions on Strengthening Undergraduate Instruction in HEIs and Enhancing Instruction Quality. It was suggested that educational administrative departments should establish mechanisms for evaluation of the quality of undergraduate instruction and system of macro-monitoring. From 2003 on, the Initiative on Instruction Quality and Instruction Reform were to be conducted.

(13) In 2010, On 29 July, 2010, the Central Committee of the Chinese Communist Party and the State Council issued *National Guidelines for Medium and Long-term Educational Reform and Development Program (2010–2020)*. The *National Guidelines* stipulated that Program of HEIs' undergraduate instruction reform should be implemented completely, management of instruction should be observed more strictly, the quality assurance system should be perfected, and instruction evaluation should be improved.

(14) In 2011, the Ministry of Education issued *Opinions on Undergraduate Instruction Evaluation in Regular HEIs*. The Opinions stipulated that in the process of undergraduate instruction evaluation HEIs' role of subjects should be guaranteed, the basic instruction data bank should be established, and normal monitoring of instruction quality should be conducted.

(15) On 16 March, 2012, the Ministry of Education issued *Some Opinions on Completely Improving Higher Education*. The Opinions regarded cultivation of talents as the foremost important task for HEIs, and took HEIs' intensive development as the core factor of enhancement of educational quality.

(16) In 2016, the Ministry of Education issued *Guiding Opinions on Deepenning of Reform of Education and Instruction*. The *Guiding Opinions* stipulated that Center for Teachers Development should be set up in each HEI so as to conduct teacher training, instruction counseling, research on instruction reform and evaluation of instruction quality.

10.7 Current Situations of the System of Quality Assurance of Higher Education

10.7.1 Accreditation of Higher Education Institutions in China

Accreditation is the qualifying evaluation of basic facilities, books, personnel and basic educational quality in higher education institutions. It is realized in undergraduate and post-graduate education.

10.7.1.1 Accreditation of Undergraduate Education

In China, accreditation is organized and implemented by the Ministry of Education. The evaluation is made when the new institution's new students have graduated for the first time in the history of the institute.

All new institutions of higher learning should satisfy the basic educational requirements prescribed by the government: (a) appointment of full time presidents with higher political quality and managerial competence and fulltime heads of the academic departments; (b), appointment of faculty members of whom no less than 10 should have qualifications above associate professorship; (c) appropriate land and school buildings for the needs of teaching, physical education and daily living; (d) library facilities—for schools of arts, law and finance not less than 80,000 volumes and for schools for science, engineering, agriculture and medicine not less than 60,000 volumes; (e) necessary capital investment and educational expenditure; (f) a university should have no less than three main disciplines (arts, law, finance, sciences, agriculture, engineering and medicine), higher teaching and research strength and more than 5000 students.

The conclusion of the accreditation process is: complete qualified institution, temporarily qualified institution and unqualified institution. In the case of the qualified institutions, the Ministry of Education publishes the list of these institutions and issues the certificate of passing the qualifying evaluation. The temporarily qualified institutions need to take measures to improve the facilities, books, staff as well as educational quality, and get re-accreditation next time. For the unqualified institutions, basing on the concrete circumstances, the Ministry of Education asks them to rectify, stop enrollment or close down.

From 1966 to 1976 no academic degree was granted at either graduate or undergraduate level. In February of 1980, the 13th Plenary of the 5th National Congress adopted "*Regulations on Degrees Accreditation in People's Republic of China*" (Editorial Board of Chinese Educational Yearbook 1985). This document is the first educational law since China adopted the policy of reform and Opening to outside world. This law followed the North American pattern, namely, a bachelor degree for all completing academic and professional programs, master's degrees requiring three years of further study, and another three years for doctoral degrees.

According to this law, colleges and universities which plan to award doctorate degrees or master's degrees should be evaluated in terms of the program's quality and qualifications of faculty members, complying with *Regulations for Academic Degree of the People's Republic of China*. Statistics show that China has more than 1000 colleges and universities providing undergraduate programs, among which over 300 offered postgraduate ones. More than 300 institutions of research also train graduates, but not all of them could award academic degrees. In order to do so, these institutions of research must apply for approval based on the evaluation done by the National Committee on Degree Accreditation.

In accordance with *Principles and Measures on the Degree Accreditation* colleges and universities must meet the following standards:

A college or university which is qualified to award the bachelor's degree should be one where the establishment is approved by the State Council and where major fields of undergraduate study are appropriate with the guiding principles of curriculum formulated by the Ministry of Education. They should:

- be capable of providing the major courses of the field, mostly taught by qualified teachers with titles above 'lecturer';
- be capable of directing the required laboratory work at a fairly high level;
- possess a certain number of teachers with titles above 'lecturer' to supervise the completion of these;
- have a sound system of examination and assessment of the results of teaching and learning.

An institution which is qualified to award master's degree must be one of the colleges or universities enrolling postgraduates approved by the Ministry of Education or by the respective Ministries of the State Council. The major fields of study must reach the following standards:

- Faculty members need to be at a fairly high academic level with fruitful achievements in teaching and research. The advisors for master's degree students are required to be professors or associate professors.
- They have to be capable of setting up the required courses and elective courses of basic theories, specialized theories and technical laboratory courses.
- They have a definite direction for research in the major fields of study, and be capable of supplying the necessary equipment for experiments, research and reference materials for the graduation thesis.
- They have a sound system of examination and assessment.

The qualifications of awarding doctorate degrees are to be limited to those colleges, universities and research institutes associated with the Ministries of the State Council. Some major fields of study in other institutions with the following conditions can also be qualified:

- They have advisors of fairly high academic attainments with prominent achievements in teaching and research.

- They are capable of providing favorable conditions of learning and research to the fullest extent, and giving assurance for the accomplishment of the studies.
- They have a sound system of examination.

On 2 June 2014, the Meeting of International Engineering Ferdaration was held in Kuala Lumpur, and China has been the signer of "Washington Accord" (the International undergraduate engineering degree agreement). The engineering education quality has been recognized by other countries.

10.7.2 Accreditation and Evaluation of Graduate Education

10.7.2.1 Examination and Ratifying of Master's and Doctorate's Degree-Granting Institutions

From July 26 to August 2 in 1981, the National Committee on Degree Accreditation called a meeting of its Groups for Assessment of Subject-Matter Areas in Beijing. It was the first meeting of this committee and was attended by 436 groups of members and scholars of natural science and social sciences, among which 162 were academicians. They examined and approved the first list of colleges, universities, and research institutes which were authorized to award doctorate's degrees, master's degrees and bachelor's degrees in particular subject areas. It was announced that 15 institutions were authorized to award doctorate's degrees, among them 812 particular subjects were authorized to award doctorate's degrees in 1981; 358 institutions were authorized to award master's degrees, among them 3158 subject areas were authorized for master's degrees, among them 812 particular subjects were authorized for master's degrees. Keeping up with the principles of "quality first, with steady progress" and "adhering to the standard with strict demands, quality assurance and just treatment", they carried out an earnest assessment. There are 358 institutions to award master's degrees covering 3158 sections for major fields of study, among which colleges and universities accounted for 84.2%. There were 15 institutions which were approved to award doctorate degrees covering 812 sections of major fields of study, among which colleges and universities occupied 75%.

At present there are 117 members on the National Committee on Degree Accreditation, including the leading figures of the Ministry of Education and nationally famous scientists and scholars (all on part-time basis). The president and the vice-president of the committee were appointed by the State Council. The Group for Assessment of Subject-Master Areas is an academic operational group subordinated to the Committee, consisting of outstanding scientists and scholars, assigned on the basis of recommendation. There were 758 members who were divided into 10 assessment groups of philosophy, economics, laws, education, literature, history, science, engineering, agriculture and medical science. They conduct regular evaluation on higher education programs.

10.7.2.2   The Quality Assessment of Degree-Granting Activities

In October of 1991, the National Committee on Degree Accreditation and the former State Education Commission (operation between 1985 and 1998) issued *"Notice on the Assessment of Degree-awarding Work and Postgraduate Education in the Discipline of Liberal Arts"* (Department of Policy and Law in the National Education Commission 1995).

The main task of this assessment was to examine and assess the ratified degree-granting institutions, disciplines and specializations and determined whether they could keep on granting degrees. The unqualified ones would be suspended temporarily or stopped completely from granting specific degree.

After several years' practice, the National Committee on Degree Accreditation issued "Notice on the Qualifying Assessment on the Basic Requirement in the Doctorate's and Master's Degree-granting Institutions". This Notice pointed out that in order to put much more emphases on the improvement of quality in degree-granting work and postgraduate education, it is necessary to make an examination of the basic requirements of degree-granting institutions because some of them would fall far behind the development of other institutions. Up to now, all of the former degree-granting institutions have been examined once.

From 1998 on, the Ministry of Education and Degree Commission under the State Council conducted the evaluation of doctoral dissertations across country. The number of doctoral dissertations was 100 every year. If there were not enough excellent dissertations, less than 100 doctoral dissertations were permitted. In 1999 the Ministry of Education and Degree Commission under the State Council issued *Methods on Evaluation of Excellent Doctoral Dissertations across Country*. In 2001 the financing methods of authors winning the excellent doctoral dissertations in HEIs across country was issued by the Ministry of Education. By the end of 2007, more than 880 doctoral dissertations were examined and approved as excellent dissertations. The evaluation of excellent doctoral dissertations was beneficial to the enhancement of the quality of higher education. It was beneficial to arouse graduates' innovative spirit and train high level creative talents.

On 29 January, 2014, the Degree Commission under the jurisdiction of the State Council and the Ministry of Education issued *Regulations on Sampling Examination of Doctoral and Master Dissertations*. The Regulations stipulated that in every year 10% of doctoral dissertations and 5% of master dissertations should be chosen to be reexamined by three experts. If one expert regards the dissertation is unqualified, then this dissertation would be reviewed by two other experts. If one of them regarded it as unqualified, then this dissertation would be regarded as problematic dissertation. Relevant universities, colleges and supervisors should take measures to improve quality of dissertations.

10.7.3   The Evaluation of Instruction at Various Levels

The evaluation of instruction is the most important measure to guarantee the quality of higher education. The evaluation of instruction takes place at the state level, at institution level, at department level, at subject level.

The National Committee on Degree Accreditation had a forum of quality examination and put forward the requirements for the examination and assessments in 2007.

It is decided to make examination of the quality in some sub-disciplines and specializations. The expert group was set up and the indicator system of quality assessment is constructed. The conclusion of examination was classified as very good, good, satisfied, failed. In 2007, the expert group conducted an examination of the discipline of metal materials. The conclusions made by the expert group were as follows: as far as master's degree is concerned, 36 specializations or 49% are very good, 9 specializations or 25% are good. Under the guidance of the National Committee on Degree Accreditation, the expert groups conducted quality examination of 25 disciplines which cover social sciences and humanity, liberal arts, engineering, agriculture and medicine.

10.7.3.1   The Evaluation of Instruction at State Level

In the 1990s, the National Education Commission organizes and implemented the evaluation of undergraduate instruction. It became the main task of the National Education Commission concerning education evaluation institutions. There were three reasons for the implementation of this kind of evaluation.

Firstly, since 1992, China began to move from highly concentrated planning economic system to market economic system. In order to adapt to the reform of economic system, China's higher education administration system needed further reform, both the macro-level administration of higher education and autonomy of HEIs are stressed. The evaluation of higher education was regarded as an important means of macro-level administration.

Secondly, undergraduate education was the basis of higher education development; the quality and efficiency of undergraduate education reflected the quality and efficiency of higher education in the whole nation. The rapid development of higher education brought some problems.

On one hand, although the quality and efficiency in most HEIs were high, in some HEIs the performances were not as good as many stakeholders expected. Some new HEIs did not have the necessary staff, building, books and other facilities, so the quality could not be assured.

On the other hand, in the period of rapid development and great reform, some HEIs made insufficient input of expenditure, time and vigor of administrators, time and vigor of teachers, time and vigor of students, so the quality of under-graduate instruction were going down.

Thirdly, these 1053 HEIs have different bases, strength and weakness, power, as well as tasks. So it was vary important for them to have their own orientation and build up their own characteristics. The academic drifts should be prevented effectively.

The Department of Higher Education in the National Education Commission issued *"Notice on the Evaluation of Undergraduate Instruction in Some HEIs"* (He 1998a, b). It was announced that 165 HEIs would be evaluated within three years.

According to differences between evaluation objects, the evaluation of undergraduate instruction is classified into three kinds, namely qualifying evaluation, excellence evaluation and random evaluation.

The target of qualifying evaluation is the new institutions, and they usually have lower starting points. This kind of evaluation aims at improving the basic construction of instruction and quality of teaching and learning.

The targets of excellence evaluation are the best HEIs; they usually have long history of development, good bases of administration and high quality of instruction. This kind of evaluation aims at the choice of the best universities and colleges; these universities and colleges will be recognized as key universities and colleges and would get additional financial support from governments.

The random evaluation is suitable for those HEIs that lay between these two kinds of institutions mentioned above; they are not too good but not too bad, either. This kind of evaluation aims at improving the quality of instruction and efficiency of running the institution.

The main criterion of evaluation of undergraduate instruction is the "Evaluation Scheme of Undergraduate Education in HEIs". These schemes we developed by various expert groups according to different HEIs. Up to now, these schemes were used for comprehensive universities and those universities and colleges which specialized in engineering, agriculture, medicine as well as other disciplines.

As far as procedures are concerned, the evaluation consists of three stages.

The first stage is self-assessment by HEI; it is the basis of evaluation. In this stage, the HEIs write the self-assessment report and present it to the Ministry of Education. The self-assessment will not only deepen the reform and construction, but also lay a solid foundation for further development through self-assessment.

The second stage is examination by expert groups. Before going into the higher education institution, the expert group will receive specific training of supervision. After going to the institution, they will read the self-assessment report, listen to the report of the administrator of the institution, listen to lecturers, interview teachers and students, visit laboratories and other places. After getting a complete knowledge about the general affairs of this institution, the expert group will write a report and present it to the Ministry of Education; in the report, they will draw a conclusion of the examination. Meanwhile, the expert group will talk with the managers of the institution and make suggestions about the improvement of undergraduate instruction.

The third stage is rectification and improvement. After receiving the expert group's opinion and suggestion, the concerned institution will make a plan of rectification and improvement, and present it to the the Ministry of Education. The institution will build up the quality assurance system and take measures to resolve the deep-seated problems in the process of running the institution.

The Ministry of Education stipulates that the result of the evaluation of undergraduate instruction is the basis for an institution to increase undergraduate specialization, or become masters or doctorates degree-granting institution. For those institutions that are recognized as unqualified institutions, they will be asked to rectify in time, or suspend enrollment, or stop granting bachelors degrees. The term of validity of this evaluation is six years, during this period the NEC would conduct supervision if necessary.

The Ministry of Education evaluated 254 HEIs till 2002, among which, 192 passed the qualifying evaluation, 16 passed the excellence evaluation, and 46 passed the random evaluation. It was decided that the Ministry of Education will make a round of evaluation every five years, since 1998.

The evaluation of undergraduate instruction in China is different from other countries' evaluation.

On the one hand, Chinese higher education is dominated by state-run or public higher education; it is necessary for the governments to control, accredit and evaluate higher education. Accreditation and evaluation are important means of macro-level management of higher education. Chinese governments rely on experts to make evaluation. The formulation of the evaluation schema, process of evaluation and making the conclusion, all depend on the expert's opinion. Therefore, evaluation of undergraduate instruction is directly administrated by governments. This is not only different from many developed countries in which governments do not involve in evaluation of higher education, but also different from some western countries in which government supervise HEIs directly.

On the other hand, the evaluation of undergraduate instruction is a holistic evaluation of undergraduate-level instruction. It is different from accreditation and curriculum evaluation as well as comprehensive evaluation of whole university or college.

In 2013, the Ministry of Education organized an expert commission on undergraduate instruction in HEIs, the expert commission made an qualified assessment on undergraduate instruction for 80 new-established HEIs.

In 2015, Report on Higher Education Quality in China was published by the Ministry of Education, this Report indicated that the most weak area of instruction in HEIs was the innovation education and entrepreneurship education.

10.7.3.2   The Evaluation of Instruction at Institution Level

General evaluation of the university performance is an all-round examination of the guiding principles of running of the institution, conditions of implementation of the policy of the government, state of institutional construction and the quality of political education, faculty development, research and social service.

The general evaluation is carried out generally every four to five years. Since the middle of 1983, the Shanghai Bureau of Higher Education has developed inter-college evaluation procedure in Shanghais municipality as follows:

In every university and college, there are two kinds of instructional supervisors, one kind is the instruction supervisors employed by universities and colleges, all these supervisors were part-time experts, some of them are retired experts, so they have enough time to make supervision on instruction in universities and colleges. In departments or colleges, experts also are employed to make instruction supervision.

Nowadays many universities and colleges have been publishing their instructional evaluation reports.

10.7.3.3   The Evaluation of Quality at Department Level

Zhejiang University has been experimenting with departmental-based evaluation in the major in fields of optical instrumental engineering. Taking the responsibilities for training qualified undergraduates and postgraduates of master's or doctorate degrees as well as making the university a center for research, the evaluation focused on the achievements, problems, and directions in teaching, research, and management. Summarization of these aspects is to be assessed jointly by administrators, experts and staff.

Tongji University in Shanghai has also experimented with a departmental-based evaluation on major fields of study. On the basis of extensive evaluation on major fields of study and on the basis of extensive discussions and interviews, the evaluation committee members vote by ballot on each of the necessary items in different ranks: excellent (grade 5), good (grade 4), fair (grade 3), pass (grade 2) and fail (grade 1).

10.7.3.4   The Evaluation of Instruction at Subject Level

Curriculum development is an important problem in educational reform and development. A great number of institutions make the subject-based evaluation as breakthrough point in educational evaluation. It is recognized that curriculum development is the basic construction of higher education institutions.

In order to guarantee the instructional quality in the whole institution, it is necessary to make sure teachers and students are doing the best in every course. Formal evaluation of curriculum will introduce the competition mechanism. The most critical problem facing curriculum evaluation is the contradiction between multiplicity of various courses and simplification of course evaluation.

Some Chinese universities and colleges make efforts to solve this problem. Beijing Light Industrial College has been making progress in this area. Its experience is as follows:

Firstly, the institution determines seven "curriculum assessment units", namely, instructional goal, teaching staff, teaching conditions, quality of teaching, caring not only for students' acquirement of knowledge and skill but also for students' moral and professional development, organization of instruction, quality of learning.

Secondly, the institution sets up nine curriculum assessment series, namely, political courses, foreign language courses, natural science courses, laboratory courses, practice courses inside of campus, practice courses outside of campus, design courses.

Thirdly, for every curriculum assessment series, the curriculum assessment unit has a common assessment element which is the same for all and a specific element which is characterized by this unit.

Tsinghua University's experience of evaluation of subjects is a good example. To begin with, 12 key university-based subjects and 33 key department-based subjects are chosen for evaluation. Two principles were laid down to make up the evaluation indicators. Firstly, evaluation indicators must be applicable to the evaluation of different types of subjects. Secondly, evaluation factors must be clear and good for curriculum development. Using the evaluation indicators in combination with on-site visit, these subjects are evaluated within one year. After four or five years all subjects would be evaluated at least once.

The evaluation of teachers' teaching quality is a very important step to improve educational quality. Many HEIs build up their own evaluation methods. Every semester, Zhejiang University makes an evaluation of every course. After mid-semester, for every course, students are given a questionnaire which consists of twelve indicators. Every indicator uses five grades (5 is best, 1 is worst). Students are encouraged to make suggestions about the improvement of teaching quality when filling in the questionnaire. In the total score assessment, every course is ranked, and the result will be published in universities website and bulitins ando form the basis for teachers' promotion and rewarding.

10.7.4 University Rankings

In 1987, the Academy of Management Science published the first Chinese university ranking. Up to now there were about 30 different kinds of university ranking made by more than 14 research institutions, among which, the famous ones are the university ranking made by the Ministry of Education, Wu Shulian and netbig.com, a private origination.

Since 2000, the Ministry of Education has been publishing the university ranking. This ranking is not a comprehensive ranking. The Ministry of Education made a ranking of universities using several performance indicators. These indicators are classified into eight parts.

Part one is the ranking of staffs; the indicators include the number of teachers who take part in the "prominent personnel planning", the number of professors and associate professors, the number of postdoctoral mobile stations, and the numbers of supervisor of post doctoral students.

Part two is the ranking of national key disciplines, and the indicator includes the number of national key disciplines.

Part three is the ranking of articles, and the indicators include the number of articles received by SCI, the number of international articles being cited, the number of national excellent articles.

Part four is the ranking of expenditure on scientific research, and the indicators include the total expenditure of scientific research, the total expenditure received from the National Science Fund.

Part five is the ranking of awards, and the indicators include the number of national scientific and technological progress awards, technological invention awards, and national natural science award.

Part six is the ranking of scientific activities; the indicator includes the number of patents asking for ratification and received.

Part seven is the ranking of employment rate of graduates.

Part eight is the ranking of first-level disciplines; the indicator includes the power of every discipline of every university.

Netbig.com, a commercial web site, has been providing Chinese university ranking since 1999. When it began this program, there were few university ranking in China; so it attracted much attention especially from universities, students and parents. Netbig.com's university ranking is a social evaluation. There are three characteristics of Netbig.com's university ranking: (1) one principle, namely objective, fair, and scientific; (2) one viewpoint, namely viewing the ranking from consumer's position; (3) one direction, namely reflecting the efficiency and effectiveness of universities and colleges. Netbig.com builds up an evaluation indicator system that consists of five first-level indicators and eighteen second-level indicators. However, Netbig.com is criticized by many people, for its only source of information is from the Internet.

Since 1998, Wu Shulian and his colleagues have published ten university rankings of the top 100 universities, and these rankings have caused great debates in China (Wu 1997). There are 25 evaluation indicators. The weights of indicators are given by 203 experts using the Delphi method. The data set is from official publications of natural science and social science activities of HEIs.

Since 2000, Wu Shulian has been publishing the comprehensive ranking of Chinese university ranking in which the undergraduate universities and colleges, the 2–3 years' vocational universities and colleges, graduate schools, disciplines, specializations were ranked. According to Wu Shulian's opinion, their rankings were characterized by the use of public data set concerning HEIs, making the comparison of different kinds of universities and colleges possible, and having the functions of accreditation and diagnosis. According to Chinese university ranking in 2016 made by Wu Shulian's Team, the best ten universities are Tsinghua University, Zhejiang University, Beijing University, Shanghai Jiaotong University, Fudan University, Nanjing University, Wuhan University, Zhognshan University, Huazhong Sci-tech University.

University ranking influences many stakeholders of higher education, such as managers of HEIs, teachers, students, parents, employers, officers of governments, fund providers. There is no great consensus about the functions, types, provides, methods, indicators, and data set concerning ranking among these stakeholders. The university ranking can provide useful information about HEIs, so it will continue to attract many people's attention and need to become a sound quality assurance means.

10.7.5   The Assessment of Key Construction Projects

Since 1978, the Chinese government has made various assessments on key construction projects; the higher education institutions that are assessed as qualified to participate in the key construction projects may get funds and other kinds of support and get an even greater competitive advantages. A great part of public funds, especially research funds, is distributed through this channel.

In 1995, the State Council ratified *The Total Construction Plan for the '211 Project'*. The government would like 100 HEIs and more than 100 key disciplines to improve educational quality, level of research, level of management and effectiveness of education. In the period 1995–2000, 99 HEIs and 602 national key disciplines received 10.894 billion RMB Yuan funds for the "211 Project", which was the biggest investment program since 1949.

In 1998, the Ministry of Education decided to initiate the "985 Project" which aimed at building up several world-class universities and colleges. Beijing University, Qinghua University and Zhejiang University were among the top ones.

The key construction projects have made some achievements. Many universities and colleges took measures to attract overseas experts and train domestic teachers. They are also eager to undertake major research programs.

On 24 October, 2015, the State Council issued *Program on Building of World-class Universities and World-class Disciplines*. The *Program* put forward to the total construction goals classified as three stages, up to 2020, some universities and disciplines should be recognized as world-class universities and disciplines, some disciplines should be recognized as disciplines at the leading position; up to 2030, more universities and disciplines should be recognized as world-class universities and disciplines, some universities should be recognized as universities at the leading position, more disciplines should be recognized as disciplines at the leading position; at the mid of 21st century, the amount and power of world-class universities and disciplines should be at the leading position, and goal of power of higher education should be fulfilled. Tasks and measures for building of world-class universities and disciplines were also put forward.

10.8   Some Problems Facing China in the System of Quality Assurance of Higher Education

Although great progress has been made in the development of higher education as well as evaluation of higher education, there remain some problems in the quality assurance of higher education that need to be tackled urgently.

Firstly, the subject of quality assurance in higher education seems to lack variety. Before the 1980s, the government became the singular subject in quality management and assurance in higher education; any other evaluation of higher education could not be recognized by government and society. Since 1980s, this situation has changed gradually, but up to now, governments still dominate the accreditation, evaluation and assurance of higher education quality. The society and higher education institutions do not play the roles matching with their positions at large. As China is building up the socialist market economy, the model of quality assurance completely dominated by governments needs to be reformed.

There are two reasons for this change. Firstly, this model cannot adjust to reform of management system in higher education. Nowadays China has built up the new management system that is characterized by both the central and local governments' control. The central government delegates much management powers to local government. Local governments are responsible for many vocational higher equation institutions. So it is not suitable for the central government to control more than one hundred HEIs. Local governments should have some rights of assessment, monitoring and control of higher education. Secondly, this model cannot adjust to the change of social needs. Since 1998, many private higher education institutions have been set up; their number is equal to the number of public higher education institutions. The structure of higher education has changed rapidly. So the external quality assurance of higher education cannot be the privilege of the governments. Social groups and non-government organizations should involve in the quality assurance of higher education.

Higher education is serving the society; as a result social evaluation is an important form of participating in higher education. If the governments control the evaluation of higher education, they will not reflect the social needs effectively and timely. As far as the sole control of quality assurance by governments is concerned, there are three disadvantages. First, the government looks for its own profits and viewpoints; they cannot represent other social group's profits and viewpoints. A buffer organization of evaluation is necessary. Second, the sole evaluation and control of quality by government focuses on the accreditation, summative evaluation, and ranking; so the formative evaluation, monitoring, enhancing of quality is neglected to some extent. Third, in the process of evolution, influenced by the status and authority of government, the evaluators are not free to make objective evaluation because they are responsible to the government.

Secondly, Chinese quality control of higher education lacks vigor. It is well known that higher education institutions are the subjects that control all factors affecting the quality of higher education within institutions. Quality control is realized by continuous self-evaluation, self-enhancement, and self-improvement. So, high quality education and teaching is the result of the efforts of all teachers and students. Without teachers' and students' efforts, the external quality assurance cannot guarantee high quality. In the present quality assurance system of Chinese higher education, great emphasis is given on the external evaluation by governments; little emphasis is given to the self–evaluation within the institution. As a result HEIs are short of internal driving force to strengthen the management of quality. On the one hand, administrators in HEIs think it is the government that cares about the quality of higher education. On the other hand, some HEIs carter to government's need; they just want to pass the evaluation; they pay attention to the evaluation items required by government and do not make great efforts to improve the quality of higher education. There are three reasons for this phenomenon. Firstly, traditionally universities were regarded as affiliated with the government; their status and characteristics were not well recognized. Secondly, government's management and evaluation was highly unitary; it leaves not rooms for autonomy of universities.

Thirdly, universities were dependent on government; competition between universities is rare.

Thirdly, theoretical research on quality assurance is lagging behind. Quality assurance of higher education was beginning in the late 1990s. Research on quality assurance is in the incipient period. There are misunderstandings about quality assurance. Some people regard it only as quality assurance of elite education, teaching quality evaluation, total management of education, introduction of ISO 9000. In practice, too much stress was laid on macro-research such as the government's role in managing a university while neglecting micro-research like teaching goals, students' achievement, etc. This is somewhat in correspondence with traditional intuitionism and the concept of wholeness, but for the examination of details, such ways of evaluating proved to be too abstract, vague and thus neither scientific nor useful in providing applicable results. This evaluation style also had something to do with the older leadership style in China. Researchers focused on evaluation indicators or indicator systems rather than on the purposes and functions of the evaluation of higher education. From the very beginning, due to the concept of the so-called 'social-self' in Chinese culture, indicators or indicator systems were placed high on the evaluation priority list.

Fourthly, the environment of quality assurance needs to be improved. It consists of hard environment and soft environment; the hard one is about the institutions including laws and regulations; the soft one is about the quality culture. Up to now China has not built up a complete legal system concerning quality assurance. There are no formal laws on quality assurance except for "The Regulations on Assessment of Regular Higher Education Institutions". Quality culture means the recognition and pursuit of high quality persistently. The traditional factors such as high concentration of power, official position-based culture, and mediocrity-based moral rationality hamper the development of quality culture.

Fifthly, there exist some problems in terms of evaluation of scientific research. In terms of evaluation of research achievements, the outcome is regarded while process is disregarded, and the quantity of research achievement is regarded, while quality of research achievements is disregarded. The evaluation of individual achievements is regarded while evaluation of groups is disregarded. The examination and support on research projects depends on what has been done in the projects. Some teachers do not make research for the sake of personal interest.

10.9   Strategies and Measures for Improving Quality of Higher Education

In order to resolve the problems facing China's quality assurance of higher education mentioned above, it is necessary to take the following measures.

Firstly, a multi-subjects system of quality assurance of higher education that consists of actors like HEIs, governments, society, and students should be set up.

Government is the main subject of external quality assurance; its main task is to make relevant laws and policies, to set various educational standards, to involve indirectly in evaluation, to make macro-management. The behavior model of government needs to change from a control model to a supervision model. In order to realize the supervision model, the central government needs to deregulate some of its powers, such as evaluation of vocational HEIs, to provincial governments, to encourage the development of social evaluation institutions, to build up the information system of quality assurance and to take part in the international network of quality assurance.

HEIs are not only the object of evaluation, but also the important subject of evaluation; they should increase the consciousness and capability of self-regulating, self-constraint, self-adapting. HEIs' self-evaluation should be stressed.

As higher education institutions become the axial institutions and the learning centers, society pays more and more attention to the quality of higher education. China will set up more intermediary evaluation institutions; their main tasks are to assess the quality of graduates. Social evaluation can help HEIs to get the information of graduates timely.

As students are paying the tuition fees for higher education, students should become the subject of evaluation; they should be involved in the evaluation of the quality of higher education.

Secondly, HEIs are the sole subject of internal quality assurance; they are responsible for the management, control and self-evaluation of quality of education and instruction. HEIs's enthusiasm for quality education and instruction should be aroused. The enthusiasm of administrators, teachers and students should be stimulated. HEIs should set up quality assurance commissions that involve many stakeholders. The colleges and departments also need divisions of quality assurance. HEIs can get engaged in many kinds of internal evaluation (Zhu Jiusi 2001).

Thirdly, China need to develop the theory of quality assurance and train staffs specialized in quality assurance. The theoretical development should focus on the following three aspects, namely theory, methods, principles and system of quality assurance; subjects, goals, structure, function and characteristics of quality assurance; criteria of standards and evaluation system. Meanwhile, China needs to build up three forces, namely the research force specialized in evaluation, the force specialized in management of education evaluation, and the force specialized in evaluation.

Fourthly, "Regulation on Evaluation of Regular Higher Education" needs to be revised because the environment of quality assurance changes rapidly. HEIs should make out regulations about quality assurance. It is necessary to make various kinds and levels of evaluation, to link performance to promotion and rewarding teachers more directly, to introduce complete credit system.

Lastly, in order to reform evaluation on teachers' scientific research in HEIs, four measures should be taken. Firstly, various criteria of evaluation should be established, and evaluation of innovation competence should be strengthened. Evaluation on scientific research should reflect research laws. Both the outcome and process of research should be emphasized. The evaluation of quality of research should be stressed. Innovation competence in research should be an independent criterion. Secondly, good environment of scientific research should be created. Scientific research stages may be classified as four stages. They are: posing problems, making hypothesis, making experiment and testing hypothesis. Failure is the mother of success. Innovative projects should be conducted on purpose. Thirdly, HEIs should establish projects within institutions and encourage teachers to conduct more preliminary researches so as to bring about more fruitful research results. Fourthly, spiritual encouragement should be strengthened, and autonomy of research should be increased. Some teachers attach too much importance to the material benefits. Under these circumstances, being overly eager for 'instant success and benefits' will not bring about great and long term scientific achievements. The researchers' motivation for achievement should be cultivated.

References

Department of Policy and Law under the National Education Commission (Ed.). (1995). *The educational policies and laws in the People's Republic of China.* Beijing: People's Education Press.

Editorial Board of China's Education Yearbook. (1985). *China's education yearbook.* Beijing: People's Education Press.

He, D. (Ed.). (1998a). *Important documents in the People's Republic of China (1949-1975).* Haikou: Hainan Press.

He, D. (Ed.). (1998b). *Important documents in the People's Republic of China (1976–1990).* Haikou: Hainan Press.

Wu, S. (1997). *The rankings of Chinese universities and colleges.* Chinese Higher Education Evaluation, vol. 10.

Zhu, J. (2001). *Competition and transformation.* Wuhan: Huazhong Science and Technology University Press.

References

Altbach, P. G. (1991). *International higher education: An encyclopedia.* New York: Garland Publishing INC.

Association of Chinese Educational Research and Association of Chinese Higher Education Research (Ed.). (1999). *Twenty years' educational reform and development in China.* Beijing: Beijing Normal University.

Cheng, F. (Ed.). (2002). *Report on Chinese educational issues.* Beijing: Chinese Social Science Press.

Cheng, X. (1999). *On educational management.* Beijing: Beijing Normal University.

Cheng, X. (1999). *Higher education research in China in the past 50 years (1949–1999).* Beijing: Educational Science Press.

Cheng, Y. (1993). *Politics of education.* Nanjing: Jiangsu Education Press.

Cheng, Y. (2003). *Evaluation of education.* Beijing: People's Education Press.

Cleverrley, J. (1985). *The schooling of China.* Winchester: George Allan and Unwin Publishers Limited.

Deng, X. (1989). *Deng Xiaoping' selected works.* Beijing: People's Press.

Deng, X. (1993). *Deng Xiaoping' selected works.* Beijing: People's Press.

CPC. (1985). *Decision on educational reform.* Beijing: Foreign Language Press.

Cui, Y. (2002). *An economic analysis of innovation in higher education institutions.* Beijing: Beijing Normal University Press.

Cummings, W. K. (2005). *Asian educational edge.* Lanham: Lexington Books.

Department of Finance under the Ministry of Education. (2008). *Development report on education expenditure in China.* Beijing: Higher Education Press.

Department of Planning under the State Educational Commission (Ed.). (1984). *Achievement of education in China (1949–1983).* Beijing: People's Education Press.

Department of Planning under the State Educational Commission (Ed.). (1986). *Achievement of education in China (1980–1985).* Beijing: People's Education Press.

Department of Planning and Construction under the State Educational Commission. (1979–2007). *Educational statistics yearbook of China.* Beijing: People's Education Press.

Du, Y. (2003). *An economic analysis of management of school.* Beijing: Beijing Normal University.

Editorial Board of China's Education Yearbook. (2008). *China's education yearbook.* Beijing: People's Education Press.

Educational Institute in Heilongjiang Province. (Ed.) (1985). *Management of school.* Haerbin: Heilongjiang Education Publishing House.

© Springer Nature Singapore Pte Ltd. and Higher Education Press 2018
M. Yang and H. Ni, *Educational Governance in China,*
https://doi.org/10.1007/978-981-13-0842-0

Fan, G. (2015). *Observation on Chinese educational reform.* Shanghai: East China Normal University.

Fan, M., et al. (2006). *On modern higher education system.* Hefei: Anhui Normal University.

Fan, W. (2004). *Retrospect and prospect of financing higher education and higher education evaluation in China.* Beijing: Higher Education Press.

Fan, X. (1999). *Economics of education.* Beijing: People's Education Press.

Financial Department of Culture and Education Management under the Ministry of Finance. (1990). *Selected data on system of financial management.* Beijing: China's Economy and Finance Press.

Gao, Q. (1996). *Educational development in the Peoples' Republic of China.* Shijiazhuang: Hebei Education Press.

Gu, M. (Ed.). (1992). *The great dictionary of education.* Shanghai: Shanghai Education Press.

Guo, F., & Wu, D. (Ed.). *On educational reform and development.* Shijiangzhuang: Hebei Education Press.

Hao, K. (Ed.). (1998). *Twenty years' educational reform in China.* Zhenzhou: Zhongzhou Ancient Book Press.

Harling, P. (1984). *New direction in educational leadership.* Philadelphia: The Falmer Press.

Hayhoy, R., & Bastid, M. (1987). *China's education and the industrial world.* Amonk: M.E. Sharp Inc.

Hayhoe, R., & H, Pan (Eds.). (1996). *East-west dialogue in knowledge and higher education.* Amonk: M.E. Sharp Inc.

He, D. (1994). *Ten years' history.* Beijing: People's Education Press.

He, Dongchang (Ed.). (2003). *Important documents in the People's Republic of China (1998–2002).* Haikou: Hainan Press.

Hao, K., & Tan, S. (Eds.). (1997). *Chinese education facing the 21th century.* Guiyang: Guizhou People's Education Press.

Hu, W. (2012). *The reform of system of running of schools.* Beijing: Educational Science Press.

Jian, X. (1997). *Economics of education.* Beijing: People's Education Press.

Jian, X. (1998). *Educational reform taken place in the process of development of the market economy.* Guangzhou: Guangdong Education Press.

Jin, H. (Ed.) (1993). *An analysis of educational management.* Xi'an: Shangxi Peoples' Press.

Lao, K. (1993). *On education law.* Nangjing: Jiangshu Education Press.

Li, D. (1998). *Economics of education in modern China.* Beijing: Economic Management Press.

Li, B. (Ed.). (2002). *On management of school.* Beijing: Higher Education Press.

Li, J. (2006). *I am a student from family of workers, peasants and soldiers.* Fuzhou: Fujian Education Press.

Lin, Y. (2006). *An innovative method.* Beijing: China's Central Radio and Television University Press.

Lu, Z. (2002). *Toward a new world in higher education.* Xi'an: Xina Press.

Ma, H. (Ed.). (1992). *An encyclopedia on reform in China.* Dalian: Dalian Publishing House.

Mao, Z. (1977). *Mao Zedong's selected work.* Beijing: People's Press.

Macfarquhua, R., & Fairbank, J. K. (1987). *The cambridge history of China.* Cambridge: Cambridge University Press.

Min, W. (2006). *Report on China's education and human resource development (2005–2006)* Beijing: Beijing University Press.

Morris, P., & Sweeting, A. (Ed.) (1995). *Education and development in East Asia.* New York: Grand Publishing, INC.

National Education Research Center (Ed.). (2007). *Green paper on education in China in 2007.* Beijing: Educational Science Press.

Neave, G., & Van Vught, F. A. (1994). *Government and higher education relationship across three continents: The winds of change.* Extert: Pergamon Press.

OECD. (2002). *Redefining tertiary education.* Paris: OECD.

OECD. (2003). *Current issues in Chinese higher education.* Paris: OECD.

Osborne, D., & Gaebler, T. (1992). *Reinventing government: How the entrepreneurial sprit is transforming the public sector*. Addison-Wesley Publishing Company, Inc.

Pan, M. (1985). *On higher education*. Beijing: People's Education Press.

Pedagogic Research Group in Educational Department of East China Normal University. (Ed.) (1980). *Reading materials on pedagogy*. Beijing: People's Education Press.

Peng, Y. (1999). *Reflection on reform of higher education*. Lanzhou: Lanzhou University Press.

Qian, Y. (2003). *Research on basic education*. Shanghai: Shanghai Science and Technology Education Press.

Qu, B. (Ed.) (1988). *Management of school*. Beijing: People's Education Press.

Research Center on Educational Reform and Development in Beijing Normal University. (Ed.). (2000). *Report on Chinese education development*. Beijing: Beijing Normal University Press.

Research Center on Educational Reform and Development in Beijing Normal University. (Ed.). (2001). *Report on Chinese education development*. Beijing: Beijing Normal University Press.

Research Center on National Education Development. (2007). *Green paper on education in China in 2007*. Beijing: Educational Science Press.

Research Group on Speeding on Implementation of the "5.4" System of Schooling. (2000). *Research on the system of schooling in basic education*. Beijing: Beijing Normal University.

Research Group on Issues on Chinese Education and Human Resources. (2003). *Stride from a country of tremendous population to a country of profound human resources*. Beijing: Higher Education Press.

Research Group on Reform and Development in China since 1978. (2008). *The rising of a country through education*. Beijing: Educational Science Press.

Research Group on Reform and Development in China since 1978. (2008b). *The main theoretical research achievement in Chinese education in the past thirty years since implementation of the policy of reform and opening up to the outside world*. Beijing: Educational Science Press.

Research Group on Reform and Development in China since 1978. (2008). *Main historic affairs in Chinese education in the past thirty years since implementation of the policy of reform and opening up to the outside world*. Beijing: Educational Science Press.

ResearchGroup on Shanghai Educational Development. (1988). *Research on educational development strategy in Shanghai*. Shanghai: Fudan University Press.

Shao, Z. (Ed.). (1993). *A theoretical and practical exploration of compulsory education*. Hangzhou: Zhejiang People's Press.

Sun, M. (Ed.). (2001). *Education administration*. Beijing: Higher Education Press.

The Ministry of Education (Ed.). (1998). *Twenty's year's education in China under the guidance of Deng Xiaoping's theory*. Fuzhou: Fujian Education Publishing House.

The Central Educational Research Institute (Ed.). (2004). *Prospect of China's education in the 21st century*. Jinan: Shandong Education Press.

The State Education Commission. (1998). *Collections of higher education laws and regulation in China*. Beijing: People's Education Press.

Guoqiang, Tian. (2014). *Educational Reform in China*. Beijing: Economic Science Press.

Unger, J. (1982). *Education under Mao*. New York: Columbia University Press.

Wan, K. et al. (Ed.) (2003). *China's non-government education research 2001–2002*. Shanghai: Shanghai People's Press.

Wan, H. (2012). *On higher education reform*. Beijing: China's Forestry Press.

Wan, W. (1998). *An introduction to modern education supervision*. Guang zhou: Guangdong Higher Education Press.

Wan, Y., & Liu, H. (Eds.). (2005). *Report on China's education development*. Beijing: Beijing Normal University.

Wang, J. (2001). *Chinese higher education facing the 21st century*. Beijing: Education Science Press.

Wang, J. (2002). *A Macro-analysis of Higher Education*. Beijing: Higher Education Press.

Wu, Z. (2000). *New Exploration of Educational Administration*. Beijing: People's Education Press.

Xiao, Z. (1988). *On management of school*. Beijing: People's Education Press.

Xie, A. (Ed.). (2003). *An study on higher education*. Chongqian: Southeast Normal University Press.

Wan, Y. (2005). *Annual report on China's education development in 2005*. Beijing: Beijing Normal University.

Xie, X. (Ed.). (1994). *Educational reform and development in Shanghai*. Shanghai: Tongji University Press.

Yang, M. (2003). *On reform on financing of international higher education*. Changchun: Jilin People Press.

Yang, M. (2005). *The quality assurance of higher education in the People's Republic of China*. Kiel: Kiel University Press.

Yang, M. (2007). *Government and market: Research on policies of financing of higher education*. Hangzhou: Zhejiang Educational Publishing House.

Yang, M. (2009). *Examination and competencies: The sixty year's development of secondary education in PRC*. Hangzhou: Zhejiang University Press.

Yang, M. (2010). *Theoretical analysis of education and implementation strategies*. Hangzhou: Zhejiang University.

Yang, Ming. (2010). *Value and choice: A study on comprehensive evaluation of regional education*. Jinan: Shandong Educational Publishing House.

Yang, M. (2013). *Beilun mechanism: A study on quality evaluation of regional basic education*. Hangzhou: Zhejiang University Press.

Yang, M. (2014). *On German educational strategies*. Hangzhou: Zhejiang University Press.

Yang, Z. (2004). *Reform and development of financing of education in China at the turn of 21 century*. Wuhan: Huazhong Normal University.

Yao, Q. (2002). *Education reform in China in the 1990s*. Beijing: Beijing Normal University Press.

Yee, H. A. (Ed.). (1995). *East Asia higher education: Tradition and transformations*. Maxwell House: Pergamon Press Inc.

Yuan, G. (2002). *Basic education reform and development*. Changchun: Northeast Normal University Press.

Yuan, G. (2012). *Typical case study on educational reform*. Beijing: People's Press.

Yuan, Z. (2015). *Review of Chinese educational policies*. Beijing: Educational Science Press.

Yu, L. (Ed.). (1994). *A history of Chinese higher education*. Shanghai: East China Normal Press.

Zhai, B. (2013). *The theory and practice of balancing development of basic education*. Beijing: Educational Science Press.

Zhan, D. (2002). *Academic power and administrative power in HEIs*. Nanjing: Nanjing Normal University.

Zhang, J. (Ed.). (1995). *New recognition of education*. Chengdu: Sichuan Education Press.

Zhang, M., & Ding, N. (2016). *A history of educational reform in China*. Wuhan: Hubei Educational Publishing House.

Zhao, D. (Ed.). (2003). *Rights and responsibilities: Research on relations between governments and universities*. Haerbing: Heilongjiang People's Press.

Zhao, L. (2000). *Chinese basic education*. Tianjin: Tianjin Education Press.

Zhen, D. (Ed.). (1994). *A history of Chinese higher education*. Shanghai: East China Normal University Press.

Zhen, Q. (1999). *Education conducted in the revolution period*. Beijing: China Youth Press.

Zhong, Q. (1993). *New progress in educational science*. Xi'an: Shanxi People's Education Press.

Zhou, C. (Ed.). (1987). *Administration of higher education in China*. Wuhan: Wuhan University Press.

Zhou, G. (2003). *Academic freedom and social intervention*. Wuhan: Huazhong University of Science and Technology Press.

Zhou, Q. (1999). *"Education revolution" in the great cultural revolution*. Guangzhou: Guangdong Education People's.

Zhou, H. (2014). *The yellow book of education in China in 2014*. Wuhan Hubei Educational Publishing House.

Zhou, Y. (Ed.). (2003). *Higher education toward a new century*. Beijing: Higher Education Press.

Zhu, J., K, Cai, & Yao, Q. (1983). *Higher education management*. Huhan: Huazhong Engineering College.

Zhu, Y. (2016). *Reinitiating the educational reform, life*. Beijing: Reading and New Knowledge Press.

Index

A

Academic
  committee, 75
  organization, 85
  power, 87, 88, 91, 92
Accountabilities in enrollment, 154
Administrative
  organizations, 17, 18, 52
  positions, 62
  power, 31, 33, 67, 87, 88, 91, 92, 181
Agricultural secondary schools, 110
Assessment of key construction projects, 303
Assurance of autonomy of schools, 54
Autonomy in HEIs, 41, 160

B

Bachelor's degree, 294, 295
Brown, 7
Budget of education, 205

C

Central Committee of the CCP, 13, 14, 23, 24, 31, 33, 34, 37–43, 47, 48, 70–73, 75, 100, 106, 109–111, 113, 115, 119, 125, 126, 150, 152, 160, 176–179, 196, 204, 214–216, 243, 266, 269
Central Government Organization Law, 23, 24
Centralized system, 13, 19, 174
Central unitary finance, 195
Central unitary leadership, 31, 41
Charging fees, 202, 210, 219
Check on courses, 240, 254, 267
Chinese Communist Party's branch, 67, 69, 70, 73, 81

Chinese Culture and Education Commission, 24
Collective leadership, 65, 66, 81
Command and control model, 55, 59
Commoditization of education, 54
Common Program of CPPCC, 21
Comprehensive education reform, 118
Compulsory education, 9, 45–47, 57, 58, 78, 117, 124, 133, 134, 136, 162, 164, 166, 167, 211, 215, 219, 220, 223, 226, 227, 229, 251, 256, 258, 268
Conference of representatives of teachers, 82, 85
Constitution, 22, 38, 67, 79, 116, 142
Control over higher education, 28, 42
Correspondence university, 120
CPPCC, 21
Criteria of evaluation, 8, 19, 256, 267, 270, 272, 277, 278, 281, 282, 307
Cultural revolution, 34, 36, 72, 114, 116, 150, 179, 180, 206, 207, 267, 288

D

Decentralized system, 13, 19, 20
Decision-making power, 13, 18, 50, 51, 289
Decision on Reform and Development of Basic Education, 45, 220
Degree accreditation, 294–297
Degree-granting activities, 296
Democratic management, 19, 59, 66, 75, 81, 82, 85
Deng Xiaoping, 35, 38, 43, 112, 152, 214, 290
Department of Culture and Education, 25, 26
Development of basic education, 52, 136

© Springer Nature Singapore Pte Ltd. and Higher Education Press 2018
M. Yang and H. Ni, *Educational Governance in China*,
https://doi.org/10.1007/978-981-13-0842-0

Devolution of power, 51, 93, 106, 204
Devolved management system, 142
Directives on Educational Undertakings, 32,
    70, 71, 107
Division of power, 18, 39, 56, 59

E
Economic system, 1, 3, 4, 6–8, 12, 20, 42, 81,
    87, 97, 148, 195, 208, 297
Educational
  administration, 9, 17, 18, 20, 22, 29, 32, 33,
      40, 42, 45, 50, 53, 58, 59, 204
  administrative departments, 17, 19, 25, 33,
      36, 39, 40, 50, 51, 56, 57, 65, 70, 78, 90,
      91, 108, 119, 134, 137, 142, 154, 158,
      165, 196, 199, 205, 207, 217, 218, 223,
      226, 238, 244, 245, 250, 254, 266, 270,
      280, 292
  decision-making system, 5
  efficiency, 19
  equity, 96, 127, 234
  expenditures, 18, 36, 40, 45, 46, 53, 129,
      165, 198, 202, 204, 205, 208, 215, 216,
      218, 220, 228, 232
  goal, 5, 19, 263
  information system, 5
  input, 2, 6, 51, 129, 218, 223, 227, 231
  institutions, 3, 6, 7, 9, 11, 19, 22, 25, 28,
      36, 51, 76, 77, 81, 90, 95, 98, 121–123,
      125, 127, 133, 137, 141, 142, 186, 193,
      194, 198, 201, 215
  investment, 13, 57, 193, 194, 215
  management, 3, 13, 17, 22, 45, 50, 54, 57,
      91, 118, 195, 257
  organization, 1, 4
  production, 6, 57
  provision, 14, 15, 57, 96–98, 128, 129, 132,
      136
  resource allocation, 7, 13, 20, 54, 55, 122,
      172, 264
  responsibilities, 57
  revolution, 35
  rules, 3, 4
  structure, 2, 4, 8, 14, 43, 118, 161, 166
  supervision, 39
  system, 1–9, 11–15, 18, 37, 42, 56, 64, 89,
      96, 117, 127, 193, 235, 258
  system analysis, 1
  undertakings, 4, 15, 20, 29, 37, 42, 50, 76,
      108, 125, 204, 207, 266
Enrollment in secondary schools, 143, 168

Enrollment plans, 146, 156, 157, 173
Entrance examination, 98, 100, 139, 143, 144,
    146, 149, 152, 159, 162, 165, 166, 246,
    249, 250, 253, 256, 259, 260
Evaluation
  of instruction, 292, 297, 299, 300
  of schools, 10, 270, 276, 280, 281
  of students, 257, 265, 267, 269, 271, 274,
      280, 283
  of teachers, 76, 79, 89, 245, 266, 267, 270,
      272, 274, 277–279, 281, 282, 301
Examination
  -based enrollment, 141
  in HEIs, 242, 249
  in schools, 167, 236, 241
  -oriented education, 164, 259, 275

F
Fast
  literacy methods, 101
  secondary schools, 142, 143, 149
Fee, 156, 165
Financing
  higher education, 59, 230
  of private education, 201
  primary and secondary education, 232
Financial management, 101, 125, 133, 136,
    140, 196, 199, 209, 222
First
  five-year plan, 23
  National Conference on Higher Education,
      287
Five-year plan, 23, 122, 123, 215, 290
Five-year system in primary schools, 100
Full-time
  education, 107, 113
  schools, 107, 109, 112
Function of education, 6, 17, 53

G
General examination, 246
Governmental positioning, 53, 57
Government-oriented educational system, 8, 9
Governments' macro-management of
    education, 53
Grassroots organization, 92, 178
Great Administrative Regions, 23, 24, 26–28,
    105, 106, 145, 146, 149, 196–199,
    203
Great Chinese Dictionary, 3
Great Educational Dictionary, 3

H
Head's taking overall responsibilities, 64
HEIs, 12, 14, 21, 26–28, 36, 43, 47, 48, 53, 56,
      59, 63, 69, 72, 79, 80, 84, 85, 88, 89, 92,
      105, 106, 111, 115, 119, 121, 126, 127,
      135, 139, 144–146, 149, 150, 153, 154,
      157, 159, 166, 175, 178, 179, 183, 186,
      189, 212, 260, 292, 299, 304, 306, 307
HEIs' accountabilities in enrollment, 154
HEIs' Committee of Affairs, 68, 71
HEIs' funds, 213
Higher education system, 4, 7, 42, 45, 50, 138,
      186, 286, 289
Higher specialized colleges, 48

I
Ideological education, 30, 75, 104, 173, 189,
      190
Information system, 5, 12, 13, 306
Institutional perspective, 11
Institutions, 3, 4, 8, 11, 17, 19, 28, 43, 45,
      47–49, 51, 52, 55, 58, 61, 66–72, 75, 79,
      80, 87, 90, 91, 109, 112, 116, 125, 134,
      135, 138, 154, 194, 213, 247, 286, 290,
      294, 298, 304, 306
Instruction plans, 28, 33, 36, 99, 101, 258, 287
Internal examination, 235, 250, 251, 253, 255,
      256

J
Job assignment, 175–178, 181, 183, 184
Job-oriented enrollment, 157, 182
Joint construction, 49

K
Key schools, 40, 108, 119, 198, 264, 267
Key secondary schools, 40, 109, 151
Key universities and colleges, 112, 288, 298

L
Land Reforms, 23
Learning load, 40, 164, 270, 277
Length of schooling, 27, 98–100, 108, 114,
      117, 120, 142, 287
Leninism, 50
Literacy rate, 21
Longman Dictionary of Contemporary English,
      3

M
Macro-management of education, 2, 13, 51, 53
Management, 3, 4, 7, 9, 12, 14, 17, 18, 28, 34,
      42, 44, 46, 48, 51, 53, 57, 61, 62, 65, 68,
      72, 73, 77, 81, 86, 88, 90, 91, 96, 127,
      135, 142, 185, 199, 205, 217, 248, 277,
      292, 304
Mao Zedong, 22, 31, 35, 106, 265
Market economic system, 98, 297
Marketization of education, 54
Market-oriented educational system, 8, 9
Marxism, 50
Master's degree, 293–295, 297
Ma Xulun, 24, 105, 143, 237
Meeting of school affairs, 66
Merger of school affairs, 137
Middle schools, 21, 66
Military Regulation Commission, 29
Ministry of Education, 13, 15, 19, 24–27, 30,
      32, 33, 35, 36, 40, 41, 47, 48, 55, 59, 68,
      73, 76, 99–101, 103, 105, 106, 108,
      109, 112, 119, 120, 125, 128, 143, 145,
      146, 148, 149, 152, 156, 158, 160, 173,
      177, 178, 181, 197, 201, 204, 207, 211,
      220, 222, 239, 242, 244, 249, 264, 270,
      292, 293, 296, 298, 299, 301
Ministry of Higher Education, 24, 28, 33, 69,
      148, 198, 203, 239, 241
Moral education, 75, 86, 265

N
National college entrance examination, 121,
      122, 127, 152, 155, 163, 166, 242, 252,
      288
National educational expenditures, 216, 218
National examination, 122, 146, 160, 240, 253
Nationality education, 24
National People's Congress, 37, 38, 77, 125,
      211
National unitary job assignment system, 174,
      178
Night university, 112, 120
Nine-year compulsory education, 38, 117, 118,
      125, 158, 182, 229
Non-compulsory educational system, 8
Non-formal higher education, 112, 120
Non-key schools, 119
Normal secondary schools, 100, 144

O
Office of Science and Education, 35
One-head system, 70, 81
On New Democracy, 22
Organization system, 6, 96

P
Pan Maoyuan, 3, 4
Party's Commission, 68
Party's construction affairs, 34

People's Daily, 36, 41, 152, 172
People's grants, 29, 198, 204, 213
Physical health examination, 153
Policy perspective, 10
Popularization of education, 39, 107
Primary education system, 7
Principal's accountabilities, 86
Principal's role, 65
Private schools, 21, 25, 31, 95–97, 103, 104,
    110, 115, 123, 124, 131–134, 137, 139,
    202, 215
Probation system, 179
Public school, 9, 36, 95, 97, 110, 123, 131,
    132, 136, 165, 202, 221

Q
Qualifications for teachers, 78, 87

R
Recommendation by schools, 151, 152, 155
Recruitment methods, 154
Recruitment of teachers, 67, 79
Reform and opening up to the outside world,
    11
Reform of political system, 73
Regulation system, 5, 13
Rejuvenational Action Plan for Education, 123
Remarks on students, 238, 248, 274
Research organization, 62
Responsibilities of presidents in HEIs, 84
Restructuring of universities and colleges, 175,
    290

S
Salary criteria for teachers, 68, 69
Scientific management of education, 2
Secondary education, 7, 8, 13, 18, 25, 31, 41,
    82, 102, 109, 110, 114, 124, 130, 165,
    166, 168, 184, 205, 226, 230, 237, 250,
    256, 258, 264
Secondary specialized schools, 31, 99, 114,
    116, 213
Second-level private college, 126, 127
Single-school, 62
Skilled labor force, 7, 12
Social intermediary organizations, 51, 270
Socialist market economic system, 7, 82, 185
Socialist transformation, 22
Socialization and professionalization of
    production, 30
Social organization, 9, 270, 274
Social service, 9, 259, 286, 299
Spare-time schools, 107
Specialized secondary schools, 32, 49, 99, 102,
    110, 148, 152

Specialty, 43, 113, 114, 186
State Council, 18, 24, 31, 32, 34, 37, 40,
    43–45, 47–49, 51, 53, 70, 71, 77, 79,
    107, 113, 117, 119, 120, 123, 126, 150,
    155, 160, 177–179, 183, 208, 211, 216,
    219, 222, 226, 246, 249, 269, 294, 296,
    303
State Education Commission, 37, 39, 43–45,
    47, 74, 76, 81, 84, 118, 119, 125, 152,
    156, 159, 212, 218, 227, 245, 247, 291,
    296
State-owned schools, 96, 131
Strategic position of education, 215, 231
Structural reform in secondary education, 41,
    102
Structural salary, 74
Subjects of examination, 144, 145, 147, 149,
    153, 158, 239, 246, 249, 250, 254, 259,
    260
Supportive organization, 62
Surtax on education, 215, 217, 220, 223
Syllabus, 25, 32, 33, 266
System of
    academic degree, 8
    administration of primary education, 25
    appointment of teachers, 74, 78, 80, 85, 86
    budgetary appropriation, 194
    certification, 8
    common enrollment, 145, 146
    direct assignment, 178
    educational administration, 9, 15, 18–20,
        28–31, 37, 44, 50, 52, 55, 56, 58
    educational evaluation, 263, 264, 266, 267,
        269, 280
    educational provision, 14, 95–98, 123, 126,
        128, 129, 131, 136, 139
    educational supervision, 8, 39
    employment, 10, 171, 183, 185, 187, 188,
        212
    enrollment, 141, 142, 149, 150, 152, 156,
        159–162, 165, 167, 212
    evaluation of students, 265, 271, 279, 283
    evaluation of teachers, 265–267, 270, 272,
        279, 281
    examination, 15, 144, 145, 160, 235–237,
        245, 248, 249, 251, 256, 294, 295
    finance, 195, 196, 206, 208, 211
    financing of education, 214, 215, 223,
        231
    governmental assignment, 174
    HEIs'committee of affairs, 68, 71
    internal management, 4, 15, 61–64, 67, 69,
        70, 72, 73, 77, 81, 85, 87, 89, 91, 101
    meetings, 83, 85
    personnel management, 7, 61, 62, 79

professional titles, 74, 76, 78, 80, 84, 85
qualification of teachers, 77
quality assurance of higher education, 285, 286, 293, 303, 306
schooling, 3, 26, 36, 44, 98, 99, 108, 117
teachers' responsibilities, 76, 86
teachers' salaries, 7, 68
unitary enrollment, 143, 154

T
Taking over private schools, 103
Teachers' law, 77, 78, 90, 91, 270
Teachers' salaries, 7, 62, 63, 68, 74, 204, 205, 223, 225, 266
Total guideline, 23
Training of teachers, 139, 268
Tuition and fees, 186, 224, 226, 230

U
Unitary system of administration of higher education, 26
United Kingdom, 1
United States, 1, 54, 88, 233
Unit's head's taking overall responsibilities, 63, 64
University rankings, 301, 302

V
Vocational education, 14, 47, 48, 115, 116, 123, 125, 129, 138

W
Winter schools, 101, 143
Work-study schools, 107, 109, 110, 112, 113, 245